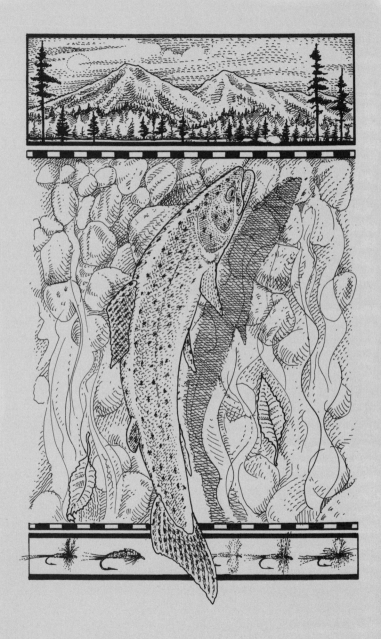

John Gierach

Death, Taxes, and Leaky Waders

A John Gierach
Fly-fishing Treasury

Illustrated by Glenn Wolff

Simon & Schuster Paperbacks
New York London Toronto Sydney

SIMON & SCHUSTER PAPERBACKS
Rockefeller Center
1230 Avenue of the Americas
New York, NY 10020
Introduction and compilation copyright © 2000 by John Gierach
Interior illustrations copyright © 2000 by Glenn Wolff

For information about special discounts for bulk purchases,
please contact Simon & Schuster Special Sales :
1-800-456-6798 or business@simonandschuster.com
Designed by Karolina Harris
Manufactured in the United States of America
17   19   20   18   16
The Library of Congress has cataloged the hardcover edition as follows:
Gierach, John
Death, Taxes, and Leaky Waders:
a John Gierach fly-fishing treasury / John Gierach;
illustrated by Glenn Wolff.
p. cm.
1. Fly fishing—Anecdotes. I. Wolff, Glenn. II. Title
SH456 .G573 2000
799.1'1—dc21   00'027650
ISBN-13: 978-0-684-86858-5
ISBN-10:   0-684-86858-X
ISBN-13: 978-0-684-86859-2 (Pbk)
ISBN-10:   0-684-86859-8 (Pbk)
All essays previously published in other media.
Additional copyright information will be found on page 415.

Contents

Even Brook Trout Get the Blues

Dances with Trout

Another Lousy Day in Paradise

Introduction

I think writing is a lot like fishing, especially when it's *about* fishing, as most of mine is. Both take curiosity, patience, persistence, lots of time, some skill, a willingness to put things together in odd ways, an appreciation of the process itself (regardless of how it turns out), and faith that it's all somehow worthwhile. What sane person would spend a whole day writing a paragraph that reads like it was dashed off in thirty seconds? The same kind who'd fish for one big trout all morning just so he can look at it and release it.

I like to think I was born to be a fisherman. There's a family story that I caught my first bluegill at age five and wanted to have it mounted. I don't remember that, but it sounds about right. By the time I was a teenager I fit the standard profile of a lifelong angler: I was lazy, shiftless, unambitious, and willing to work hard only at things that were widely considered useless. My folks thought I'd grow out of it.

As for writing, I don't remember why I first thought I'd like it, but I have to suspect it's because writers weren't very well thought of and because they didn't seem to work. At a certain age, playing hard, not really working, and living up to a bad reputation seemed like the way to go.

My first revelation was that writing *did* involve some work. Lots of it, actually. Some people have a warped view of writers in general, and outdoor writers in particular. Now and then someone will say to me, "Boy, what a life you have. All you do is fish." Usually I nod and smile because that's what I used to think myself and because it's not entirely wrong, but there's a mood I sometimes get into that makes me ask, "Who the hell do you think writes the stories?"

Then there are those who'll tell you you're blessed with talent, which is another way of saying you don't work. If you explain that whatever talent you may have now is the result of decades of toil, they'll say that kind of patience is a gift. There's no talking to some people. If they want you to be blessed, then you're blessed, god damn it! Don't argue.

Then again, one of my more levelheaded friends once said, "Look, if someone thinks you don't work, maybe it means your writing seems effortless, so you should take it as a compliment." I wouldn't mind having more levelheaded friends, but when eventually almost everyone you know is a fly fisher, guide, writer, editor, or publisher, you take what you can get.

I didn't start out to be a fishing writer; I started out to be a "serious" writer, back when I was much younger and still liked the sanctimonious sound of that. I wrote my first stories for outdoor magazines out of curiosity; to see if maybe that wouldn't be a better way for a struggling writer to support himself than driving a garbage truck—not that driving a garbage truck was all that bad.

That didn't work out the way I had it pictured because writing for a living turned out to be a full-time job that left less time and energy for art than real work had. On the other hand, I found that writing was writing and that any subject—with the possible exception of golf—could open up on grand themes if that's what you wanted it to do.

I remember two milestones now: the first story I sold, and the first story I sold that seemed to be about grayling fishing in Canada but that was really about death. At the time I thought I'd fooled the editor who bought it, but years later I ended up fishing for salmon in Scotland with him and he said, "Remember that story you did once about death and grayling? I liked that one."

Some of these stories began in the "Outside" column I've been writing for the *Longmont Daily Times-Call* newspaper for the last seventeen years and also the one I did for the *New York Times* for a short period in the early '90s. Being a weekly columnist is grueling, but it's a good job for a writer. If nothing else, it's steady work, and it also keeps you in shape, like hiking two or three miles a day unless there's a good reason not to, which I also do. You know that whatever else happens in a week's time, you'll write one reasonably coherent, 800-word story, and in most cases you'll go fishing at least one extra time so you'll have something to write about.

It really *is* grueling at times—the writing, not the fishing—but by now I'm so used to it I'd probably miss it. I didn't even realize how long I'd been doing it until a few years ago, when, during my rare appearances in the newsroom, some of the younger people there started calling me "sir" and a man in his thirties told me he'd grown up reading my column.

Anyway, some of those short columns hinted at something more, so they went on to become magazine stories, and then finally book chapters, usually getting longer and more genuine in the process. A book is the only place where I don't run into constraints on length, language, or content, and in a few cases book chapters have served as revenge against editors who located the heart and soul of a story and removed it before it appeared in the magazine or who just chopped it for length and accidentally hit a vital spot.

I hadn't read most of these essays since they were published, because by the time a book comes out I'm done with it. For one thing, I've moved on to other fishing trips and other stories. And I've already read the thing dozens of times, carefully, critically, changing this and that, then maybe changing it back to the way it was to begin with. Then I read the copyedited manuscript. Then I proofed the galleys. When the actual book arrives in the mail, I'm happy to see it—even get a little glow of satisfaction—but I don't feel like reading it again.

Then I have to pick a nice short chapter to read aloud on the brief publicity tour my publisher now sends me on when I have a new book. (I read the same one over and over so I come to know it by heart and don't stammer too much.) I'm fairly new to book tours and I guess they're not my favorite part of being a writer. There's something in my Midwestern Protestant upbringing that makes me shy about being the center of attention, and of course book tours are almost always scheduled when the fish are biting back home.

Still, I've come to terms. It's fun traveling on an expense account—even if you don't have much time to abuse it—and some neat things usually happen. I get to see some of the great independent bookstores—Tattered Cover, Elliott Bay, Powell's, Boulder Bookstore—meet guides, fishermen, book people, and other writers; sometimes get an invitation to come back later and go fishing; or maybe even accidentally say something that could be construed as brilliant. And once I ran into an old girlfriend who somehow hadn't aged a day in more than twenty years. She asked if I remembered her. How could I forget?

A few pieces of advice about book tours from more experienced writers helped a lot. Specifically: "Don't start believing your own dust jacket copy" and "Don't let the bastards put you in a necktie."

I enjoyed reading these stories again because I'd all but forgotten about some of them. Sure, a few I remembered nearly word for word and a few more started to come back after I read the first paragraph, but some of the oldest ones were almost new; by now, no more than vaguely familiar. Not surprising, I guess. I figure that since I finished *Trout Bum* in 1985 I've written over eight hundred newspaper columns, somewhere in the neighborhood of three hundred magazine stories and nine books.

I'm almost sorry now that I stopped to figure that out (and also surprised I kept such good records), because adding up numbers is no better a way to look at a life spent writing than one spent fishing. The fact is, I either don't work as hard as it seems, or I do, but I enjoy it so much it doesn't really qualify as work. Years ago Charlie Waterman admitted that writing about fishing can be more fun than actually fishing. Up until then I thought that was my little secret.

I think I'm a better writer now than I once was, but I can't put my finger on anything I do differently. I've always tried to figure out what a story is actually about—usually it's something other than the fishing, but that wouldn't have come up *without* the fishing—and I've tried for the sound of real, spoken language.

I think a good fishing story is like any good story: It either gets at something that wasn't immediately apparent or it gets at something obvious in a way you never thought of before. Beyond that it's honest, plainspoken, and avoids being a billboard for the author's ego. Of course that last one is the trickiest, because your own motives are always the hardest to see and because without a pretty healthy ego you wouldn't be writing in the first place.

Still, you come to understand that if you compose something that you think really shows off your skill as a writer, you should get rid of it because it's self-indulgent and, worse yet, it won't fool anyone. At its worst, this can become what Garrison Keillor recently called "stuff in which there's nobody home," and Jim Harrison could have been talking about fishing stories instead of poetry when he said that most of it was "elaborate harness that never smelled a real horse."

There have been times when I dashed off columns on a portable typewriter set up on a picnic table or tailgate and filed them with datelines like "Last Chance, Idaho," but I do most of my writing at my desk at home. It's best for me to take a good, long time to write a story, and also to let a trip sink in for a while and then see which parts of it float to the top by themselves.

I do keep a fishing journal that I sometimes refer back to—usually to find something like the correct spelling of "Agulukpak River"—but besides making short daily entries in that, I really try not to write on the road. (If I did I'd have graduated to a lap-top by now, and although I think typewriters are charming, computers annoy me.)Whatever contraption they're written on, the stories are almost always cleaner and more honest if I don't try to orchestrate them as they're happening, but just go fishing to see what happens and then think about it later. If a trip somehow doesn't *produce* a story, that just means I have to go fishing again right away. It's my job.

Jim Harrison (obviously one of my favorite writers) recently described the process of editing a collection of his own work as "brain peeling," but for me rereading the six books I've drawn on in this volume was fun, like going back through old photos—even though a few were the inevitable snapshots of people who are now dead but back then were holding big trout and grinning. Since no one told me to choose the best stories based on some objective standard—let alone what that standard might be—I just picked the ones I liked the most, for reasons of my own.

Writers are compulsive tinkerers, and I did feel the urge to edit here and there or maybe revise in light of what I've learned since, but I resisted. If there's ever a time when a story is irretrievably finished, it's when it appears between the covers of a book. And anyway, I like them all the way they are, especially the parts that let you fill in things like the actual size of a fish for yourself, thereby almost surely making it bigger than it really was. A man I've fished with for years was once asked if all my stories were true. He said, "You bet they are—in a way."

I also noticed that I kept drifting back to old familiar fishing spots in one way or another: the St. Vrain, Platte, and Frying Pan Rivers, some local bass and bluegill ponds and pocket water streams. Fishing writers dote on their home waters and compare everything else to them. (What's the Moraine River in Alaska like? It's like the North Platte in Wyoming except with tundra instead of prairie and brown bears instead of cows.) The home water is where we do our casual, day-to-day fishing, where our friends are most likely to say the offhandedly profound things we end up making our own, and where we sooner or later take on the coloration of our environment.

But there are plenty of new places, too, because writers and fishermen are restless, always sniffing out something unfamiliar to compare with what we think we already know. I remember some of those new places clearly, even if I only fished them once years ago and never quite got around to going back, but some others have pretty much faded. That is, I can picture them well enough, but I don't recall their names and I don't think I could find them again without help. I'm not sure how I feel about that. A little wistful, maybe, but also happy I've done so much fishing that I've managed to lose track of entire rivers.

Naturally, some of the old familiar places I wrote about fifteen and twenty years ago are even more familiar now, but then some waters you could once get on because no one much cared are now fenced and posted, and there have been changes in regulations, overcrowding, floods, fish kills, natural cycles, new fish stocked in some places, an end to stocking in others, and lately whirling disease. Proposed dam projects were defeated on two of my favorite streams, but the rivers seem more fragile now. There are days when I stop casting and think, This could have been under fifty feet of water—and it might be yet if we're not careful.

But then some places are still the same as when I first saw them, either because they're that resilient or they've somehow been overlooked. A few even seem better than they were, with more and bigger fish, but that's probably just because I'm a better fisherman now. And of course they're as beautiful as ever, like the ageless former girlfriend in Portland. Or was it Eugene?

Trout Bum

Camp Coffee

I use a common American brand of coffee that you can get in big, three-pound cans. It can be found on the shelves of stores, large and small, throughout the West. On road trips I carry a pound of it. In my backpack I carry some in a four-ounce tin that once contained tea grown in India and packaged in England. It's enough for several days out and the tin fits neatly inside the coffeepot. The pot, in turn, goes in a heavy plastic bag to keep carbon smudges off my clothes and other gear. Tidy, efficient.

A few years ago I experimented with some exotic—and expensive—kinds of coffee for fish-camping but found them unacceptable for a number of reasons. For one thing, the cost was prohibitive. Not long ago I spent three-hundred dollars on a fly rod, but an extra seventy-five cents for a pound of coffee still rubs me the wrong way. Once established, priorities must be maintained.

There was also the extra care and attention that brewing up a pot of some strange blend required in the field. The coffeepot is the hook from which a good, comfortable, homey camp hangs, but it should be as thoughtless as a rusty nail, not a big production.

And then there were the aesthetics of the situation. My gear, with some notable exceptions at both ends of the scale, is largely of moderate quality—serviceable, but not extravagant—and my camps are cozy, but far from posh. Espresso seemed out of place.

For me, coffee has always had at least a hint of the woods and rivers about it because I started drinking the stuff on fishing trips at what many would consider a too-tender age. I had my first cup in the kitchen of my Aunt Dora and Uncle Leonard's farmhouse before dawn on the morning of a bass fishing trip—or maybe it was a pheasant hunt. That's not the part I remember so well. What I recall is the oilcloth on the table, the straight-backed wooden chairs, Agnes the pet raccoon scratching at the back door, the whole no-nonsense atmosphere of the familiar, working Midwestern farm kitchen, the darkness outside the windows, and the morning chill. The cold is what makes me think it might have been pheasant season.

Bass or pheasants, it doesn't matter. I remember the coffee, in a chipped, heavy, well-used cup, as one of the early rites of manhood. There were others that have not served me as well.

That first cup (and many thereafter) was brewed by Aunt Dora. Though I paid no attention to the brand or the method used, I've judged all coffee since then by that standard, in the same way I've judged my own conduct in the field, and that of others, by the relaxed, competent, unhurried, droll example set by Uncle Leonard.

I especially remember the teen-age years when things like girls and fast cars were more on my mind than shotguns and fishing rods, but when fishing and hunting became what they remain for me today—a way out of, a way back from, a world that's faster, more complicated, and more ruthless than it needs to be—there was always a pot of coffee simmering in the coals of the campfire or nuzzling around in the mysterious depths of a thermos bottle.

Between then and now I've consumed many more cups of coffee in civilized settings than out in the woods, but the aroma of the stuff is so inexorably tied to flushing birds, rising trout, giggling loons, drifting woodsmoke, and so on that they cannot be separated, even when the cup is made of styrofoam.

There was a time when I carried instant coffee in the field for the sake of speed and convenience. It worked for a while. In those days I was somewhat younger and more eager for the kill. Drives, hikes, camps—they were nothing but means to an end. I was very businesslike and something of a guerrilla. Now that I think about it, I was also wet, cold, hungry, and/or lost more often than I am now and not as successful. I was in the process of proving something then that has now, apparently, been proven and forgotten. Going through a stage, they call it.

I think I started brewing real coffee in camp about the same time I began releasing all but a brace of trout because they're best fresh and because two is enough. "Enough" is a useful concept for the sportsman, especially the young one. I used the small aluminum percolator that saw me through college, when my main goals in life were to mess up my brains, get girls, and overthrow the government, not necessarily in that order. It did an adequate job.

It took A.K. to teach me how to make real camp coffee: bring one pot of lake or river water to a rolling boil, add two palmfuls of generic coffee, and remove the pot to the edge of the coals. If it's the breakfast pot, throw in the eggshells. When it's done (five to ten minutes), add a splash of cold water to settle the grounds.

Like whiskey, it should be drunk from a tin cup.

A.K.'s coffeepot goes back a long way. It sat on the banks of trout streams in Michigan for many years before it came to the Rocky Mountains and is now in its third stage of its evolution as a camp utensil. First it was clean and enameled in some color that is now lost to memory. Then it got all black and stayed that way for a long time. Now the accumulated black gunk is flaking off, exposing the battleship gray of the bare metal. Someday the bottom will drop out and an era will have ended.

A.K. and I have drunk from this pot around countless fires across several western states, but it has now become almost synonymous with winter trout fishing in Cheesman Canyon. That's a stretch of the South Platte River, one of those tailwaters that stays open and more or less fishable throughout the year. It's famous water and almost too crowded to fish in the summer, but still nice and lonely on most days between Christmas and, say, the end of March.

We've built coffee fires in several spots, but there's one place that has seen the majority of them. It's where trout are often rising to sparse midge hatches—slow, hard, technical fishing. Sometimes we'll take turns on a pod of risers, one guy tending the fire, sipping coffee, the other casting and slowly freezing in the cold water. It was there that I hooked and landed my one-and-only good-sized trout on a #28 fly and 8x tippet.

We use dead, dry willow twigs, and it recently occurred to me that the few of us who build fires there have been inadvertently pruning the little bankside brush patch, keeping it healthy enough to provide the modest amounts of firewood we need—a delicate and accidental balance.

A few years ago I made a comment in a magazine article about A.K.'s bankside boiled coffee, something to the effect that it was okay when you were cold and wet but that if you got a cup of it in a cafe—too strong, with pine needles and nymph shucks floating in it—you'd refuse to pay.

It wasn't more than a few weeks after the article appeared that we ended up in the Canyon again. It was February, cold, blustery, bitter, with drifts of snow right down to the water. Sensitive to the early signs of hypothermia, I had left the river when I began to shiver a little and headed upstream towards the slightly bluish curl of smoke that told me A.K. had the coffee on. I rummaged through my pack for my tin coffee cup, finding that, amazingly, I'd left it at home. A.K. was delighted, saying it didn't matter anyway, since the coffee was no good. There was a lot of good-natured hell to pay before I could get my hands on his cup, all of which I deserved. Best damned cup of coffee I ever had, strong and black.

I can drink good coffee black, but I prefer it with cream. In a full camp I use real milk, but when working from a pack I vacillate between evaporated milk and that powdered, "non-dairy creamer." The powdered stuff is the most efficient, but I remain suspicious of it.

Coffee is okay on warm mornings when the wool shirt is shed while the bacon sizzles, but it's best on cold, winter trout streams, or during claustrophobic storms when the almost painful sting of its heat telegraphed through the thin walls of a tin cup seems like the center of the universe, a very real element of basic survival.

My first wife used a sterile-looking glass pot—more of a carafe, actually—and the coffee dripped with agonizing slowness through paper filters. It was always cold before it was ready to drink. My second wife used a tall, elegant electric percolator with a spout as long and graceful as the neck of a Canada goose. The noise it made while working was vaguely industrial. Once she gave up coffee entirely in the belief that it wasn't healthy. Of course it's not healthy; what is anymore? As Aunt Dora used to say, "Everything I like is either illegal, immoral, or fattening."

The coffeepot I've carried and camped with for more seasons than I've kept track of is of the old style: sturdy, heavy, enameled in the classic midnight blue under specks of white that are now fire-singed to a mellow brown around the slowly growing black patch under the spout—midway through evolutionary stage two. I bought it for pocket change at a yard sale and discarded the guts as soon as I got it home. It has been rinsed thousands of times but has never really been "washed."

Once I drop-kicked it twenty yards across a mountain meadow in Colorado (for reasons I won't go into here). When I retrieved it, the mineral deposits that had built up inside it rattled out like flakes of shale. The small dent it bears from that incident still shames me sometimes. Uncle Leonard would never have kicked the coffeepot.

For years that pot reposed with the rest of my camping gear and was brought out, along with sleeping bags, waders, fly rods, shotguns, etc., for what amounted to special occasions. Now it sits proudly on the stove in the kitchen as a symbol of freedom and simplicity. Why would anyone need more than one coffeepot?

At home I use tap water, but otherwise the coffee is made the same way as in the field. The glass knob in the lid of the pot disappeared long ago (in that meadow, maybe?), and just glancing into the kitchen I can tell the coffee is ready by the curl of steam coming from the hole it left.

Kazan River Grayling

T H E Kazan River in Canada's Northwest Territories is a strange one, as rivers go. It rises in the interior at sprawling Snowbird Lake and eventually empties into Hudson Bay some 900 miles to the east, but up near the headwaters it's nothing more than a series of channels draining one lake into another. What is cavalierly referred to as The River is, in this area at least, largely a figment in the imagination of some cartographer. Its course, if you can call it that, is difficult to locate on a map and downright incomprehensible from a boat. It's worth finding, however, because these little stretches of river—some no more than a few hundred yards long and separated by hours on a hard boat seat—hold some world-class Arctic grayling.

There are grayling in most of the lakes too, usually in the shallow bays and coves and around points of land, but the largest ones in this particular part of the Northwest Territories are typically found in the stretches of fast water known collectively as the Kazan River. According to the guides, the grayling stay out of the deep water to avoid the enormous lake trout, and they shun the weedy backwaters for fear of the northern pike, or "jacks," as they're called.

Now that's a homespun theory attributing more thought to the fish than they're capable of, but I still like it, and the larger fish (those weighing in at between 2 and 3 pounds) *are* in the river. In fact, two fly-rod world-record grayling came from the Kazan. Both weighed just a hair over 3 pounds when caught and an ounce or two under by the time they were officially weighed. For comparison, the all-tackle world-record grayling—the largest specimen ever recorded—weighed in the neighborhood of 5 pounds, about the same as the world-record bluegill.

I was working out of a fishing camp on Snowbird Lake in the company of Wally Allen and, typically of both of us I suppose, we were clearly doing things backwards. The main attraction for most anglers in this remote area (130 miles by float plane from the nearest settlement, 275 miles from the nearest road) are the lake trout, or mackinaws. They're not called macks up there, though, probably because it would rhyme with jacks and cause a lot of confusion.

Whatever you call them, fish in the 30-pound class aren't uncommon, and that's what most people come for. The grayling aren't exactly looked down upon, but they tend to be viewed as something to amuse the sports when the lake trout are off or when they've become jaded from taking too many huge fish on 3/4-ounce jigs and T-60 Flatfish. My friend and I, however, had come loaded with fly tackle mainly in pursuit of grayling and so were considered by the camp staff and guides to be harmless, though definitely odd.

The Kazan rises near the southern end of the 70-mile-long lake, about a twenty-minute boat ride from the camp. There's a half mile of brawling, marginally navigable river before you come to the next lake, which remains nameless on the best local map. This is the only part of the Kazan that anyone from the camp had ever felt moved to fish, and it's a fine piece of water with pools, glides, pocket water, riffles, and one set of genuine standing-wave rapids. It's just like a real river except that it begins and ends too abruptly.

This is the stretch we fished for the first few days, heading out across De-houx Bay towards the river while the other guides and sports—some flashing us puzzled expressions—motored out to fish the submerged glacial eskers for the Big Fish. We had it to ourselves for a few days, but it wasn't long before we began to pick up some company.

During the inevitable talk over supper at the camp, it came out that we were taking some grayling that nudged current records. (In my limited experience with guides, I've found that you can bribe or beg them into just about anything except keeping quiet about the big fish they've put their clients onto which, after all, is fair enough—it's like asking a painter not to sign his work.) An International Game Fish Association record book magically appeared and was studied carefully by some of our colleagues, who admitted that the lake-trout fishing had been a bit slow. As Colorado fly-fishermen and, more recently, grayling specialists, our mildly oddball status was revised to the tune of several lukewarm Labatt's beers, and we were summarily pumped for details.

Grayling are an exotic species of fish to most American anglers. In appearance they fall somewhere between a trout and a whitefish but are in their own class with that beautiful, flamboyant dorsal fin used in mating displays. Whether they also use it for navigation is, apparently, arguable, but I believe they do—it *feels* like it when you have a good one on the line. I'll admit that's less than a purely scientific observation, not unlike assuming the fish live in the fast water to hide from the pike.

The color of an Arctic grayling is hard to describe and can only be hinted at in color photographs. They're subtly iridescent with hints of bronze, faint purple, and silver, depending on how you turn them in the light. They have irregular black spots towards the front of the body and light spots on the bluish dorsal fin which, on many of the larger Kazan River fish, is rimmed with a pink stripe at the top. They're so pretty, I never quite got used to them.

In Latin they're known as *Thymallus arcticus* because they're supposed to smell like thyme, though I can't say I ever noticed that, even though I sniffed a few fish when no one was looking. My olfactory memories of the trip are confined to pine, mosquito repellent, and the fabulous aroma of shore lunch: baked beans, homemade bread, onion rings, fresh fish breaded lightly in cornmeal, and industrial-strength camp coffee. Although the delicate white meat of the grayling is excellent, it still comes in second to the pink-fleshed lake trout.

For the record, we used barbless hooks and released most of our fish, as one is encouraged to do by the management of most camps and by the Northwest Territories Wildlife Service, whose conservation policies are very up to date though difficult to enforce in a largely roadless area covering well over a million square miles.

A phrase like "a million square miles" is like "a billion dollars"—you know it's a hell of a lot, but beyond that, it's meaningless. The poetry of the word "wilderness" makes a lot more sense to me, and when I try to conceive of the incredible size of the Northwest Territories (most of the water in which has *never* been fished, by the way), what comes to mind is the cairn of shed caribou antlers that stands on the beach in front of the camp.

This area is big enough and wild enough that herds of these animals can migrate across relatively small pieces of it and remain more or less ignorant of the existence of human beings on the planet.

The Kazan River grayling behaved almost exactly like trout except that they were much easier to lure up to dry flies (when they weren't already rising) than any of the trout I've ever personally known. In fact, dry flies were consistently more effective than nymphs, even for the larger fish, and going under water didn't move larger fish, as it often does on a trout stream.

They weren't exactly selective, but they weren't idiotic, either. Yellow Humpies and Elk Hair Caddises in sizes 16 and 18 worked consistently, but when we got too far from those two in either size or color, the action dropped off noticeably. The Kazan is largely a caddis river (we saw no caddis flies larger than a size 14, most smaller) with a liberal smattering of mayflies, midges, and even stone-flies, but the caddis seems to be the main food source. By the way, all aquatic insects are collectively referred to as "fish flies," as in "big brown fish fly" or "little yellow fish fly."

I can't remember when it was that we got the itch to explore more of the Kazan than just that first stretch. Maybe it was on the third or fourth day. That far north the days run together, literally as well as figuratively, with almost none of what you'd call "night" and sunrises and sunsets that would last for hours and almost run together. It was a little dreamlike at the time, and in hindsight it's close to hallucinatory.

Going down the Kazan was not the usual procedure; in fact, no one had ever wanted to do it before, and so there was some discussion about it. Eventually, the camp manager located some waterproof maps in the storeroom, suggested we make this our last beer, and told us we'd be going with a different guide in the morning.

After breakfast the next day we lugged our gear down to the beach and were greeted with, "I am Guy LaRoche, forse class Franch Cunadium feeshing guide; get in zee boat, eh?" The man was young, hard as nails, steely eyed, good on rivers, and all business. Terrific.

We crossed the bottom end of Snowbird, white-knuckled the short rapids in the first stretch of river, and set out across the nameless lake. It was bigger in reality than it looked on the map, was spattered with small islands, and had at least one pair of bald eagles nesting on its banks. We fished the channel at the bottom end and then set out across Obre Lake. Obre, dotted with larger islands, was long and deep enough to land a float plane on, and so it had a camp. We stopped, but it was deserted, and in the middle of the season, too. Obviously the owners had gone under. Running a fly-in wilderness camp is an expensive proposition: I was told that by the time the gasoline for the outboards was barged up to Stony Rapids and then flown into the camp at Snowbird, it ended up costing between seven and eight dollars a gallon. No figures were available for beer.

We spent something like a twenty-four hour day (most of it riding across lakes at full throttle) in order to fish three stretches of river that, laid end to end, might have been two miles long. I couldn't help thinking of that chapter in Richard Brautigan's *Trout Fishing in America* in which he describes a hardware store with hundred-yard sections of trout stream stacked out back and of the fact that that book—one of the great pieces of modern surrealism—has been innocently filed under "Fishing" in the Longmont, Colorado, public library.

The second channel down from Snowbird was long and wide with an easily wadable shelf; it was big, slow water that called for some long casts.

The next channel was a fast, deep rip of three or four hundred yards that we located first by cruising the bottom end of the lake until we found the spot where the weeds began to lean in the imperceptible current and then by the sound of the white water. It was a treacherous spot full of big grayling. We landed few under 2 pounds and a fair number pushing 3. It was here that Wally took one of the fish that would become a new fly-rod world record, and it was at the bottom of this stretch that we found the remains of what had once been a crude but very serviceable wooden canoe and a hand-carved paddle—a chilling find, especially so because a search was going on at that very moment for a plane that had gone down somewhere in the area. It was never found.

It was also in this stretch of fast water that I got myself into a spot from which I had to be rescued. I'd hooked a lovely big grayling about midway down the rip on a #16 dry fly and a light tippet. The fish jumped once and headed down into the fast current, peeling off line and starting on the backing, of which there suddenly didn't seem to be nearly enough. The bank was too steep and overgrown for me to get out and follow him, so without thinking, I started downstream and quickly waded into a scary spot that I couldn't wade back out of: I ended up at the top of the rapids in nearly chest-deep water, unable to move an inch towards shore and in the slow but steady process of being sucked into the white water (where I would have gotten a brutal dunking at best, and might easily have drowned).

As luck would have it, Wally came along about then. Assessing the situation immediately, he sprinted off through the trees to find the guide, who would have to interrupt his afternoon nap to, as it was told later in the guides' shack, "save the miserable hide of the dumb American."

I didn't know how he was going to handle it, but I was immensely relieved when I saw Guy push off from the bottom of the rapids and—first things first—swing out around my line so I wouldn't lose the fish. He motored up through what passed for a channel in the rapids, deftly flipped sideways (presenting me with a fast-moving gunwale at the level of my forehead), and yelled, "Get in zee boat!"

So, I got in zee boat, scattering rods and tackle boxes, and Guy, with absolutely no expression on his face, calmly handed me my fly rod. Out in the still water of the next lake I took up the slack, and the fish came out of 15 feet of water to make one more beautiful jump before I landed him, whopped him on the head with a knife butt, and tossed him in the cooler for lunch.

One of my clearest memories from that trip is that fish's last jump. Grayling are great jumpers, usually coming out of the water three or four times before they're played out, and they do it with fantastic grace and style. They actually *look* like the paintings of leaping fish you see on calendars—seeming to freeze for an instant in that perfect arc before diving cleanly back into the river.

While I was dealing with the fish, Guy was examining the outboard—seems he'd dinged the scag, that blade-shaped piece of metal that protects the prop. Actually, it was broken clean off, but guides never "break" anything, though they may "ding it up a little."

If he *had* wrecked the boat or motor, stranding us in the middle of nowhere, it would have been my fault, but he paid me the supreme compliment of not giving me a lecture, assuming that, although I was a jerk, I was at least smart enough to know it. A lot of information can be conveyed by a single blank look.

He did, however, stop off at a local shrine on the way back to the camp. It's a pair of graves set on a low hill overlooking the southern end of Snowbird Lake, the kind of place that's chosen not so much for the benefit of the deceased as for those who'll come to visit. No one knows who's buried there, maybe French trappers or some folks from the party of Samuel Herne who discovered and named the lake on his way to the Arctic Ocean. It's clear they've been there a long time, though: the inscriptions on the wooden crosses have long since weathered away. When the camp is opened in the spring, one of the first orders of business is to send someone over to clean off the graves and straighten the markers. The hill is near the place where the fish are cleaned, across a small bay from the camp, to keep the wolves at a respectful distance.

It wasn't as heavy-handed an object lesson as it might seem; every sport is taken there once during his trip, and we'd already had a good laugh by way of writing off the incident in the rapids as a harmless screw up. Still, there *was* something about the timing. I guess I should have felt lucky, or realized that perhaps I'd just blown my last chance for a truly glorious death—something few of us get a shot at anymore—but none of that occurred to me until later. At the time we were tired and happy, and Wally had a world-record grayling down in the cooler. It was a pretty spot, though, just a nice, peaceful place in the north woods.

Headwaters

A s you follow the stream up into the canyon, it seems to get smaller and colder all at once, an illusion caused by leaving behind the civilized water where the pools are named and where there are places to park. Going upstream here, where the cliff forces the road away from the stream, feels a little like going back in time, and the trout—still mostly browns—seem as liquid and transparent as the water. You're elated, still on your first wind.

This is pocket water and there's lots of it—miles and miles of it—so rather than fish it thoroughly, you keep moving, now and then casting a dry caddis (an obscure local pattern named for the stream you're on) over a good-looking spot. It seems appropriate and it works. Later there will be a hatch of caddis or maybe even mayflies and you'll stop and get down to business, but since you're more interested in distance now, you fish casually from the bank in hiking boots with the pack on your back.

You go carefully because you're walking with the rod strung, sometimes having to thread it through the brush and low limbs ahead. The cloth bag is stuffed in your pants pocket but, in the interest of lightness and mobility, you've left the aluminum case at home.

It's your favorite cane rod, a 7½-footer for a #5 line. You debated over the choice, weighing the risk to the rod against how perfectly suited it was to this little stream. Finally the honey-colored rod with its English reel won out. It's idiotic, you thought, to spend hundreds of dollars on a fine rig that you're afraid to use. And now you're pleased: the wood rod casts beautifully, and through it you can almost feel the heartbeats of the small trout. When you stop for lunch you lean it very carefully against the springy branches of a short blue spruce.

You've been walking easily and haven't gone far, but already it feels good to have the pack off. It's not as light as it could be—they never are—but considering how long you'll be out, it's not bad. You're figuring three days, maybe four, and you were very careful not to say exactly when you'd be back.

You haven't had to rummage in the pack yet, so it still seems a model of efficiency, ever so slightly virginal, leaning in the shade of a lichen-covered ledge. Tied on top are the rolled-up sleeping pad and the poncho which can be worn to cover you and all the gear or made into a serviceable free-form rain fly. The down sleeping bag is tied to the bottom and the old number 44 "Cold Handle" frying pan is strapped securely to the back. The pan always seems a little too big, but it will hold two butterfly-filleted, 8- to 12-inch trout perfectly. You'll eat fish on this trip or come back early; your provisions are composed of just-add-water starches and soups with some coffee, one can of pork and beans (a treat), some oil, salt, pepper, and lemon juice. Side dishes. The main courses are still in the water.

Beyond that, there isn't much: clothing you can wear all at once if necessary (wool shirt, sweater, down vest, wool hat), coffeepot, fork and spoon, spare socks, flyweight waders, wading shoes (low-cut tennis shoes, actually, because they're smaller and lighter than the real thing), and your tin cup. It's in the side pocket now, but if you were farther north you'd tie it next to the frying pan as a bear bell. Packed in the coffee cup is a heavy plastic bag to put the tennis shoes in once they're wet.

There's a camera in there, too, and the pack is so pretty in the mottled shade you think about digging it out and taking a shot, but it's only a thought. At the moment you don't feel like looking at the world through a piece of glass, even an expensive piece.

The only luxuries you've allowed yourself are a full-sized coffeepot, a notebook, and a modest-sized bottle of good bourbon—but maybe they're not entirely luxuries, at that. The coffeepot doubles as a saucepan, and holds enough water to completely douse the campfire in three trips to the stream. Your life has been such that there's the normal background noise of guilt, but so far, you haven't burned down a forest and don't plan to; you are meticulously careful with your fires.

The bourbon is still in the glass bottle because it just doesn't taste right from the lighter plastic flask, and whether the whiskey itself is a luxury or a necessity isn't worth worrying about at the moment. The notebook might be considered nonessential except that you generally use more of its pages to start fires than to jot down lines of poetry and notes of cosmic significance.

After lunch—a deli ham-and-cheese sandwich in waxed paper—you put the rod in the bag and walk. The trail is gone now, and the country is more rugged. Dippers splash in the stream; you spook a doe mule deer coming around a bend; and you get very close to a marmot sunning on a rock before he wakes up and bolts, giving the warning whistle, even though he seems to be alone.

At one point you find yourself within five feet of a pair of typically innocent blue grouse. You consider the possibility of getting one with a rock and have a momentary olfactory hallucination: roasting grouse and frying trout. You decide against it, though, probably because it's illegal.

And then it's late afternoon, the canyon has begun to level out a little, and the stream has a distinct shady side. The pocket water has given way to a long run, the bank on one side of which is open and grassy. There are delicious-looking undercuts. With several hours of daylight left, you find a level spot away from the stream (away from mosquitoes and morning dew or frost) and lean the pack against a tree, unroll the sleeping bag to air out, clean out a fire pit, gather wood, and set out coffeepot, frying pan, and tin cup.

The spot you've chosen is a tiny meadow stretch only a few hundred yards long. The open sky is pleasant after the closed-in, forested canyon below, and ahead, for the first time today, you can see the snowcapped high country. The weather is still shirt-sleeve warm with a comfortable hint of evening chill. There is as much spruce and fir as pine now on the hillsides, and you can see patches of aspen. You think you hear the screech of a hawk but see nothing when you scan the sky.

You could probably fish the stream here without wading, but you dig out the waders and put them on because you carried them in and are gonna use them; it's important. There's no fly vest; instead, you're wearing a four-

pocketed canvas fishing shirt which you load now from the side pocket of
the pack: three spools of leader material in the lower right-hand pocket,
bug dope, fly floatant, and clippers in the lower left. Each breast pocket
holds a fly box—one with nymphs and streamers, the other with dries. In
the interest of razor-sharp efficiency, you wanted to have a single box, but
the bigger ones didn't fit anywhere and you only toyed for a few minutes
with the idea of rebuilding the fishing shirt. Anyhow, the bulges are more
symmetrical this way.

You saw two small rises at the tail of the run when you first arrived, and
now you notice what looks like a bigger fish working along the far grassy
bank. There are a few tan-colored bugs that you assume are caddis flies fluttering over the surface, but without pondering the situation further, you tie
on a #16 Tan-Bodied Adams. The trout in these mountain streams see few
anglers and are seldom selective (though your two fly boxes are evidence
of the occasional exceptions) and the Tan Adams is a favorite. The tails are
of medium-dark moose body hair, the body of light raccoon fur; the grizzly
hackle is mixed with ginger instead of brown, and the wings are wide and
darkly barred—from a hen neck. It's a personal variation you often think of
as a "generic bug," an excellent high-country pattern.

You work the tail of the run first and, on the third cast, take a tiny rainbow that still has his parr marks, a wild fish. Then you take a slightly larger
one that wasn't rising but came up to your fly anyway, and then you take
the fish along the bank—a 9-inch brown.

The fish are eager, slightly stupid, and not large; you get a strike nearly
every time you put a good cast over a rising trout. Then you land and release
a fine, chubby, 10-inch brown and remember what a friend once said: "If
you're gonna keep fish, go ahead and keep 'em. If you wait till the last two,
you'll be eating beans." So the next good fish, a fat, bright rainbow of 10 or
11 inches, is tapped on the head and tossed on the bank in the direction of
camp. This is something you seldom do anymore, but it doesn't feel too
bad. In fact, it feels pretty good.

After five or six more fish, you take a firm brown that reaches the full 12
inches from the butt of the reel seat to the first T in the name on the rod. It's
a male with a slightly hooked jaw and colors that remind you of a Midwestern autumn. You clean him, along with the rainbow, wrap them both in
wet grass, and lay them in the shadows that have now swallowed the
stream and half the eastern ridge. You're camped on the west bank to catch
the first morning sunlight.

You think of going to a streamer then, of running it past the undercut to
see if there's a big brown there, but the dry fly and the wood rod are too

hypnotic. You take a few more small fish and quit with just enough light left to get situated in camp. You clip the tattered and now one-winged fly from the leader and drop it in the stream, like you'd smash a glass after a toast.

Supper is trout fried in oil with pepper and lemon juice, rice, and whiskey cut lightly with stream water—eaten by firelight. Then, lying in the down bag, you let the fire die to coals, think of the trout, the hike, home, people, career, the past, and you are asleep.

The morning is gray and cold, but blue holes perforate the clouds to the west. You put on the wool shirt and vest, build a fire, and start water for coffee. After one cup you go to the stream, waderless, and without ceremony take one 9-inch rainbow for breakfast. You roast him over the fire on a stick so as not to dirty the pan, and on another stick you make Bisquick muffins—a bit dry, but just fine. As someone (probably French) once said, "Hunger is the best sauce."

With the fire well doused and the pack loaded, you take one careful look around to make sure nothing was dropped or forgotten, then head off upstream with only a single look back at that undercut bank where you never did try a streamer.

By midmorning the sun is out, and you stop to shed some clothes before you get too sweaty. While putting the stuff in the pack, you're struck with the sudden certainty that you forgot the roll of nylon cord with which you can turn your poncho into whatever-shaped rain fly the terrain and handy trees allow; you can clearly picture it lying on the kitchen table at home. But then a short, carefully unfrantic search turns up the cord, as well as an apple you'd forgotten about. At least one attack of backpacker's paranoia per trip is normal, but you don't mind because it has served you well. You've never forgotten anything important.

With the rhythm of the walk broken, you decide to fish, and with the Tan Adams you take the first brook trout. But since you've taken only two other small fish after fifteen minutes, you shoulder the pack and move on.

Shortly you come to a road and, although it breaks the spell a little, you're glad it's there. On the way out you'll climb the grade and hitch a ride to the nearest cafe for pancakes or maybe a big, greasy burger, and then on into town. But now you go under the bridge with the stream, listening for the whine of a car and being glad not to hear one.

Above the road you come into a high, marshy meadow. Here the trees stop as the land levels out, giving way to tangles of willow; the only way to walk through it is up the stream, in waders. Wading and casting with the pack on and the hiking shoes dangling in back is clumsy but not impossible. You work only the best-looking spots at first, slowing down and concentrating a little more after you've spooked some good fish from what looked like uninteresting water. The trout are brookies now, with the occasional rainbow.

By the time you hit the beaver ponds, your back aches from the pack; so you set up camp on the first level, dry spot you come to. After a short break, you switch to a streamer and creep down to the nearest pond. The fly is a little brook trout bucktail, and your past success with it has convinced you that brookies do, in fact, eat their smaller relatives, even though more than one fisheries biologist has told you that's not so. You think, science. *Truth.* The fish take the fly, so it's true; or maybe it's largely false but still works, and so might as well be true—like politics or religion. It occurs to you that the Great Questions are probably a hell of a lot more fun than the answers, but by the time you've made your fifth cast, you've forgotten about the whole thing.

Four ponds and a dozen fair-to-middling trout later, you hook a heavy fish back in some flooded brush—a *heavy* fish. He fights well but stays in the open, where you play him carefully. You wish you'd brought a net, even though you'd have snagged it in the brush two-hundred times by now. You play the fish out more than you'd like to, finally hand landing him as gently as possible. As you hold him by the lower jaw to remove the barbless hook, he wiggles and his teeth cut into your thumb, starting a small stain of blood in the water.

Laid against the rod, the trout's tail reaches well past the 12-inch mark, well past. Sixteen inches? Possibly, and fat, too, and deeply, richly colored; the orange flanks are like a neon beer sign shining through a rainy night. You sit there like an idiot until the trout's struggles indicate that he's recovered from the fight. You release him then, and he swims away, leaving you with a momentary sense of absolute blankness, as if the synapses in your brain marked "good" and "bad" had fired simultaneously, shorting each other out.

Then you're hungry, and cold. You backtrack down the channel below the pond and keep the first three small trout you hook, trying to picture the exact size of the frying pan. Supper is eaten in chilly twilight; the waders are hung to dry; the rod, in its cloth case, is hung out of reach of porcupines who would chew up the cork grip for the salt, given half a chance. The dishes are washed, by feel, in muddy gravel.

The next morning you wake before dawn, soaking wet, freezing, and covered with mosquito bites, having slept dreamlessly on the edge of a bog through a substantial rain, with the poncho lying uselessly under you as a ground cloth. The curses you utter—the foulest ones you can think of—are the first words you've spoken aloud in two days.

Luckily the sky is clear now, and the sun comes up warm over the eastern ridge, helping along the effects of the smoky fire that took fifteen minutes to start. You recover by degrees, aided by coffee, and drape your gear in the willows to dry, everything angled to face the sun like the heads of flowers. Even the notebook was damp, towards the back, so you started the fire with pages that were written on, pages you did not read before lighting.

Breakfast is big and starchy, mostly half-ruined rice mixed with pond-water chicken soup, a shapeless candy bar you found while emptying the pack, and the apple. The candy bar wrapper is burned in the fire, but the apple core is tossed in the brush for a squirrel or maybe an elk. After fluffing and turning the sleeping bag, you slog the half mile to the head of the ponds and fish the stream, where you hook the first cutthroat—small, bright, and confused looking. You feel a little more in touch with the place, having been soaked and frozen with, apparently, no ill effects.

Back in gear—the pack tight, dry, and efficient again—you leave the stream and hike the dry ridge side towards the lake. Most of the time you can't even see the stream in its tunnels of tangled willow. You're moving well, feeling free on the dry ground in the shady spruce and fir, sensing the curves and cups of the land now instead of the bottom of the trough where the water runs.

You angle up unconsciously (almost always better to gain altitude than lose it when walking in the mountains) and come on the lake a little high, from a vantage point of no more than fifty extra feet. You wouldn't have planned that just for the view, but the view is excellent, with the small lake hanging in its tight cirque, smooth and blue-gray, with snowfields on the western slope and a soft-looking lawn of tundra around it. The trees here are short and flagged, bare of branches on the windward side.

You set up camp on a perfect, level spot, rigging a clumsy rain fly (thinking of last night) though the sky is cloudless. It seems early, *is* early, in fact, but the looming Continental Divide means dusk will come before it seems right. You stroll down to the outlet, the logical place for fish to be since the inlet is only snowmelt from a scree slope, and sure enough, you spot a few rising cutts. You've tied on a #16 Michigan Chocolate Spinner, based on previous experience, time of day, location, and hunch. You've also put on the wool shirt and hat because it's cool away from the shelter of the trees.

You stalk up to the water too quickly, too erect, and the trout don't exactly spook but solemnly stop rising. They don't know what you are, but they don't like you—a thought that cuts through the magazine-feature-article glitter of wilderness fly-fishing for the ten minutes it takes for two of the smaller fish to start feeding again.

The first cast is a good one, straight and sure with a downstream hook on the admittedly easy, uniform current, and a 13-inch cutt takes the spinner with a casual, unsuspicious rise. The fight is good, but because the fish has no place to go, you land him easily. It's supper and the last fish of the day; the others have vanished in that supernatural way trout have—they don't run like deer or fly away like grouse; they're just gone.

In camp you fry the trout, sitting close to the fire that seems to give little heat in the thin air. Camping alone isn't something you normally do, but you've done it often enough that it's familiar; you no longer get the horrors at night. You've gone out alone before because you were sad or happy, or neither or both—for any reason at all, the way some people drink. The lake is black now, and for a long moment you can't remember why you're here this time.

The Adams Hatch

PART 1 — GETTING THERE

I'M speaking to you from the cab of a faded-blue, 1970 Chevrolet pickup truck heading west on I-70 towards Basalt, Colorado and the Frying Pan River—speaking, that is, into a small tape recorder I borrowed from a friend's teen-aged daughter. The plan is to amuse myself and also to determine, once and for all, whether those insights, ideas, observations, and blasts of Pure Truth we all get on long, solitary drives are really profound or just the symptoms of white-line fever. The tape recorder doesn't lie.

I've been staying in the right lane most of the time (the slow lane where a fourteen-year-old pickup belongs), and I'm being passed on the left at the moment by an enormous camper, the kind my lawyer calls a "Wyomingoid road slug." The woman in the passenger seat (the wife, I assume) is looking at me now with an expression of undisguised horror.

"Bearded man in a pickup truck talking to himself—and he's got a shotgun in the window rack, too," she seems to be saying to her husband.

The husband looks over and says something. "Oh, I don't think he's dangerous, Martha."

Nice-looking, upper-middle-class couple, probably retired. Somebody's grandma and grandpa. Illinois license plates. Chalk it up to local color, folks, and it's not just a shotgun, it's a Parker. It happens to be dove season here in the Wild West.

I'll have to negotiate with dozens of these four-mile-to-the-gallon land yachts today, but it won't be as bad now as during the regular summer infestation.

So, where was I? Right, an hour from home, having made the right turn at the Point of Geologic Interest parking lot that takes me west, over the Continental Divide, and down into the Colorado River drainage on the Western Slope. That lot is a convenient place to meet fishermen coming out of Denver, and I've spent some time sitting there in the predawn dark and cold, mostly waiting for the legendary Charles K. (Koke) Winter and guzzling coffee from a thermos. You can see Koke coming a long way off even when he doesn't have the john boat on the roof of the car. He's a cabbie and drives with his interior lights burning. For some reason, I've never been moved to go over and see what's so interesting about the geology there, though you can clearly see the stripes in the rock where they blasted a ridge away for the highway.

I enjoy driving alone, especially through beautiful country on the way to a fine trout stream, and with the radio broken. I twisted the tuning knob off last winter in a fit of early-morning impatience and never got around to fixing it. It's okay, since nothing much of value comes through the air anyway. When I'm on the road I like to hear the blues, and they don't play it much anymore. Allow me:

Look on yonder wall
Hand me down my walkin' shoes.
I hear my telephone ringin' (lord, lord)
Sounds like a long distance call

It's a shame you can't hear this and, by the way, what *does* a long distance call sound like?

As on any trip, I'm experiencing a split consciousness: I'm here, west of Silver Plume now, heading for the Eisenhower Tunnel, and I'm also projecting to my destination so much that I can hear, smell, and see it.

The Frying Pan River and the guy I'll be meeting there (A.K.) are both old friends, so I pretty much know what to expect: a whoop and a wave from A.K. when I find him and a river full of trout and red rocks, down and clear at this time of year. The hatch (and there *will* be a hatch) will be some small mayfly: the Blue-winged Olive, maybe the Red Quill, or, if nothing else, midges. The fish will be hard, but I'll catch some—perhaps not a lot, but some.

It's after Labor Day and after the famous Green Drake hatch, so the river and the campgrounds will be more or less deserted, even though the fishing is every bit as good now as it was earlier (if not better by virtue of not being elbow to elbow). The nights will be cold. If the sun stays out, like it is now, the fish will be spooky and cautious, but the water will have that almost unbearable crystalline quality it gets in September—freezing cold and full of light.

When I think of the Pan now, juiced up as I am by anticipation, I get some precise mental images, complete with sound and color, geared to my momentary visual attention span: the 16-inch brookie from two years ago with the pretty burned-wing Green Drake dry fly in his jaw; Dave Student tying flies on a kitchen table all but obscured by Miller beer cans; certain rocks, certain swirls of current.

That's probably because my mind, in spite of itself, has been trained by television, an impression heightened by the fact that the Frying Pan River has *been* on television more than once. It's among the best, and best known, trout streams in the state, and those roving-reporter types at the local stations come up once a year for a story and, one would hope, a fishing trip on the company. It's considered cool—in a no-risk, Gonzo journalism sort of way—to do the story from midstream, in hip boots. They always interview Bill Fitzsimmons, the local hot guide and fishing entrepreneur. In recent years Bill has studiously avoided grinning into the camera and is looking very hard and professional. A famous fisherman.

Bill has a classy fly shop in the town of Basalt—cozy, clean but funky, with Del Canty mounts on the walls and the Pan right out the back door. The last time I checked, I couldn't find a fly in the place that had a barb on the hook.

There's a little-known law in Colorado that every fly shop must have a bird dog on duty during business hours, and that job at Bill's is filled by Tonkin, a Chesapeake Bay retriever so named because as a puppy he went to sleep in a display case full of split-cane rods, inadvertently saving his young life by not chewing them up or peeing on them. Tonkin is the son of old Trapper, not much of a distinction since half the dogs in the county have that curly bronze-colored hair and brown eyes. It's a local tradition.

The place is called "Taylor Creek Angling Services," and you may consider that a blatant plug.

Still, I kind of miss the old place, the one that was actually *on* Taylor Creek. It was a garage-sized cabin where Bill tied the flies he sold, but which may or may not have been open for business in the traditional sense. You could find him there sometimes and were always made welcome, but the feeling you got was somehow not quite like that of a store. If you just strolled in, you always felt like you should have knocked first. If you knocked, you felt a little silly.

Mostly he wasn't there. You'd go over to the house and his wife, Gerry, would say he was "out on the river someplace," usually with a sport. You'd pass the usual pleasantries while tossing a ten-pound piece of firewood for Trapper, a dog whom it is impossible to ignore even if you wanted to. You were made to feel welcome in the front yard too, even if you were just one of the hundreds of fishermen passing through every year who were so enamored of the scene that they just had to stop by and say hello. On the practical side, news of the hatches, of which there are many, was updated hourly.

It was nice, as, through the passage of time, the way things used to be always seems a little better, but I don't begrudge Bill getting all the yahoos off his front lawn and down in town at the shop. I'm also glad to see him doing well. He's often down in Florida now, fishing for tarpon and bonefish, though he hasn't lost his touch for regular old trout.

There's the Eagle River, the first of either three or four times I'll cross it on this road; I can never remember how many.

As trips go, this one was badly organized and got off to a poor start. A.K. and I had planned to do a week on the Pan like we did last year and the year before. It's developing into a tradition for the month of September, but our schedules didn't mesh, just like they didn't mesh last month when we were supposed to meet Ed Engle down on the Animas River and I ended up going by myself. I remember us wondering then if we weren't getting too busy for our own good and speculating generally about the nature and meaning of success. Is a man who's too busy to go fishing a success? We decided that, in this case, it was a passing inconvenience, but something that needed to be monitored carefully.

***

A.K. drove over yesterday and will be camped on the Pan alone for a week. He's one of those people who *can* camp alone for a week, tying flies by lantern light or gazing into the fire and sipping whiskey night after night, happy as an old mossy rock with no particular desire for company. This time *I* was the one who was too busy to spare a week but, in the interest of keeping my priorities realistic, I've stolen an indeterminate number of days anyway. Just making that decision has made my poor overworked heart soar. It's interesting how the power of responsibilities fades in direct relation to the amount of windshield time you put in going in the opposite direction. Errands, creative excuses, and phone calls kept me in and around town until eleven this morning, but if I don't stop to fool around, I'll make the evening rise.

I packed in record time this morning, but looking over at the gear stacked on the seat next to me, it looks like I've got everything: rods, reels, vest, waders, camera, rain gear, warm clothes, and sleeping bag. Anything less essential than that I can bum from A.K. or do without for a few days. Coffee cup? I think so, but I'm not going to stop to check now. The little book with addresses and phone numbers? On the desk at home. To the inevitable question, "Where can you be reached?," I answered, "I *can't* be reached." Not entirely true, perhaps, but true enough if that's how I want it.

Just made a pit stop in the thriving metropolis of Eagle, Colorado, for gas, oil, and air in the slowly leaking right-front tire, and a cup of what turns out to be really bad coffee. I know from experience that if I try pouring it out the window at 60 miles per hour, I'll get half of it in the face, so I'll just let it sit here and clot.

I guess I shouldn't be sarcastic about Eagle. It's a clean, quiet little burg where you can catch trout and shoot elk more or less right out the back door and where nothing much ever seems to happen. It's not the kind of place the kids stay in once they're out of high school but, to be fair, I'm sure you could get your life just as screwed up there as you could in, say, San Francisco. This is, after all, the last quarter of the Twentieth Century. It's a fine little town; it's just that the coffee is bad.

The Eagle River looks good here—clear—a stream I've somehow never fished, though I hear it's a lot better than most people think. Pretty soon it will get swallowed up in the Colorado which, even at this time of year, will be the color of an old banana daiquiri. We're into that stretch of alternating dirty-gray-colored badlands and crisp red cliffs west of Eagle, east of Gypsum (the same red rock that lines the Frying Pan). Geology again. I don't know anything about it except that it's down there underneath everything, it's meaningful, and it gets exposed by running water and dynamite.

It's not too far to Glenwood Canyon, which is near Glenwood Springs, which is not too far from Basalt. Still a ways to go, but easier to think of in segments. I should make it by four o'clock. I'll stop at Bill's to get the word on the River (he'll say the Adams hatch is on), find out where A.K. is camped in case I miss him on the water, and decompress from the road a little. It should take all of fifteen minutes and is a required stop.

Missing A.K. on the river isn't likely. He'll be at the Picnic Pool or on the Flats, and if I do miss him, I guess I know exactly where he'll be camped. When I find him I'll say, "Are they bitin', mister?"—an old and somewhat obscure private joke.

Here's Glenwood Canyon, one of Colorado's prettiest, seriously marred by the road I'm on now, though less so by the railroad tracks across the river. Still that residual romance of railroads. The road is in the process of being widened into a big, futuristic-looking super highway which is genuinely unattractive and probably environmentally unsound, to boot, though some of the highway department flag women are real pretty—darkly tanned, waving and smiling.

I'm south of Glenwood Springs now, following the Roaring Fork River up to its confluence with the Frying Pan at Basalt, feeling a distinct lack of guilt at playing hookey. As I said, A.K. will be up here for a week, catching trout, frying beans on the fire, and speaking nary a word out loud, but in a day or so I'll begin to feel that vague gravitational pull that means I'd better get back. There are deadlines to meet, money to be made after all, and, if the truth be known, there's this lady law student with long black hair. She's not entirely sure she wants to get involved with me; however, it occurs to me that our relative positions when we had that conversation last night might indicate that we're already "involved" in some sense.

Be that as it may, at the moment there's nowhere I'd rather be than driving six miles per hour over the speed limit (about all the old truck can muster without shaking apart) down Highway 80 towards the Frying Pan, going fishing in spite of everything. One is tempted to speculate here on the meaning of life, but why bother? Oil pressure's good, battery charging, half tank of gas.

Nearly there now, and things are getting more familiar. There's the bridge where you can put a boat in, and right up here is the hole where A.K., Dave

Student, and I caught all the whitefish that time. We were up here in April staying in one of Bill's cabins, and the fishing on the Pan was unusually lousy. After two days we came down here to the Roaring Fork, caught a mess of firm, cold-water whitefish, went back to the cabin, and made a huge pot of Chippino, a strong Italian fish stew designed to mask the taste of marginal seafood. Bill said the cabin stank of it for weeks afterwards.

PART 2: LEAVE MY MOTHER OUT OF THIS

I found A.K.'s pickup parked at the Flats under the dam, the only car in sight. It was half past four, just right. I rigged up slowly and carefully, deliberately not rushing—the equivalent of taking a few deep breaths to relax. A trout stream should be approached with a degree of reverence, for practical as well as aesthetic reasons: if you jump out of the truck after five hours on the road and hop into the stream, you'll not only wade right through a pod of rising trout, but will probably fall down and get your ass wet, too. Be calm—you're there. Squint at the sky, sniff the air, listen to the water. Tell yourself there's no rush, even if there is.

A.K. had seen me drive up and was coming down the far bank. I waded out to meet him with my flyless leader held against the cork grip. With some streams I'm confident enough to tie on an Adams before stepping into the water, but the Pan isn't one of them. There's too much to be wrong about. I could have put on a Blue-winged Olive dry or the emerger and been making a reasonable bet, but tying a fly on the tippet is the kind of commitment that needs to be honored for an appropriate amount of time. For one thing, you don't want to appear flighty and indecisive, even to yourself. For another, furiously changing flies is a sign of panic, and fishermen in a state of hysteria seldom catch trout. It's best to wait, even though wading a stream with no fly on the leader is a little like deer hunting with an unloaded rifle.

A.K. and I met in the middle of the ankle-deep ford. We did not shake hands. That ceremony is reserved for more unique occasions than convening on a trout stream. "Are they bitin', mister?" I asked. "As a matter of fact,

yes," he said, though apparently not at the moment, or he wouldn't have
come to meet me.

The word was Blue-winged Olives (ah-ha!) mixed with some little Red
Quills, some midges, and the odd caddis fly, blending into a mixed fall of
spinners—a drawn-out, sparse, multiple-hatch situation not atypical of this
water. A.K. had also taken some fish, including a 20-inch cutt/bow, on a
#12 March Brown and had seen a few of the big mayflies. That wasn't sur-
prising, though there's some debate about exactly what this bug is.

For all practical purposes, the Green Drake emergence was over, the famous banker's hours hatch, starting predictably at ten o'clock in the morning and lasting till three o'clock in the afternoon, the one that seems to be
attended by half the fly-fishers in the state. But even weeks after the major
hatch, one can still pound up fish using the Drake pattern, presumably because trout remember the big mayflies and also because there are continued, sporadic appearances of a big fly that some consider to be a residual
Green Drake and that others confidently refer to as the Great Slate-winged
Red Quill.

To my eye, the later flies are identical to the Green Drakes except that
they're noticeably lighter in color and have a faint rusty instead of grayish
green cast to them. It's also significant that the March Brown produces a bit
better than the standard Green Drake tie. A #12 Adams has been known to
work also on both hatches.

Be that as it may, I guess I'm only mildly interested in whether this later
fly is the real Green Drake or a different insect, my only firm opinion being
that "March Brown" trips off the tongue more lightly than "Great Slate-
winged Red Quill," a considerable handle for what anyone but a fly-
fisherman would call a brown bug. It *is* a nice little secret, though, both
the obscure, late hatch and the lighter pattern. It's what anglers are ultimately after—a shred of understanding with a practical application.

So, the latest word on current conditions. This is one of the advantages
of showing up a day late.

Nothing much was happening on the Flats (there were two guys drifting
big caddis dries over a pod of three or four trout who were clearly taking
midges) so we worked our way downstream. There were some fish working in the Gauging Station Pool as well as some in the braided water downstream. A.K. said he'd taken his 20-incher and seen some other good trout
in the pocket water below the channel and so, understandably, headed off
in that direction, trailing plumes of pipe smoke that hung in the still, cool
air.

I stood at the Gauging Station watching trout rise with a lazy but deliberate head-and-tail roll, fingering the zipper on my vest, beneath which reposed a whole box of Adamses, sizes 10 through 20. The Pan has the reputation of being a persnickety, match-the-hatch-or-else kind of stream, and it *is* that, though you can still find codgers fishing with Phillipson or Granger rods, sometimes fitted with ten-dollar automatic reels, taking trout hand over fish with a #12 Humpy. I've conducted some serious business on nearly half a dozen mayfly hatches here using an Adams in the right size (Bill is only half joking when he talks about the Adams hatch) but have just as often spent the evening tying Blue Duns with lighter bodies and darker wings than the ones that didn't quite click that day. It's a stream that can teach you about the frailty of your beliefs.

I tied on an Adams, size 20.

It became obvious in a few minutes that this was one of those times. The fish showed some interest, doing bumps and short inspection rises, but not taking, something you see more often on a heavily fished stream than on a wilder one where, when a trout moves for a fly, he usually hits it. Trout who get fished for often develop the capacity to commit in a considered way, allowing for a last-minute change of mind.

Okay. It's probably the spinner. A quick look into the current at my feet revealed a good number of them, mixed with the last scattered duns of the Olive hatch and the odd little Red Quill. I should have known that, *did* in fact know it, but the belief that trout aren't really all that selective needs to be hauled out and tried by way of an observance.

The religious symbol of this belief is the Adams dry fly. It's a pretty thing, with its mixed hackle and grizzly wings, the universal favorite of all but the most exacting fly-fishers. The pattern was originally tied as a caddis by Len Halliday on Michigan's Boardman River but has since gone far beyond that to straddle the line in the minds of anglers between the imitative fly and the attractor. It looks a little like everything, not exactly like anything, and seems to have great totemic power. Pinned to the wall above A.K.'s fly-tying bench is a slightly out-of-focus snapshot of a rather ordinary-looking piece of water, not worth a second glance until you learn that it's the famous Adams pool where the fly was first fished, at which point it becomes a kind of icon.

In fact, the Adams is symbolic of fly-fishing itself, a sport that, at its best, mixes the basics of science with dark powers on one hand and bumbling luck on the other. It's a good pattern for fishermen who catch trout by suspending belief in any particular system and who don't feel driven to know everything. It's a cowboy's fly, notwithstanding that it comes from Michigan. For that matter, so do pickup trucks.

***

Between clipping off the Adams (a little sadly) and replacing it with a #18 Rusty Spinner, I glanced downstream to where A.K. was holding a deeply bowed and nicely throbbing rod, the only sign of his excitement being the shorter, faster puffs of smoke from the pipe. Very pretty.

It occurred to me that I was standing in exactly the spot I was standing in several years ago in April when I mistook a bear for Koke Winter. We'd separated on the river and I had slogged down to the Gauging Station through the deep, crusty snow to fish a nymph. After a troutless hour, I heard footsteps crunching through the snow behind me. As far as I knew we were the only two fishermen out that day (a cold and dreary afternoon in midweek) so I said over my shoulder,

"Doing any good, Koke?"

"Grunt."

"Uh . . . Koke?"

It was a little cinnamon-colored black bear—I remember him as kind of pretty, now that he's not breathing down my neck. We were both terrified, but he ran up a scree slope while I stood where I was, somehow maintaining control of my bladder. I'd have jumped in the river if I'd thought of it.

Not a big deal, of course, the kind of thing fishermen get used to. Later I simply mentioned to Koke that I'd seen a bear, though I had the unreasonable suspicion (the same one you'd have if you knew him) that he'd somehow staged the whole thing.

I shook myself out of this reverie, incidentally glancing over my shoulder, and cast the spinner to a steadily rising trout just on the near side of the fast current. He took, I set, and suddenly, finally, I was fishing. Just fishing. The roar of wind from the open truck window was replaced by the liquid roar of the stream, and all concern for money, women and other personal demons was gone. Of course it was the spinner fall. I just hadn't been paying attention.

In camp that evening A.K. was orchestrating supper and drinks while I built the fire and admired the setup. He'd picked a spot near a little creek, for the music at night, he said, and also to cool the beer. The tent was next to the picnic table, on which sat the venerable old Michigan camp kitchen. This thing is a large, well-built pine box that can be padlocked shut and also bicycle-chained to a tree. The side folds down to form a working surface and to reveal a Coleman stove, pots and pans, staples and spices, coffeepot, and a bar consisting of a bottle of Canadian Club and some tin cups, all set securely in their own cubicles.

Inside the tent was A.K.'s air mattress and sleeping bag, and on the other side of the entrance sat a chair and table for tying flies. There was a lantern for light. Just outside, a bare tree held a set of wader hangers. A.K. belongs to the base-camp school of living outside. His camps are there for a reason (usually fishing) and the implied motto is, "suffer if you must, but not if you don't have to."

We were in the big campground above the dam, alone but for one other camper down closer to the reservoir. In another week the iron gate with the "closed for the season" sign would be swung across the entrance, and soon thereafter the place would begin to slowly and quietly fill up with snow. Grounds like this are worse than towns in the summer, but in the off season they're nicely deserted, eliciting the same kind of pleasant loneliness as a single ranch yard light burning across otherwise empty country at three in the morning. In September the deer start coming down at night.

It was empty enough that when two guys in a well-used old van pulled in near us, we gave the casual howdy-there-pilgrim wave, basically unoffended by the company. They were grouse hunters, maybe, or even fellow anglers, though the latter was doubtful, as they didn't come over to ask about the fishing.

Since they didn't start playing rock and roll, we promptly forgot about them, stuffed ourselves with beef stew, wheat bread, and canned peaches, and settled down to poking the fire and rambling. Two hours and several drinks later, we were reliving the time when we were marginally stumped by a mayfly hatch, a season or two ago on this very river, and spent the better part of an evening at our respective fly-tying travel kits reinventing the Quill Gordon.

Then we noticed the sounds of a scuffle coming from the van—thumps, grunts, muffled profanities. We carried our drinks over for a closer look and a better listen. It may have been in our minds to try to break it up if that seemed appropriate, though we'd both have dived into the bushes if knives, axes, or shotguns became part of the deal.

There was obviously a fistfight going on in the van (it even rocked on its springs a time or two), and during one lull in the action, we clearly heard one of the contestants say, "You leave my mother out of this, you (deleted)."

Things then quieted down to a low grumbling argument that sounded plenty combative but essentially harmless. A.K. and I decided this was not something we cared to get involved in or even learn any more about. The world, we agreed, is certainly full of trouble.

* * *

The next morning, I awoke to the sound of A.K. wrestling into his clothes while sitting on his sleeping bag. This awkward performance is a holdover from past days; the new tent is tall enough to stand up in, but it will take a few seasons for that to sink in. At first it seemed to be pitch dark beyond the tent flap, but a second look through more open eyes revealed a faint, cold, rosy glow along the horizon.

This is the only part of camping with A.K. I don't enjoy. He's one of those guys who spring to their feet an hour before dawn, happy, hungry, cheerful, exuberant, and minus a hangover. "Good morning," he'll shout, "you gonna lay there all day or you gonna go fishing?" It's enough to make you puke, but at least the coffee's ready when I drag myself out into the open, trailing untied bootlaces, blinking at the last frigid stars.

Coffee, breakfast, sandwiches for lunch, and the squaring away of camp were accomplished in a typically unhurried but brisk way. One does not dawdle around camp when there are trout to be caught. During these chores the van pulled past us and headed up the road. A.K. swore there was only one person in it, so I walked over to their spot to see if there was a body. Dealing with a murder would have killed at least a half day's fishing, but I supposed one did have certain civic duties. There was no corpse, though I'll admit to not looking under every bush.

On the water, A.K. wanted the Picnic Pool, while I decided on the long run upstream—there were trout rising all over the place. In that last moment before splitting up, when some words of encouragement are considered proper, A.K. turned to me and said, "By the way, leave my mother out of this."

This is how crazy old coots evolve. Leaving mother out of it will join "Are they bitin', mister?" and other vague allusions and mispronunciations— like sounding the "P" in Pflueger—taking us one step closer to the point where people will begin to wonder just what the hell we're giggling about.

There were scattered small mayflies on the water (surely the Olives) and a few ubiquitous midges. The trout were working in the current—hungry, eager. With supreme confidence, I tied on a #20 Adams.

Night-fishing

T H E girl singer on the late-night television show is a knockout—busty, willowy, all but coming out of her dress as she giggles and bounces around in her chair. The kind of woman that, as near as I can determine, does not actually exist. I'm beginning to lose interest.

"I understand you have a concert tour coming up."

"That's right, Johnny. . . ."

And that's all I can take.

I turn off the set, down the last of a cup of strong coffee, grab my hat, and go for the door. Out in the darkness the gear is already stowed in the pickup, which is aimed in the right direction. With my hand on the doorknob, I turn and tell the dog to stay. He opens one eye and looks at me as if to say, "And where would I be going at this time of night?" or maybe, "You never take me anywhere. You don't love me." It's hard to tell.

Five minutes later I'm parked off the road above the lake and am rigging up in the headlights, after which I have to wait another five minutes or so for my eyes to get used to the dark. There's a light across the lake, and I try to picture the fisherman dozing in a lawn chair with his lantern resting on the beer cooler, waiting for a catfish to pick up his golf-ball-sized gob of worms or, if he's a purist, aged chicken guts. Fun.

Then again, what the hell. He's not hurting anything, and if I have to change flies, I can silhouette the eye of the hook against his light rather than blind myself with the flashlight. If there's a trick to night-fishing, it's to get into the darkness, although, having said that, I'll have to admit to carrying not one, but two lights: a little AA battery job that I can hold in my mouth, leaving my hands free for unavoidable chores, and a great big bright sucker for finding the truck again and for determining quickly whether that big, vague, heavily breathing shape in the darkness is a cow or a grizzly bear. There hasn't been a grizzly around here in a hundred years but, in the middle of the night, one likes to make sure.

My gear is spartan and stout, well thought out. There are the two flashlights (the little one in a breast pocket, the big one clipped to the belt), a pair of toenail clippers in the right pants pocket, and a sheepskin hatband full of flies—poppers on one side, streamers on the other. No fly is smaller than a size 4. I'm after bass.

The rod is a heavy 9-foot split cane with an 8-weight forward line. I'm not using a cane rod to impress anyone (I would, but no one is going to *see* me); I'm using it because this particular one is slow and heavy and I can feel my backcast, a distinct advantage when you can't see what you're doing. It's also long enough to keep the big flies with their deeply gapped, lethal hooks away from my head.

The whole thing is a model of efficiency, which only illustrates that I don't do this very often and am not very good at it. It's eleven-thirty, too early, but if I'd stayed home any longer I'd have had to have a drink or two, and night-fishing is problematic enough when sober.

It's a warm, clear night, moonless but with stars. I can see the lake as the near edge of a purplish disk and can make out the closer cattails. I know from having fished here for six or seven years in daylight—and a handful of times at night—that I can go down to the water at the sandy place and cast to my left up against the cattails. I'll work a wedge-shaped piece of water twice or three times before I move down the bank a little, pushing the wedge ahead of me (and will naturally drop that plan at the sound of a splash or the spreading rings of a heavy swirl in the starlight). I'm wearing only hip boots to keep me from wading too deep. The idea is to work the shallows where, presumably, the big fish will be.

Night-fishing can be a pain in the ass, literally and figuratively, because you can't see where you're going or what you're doing. I refuse to night-fish water I'm not familiar with by daylight, but even so, stumps and barbed-wire fences change position and the drop-offs creep in closer to shore. The whole place seems different, and you find yourself doing things that are analogous to getting up in the middle of the night to go to the bathroom and ending up in the hall closet. I always feel like I'm very close to, as they say, "stumbling around in the dark." It goes without saying that the blackest nights are the best for fishing.

There are some things you can do to simplify the situation. You can keep your gear to a bare minimum to reduce the amount of fumbling, and you can plan routes to and from the water that keep you away from known pitfalls like forgotten fences shrouded in vegetation, sinkholes, deadfalls, and all those other things you lightly and casually step around when you can see them. On this lake I'll go in at the sandy spot, wade north along the cattail bank (where the bottom is mucky but of uniform depth), get out at the far end where the cattails give way to high grass over firm ground, swing up to the road, and back to the truck. If I'm not ready to bag it at that point, I can go on up the north bank, which is open, sloping, and less interesting but sometimes productive anyway. This particular spot is a piece of cake, comparatively, and I can probably do the whole thing without using a flashlight unless I get spooked or take a bass I just have to get a look at.

The preparations—scouting and gearing up—are essentially intellectual pursuits, the kind of thing that can look good on paper. At some point, however, you're faced with actually going out there, and that takes some getting used to.

For one thing, the hours are freaky, so much so that in some circles "night fishing" is a euphemism for catting around. What we're talking about here is the kind of night-fishing you do with a fly rod, and the best time is in the darkest, quietest hours between midnight and false dawn. Going fishing at midnight and coming back before sunrise doesn't easily fit into many schedules, and that may be what keeps so many fishermen away from it.

Something else that discourages would-be night-fishers is a basic fear of the dark. This comes in two overlapping varieties: the fairly rational dislike of operating blind (the fear of real physical injury) and that deeper, darker thing that made our ancestors get into fire in the first place and which has made bats symbols of evil instead of, say, bluebirds.

Now, I know in my mind there's nothing out there that will hurt me. What's abroad at night? Rabbits, mice, voles, foxes, coyotes, owls, house cats, deer, bats, frogs, and all manner of insects, including mosquitos, which aren't especially pleasant but are far from sinister. Bats can be spooky at times, but they're actually kind of cute. The only dangerous animals around here are the rattlesnakes, and even the balmiest summer nights are too cool for them.

It's really lovely out there at night, pleasantly cool after the hot, dry days, and blissfully quiet. There is, of course, no real silence in nature, only layer after layer of softer sounds: the rustlings, ploppings, and buzzings of God knows what, the sighing of the air and the water, punctuated now and then by the bark of a farm dog in the distance, the unearthly yowling of coyotes, or the muttering of a lonesome duck with insomnia. It's peaceful, and if I happen to get scared, I always have the big flashlight hanging on my hip like a .44 magnum. Ultimately the fear is a little thing, a subtle spice without which the experience would be just fine but still not quite as good. We human beings don't belong out on the water at night any more than we belong in space, but we go anyway, just because.

Well, just because the big fish feed at night—the largemouth bass, the brown trout, and some others, too—I usually fish for bass in the evenings, expecting, and often finding, a flurry of activity in the hour or so between sunset and actual nightfall. That's a transition zone, as real as the one between deep and shallow water, and the fish like it, regardless of the biological reasons. They come in and charge around, bigger fish than during the day, taking bigger flies.

That's the closest to night-fishing most fishermen get: staying on the water until it's dark. But as night comes on they notice that things slow down and it gets cool, and they're tired and a little hungry. You know, the energy fades and it's time to go. You could use a drink and, anyway, it's *dark*.

Things do slow down early in the night but, the way I figure it, about the time I'm ready to turn on the tube and see who the latest girl singer with the obvious charms and doubtful talent is, the big bass are just beginning to nose up into the shallows. These are the fish that are as much as twice the size of the best ones you'll take there during the day (in the case of my local bass lake), maybe as heavy as 6 or 8 pounds. In better water, who knows.

It's an article of faith among fishermen that any body of healthy water holds some monsters, fish that no one ever catches but that are, nonetheless, there. In most cases, this faith is justified. These are the bass that loom out of the darkness at three o'clock in the morning looking for mice, frogs, baby muskrats, and 2/0 bass poppers. Any fisheries biologist will tell you they're there, though the information will likely be couched in terms of statistical anomalies, meaning there aren't a lot of them. Their dietary preferences seem shocking on one hand, but we do not laugh at the flies tied to imitate such things, and bass flytiers are in a constant unspoken competition to see who can tie the most adorable mouse.

All fishermen know this: that the biggest bass eat (or would prefer to eat) food organisms just below those favored by alligators, i.e., dogs and small children. Just look at the fish. He's designed to take the biggest mouthful possible. The gape of his jaws roughly equals the circumference of his body. Fishermen also know the lore of night-fishing, but most of them still ignore it.

The whole night-fishing for bass procedure was impressed on me early in life by my Uncle Leonard. I remember the first time we went out at night (it may have been the first time I had *ever* gone out at night). The fish were enormous, though certain details, like Uncle Leonard's turning the car lights out when we turned off the main road and his telling me to be quiet so we didn't scare the fish while we were still half a mile from the pond, make me suspect now that we might have been poaching. Night-fishing is not only a way to get at the bigger fish, in some circles it's also a way to keep from getting caught. In my youth I was led to believe that only dilettantes and outright chickens fished for bass in daylight.

Night-fishing isn't something a lot of us get into seriously. It takes the kind of dedication to actually catching fish that many of us don't have; but it should be done from time to time, if for no other reason than that it's *there* to be done—an easy adventure. If you ignore too many things like that, you'll eventually end up with a general dissatisfaction with your life. You'll go sour and won't know why. It will be because you never fished at night.

Tonight I'm using a standard night fly. It has a heavy black fur tail (dyed rabbit in this case, though it could be anything) and a body of tightly palmered black hackle, maybe six or eight feathers wrapped on the shank of a #2 stinger hook. It looks like a bottle brush with a fuzzy handle and, with the addition of some rubber legs, might pass for an all-black version of the French Tickler streamer Russ Kipp designed for Montana's Beaver Head River. With hackle-point tails it would be a Marsh Hare. I call it the Night Fly, having temporarily run out of better names.

Night flies are traditionally black, or at least dark in color, and heavily dressed, the idea being that dark colors produce sharper silhouettes against the night sky and that the heavy dressings make more noise as well as increase visibility. Noisemaking is an accepted function of surface bugs but it's often ignored in the design of streamers. A lot of the old-timey bass streamers, and some for trout, too, had gold or silver spinner blades attached to the front ends. This was apparently done to add flash, but it also made the flies run louder. Putting propellers on my night streamers is among the things I'm meaning to try but have yet to get around to.

My only other standard night fly is the classic Arbogast flyrod Hula Popper, the black one. I fish a #2, the biggest they make, even though they're a little hard to cast on anything short of a 9-weight, weight-forward line. This fly (or "lure," if you prefer) is the loudest of the hard-bodied poppers, much louder than any struggling mouse or swimming frog. In fact, the sound it makes is more like the chugging strike of a big bass, and I think it attracts fish by mimicking feeding activity. Think of it as a bass call. Lately I've taken to removing the rubber skirts from these things and replacing them with long feather tails and hackles. They look a bit more traditional that way and may even be a little easier to cast.

Many other things will work, of course, and if you go out at night only occasionally you don't have to develop a whole new set of patterns for it. Still, this big black fly business is part of the mythology of night-fishing, a strange and solitary sport in which even the fish remain mythological most of the time. If the truth were known, even the truly serious night-fishers don't haul in enormous bass on a regular basis, and those of us who only dabble in it hear and feel them rarely, landing them almost never.

Tonight I'm fishing the streamer in the interest of efficiency. Striking by sound, as you have to do with a popper, is too much like playing chess without looking at the board—something best left to those who actually know what they're doing. A streamer is fished on a tight line, enabling you to feel the strike, so your only problem is casting the thing.

In front of me now is a stretch of relatively open shallow bottom immediately adjacent to deep water bordered on the dry-land side by a narrow cattail marsh populated by frogs, mice, snakes, fingerling bass, crappies, and bluegills, as well as golden chubs. Most of these feed on insects, some of which are predatory, feeding on other insects who, in their turn, exist on vegetation or zooplankton, which, somewhere down in the elusive depths of creation, generate life from mud, water, and sunlight. Or at least that's how I understand it. I'm here doing my level best to complete the food chain by taking a fish so big and so far up the system that he has no enemies except me and the guy across the lake in the lawn chair, who is probably deeply asleep and dreaming by now. If he's good he has a little tin bell on his rod tip to alert him to the fact that the battle has begun.

If I do connect tonight, my place in the food chain will probably be symbolic, as I'll almost surely release the fish. I have sworn to kill, stuff, and mount any bass approaching 10 pounds caught fairly on a fly rod anywhere in the state of Colorado, even if I have to mortgage the truck to pay for it, but it's highly unlikely that I'll get called on that, and to just *eat* a statistical anomaly is probably sinful.

I'm casting up close to the cattail, which reveal themselves as a taller, more substantial darkness. The water there is less than two feet deep. A bass could be cruising the edge or even back in there, swimming among the stalks. Once, in late evening light, I spotted a big largemouth by the movements of the weeds as he shouldered his way through them lazily, maybe eating damselfly nymphs or looking for something bigger. I cast a deer-hair froggie with spots and eyeballs to a little open patch of water he was headed for, jiggled it once just as he got there, and he swallowed it with a heart-rending burble. For once it was a bass and not a muskrat, and I felt like Dave Whitlock. But tonight I can see nothing, and imagining you can *hear* a bass moving the cattails is a good way to give yourself the screaming willies.

I'm looking hard, though there's little to see, and am listening anyway. Whether or not I want to hear the heavy splash of a strike to anything besides my streamer is debatable. I'd cast to it, but it could be a huge bass who has just consumed a quarter of his weight in raw bullfrog and is, consequently, not all that hungry anymore. For that matter, it could be a beaver. I'd cast to it anyway.

The fly is only lightly weighted, enough to get it under the surface but not enough to slam it to the bottom or ruin its action. It's so quiet I can hear the blip as it hits the water. I wait until I think it has sunk a few inches (during which time a fish could hit it, so I strain to listen, tightening my scalp muscles, as if that would help) and then begin the retrieval with a hard pull. I imagine the sound it must make: "voooooop." A 2-foot-long bass has heard this through his sensitive lateral line. Safely covered by darkness, he ponderously waves his tail and approaches the victim silently, hideous jaws already opening. Then again, maybe not. There is no strike on this cast nor on the next twenty.

Sometime later there is a tug on the line when I strip it and, though I thought I was relaxed, I set the hook too fast and way too hard. The gob of weeds comes loose reluctantly, by the roots, and when I clean the hook I notice that the water is almost exactly the same temperature as the air. The only way I know my hand is in it is by the slight liquid resistance.

I think this could be the wrong night. Intense night-fishers figure the phase of the moon, the barometer, and all kinds of other great movements, the proper combination of which will bring the bass of local legend to their feet like puppies. For me it's the dark of the moon and nothing much to get up for the following morning, period. Then, on the water, ignorance settles on me like a fleet of leeches. It occurs to me that all the bars are closed.

Half an hour later (intuitive time) it actually happens. I let the fly sink and when I begin to strip it in, there's a moving weight attached. I set the hook smartly, feel a ponderous wiggle, and cinch it once more to sink the point to the bend. The fish runs slowly for open water and turns grudgingly against the palmed reel.

Turning him out there was a stupid move. In the open water he would only pick up those flimsy weeds that aren't enough to break my short, 17-pound test leader. I'd have cranked him in as an almost dead weight and peeled him out of the crap like a banana. Now he's going for the stout tangles in shallow water, where I will lose him.

I'm sidestepping slowly but frantically out away from shore, and the water that slips into my hip boots cannot be the same water that seemed so warm before. The rod is above my head, in both hands. I imagine I can feel the molecular structure that holds the linear cells of the bamboo together giving way, atom by atom, bringing closer by the second the day when this already thirty-year-old rod will become a useless noodle. I'm playing this fish like an idiot but can't come up with anything better. I catch myself thinking about a friend who used to drive a garbage truck for a company known as BF&I. "What's that mean?" I asked him once. "Brute Force & Ignorance," he said.

A few yards from the cattails the fish turns, miraculously. Not miraculously, I realize. If he was as big as I want him to be, he would *not* have turned. Still a good fish, but, suddenly, it gets easier.

I hand land him by the lower jaw and shine the big light on him: stubby, fat, glassy-eyed. I think, 5 pounds, so let's say 4½—but then, thinking of all those magazine articles, I stick my fist in his mouth, and it fits. So let's go ahead and say 5. For this water, a hell of a bass.

A friend who lives nearby would consider it proper to be awakened at this hour to have a 5-pound bass flopped on his kitchen table. He would produce a couple of cold beers and his wife, being a sport herself, would be of good cheer.

But by morning it would pale to a "nice fish," which is exactly what it is, and the bastard would probably get out the scale. The bass I want would be worth waking up the whole town for and would establish me forever as mucho hombre, the man who is *out there* while the rest of them are safe in their little beds.

When I release the fish he bumps my leg once in his confusion before he is irretrievably gone.

Cutthroat Pilgrimage

T H E lakes are small, rocky bottomed, cold, scattered blue spots on the topographical maps, lying in a north-south band up near the Continental Divide. Most are named, but a surprising number remain anonymous.

There are brook trout here, some rainbows, even a few browns at the relatively lower altitudes, but the romance lies with the cutthroats. Just the sound of the word suggests the wild and untouched. "You get far enough up on the Middle Fork and you start running into cutthroats." Hearing that, you can smell the refrigerated air coming off the snowfields and hear the lazy honking of ravens, the implication being that the place where you start running into cutthroats is too far into the backcountry for the lazy or faint-hearted. That's not always the case, but it's a nice thought.

One June, to no clear purpose, but on something slightly more substantial than a whim, I walked to the top of Niwot Ridge for a view of the lake country. It was appropriately mystical. Standing on the spine of the Continental Divide, I urinated into the drainages of two oceans more or less simultaneously (a little childish, maybe, but a required ritual) and then perched on a flat rock that would be the ideal vantage point for someone who decided to just sit and watch the universe run down.

I chose that particular hill because it's the easiest place in the area to achieve the Divide on foot and because it's a walk instead of a climb—long, gruelling, tedious, but still a walk. My early flirtation with real climbing ended suddenly some years ago when I learned, by way of one of those horrible, life-jolting, late-night phone calls, that the man who'd been teaching me had fallen to his death. That call was among the things that have made me a more serious and dedicated fisherman, a sport in which life and limb can be risked on an occasional and usually voluntary, rather than a regular, basis.

On a long, trudging hike to 11,000 feet above sea level, one finds things to think about: that, for instance, Niwot, for whom the mountain is named, was an important Indian hereabouts back in the old days when Haystack Mountain was known as Peckers Knob and when other things were also still as they should be. The word means "left hand" and left-handedness was considered by the Indians to be very big medicine. I dismissed as idle the thought that I was righthanded and didn't have a mountain named after me. As I said, it was a long walk.

This area hides approximately sixty lakes. I say "approximately" because I've never bothered to count them and because I try to ignore the artificial boundaries where a national park becomes wilderness area and where a wilderness area becomes national forest, so I wouldn't know where to stop counting if I ever got started. There's also the problem of definition. The majority of these are cutthroat lakes, some hold other species or a mix (cutts and brookies is my favorite combination), and a few are devoid of fish for one reason or another. Whatever the cartographers say, a body of still water that doesn't hold trout isn't a lake, it's a pothole. After fifteen years in the area, I still haven't determined which is which in all cases, though I will if my legs hold out.

At first I was disappointed that I couldn't see more water from the hard-won summit of Niwot Ridge. I expected the whole thing to be laid out for me, but then I realized that that's possible only when viewed from the air or the implied aerial view of maps. After a little while the idea that the lakes were lying hidden in the trees, over the far ridges, and hanging in cirques began to appeal to me. It was either that or climb a higher mountain. The few I *could* see were enough and, after all, a lake is only truly meaningful when your backpack and rod case are lying on its bank.

Fishing these high cutthroat lakes can be about as problematic as fly-fishing gets, though in a different way than some of us are used to. At the highest altitudes, the fishing season—that period of time between ice-out and the first winter storms—can be as short as six weeks. Farther down the slope things start earlier and last later, but it's still easy to get blown out on either end, especially when you have to hike in some distance.

Some friends and I have tried to deal with this by developing the concept of the test lake. Test lakes have the virtue of being easily accessible by road or short trail while at the same time being at roughly the same altitude and on the same slope as more remote ones. In many cases the test lakes hold brookies or stocked rainbows, while the ones deeper into the country harbor cutthroats, but otherwise they're comparable. Rather than make a completely wild guess, you can drive up to, say Sprague Lake and if the ice is off there, you can figure it's off old Lost Lake too.

This isn't exactly a foolproof procedure, but it beats basing an expedition into the high country in the early summer on nothing more than the fact that you're, by God, ready to catch some cutthroats. It's an attempt at understanding—which is what fishing in general is—but, like fishing, the test lake theory allows for its misadventures.

If you hit a good high-country cutthroat lake within a few weeks of ice-out, you may find yourself in the midst of some of the easiest fishing you'll ever see, incredibly easy compared to normal cutthroat fishing. If you hit it just right, the trout are as hungry as spring bears and haven't yet begun to spawn. If they *are* on the beds, you take one or two, just to have a look at them, and then force yourself to leave them alone. Sometimes the fish are a bit skinny and a little weak from the long winter under the ice. At times you'll play a nice one too long and release him with the small, gnawing suspicion that you've done him in. Even the gentle art of fly-fishing has its little moments of tragedy.

Maybe you quit then because you don't quite feel right about taking unfair advantage and because the catching is too easy to be proud of. The victory here isn't landing fish so much as it is arriving at the lake at *the moment* through the exercise of (you tell yourself) your considerable steely-eyed, wood-smoke wisdom. With trout still rising, you can assemble a twig fire, brew a pot of coffee to cut the still wintry-feeling chill, tell yourself, "I am one smart s.o.b. and kindhearted, to boot," and sit there reveling in self-righteousness. At these rare times I typically dismiss the thought that an angler who has reached the highest levels of enlightenment might be tempted to leave the fishing tackle at home and just go up to have a look. As it stands now, though, I'm a fisherman, not a saint. You can ask anyone.

In any event, occasions for that kind of self-congratulation are not to be passed up and so, once or twice every spring, when anyone with the brains they were born with is down at the farm ponds catching bedding bluegills or bass, a few of us scope out the appropriate test lake and then slog into the high country in search of the first cutthroats. The self-congratulation is well earned when you figure that out of two trips every spring, you hit it right once every other season.

Last May A.K. and I decided to try it on Little So-and-So Lake, which is just east and a little downhill from *Big* So-and-So Lake. It had been a heavy snow year, with the lowland streams deep in muddy runoff. Even the road up to the trailhead parking lot was closed, adding a round trip of about three miles to an already healthy day hike.

We pushed it hard, the usual trail chatter degenerating into concentrated silence as we alternately swung along and waded the drifts. There was too much snow to walk in, but not enough for snowshoes or skis. There was also enough of the crusty white stuff to obscure the trail, and we walked right off it when it made the ninety-degree turn to the northwest.

It was about an hour later when A.K. stopped in his tracks, looked around, and said, "This doesn't look right. This slope is too steep. And see that ridge? That's supposed to be a lot closer."

True enough. This, as we agreed later, is the rather significant difference between being lost and just "sort of turned around."

We agreed on the proper direction and picked a slope that looked like it would be easy going. Less than half a mile to the north, we topped out on a shelf we took to be on the level with our destination and found ourselves standing on the bank of a new and strange little lake. It was a lovely thing, maybe two or three acres, roughly round, sitting in a little basin with a steep pitch on the west side and heavy spruce and fir woods around it. Another hundred yards to the east and we'd have strolled right past it. A single trout rose against the north bank.

Blinded by our original plan, we carefully noted the lake's location (south of that, just under this) and headed on to where we were going.

We arrived at the second lake instead of the first but, since they're only a little ways apart, we declared it a direct hit. By now it was drizzling, the wind was up, and the air temperature had dropped into the forties. As it turned out, it didn't matter which lake we found because both were free of ice but dead, in that monumental way the high lakes have, as if the trout had all slipped into another dimension. The water in both lakes was stinging cold and sizzling in what became a steady rain. Considering our ration of daylight and the absence of fish, we cased our rods and hiked out, reexperiencing the fact that wading through snow is only a little easier going downhill than up.

Back at the truck (finally) we drank warmish coffee from a thermos and dripped and steamed as the heater took hold. Whipped. We were forced, as fishermen often are, into a poetic interpretation of events: it had been beautiful, lonely, wild, not another human footprint, but some of a mountain lion.

It was about then that a red sports car with New York plates arrived, spilling heavy-metal rock and roll into the wet air, drowning out the pounding of rain on the roof of the pickup (one of the finest of sounds). Two college-aged boys hopped out and began passing an enormous joint back and forth. "Far *out*," one of them said, "get a load of *this*."

It was clearly time to leave. In all the conversation on the way back to town we managed to avoid mentioning that we'd put in twelve hours, hiked between eight and ten rugged miles, and had blissfully walked away from the only rising trout we'd seen.

Of course, such stories never really end. We made plenty of points with the boys for even trying it ("You mean you went *up there?*") and handled it the way you deal with making a fabulous rifle shot while squirrel hunting: by acting as if we mountain men do this all the time, it's nothing. We also found the new lake on the map (it was there but lacked a name), went back twice, and caught some trout both times. They were rainbows, oddly enough, the results of airdrop stocking.

"What's your survival rate on airdrops?"

"Well, it's pretty good . . . when we hit the lake."

We took to calling it Lost Lake, for obvious reasons, but that's getting a little confusing. We call them all Lost Lake when other fishermen are within earshot. The high-lake anglers I know come in only two varieties: those who generously tell all but a minor secret or two to whoever asks, and those of us who guard what little we *do* know with psychotic skill.

Once high summer is on—the short but dependable season lasting at least through most of July and August—things get easier. That's not to say you'll always take fish, but because the trout are feeding daily, you have a fair shot, which is all you can reasonably ask for.

As I see it, the psychology of our local cutthroat is paradoxical. The fish tend to feed opportunistically, the result of lives passed in comparatively sparse waters where there may be a fair diversity of insects and other food organisms but where heavy hatches and other concentrations are rare—waters where survival depends on a distinctly nonselective approach. The few times I've killed and cleaned high-lake cutthroats, their stomachs have contained a bouillabaisse of flying ants, beetles, caddis flies, scuds, midges, snails, backswimmers, spinners, various nymphs and pupae, maybe an odd leech, as well as the inevitable green goo with legs and eyes in it that could be anything.

At the same time, they have a distinct retiring streak. Cutthroats are not the shyest of trout (that distinction probably goes to the golden), but they do seem to have a genetic cautiousness, not to mention the ability to vanish so completely you could swear the lake didn't have a fish in it. When they're working, they are not often selective to fly pattern (with, of course, the usual periodic exceptions without which the sport would be no fun), but they can be maddeningly picky about things like fly-line shadows on the water, speed and depth of retrieval, and so on.

If the trout are up and working, you'll usually find them in the shallows, the littoral zone where sunlight penetrates, aquatic vegetation grows, insects and crustaceans thrive, and where most of the transactions in the food chain take place. If they're rising—that heart-lifting sight—you're in business. If not, they still may be there, noodling around the bottom in a few feet of water, picking up whatever they can find. It's not unusual to find them concentrated along a certain shelf, against a drop-off, or at a stream inlet or outlet.

You look for them, walking back from the bank if you can, carrying the rod tip low, keeping your shadow off the water, peering through polarized glasses and keeping in mind that a trout is well camouflaged on the side he shows to eagles, ospreys, and fishermen.

Maybe they're *not* concentrated. Maybe they're everywhere, with rises and boils blanketing the lake, or maybe the only trout you see is sucking ants along a shady, overhung bank. You fish for them where you find them, but you have to find them first. Blind fishing in the dark water over the drop-off shelf is a last resort—sometimes profitable, usually not.

There's a local story about deep water in high lakes. A man hereabouts heard that one of the nearby subalpine lakes had been plumbed at something like eighty feet. With visions of 30-inch cutthroats in his head, he hauled a canoe in there, paddled to the center of the lake, lowered a large hook baited with half a sucker, and settled back to watch his bobber. After several fishless hours, he reeled in to check his bait, only to find his sucker meat frozen solid.

If the fish are feeding, they'll be in or near the shallow water. They'll also be moving, maybe fast, maybe slow, because there's no current to deliver the bugs except at the inlet and outlet. This means you have to cast to where they'll be, not to where they just were, leading them like you do a duck with a shotgun. This can be easier said than done.

With only the rarest exceptions, I fish nothing but wet flies in these lakes, regardless of what the fish are doing—wet flies just under the surface film when the trout are showing on top, or crawled along the bottom when they're working deep. The pattern hardly matters; the size matters some. A #14 seems like a good compromise. While it's big enough to be worth the trouble to bite, it's not so big as to be puzzling or even frightening. If they don't like it, I usually go down instead of up, to a #16 instead of a #12.

Did I say the pattern hardly matters? Let's say it hardly matters *objectively*. I'll use anything as long as it's a Hares Ear Soft Hackle, a Zug Bug or other peacock-bodied fly, a little tan midge pupa, a pink or olive scud, or one of a pair of small streamers. These are established personal favorites, not so much fly patterns as articles of faith generating much magic. I actually believe in the magic, but I try not to talk about it too much. People give me funny looks.

The rationale for wet flies in general is that a fish is more likely to take something that's right in front of his nose than something he has to move to the surface for. It seems logical and works for me most of the time, notwithstanding the fact that A.K. can fish right next to me and take them on dry flies.

I carry some other patterns, of course. I now have my high-lake selection down to two boxes, one containing flies I'll use and the other with flies I will *not* use. I have more than once caught cutthroats by fishing a Hares Ear Soft Hackle through a spinner fall, but it would never work if I didn't have some spinners along that I declined to use. It's like a friend of mine who couldn't stop smoking cigarettes until she started carrying a full pack in her purse. It's the same thing, or close to it.

Finally, there's the mood of the fish, the ultimate hieroglyphics in all this. When the conditions are right, the fish will feed, and when they're feeding you can probably catch a few, given a modicum of caution and a little bit of a feel for it. A hatch, spinner fall, mating flight of caddis flies, or a weed bed full of shrimp will help, and cloudy, cool, breezy, drizzly weather is better than a bright, warm, calm day.

Both are good bets, but neither is a guarantee. I have now and then caught scads of cutthroats on blistering, sunny days from glass-smooth water without a sign of a bug, having no idea why or much curiosity, either. One has one's theories, but it's hard to speculate in the face of success.

The crack high-country cutthroat fisher is a good hiker, a fair-to-middling caster, a poor aquatic entomologist, and a hands-down master of the educated guess and the long, quiet bank sit. He also needs a working sense of humor, even if at times he aims his jokes with the coldheartedness of a sniper.

* * *

What makes it all worthwhile is that the fish are cutthroats, the native trout of the Rocky Mountains, sometimes called just that: natives. The ones here are of the Yellowstone variety. I know that because they have large spots that are heavier towards the stern of the fish, and also because people who actually know about such things have told me that's what they are. If the spots were smaller and more evenly distributed, I'd say they were more like Snake River cutts, thus just about exhausting my expertise on the subject. There are many varieties of cutthroat (fifteen by one count), some common, others extremely rare, a few extinct, still others hybridized to the point of being generic. The taxonomic distinctions that mark them are usually too subtle for this basically simpleminded fisherman. I'm frankly more concerned with how big they are or where they live than with what kind they are.

Around here the cutts are not typically of magazine-cover-photo size. Trout in the 9- to, say, 12- or 14-inch class are the rule, though the wall hangers do show up. Wall hangers? Well, cutthroats in the 18- to 22-inch class come out of here every year, each one being newsworthy. Sometimes they fall into the hands of kids who haven't yet learned that these fish are impossible to catch, though more often they come to hardworking, careful anglers who have more than earned them. Most are taken somewhere in the 73,391 acres that comprise the Indian Peaks Wilderness Area, and I dare not say even what little more I know about that. You understand.

To put it in its proper perspective, if you release a 15- or 16-inch cutt, you have the right to whoop and scream and give your buddy a big, platonic kiss.

We Western fishermen tend to have a soft spot for the trout that evolved in these mountains, and fishing for natives, especially in what passes for wild country, constitutes a kind of regular pilgrimage. Cutthroats have an aura about them of being "out there" where the wind blows free, where men are men, and all the rest of that Western movie crap.

Interestingly, this is largely an illusion. The fact is, most of these lakes (not to mention the streams connecting them and the beaver ponds that come and go in the meadows) were devoid of trout of any kind a century ago. The few that *were* up there were greenbacks instead of Yellowstone cutts, and most of those were quickly fished out by civilized human beings, poisoned and/or smothered in mine tailings, or outcompeted by introduced species—the then-foreign and exotic brookies, browns, and rainbows. It's a chilling thought, all that water without trout.

The fish that are there now nearly all came from some stocking efforts, either by anonymous individuals, the Division of Wildlife, or the 73-year-old Boulder Fish and Game Club. The latter is a private group whose main activity involves backpacking fingerling cutthroats into remote alpine lakes.

Think about that for a minute.

The fish and game club is among those few organizations which, without newsletters, magazines, conventions, office space, general fanfare, or plaques commemorating the fact, are just quietly and efficiently *doing something*. It's refreshing. They work with the blessing and assistance of the Colorado Division of Wildlife and have benefited countless anglers, many of whom have never even heard of them.

Another trout you'll find in the wilderness, in two lakes and a few miles of stream, is the Emerald Lake rainbow. This is actually a natural cutthroat/rainbow hybrid that was introduced here recently because it spawns well in lakes, using both the inlets and the outlets, and otherwise does well and grows large in high-lake environments. A biologist connected with this project told me the fish can spawn in water as cold as 38 degrees, giving them a good jump on the short growing season. They look like rainbows (most of them, anyway), act like cutthroats, and fight as well as both put together, lacking only the rainbows' propensity for jumping. A wonderful fish.

The poor little greenback cutthroats, so beaten down they were once thought to be extinct, have now been reestablished a little ways north in Rocky Mountain National Park where, in a few areas, you can fish for them on a strictly catch-and-release basis.

This is a classic success story: a species of wild creature brought back from the brink of oblivion by a typically undermanned, underfunded group (the Greenback Trout Recovery Team), now more or less thriving in waters where they may not have lived originally but which are nonetheless within their native drainage.

There was some controversy recently over a string of beaver ponds in which the greenbacks were stocked up in Rocky Mountain National Park. The brook trout who were living there were poisoned out, and the rare cutthroats were stocked in their place. Fine, but before too long the brookies started showing up again. It was speculated that some enterprising angler had reintroduced the brook trout, but one member of the Recovery Team told me he thought they'd poisoned the brook trout too late in the fall, killing the fish themselves but leaving the fertile eggs.

In any case, the brookies came back and began to grow to large size, while at the same time the cutthroat population began to decline. Were the brookies growing large on a diet of little greenbacks? The evidence seemed to point to that, but the biologists said no, the more aggressive brookies were simply outcompeting the cutts.

After a closure of nine years, the ponds were reopened to sport fishing, partly to see how anglers responded to the cutthroats, but mostly as a means to remove the brookies without harming the greenback population. The regulations were flies and lures only, catch and release on the cutts, a regular limit on the brook trout.

Is there *always* a glitch in the system when it comes to fisheries management? It looked perfect on paper, but the one thing they didn't count on was that lots of fly-fishers would show up on the ponds, gentle, easygoing types who found it difficult to kill those big, beautiful brookies, even in the name of science.

Back at the parking lot, volunteers armed with clipboards were taking an angler's survey.

"How many fish did you catch?"

"Eight cutts and six brookies."

"May we see the brook trout?"

"Uh, we put 'em back."

"Groan . . ."

Most of the groans came from Bruce Rosenlund, head of the Recovery Team and a genuinely nice man. The unofficial slogan for the project became: "Kill a brookie for Bruce."

A fair number of the brook trout have been taken out now (they're delicious, by the way), but it doesn't seem to have helped the greenbacks much. In fact, with the big brooks pretty much "cleaned out" (a phrase I don't especially like), fishing pressure on the ponds has dropped. The greenbacks may be rare and exotic, but they have turned out to be a wimp fish: pretty enough, but small and poor fighters. I know some of the people on the Recovery Team and we all applaud their efforts, but I think they'll now admit that the greenback cutthroat is of more interest to the biologist than to the fisherman.

Backpack stocking, airdrop stocking, introduced and reintroduced species.

It may be that the concept of a place as being truly wild and untouched is no longer useful in areas like this. Whenever I'm up there and get myself into the standard quasi-mystical wilderness head, it's a sure sign I'm about to run into a mob of screaming kids, trip over a bean can, or be intruded upon by the whop-whop-whop of a helicopter—though it may well be a helicopter full of trout, and I always watch where it goes.

I was recently told that the Indian Peaks area annually entertains something like 95,000 visitors, which leads me to suspect that the United States government defines the word "wilderness" differently than I do. The same ranger who gave me that figure said the bears had been acting funny, something that seemed to puzzle him but that makes perfect sense to me. I've been acting a little funny myself lately.

The official map of the area is covered with various crosshatch patterns indicating no fires, no camping, no "recreational livestock" (otherwise known as horses). You need a permit to camp there; you can get it at the same place you get tickets for rock-and-roll concerts.

So much for the unspoiled wilderness, although I don't turn my nose up at having four or five species of trout where there was once only one—and precious few of those—nor can I quite bring myself to think of a once-empty lake that's now full of fish as having been "spoiled."

All of this has been necessary and I can't argue with it except to say that locals should have something like diplomatic immunity from all those permits and paperwork, and to point out that the powers that be may have brought a lot of their people-management problems on themselves. For what it's worth, a wilderness area should be handled as follows:

First, remove the "sanitary facilities," also known as outhouses, plow up the roads and parking lots, reseed the trails, and otherwise vacate the interior. Then build a dirt parking lot at the area boundary and erect the following sign:

Howling wilderness beyond this point
Caution
Bad weather
Rough terrain
Bears that act funny
No rescue facilities available
Enter at your own risk
Have a nice day

Naturally, there are ways to circumvent at least some of the crowding problems. You can go to the more popular areas early or late, before or after the brilliant summer days of endless sky and gleaming snowcaps, when you're more likely to meet only others like yourself—an aristocratic but useful device.

You can and should go on days with what, in another circumstance, would be called "bad weather"—gray, thundering skies, drizzle, wind, rain clouds pouring through the passes like syrup. Tourists don't like that much and will run squealing from it when it happens suddenly, as it often does. The trout, on the other hand, seem to love it, rising and boiling almost imperceptibly in the iron-blue choppy water. You fish on the windward side of the lake where floating bugs collect and where the wave action stirs up nymphs, casting into the breeze. You do this after you've reached into your daypack for the wool shirt, sweater, and rain gear that are always there, even in the warmest, sunniest weather. You wait out lightning under cover on lower ground. Lightning is the only outside force in the mountains that is actually dangerous, regardless of how well prepared you are, and a man standing out in the open, in the water, waving a long stick is a prime candidate for termination.

You can avoid the big lakes with names and well-marked trails and fish the anonymous blue spots on the maps around them, lakes for which information is sometimes scarce. You can get skunked in the most hideous way doing this: by not only failing to catch or even see any trout, but by walking away with the fretful intuition that they're in there anyway, doing whatever it is cutthroats do when you can't find them. Thus, in your secret heart, you can never really write off a lake, even if you never go back.

If you do take fish, you keep your mouth shut except in the most trusted company. This is a further advantage of releasing your catch—you can always claim failure. Just try to keep a straight face.

You can be aware that most human activity takes place along trails and within a few miles of official access points. Even in heavily used areas, there are lakes and stretches of stream that are hardly touched.

Remember also that wilderness areas and national parks draw heavily. Going farther than everyone else is one way to beat the crowds, but stopping short of the trailheads can also work. Follow the streams out into the less glamorous surrounding country.

You can stay home and do chores on weekends and major holidays.

Finally, you can learn to live with the fact that these lands belong to the people and that it shouldn't be surprising to find some of them walking around up there. You'll now and then run into folks with more guts than brains, but most people obey the rules and stay out of the more rugged areas. What it boils down to is, if I feel like I'm better than some of the people I meet on the lower trails stumbling along in smooth-soled street shoes, that's my problem; and if I disagree with some of the management programs, it's at least partly because I'm a radical with a radical's simple solutions. That, by the way, is not an apology.

So I hike and fish because it's pretty country and the trout are out there, with the red slashes on their jaws and their fine, efficient coloring that changes from lake to lake. I look for two things, mostly: trout and solitude, in that order.

On the Road

T H I S was supposed to be an on-the-spot report from somewhere in Montana—one of the spring creeks or maybe the Missouri River, if the weather held. It's the last week in October, and Gary LaFontaine had invited me up to sample some of the not so well-known but sometimes fabulous late-season Montana fishing. As I'd never fished Montana this late, I jumped at the chance, even though I knew that an extended trip at this time of year involves something like a crap game with the weather. When I asked Gary what to bring, he said, "A light rod, a heavy rod, and lots of warm clothes."

I had the warm clothes packed—layers of cotton, chamois, wool, canvas, and down that I could wear all at once if I had to—but the crap game never even got started. I'd been watching the weather maps for a week, and they were starting to look grim. I'm no meteorologist, but I know what those big black lines and arrows mean. Sure enough, the night before I was supposed to leave, I got the call from Gary.

"Cash in your ticket; the Siberian Express is coming."

The Siberian Express isn't a passenger train; it's a storm that comes right down from the Arctic Circle to slam that open Montana country with gale

winds, freezing temperatures, and horizontal snow. A storm that will make
the national news. "Schools and businesses were closed all over Montana
yesterday as a major winter storm entered the state," etc.

I guess I'd seen it coming, but my mind still groped around frantically for
something to grab on to, even though I knew deep down that a trip into
that would mean, at best, a week spent sleeping on a hard bench in a small
airport. When we'd first talked about this trip, Gary had said he was as macho as anyone but that he drew the line at fishing in conditions that could
be dangerous, and as we talked on the phone that night (rescheduling the
trip for spring), I thought of something A.K. had said on the same subject.

"I enjoy fishing too much to risk my life at it. Death can really cut into
your fishing time."

Okay, fair enough. I was beaten by logic and reasonableness, but I didn't
feel good about it; I've actually been accused of being *un*reasonable on the
subject of fishing trips. As we talked, I kept eyeing my gear, stacked ready
to go, next to the door. There was a light rod and a heavy rod—a 7½-foot 4
weight and a 10-foot 8 weight—as well as the 8½-foot 5 weight I take everywhere these days and usually end up using. Clothes, vest, and waders were
stuffed in a duffel bag with the wooden landing net snugged in the middle
of everything to keep it from getting crushed. The cameras and film, along
with reels, spare spools, and some extra leader material, were in a small
daypack. The daypack would fit in the duffel, but I would have carried it on
the plane, making my usual scene about not letting the cameras and film get
X-rayed. It's a scene that immediately brands me as a terrorist, but I've gotten used to it. And anyway, how many P.L.O. types would hijack a flight
from Denver, Colorado, to Missoula, Montana? ("Take me to Last Chance,
Idaho, or I'll waste the stewardess.")

I could picture the flies. There was the usual stuff, heavy on the little
mayflies and midges for the spring creeks, and a whole box of big, ugly,
heavily weighted streamers for those 20-pound browns on the Missouri. Or
were they supposed to be rainbows? I won't find out this year.

I had my feet propped up on the desk, there was a nice fire going in the
stove, and I was holding a beer in one hand and scratching the dog with the
other. I figured the dog to be about the length and weight of one of those
monster Missouri River trout. My heart was breaking.

When I finally hung up I immediately went into a state somewhere between jet lag and culture shock. For the last week I'd been slowly but
surely working myself into an on-the-road head, preparing myself for the
jolts my system would have to take from hurtling north in a plastic-and-
chrome projectile that, by all rights, shouldn't fly, and then, only hours

after my arrival, finding myself standing in a trout stream amid wind, water, ducks, trout, trees, mayflies, and the famous Big Sky you're always reading about on license plates.

It would have been weird, but I was ready for it—the jammed parking lot and crowded airport in Denver, sticking out like a misfit in a Woolrich shirt, blue jeans, and hiking boots in the middle of all those tired businessmen in suits.

I've always thought there was some obscure religious significance in the fact that you sometimes have to get right in the thick of it in order to get away from it, an impression that's heightened by my dislike of flying, a dislike that, to be honest, borders on fear. I'll fly when there's a good trout stream in the deal, but I don't like it. They say the bigger planes are safer, but I figure the bigger ones are *heavier.*

There are people in my life who sometimes worry about me when I go off into the fields and streams, not realizing that the country is a calm, gracious, forgiving place and that the real dangers are found in the civilization you have to pass through to get there. When I take off on a trip I always think, Please, if I'm going to get killed on this one, let it be on the way back, after I've caught some fish.

This state of what you'd have to call negative culture shock (emotional exhaustion caused by *not* going somewhere) seemed to be another subtle way of getting cheated by the world, not unlike getting venereal disease from a toilet seat. I put another log in the stove, opened another beer, and consoled myself. There had, after all, been other trips.

Less than two months before I'd been on the San Juan River in New Mexico with Ed Engle. I'd driven down to Durango on a bright, cool, August day—an uneventful nine-hour trip more or less right down the spine of the Colorado Rockies—following directions I'd gotten from Ed's wife, Monica. They were lovely directions. She didn't know the numbers of the highways, but she knew the rivers: "Go down to Golden and turn west like you were going to the South Platte, then keep going at Pine Junction like you were going to the Tomahawk lease. Take the turn for Buena Vista like you were going to the Arkansas . . ." and so on to Del Norte at the North Fork of the Rio Grande and then over to Durango, crossing the Piedra, Los Pinos, Dolores, and Animas rivers. Thank you, Monica, I don't know the names of the roads either.

The idea was to do a fishing tour of the Southwest part of Colorado, an area I'd fished only once a long time ago, but this was a record wet year for the state, and all the rivers were too high and muddy to fly-fish. That evening Ed told me that "Animas" was short for a yard-long Spanish name meaning "The River of Lost Souls" and that the Dolores was "The River of Despair." It seems every time the Spanish explorers discovered a river, someone fell in and drowned. Moral: don't try to wade a river wearing armor.

And, as I'd noticed driving over them, they were muddy. Rivers of lost souls and despair indeed.

So, we ended up over the New Mexico line on the San Juan, a tailwater stream below the Navajo Dam that would be, if nothing else, clear.

It was clear, all right, and full of big trout that a guy could catch with some regularity if he was careful. It was also jammed with other Colorado fishermen who, like Ed and I, had come south to escape the mud. There were also plenty of locals on the water, and it wasn't long before we realized we'd waded into something of a cultural clash.

The first stretch of river below Navajo Dam is designated catch and release, the second stretch has a limit of one fish over 18 inches (I understand that's recently been raised to 20 inches), and below that it's a regular limit. The special-regulation water is restricted to barbless flies and lures only, and when you take your one fish in that second stretch, you're through fishing for the day. This rule is designed to keep people from stringing up an 18-inch trout, only to switch it for a bigger one later on, a procedure that almost invariably results in the useless death of the first fish. In spite of the regulations, there was a fair amount of that going on.

Most of the out of staters were well-dressed, well-equipped, catch-and-release fishing types, while most of the locals were clad in work clothes, fishing spinning rods, and looking for that one legal fish. The common greeting was, "Any keepers?" For the record, most of the fishermen there were acting within the law, though some were more than a little discourteous, but we did witness several flagrant violations. The award goes to the man who took a 20-inch rainbow in the catch-and-release water, strung it up, lashed the stringer to his ankle, and waded down into the one-fish-limit water, limping badly and looking guilty as hell.

There was no real trouble, but there were a lot of evil looks exchanged. Ed and I, dressed rather shabbily but nonetheless fly-fishing with snazzy tackle, were at one time or another given the hairy eyeball by just about everyone on the river.

It was a little strange, but, oddly enough, there is a distinct lack of emotion connected to those memories. We caught trout—big ones—and quickly accepted both the meat hunters and the snobs as facts of life, like mosquitos. The fact is, I can get just as aggravated with fishermen who are *more* snotty than I am instead of less so and it may be, in the final analysis, that there are only two kinds of anglers: those in your party and the ass-holes.

Now, only a few months later, what I remember about that trip are the trout—up to 4 pounds on flies down to #16—and the typically wild, cir-cuitous, convoluted conversations Ed and I have always had together. The talk after a good day on a good river seems brilliant and probably *is* brilliant in context, especially between two fishermen who go back together far-ther than either of them can clearly remember—all the way back to live bait. It's the talk of two old friends, men who are no longer exactly young but who are not yet old farts, though some of the early signs are there—talk that might just indicate the beginnings of something like shared wisdom. Of course, I don't remember much of what was said now, which only means we'll have to do it all again soon.

It's funny how the details you remember from a trip so often seem to be of superfluous things. The fishing from that New Mexico trip is filed solidly in my mind and in five boxes of Kodachrome slides, but one of my clearest recollections is of a half-hour lunch break in the town of Saguache (pro-nounced "so-watch"), Colorado, when I ate in one of those "Cafe Eat" places across the street from the old historic jailhouse and museum. The food was excellent and the cook/waitress/probably owner felt compelled to point out, "You ain't from around here." A statement, not a question.

No ma'am, I ain't, and what's so memorable about that I'll never know, except that it's all bound up in the headlong romance of a road trip.

I still do most of my traveling by car, mostly by choice, sometimes through economic necessity. Even with all their failings, automobiles still have it over airplanes because they're attached to the ground and because in them you experience the subtle changes in the countryside, see wildlife, get stiff legs, and feel deliciously far from home.

When you're in the country, which is still most of the time here in the West, you get to stop now and then at those wonderful joints, the taverns, cafes, gas stations, and sprawling combinations thereof. These places are usually unremarkable from the outside except that they look lived in, with their collections of trailers, abandoned chicken coops, smokehouses, re-tired pickup trucks, and outbuildings of indeterminate purpose. The sign out front might say just about anything, but the classic is: "GAS WORMS COLD BEER."

Like most things that fall under a single heading, no two are exactly alike, but there are some similarities between them. For instance, none of them are Orvis shops, but virtually all of them sell supposedly humorous postcards with fishing themes. Some are more friendly to strangers than others, but all of them lack that brightly lit sterility of the so-called convenience stores.

Those of us who have fished for a long time grew up around places like this and hatched some of our early dreams amid their dusty displays of outdated, cheap tackle, poorly tied flies, and spools of monofilament made brittle by time. The worst of them simply fill our momentary needs for gas, coffee, and other forms of go-juice, but the best of them—the ones with hound dogs sleeping in front of the doors—are friendly, cozy repositories of local history, the kind of oral tradition that elevates average deeds and fair-to-middling-sized fish to the status of legend. We can spot them a mile away for the simple reason that they are outposts of the subculture to which we belong. You know you can go in wearing hip boots and they'll just figure you've been fishin' or irrigatin'.

They can spot us just as easily, even when they've never seen us before and probably won't again. There's obviously something about the excited energy if you're going and the profound philosophical calm if you're coming back, not to mention the fact that, though no one actually fishes in tweeds anymore, fishing clothes are usually just a cut above regular work clothes.

There are other clues. Once, coming back from a trip to southern Idaho, I stopped in at a little joint for something or other that I didn't really need but wanted to play with on the road, maybe a cigar, or a cup of coffee. When I paid for it, the woman behind the counter asked, "How was the fishing?"

"The fishing was fine," I said, and then, out of genuine curiosity, added, "How did you know I'd been fishing?"

"Wet dollar bill," she answered, without looking up from her newspaper.

The joints I'm talking about are seldom on the main drags, and many of those that are have diluted whatever real character they once had with too much "Howdy, Y'all" cuteness and too many genuine Wyoming jackalope mounts. The good places are often on what *used* to be the main drag before that new four-lane was built and are the remnants of the once great herds of these things that inhabited the country roads near the fishable waters of America. Like fishermen, they're a little out of synch—on roads that, to the uninitiated, don't seem to go anywhere. Some of them would be pitiful if they didn't have that vague sense of dignity about them, and when I see one boarded up I know it will never be replaced by anything like the real article.

I love them, but I wouldn't care to own one.

I remember a place in Montana, somewhere along the Madison River, that is fixed in my mind as the archetypal worms-and-cold-beer store, Western style. The four of us were lost, three back in the camper, one up in the lead car. We were driving up and down a dirt road in the dark looking for a certain cutoff that would put us at a certain place on the river, a little dirt track through the trees that had eluded our lead man for the better part of the evening.

Finally we turned in at a joint—a neon beer sign glimmering through the darkness—to ask where the hell we were. Stretching and blinking in the unlighted gravel parking lot, I could hear the quiet but powerful sound of the Madison and could just make out the dilapidated outbuildings (once actually used for something, now filled with old horse tack and rusty tools that will someday be unearthed by archeologists).

The inside was cluttered and a little smoky, with moths attacking the overhead lights. The few trays of flies were of better quality than usual (this was Montana, remember), and there were several enormous old fish mounts on the walls: rainbows, brown trout, and the obligatory monster whitefish. Two guides were playing for money on a lumpy, quarter-slot pool table.

How did I know at a glance they were guides? Well, there were the clothes (faded chamois, bandanas), the leathery tans, the uniform age (late 20s), the bulging biceps from rowing float boats, the professionally cavalier attitude towards trout and trout fishing which somehow seems to throw arcs of conspiracy between the men and the fish on the walls, the level, appraising gaze at the four of us "sports" as we walked in, and an indistinct something (possibly an aroma) that said, these men are hard as nails, competent, use colorful language, drink a bit but can hold it, will fight if they have to (fairly if they can) but only when properly provoked, have a working, functional sense of humor and, in the finest grassroots existential tradition, don't give a good God damn about much of anything, thank you very much. They were fishing guides all right, no doubt about it.

It was one of these gentlemen who gave us the directions we needed. They were accurate. Strangers don't often get a lot of free, voluntary information in places like this, but what they *do* get is usually fair and honest, as if some secret sign had been passed.

Trips. There's something about throwing the gear in the pickup or, rarely, in an airplane, and *going* that plugs into our national consciousness as well as into that sublime craziness we discover in adolescence and carry through

the rest of our lives, like it or not. Every generation since civilization began
has thought they invented sex and leaving home. In a way, they all did. Vol-
untarily packing up and leaving home never quite loses its charm. And
sex . . . Well, you know.

Just to be on the road is good in a deep American way, but to be on the
road going fishing is almost too good for words. You're exposed, extended,
on a scent. Maybe you're going to a favorite place you know to be good, or
a place you've *heard* is good, or maybe noplace in particular, like
"Wyoming." Things are in perspective because you're on your way to seriously and diligently pursue success in an endeavor where success doesn't
matter in any normal way. Whatever happens, you will come back without
fish.

A trip is an adventure, and on an adventure things should be allowed to
happen as they will. Still, I have developed some guidelines.

Bad camp cooks are okay as long as you can keep them away from the
food, but bad cooks who mix cans of spaghetti and chili together in the same
pan as a way of continuing to punish their mothers for something should be
avoided, as this tendency may show up in nonculinary areas as well.

Whiners of all sorts should not come along. People who cannot deal
with the standard adversities—either real or imagined—can throw a serious clod in the churn.

Compulsive score keepers should be avoided: people who refuse to
have had a good day unless they've hit some preconceived mark, like "25
fish boated" or "at least one 20-incher."

Never go fishing with someone else's kid unless you enjoy kids a lot
more than you do fishing.

People who claim to own "fishing dogs" are all blinded by love. There's
no such thing as a good fishing dog. Most of these beasts are retrievers who
think they can do to trout what they've been trained to do to ducks. It may
sound cute, but it's not. Stay away from people who take their dogs fishing.

Do not go fishing with someone who is so set on being back at a certain
time that he will refuse to invent a case of car trouble to keep you on the
water an extra day.

Don't travel in large or even medium-sized groups. A typical gang of six
fishermen will include a bad cook, a whiner, a score keeper, someone who
absolutely has to be back by Thursday noon, his five-year-old son, and his
dog, Gonzo.

In the end, it's probably best to travel with established fishing partners,
no more than two at a time. The old hands are like your regular brand of
beer—less than perfect, perhaps, but predictable.

And never say exactly when you'll be back; that way it's not possible to be late.

Money is seldom a problem between friends, but to avoid confusion it's a good idea to have everyone put a certain amount of dough ($50, $150, depending on the trip) into an envelope marked "kitty." Group expenses come from the kitty, while personal expenses come from the pocket of the person in question. If there's anything left in the kitty at the end of the trip, it gets divided equally; if it runs out too soon, you all ante up again.

Try to eat and sleep reasonably well and don't whoop it up too much, while bearing in mind that a *little* whooping is unavoidable and probably necessary.

Fishing trips involve certain rituals, not the least of which is packing. For easy local jaunts, I have it down now to where I can be out the door, fully armed, in no more than five minutes, starting from a dead stop. I have a mantra that I recite: "rodreelvestwaderscamera," and I never forget anything. Once the season is under way, I usually have a broken-down rod, with reel attached, lying conveniently on a table near the door, and I can be on the St. Vrain River across the street almost the instant the inclination strikes. I once thought about leaving a 7½-foot, 4-weight strung up on the porch through the summer but was warned by a well-known rod maker that if I did that it would take major surgery to unseat the ferrules in the fall.

Longer trips of course seem to require more extensive planning. The preparation for, say, a ten-day trip to southern Idaho can be a logistical chess game in which the possible usefulness of every piece of fishing gear, camping gear, and clothing you own is weighed in the days before your departure. The final decision depends, as much as anything, on the size of the vehicle you're traveling in.

In addition to everything else, trips to strange or notoriously tricky waters require the presence of a fairly substantial fly-tying kit filled with bits and scraps of fur and feathers gathered from at least three continents with examples of Norwegian and English metallurgy, most of which you won't use but wouldn't feel comfortable without.

I've done a good deal of traveling with A.K., who, being a professional flytier, has a much better travel kit than mine. At least once on every trip I find myself saying something like, "Arch, you got any hooks?"

So far I've never forgotten anything vital on a trip. I tend to err in the other direction, hauling along things I have no earthly use for, like five rods besides the one I'm going to be fishing with.

This is another advantage to traveling in an automobile of some sort— you can carry a lot more junk. You can also keep an eye on it. An airline is much more likely to smash, lose, or reroute your stuff than you are. No, it's never happened to me, but I've heard all the horror stories.

Another thing I don't like about airplanes is the level of culture shock they inevitably produce. Travel shouldn't be that fast, that antiseptic, or that easy. My mind has not entered the late Twentieth Century sufficiently to be able to translate time spent sitting in a sealed capsule with distance covered. When I step into the thing in Denver and step out of it somewhere else, I feel like I've gotten to a place without actually *going* there in any kind of reasonable way.

A lot of modern human beings have gotten used to it, and I suppose *I* could get used to it too, though I'm not sure I want to.

Of course, culture shock on the outward-bound end of a trip is softened by the directional energy of "going fishing." Ultimately it will be you, your fly rod, and some trout, mackinaw, pike, or whatever, and that, at least, makes sense. Whatever strangeness there is to the place penetrates your aura of purposeful concentration at an acceptable rate. When it hits me the hardest is on the way back, when I'm tired and my sense of purpose has dissolved.

It happened a few years ago when three companions and I flew into Canada's Northwest Territories to spend a week in a fishing camp on a remote lake. We flew from Denver to Winnipeg, stayed overnight in a hotel that was much too posh for a gang of fishermen, and, at dawn the next morning, were driven to the airport to be loaded onto some kind of World War II transport—a DC-3 maybe. I don't know planes. All I know is the thing was sitting at enough of an angle that you had to climb the aisle, and I remember peeking into the cockpit, expecting to see John Wayne at the controls.

This lumbering old crate flew us north to a place called Stony Rapids, the last settlement in that direction. Next stop, the Arctic Circle.

From the dirt airstrip at Stony Rapids, we walked down to the river to catch the single-engine float planes that would take us two hundred-some miles farther north into North America's last great wilderness.

At the end of the third flight in the space of two days, I was found to be seized-up, frozen like a rabbit in the headlights of a car, and had to be pried from the plane by the guides when we arrived at the camp.

I soon got my color back, though, because I was on the ground—safe for the moment—and because the place was familiar enough: coniferous forests, lakes, streams, ducks, mosquitos, more of it than I was used to, but otherwise the same old stuff. The guides even spoke English, albeit

Canadian English, where every sentence begins with "You know" and ends with "Eh?"

The only floral or faunal incongruity involved the wolves. I remember once stepping outside to relieve myself in the middle of the short, Northern night, hearing a wolf go off like an air-raid siren at what seemed to be very close range, and deciding it could wait until morning.

It was a fine trip, as expeditions into the real backcountry typically are. The catching of fish was nicely balanced against the not catching of fish to produce the proper level of drama, and it was all set against a backdrop of wonderful, wild loneliness.

What was hard on my mind, culture-shock-wise, was the brutal unreality of the return trip. I woke up one morning in a comfortably rough camp in the territories and ate supper that night in an expensive hotel dining room in downtown Winnipeg.

Back up in the room, the boys were watching television—there were gunshots from snub-nosed revolvers, car chases, lots of griping and yelling. It was a bit too much, so I did what any seasoned outdoorsman would do: I took my small wad of exotic Canadian money down to the bar. In our week in camp I'd developed a taste for a certain brand of inexpensive Canadian beer, and I figured about fifteen of them would ease my troubled mind.

I was deep in an internal fog, so I was on my second beer before I realized something like a wedding reception was in progress. I was the only one there not in a tuxedo or an evening gown. I was dressed in week-old fishing clothes and, in spite of the fact that the place was jammed, I was all alone at the bar.

There was a group playing under blue lights at the far end of the large room, and they sounded strangely familiar, so familiar that I began to study them and, two beers later, realized, "My God! It's the Ink Spots!"

Now I wouldn't even be old enough to remember the Ink Spots except that they were my father's favorite group. He played their records all through my childhood and once told me how he and Ma had listened to them before they were married, when she was in high school and he was jerking sodas at a drugstore. He used to make some fantastic ice-cream concoction called the "Gierach Special" and probably never dreamed that his boy, years later, would also make Gierach Specials, except that mine would be trout flies.

It doesn't sound like much now. There was only one guy in the band old enough to have been an original member—the lead singer was about my age—but it was the Ink Spots, all right. It even said so on the bass drum.

Somehow it was what I was looking for, a connection of some kind. I remember thinking, okay, it's over, I'm back.

The View
from Rat Lake

The Big Empty River

L A S T summer the notorious Charles K. (Koke) Winter bought it on the Henry's Fork in southern Idaho, by which I mean he took a fall and broke his leg. "A word of advice," he told me recently. "If you're ever walking along the banks of the Henry's Fork and a pair of sandhill cranes fly over, stop walking first, *then* look."

If Koke was going to break something while fishing (and anyone who knows him would have told you it was just waiting to happen), it's like him to do it on one of the most famous trout streams in the world. He has a way of doing things like that; of engineering even his accidents so that, in the retelling, they can't help but sound heroic.

He somehow managed to achieve a spiral fracture—the classic downhill skiing injury—and so naturally someone down at the health club asked him, in that snide way people have when you're hurt, "How's the skiing?"

"I don't go in for sissy sports," Koke answered, "I'm a trout fisherman."

That kind of style is something you have to be born with.

I've never broken anything on the Henry's Fork, not even a fly rod, but I've fished it every year since the first time I laid eyes on it. That puts me in the company of thousands of other fly-fishers from all over the country and even in the rest of the world—the people whose cars and trucks, during the Green Drake hatch at least, make that little patch of gravel in front of Mike Lawson's fly shop look like the parking lot at the United Nations building.

I first fished the river because it had become unavoidable. Everyone talked about it, quoted magazine articles about it, showed pictures of it, and even drove up there to fish in it now and then. More to the point, they all used it as a kind of measure against which all other trout streams were judged. A great rainbow trout was "like a Henry's Fork fish," a heavy mayfly hatch was "like you'd see on the Henry's Fork," a wide, slow section of any river was "just like the Fork above Osborn Bridge." I got the feeling they must have a 100-yard stretch of it on display at the Bureau of Standards as an example of *the* trout stream, right next to *the* foot, *the* pound, and so on. I finally had to go fish the thing just so I could hold up my end of the conversation.

That first trip was something of a turning point. It wasn't my first famous river, but it was my first truly mythological one. It was also the first time I fished with Koke and began to get an inkling of how famous *he* was. Everyone knew him and everyone who took the time to talk had a story, each one less believable than the last. Enormous trout, convoluted ethics, feats of strength and daring, elaborate practical jokes, and other things, too. Koke Winter stories could fill a book, and I hope they do someday. Of course, Koke will have to write it himself. No one else would dare to say half of it in print.

Some years later, while I was working in a fly shop in Boulder, Colorado, Koke came in doing his jerk act—asking about our live bait selection, referring to the fly rods as "crawler poles," and so on. It was clear to the other customers that we knew each other, so when he left someone asked, "Who the hell was that?"

"His name is Koke Winter," I said.

"*That* was Koke Winter!?" the man said. "Jeeze!" And then everyone gazed reverently at the empty spot where his car had been parked.

This was also the first long trip (the first of many) that I took with Archie (A.K.) Best. A.K. and I had been fishing together before, but it was the first Henry's Fork expedition that sealed us as partners.

A road trip can do that by getting all the cards on the table. It can also accomplish the opposite. The usual hardships of getting out early, getting in late, getting lost, getting rained on, getting skunked, and all the other things you can get tend to reveal character in a matter of days. Creeps and idiots cannot conceal themselves for long on a fishing trip.

A.K. and I have been all over hell together since then—mostly just the two of us, based on our shared perception that two fishermen are a partnership, while any more than that constitutes a committee. We now set up our camps with such wordless efficiency that spectators sometimes think we're mad at each other. I've learned a lot from him, from the nuts and bolts of fly tying and casting—both of which he's damned good at—to philosophy. It was while fishing with A.K. that I discovered you could tell the plain truth about fly-fishing and still be a humorist.

I've learned a lot from him even though he's never *taught* me a damned thing, and although this didn't exactly start on the Henry's Fork, it was there that it hit cruising speed.

The first time I saw the river my mind was boggled more than that of the normal pilgrim because of what Koke had done to us. Koke, A.K., a man named Tom Abbot, and I set out from Colorado in a borrowed camper: an enormous six-mile-to-the-gallon land yacht that, in a single two-week trip, soured me on these vehicles forever.

For one thing, it wouldn't go over forty-five mph, even across Wyoming where most drivers change flat tires at forty-five.

It ate gas as if it was still the 1950s.

It was supposed to "sleep six comfortably" but was actually about big enough for two or three close (and I mean *close*) friends with their gear and a change of clothes each. The fourth man was too many, and it was never quite clear who the fourth man was.

The thing was also furnished in late cafe gothic, so that even if you were parked in the middle of fabulous scenery, you felt like you were camped with a bunch of declining rock musicians in a sleazy motel on East Colfax Avenue in Denver.

And there was the unbearable suspense over whether the thing would start in the morning.

But the worst part was that it was slow. I've since learned that the drive to the Henry's Fork is a crisp twelve hours with six driving shifts between two people and as many piss, gas, and coffee stops. A breeze in a real road car or a serviceable pickup. Now I'm not the speed freak I once was—not like when Ed Engle and I would get off work at our landscaping jobs, hop in his car, blast from Boulder, Colorado, to Laramie, Wyoming, find a truck stop, order coffee, ask the waitress what state we were in and what the date was, and be back in time for work the next morning—but I do like to get where I'm going, and so does A.K.

In fact, A.K. gets downright kittenish about it sometimes. He's even been known to drag race occasionally when one of those rural hot rodders in the fifteen-foot-tall pickups, with the balloon tires, chrome stacks, and pinstriping revs his engine at us at a stoplight. A.K.'s pickup is rather hot, and he's been known to win, much to the dismay of several teenagers across the western United States.

You can never tell about those old guys in fishing hats.

So there we were, cooped up in this lumbering dinosaur, creeping across Wyoming, being passed by one little old lady in a Volkswagen after another. After about eighteen hours of that, you start to get a little testy.

Koke let that work on us all by itself until we came down off the pass into Idaho on the long-awaited last leg. Then he started. There were places where we had to stop and look at the scenery—and with Koke you don't just look, you speculate on the place's geologic history and determine which plants are edible and which are not. It can take an hour.

Then there was the final gas stop in Tetonia or Driggs (known as Dregs by the locals) or one of those other little towns that are an hour or so from the final destination. Koke had to tour all the gas stations to find the cheapest price, then he had to check the air in the tires, and the oil, and the water in the radiator—all of which were, of course, fine.

Then he had to have an ice cream cone. It took him fifteen minutes to pick one out, and then he started with the clerk. "Tell me, sir, is this ice cream 'quiescently frozen'?"

We had to stop to look at a single trumpeter swan in a puddle by the side of the highway, which I'd have been happy to do at any other time, except that by then we were twelve miles from the Henry's Fork for Christ's sake! Gimme a break, Koke.

When we finally arrived at the river, three of us exploded from the camper, hit the water running with fly rods still unstrung and wader suspenders unfastened, and proceeded to fall in, not catch fish, and otherwise make fools of ourselves, while Koke sat quietly on the back step of the camper and calmly took forty-five minutes to tie up the perfect leader, smiling to himself all the time.

The bastard.

In seasons since I have come to learn that Koke's sense of humor is among the most dangerous in existence, because it's practiced for his own amusement alone. It doesn't matter if you get it or not. In fact, it's probably

better if you don't. And the funniest thing imaginable to him is to shake
your composure while retaining his.

All that notwithstanding, there it was: the fabled Henry's Fork, and in the
last week in June, too, at the height of the Green Drake mayfly hatch. In all
of human experience there are only four metaphysical summits: Valhalla,
Heaven, Nirvana, and the Green Drake hatch on the Henry's Fork.

The Henry's Fork is known as the river where insect hatches come off
not only heavily, but regularly, "like clockwork." That's probably close to
true, but it would be more accurate to say they come off *more* like clockwork there than on most other streams. There are glitches even in paradise.

For instance, there was a season in recent memory when the Green
Drakes didn't come off at all, for reasons that may never be reliably determined. It just didn't happen. Another year the hatch came off just fine, but
a million sea gulls arrived and ate most of them. They didn't eat all of them,
of course, but even though there were still some bugs on the water, the
swooping, diving gulls spooked the trout and the fishing was lousy. I
missed that year, but I understand several thousand fly-fishers were seriously bummed out.

Relative to that season, I once overheard the following conversation in
the A-Bar on the banks of the Fork at Last Chance, Idaho:

First fisherman (obviously inebriated and a bit sentimental): "You remember the year the sea gulls mucked up the hatch?"

Second fisherman: "Yeah."

First fisherman, after a long pause: "You know, life is like that."

Second fisherman: "Like fishing?"

First fisherman: "No, like sea gulls."

The point is, if it happened on the Henry's Fork, it was profound.

The Henry's Fork is the favorite trout stream of so many fly-fishers because
it's exactly what you'd dream up for yourself if you could invent the perfect
place using only thin air and the loftiest elements of the fly-fishing tradition.
It's big and sprawling—some say it's the largest legitimate spring creek in
the world—and it's not fast and brawling like many western rivers. It is, in
fact, a sedate, quiet river, at least below Box Canyon. In most places the
wading is between easy and effortless, and it's been described as like a
flooded parking lot. I'll buy that if you take that parking lot and scatter a
few tripping-sized boulders and some surprise holes around in it. There are

a few places where the wading fisherman can't go, but there are damned few he can't at least reach.

And that's a good thing because the trout are everywhere. Sure, some spots are better than others, but most of the river bottom is matted with thick vegetation which is, in turn, grazed upon by a staggering number of aquatic nymphs that periodically emerge to become some of the most famous hatches in the literature of the sport. There are the real glamor bugs: the Green, Brown, and Gray Drakes, Blue-winged Olives, Pale Morning Duns, Callibaetis (Speckled Duns), tiny Black & White Trikes, Mahogany Duns, and others. There are also the spotty and mysterious flying ant falls, the bankside ants, beetles, and hoppers, and, of course, the workmanlike caddis hatches, which can be as delicately technical as any of the supposedly classier mayflies.

If you catch any of these bugs at their best on the Henry's Fork, it will be "the heaviest (fill in the blank) hatch I've ever seen," and you will babble on about it for weeks afterwards to anyone who will listen.

The trout, mostly rainbows, are large, fat, healthy, and hard fighting, and they continue to feed on insects even when they've grown well past the 20-inch mark. That, one assumes, is because there are so many bugs and so many slow currents where the fish don't have to work their little tails off to get at them.

As if the river wasn't pretty enough, it meanders through sweepingly beautiful Idaho country that is stalked by everything from sandhill cranes (stop walking, *then* look) to moose.

Given the power, this is what you'd create for yourself, but, because you're not dumb or lazy, you'd also include a few whitefish so you'd have to learn to tell the difference between their rises and those of the trout; you'd make the rainbows maddeningly picky about fly patterns and presentation to keep things interesting; and you'd include a mechanism by which the hatches were predictably regular, but still moody, so that even working from the hatch chart in the back of Mike Lawson's catalog, it would still be possible to miss them.

It would be perfect, if you agree that perfection must include the dramatic element of chance, or, put another way, the possibility of failure.

You probably wouldn't include the crowds, however. In my own fantasy, the river is owned by me, the way Averell Harriman once owned the Railroad Ranch stretch, except that my guests wouldn't be magnates and diplomats. They'd be a ratty congregation of fly-fishers who would stay for months, camped next to their pickups at discreet distances from one another, now and then coming to the lodge to use the shower. If I didn't want my ducks and moose eaten, I'd have to check firearms at the front gate.

Okay, back to reality.

The first time I fished the Fork, and a number of times thereafter, I was as intimidated by the crowd as by the river itself. There was neoprene, Gore-Tex, and graphite from horizon to horizon, punctuated by the occasional spot of rubberized canvas and the odd wheat-colored gleam of split cane. During the Green Drake hatch, one of the most heavily attended events in fly-fishing, there are literally hundreds of fishermen on the water on any given day. And many of them are very good. Last summer, Mike Lawson told me, "Not only are there more fishermen on the river now than there were ten years ago, there are a lot more *good* fishermen."

It *is* the kind of place where experts gather and the competition—if you care to engage in it—can be wilting. It can be quite the fashionable scene, and there seem to be a few hotshots who travel all the way to Idaho every year just to hold court; to stand around on the bank with their entourage offering critiques of their colleagues' casting styles and fishing tactics. Now and then you'll actually see one of these guys fishing.

Of course, the people are all fly-fishers and, therefore, mostly nice guys, but the sheer numbers can be daunting. You can get into them on a one-to-one basis, though: you meet someone, exchange the usual news and pleasantries, and in a matter of minutes you're pals, complaining about the crowd as if you weren't both part of it.

Ultimately, if you're going to fish the Green Drake hatch, you have to accept and even come to enjoy the people, otherwise the fishing will be a chore, no matter how good it is. This is, after all, a hastily assembled subculture, and as such it's not a bad one. For one thing, values are unquestioned: mayflies and rising trout are good, wind and sea gulls are bad, period. By being even mildly sociable, you can learn a lot about insects (in both English and Latin), fly patterns, fish behavior, casting, stalking . . . In fact, if you don't come to think of yourself as "something of a fly-fisherman" and start making snide remarks from the safety of shore, you can learn more in a week than you can in a whole winter of reading.

Even on that first trip, however, I learned that there are ways of fishing the Henry's Fork in relative solitude. We'd come for the same reason everyone else had—for the Green Drakes—and it was actually just fine. The big mayflies would begin to come off at about ten in the morning and continue sporadically until about three in the afternoon.

Naturally, the bugs themselves were fantastic: big, grayish-olive, long-winged flies that, as the legend says, lured even the largest of the trout to the surface where they could be hooked on dry flies. Some angling myths are actually true, and this is one of them.

Considering that the trout were spoiled, bored, spring creek fish, they rose greedily, but, as in most situations like this, no one was hauling them in hand over fist. Both the fly pattern and its presentation had to be close to perfect, and even then it wasn't a lock. Even the steadily rising fish would let a few naturals go by now and then, out of spite.

It took a good eye, too. Those of us with little previous experience with the mountain whitefish often wasted a good deal of time casting carefully to these much-disliked nontrouts. Whitefish are edible, and native, but they're still the fool's trout; like fool's gold they can be the source of some disappointment and considerable embarrassment. They're also sometimes known as "turd knockers."

If there's one secret to fishing the Henry's Fork (there are actually many secrets), it's the downstream drift. My first impression of the Green Drake water across from Lawson's was, "These people are all fishing backwards," but an hour later I was doing it myself because it was the only way to get a good, long, drag-free float in all those conflicting currents.

That year the hot fly was the big green Paradrake, as designed by Messrs. Swisher and Richards and as tied by the thousands somewhere in the Third World. It's a complicated fly with a dyed elk-hair body—complete with extended abdomen and tails—an upright hair wing and parachute hackle. It was a fly none of us had with us and one I still can't tie so it *stays* tied for more than a few minutes.

When we pulled in that first day, we went over to Lawson's shop to get The Word. The Word on events like this is usually brief and somewhat simplified for mass consumption, but still useful, generally consisting of hatch times and patterns.

We'd no sooner walked through the door when a man burst in behind us. He held a strung-up fly rod with a dangling, flyless leader, his waders were dripping Henry's Fork spring water on the carpet, and his eyes were big and glazed. He dashed to the counter and dipped his hand into the large fishbowl that held hundreds of loose Paradrakes, dumping about a dozen of them on the counter along with a fifty-dollar bill. And then he was out the door, heading back toward the river in the waddling trot peculiar to men in baggy waders.

"That must be the pattern," I said to Mike.

"Yup," he answered.

I bought a half-dozen and so did A.K., but it was harder on him. To A.K.,

fly-fishing involves catching fish with a split bamboo fly rod using flies
you've tied yourself. It's something between a matter of pride and an esthetic judgement. Don't get me wrong. He doesn't care what *you* do. In
fact, he's a professional flytier and would starve if the majority of fishermen
didn't buy at least some of the flies they fish with.

Still, as he peeled some bills from a modest roll and handed them over,
he announced, "I've tied twenty-five-hundred-dozen flies this year and it
burns my ass to have to buy these!" The assembled customers stopped talking and looked up for a moment—but only for a moment. Fishermen get
used to the occasional emotional outburst.

In case you don't have your calculator handy, that's 30,000 individual
flies.

There are, naturally, other drake patterns. There's the Green Drake
Wulff, Mike's extended body Green Drake, and the pretty Harrop Green
Drake, not to mention various hackle-tip-winged flies, a number of emerger
patterns, the Iwamasa Dun, and, of course, the size 10 Adams. (Apparently
there are a number of very proficient, mostly local Henry's Fork fly-
fishers—born-again presentationists—who use nothing but the Adams dry
fly in sizes 10 through 24 on all of the river's confusing hatches and who
catch more fish than anyone has a right to.)

In the end, it's a matter of personal style as practiced by people who
have given it a lot of thought. This is why you can hear heated discussions
between two flytiers—both of whom are catching fish—about the "correct" color of the Drake.

"It's a yellowish, olivish, tan with a hint of pale dun."

"Are you blind? It's a tannish olive with a hint of pale yellow."

It was fine, not unlike attending a convention, but then one evening Koke
suggested we go to a place he knew about downstream to see if the Brown
Drakes were hatching. "There may not be as many people," he said.

We walked in to a stretch of river so slow flowing it was almost glassy.
I've since learned that all the regulation bugs hatch there and are eaten by
trout, but it's prime Brown Drake water because its bottom is silty and the
Brown Drake nymph is a burrower, rather than a rock clinger.

I'd never seen the Brown Drake mayfly before, but I'd heard of it, and all
the stories were true. It's a huge bug as mayflies go and, although they
hatch in the low light of dusk, you can clearly see them sitting on the water
at fifty yards. They look like sailboats.

I know that comparison has been overused, but that's what they look
like. It's not my fault.

Once the hatch has been going on for a night or two, there's also a simultaneous spinner fall. All at the same time, there are nymphs rising from the bottom, emergers at the surface, hatched duns *on* the surface, and last night's bugs, molted into their sexually mature form, mating in the air, laying their eggs on the water and dying. And the trout are eating all of them.

If it wasn't for that last part—the part about the trout eating up the bugs—a guy could probably get all misty and reverent about this great orgy of birth, death, and rebirth; but these are really big trout. Sympathy for the insects is not the emotion that comes immediately to mind.

It sounds great—and it is—but it's also something of a problem because the trout get selective to one particular stage. And not *the trout* as a group, but each individual fish. You want to fish the dun pattern because the bug itself is so handsome, with its brownish body and wings mottled like the breast feathers of a grouse, but then there's a bigger fish eating the emergers, and, once you've switched to that pattern, an even bigger one sipping the spinners. The hatch can last for an hour or two and it's possible to spend that entire time changing from one fly to another and then back to the one you started with. Believe me.

The next day I bought some Brown Drake flies at Lawson's. I found them not in a fishbowl on the counter but in a modest bin with all the rest of the flies; a few dozen rather than hundreds. The way the flies were displayed in the shop was a perfect model of the rate of fishing pressure on the two hatches.

We fished the Brown Drakes for several evenings running, during which time I learned that you settle on a certain pattern—say, the spinner—and try it over one fish after another until you find the one who wants spinners. If nothing else, it keeps you fishing instead of changing flies. I caught a fish or two, but that's not what I remember so well. What I remember is the loneliness and the quiet.

We weren't exactly alone there, but we were part of a manageable number of fishermen. There was enough for everyone and there were owls moving soundlessly through the trees and sandhill cranes making that chilling, prehistoric clatter. One night there was a crashing back in the woods. A moose, probably, but in that country there's always the possibility of grizzly bear.

In years since, in the evenings after other Green Drake hatches, A.K. and I have gone downstream to fish until past dark. We've never hit the big Brown Drakes again, but we will. We both carry boxes of the flies.

What we have found are the spinners of the Pale Morning Duns, and sometimes caddis. We've never caught a lot of fish there at night, but we've caught some big ones and have seen some even bigger.

It has never been crowded, and I don't know why. It might be the darkness. It's surprising how many fishermen, and very serious ones, too, will just not go out at night. I won't say I don't understand that because I now and then get spooked myself, but it usually turns out to have been worth it.

Once, on the Henry's Fork, I had stayed out later than everyone else. I didn't catch the fish I was after, and he finally stopped rising, so I struck out across a meadow toward the road and the truck where my partners were waiting.

Somewhere out there I stepped on a pair of nesting cranes. Two of them. Four feet tall. I screamed bloody murder, fell on my back, and lay there for five minutes trying to let it sink in that I wasn't dead, it was okay, it was just dark, that was all. Back at the truck someone said, "Heard you yell. Thought you were eaten by a bear. We were just gonna divide up your stuff."

But then some nights you *do* catch the fish, and it's incomparable. Reaching out into the dark river and feeling that tugging from what seems like another dimension is too eerie to describe. It must be experienced. Hooking a big trout at night seems like something that can't be done, but you just did it. For some reason, though, most don't even care to try it, and those who do night-fish don't seem to talk about it much.

What clouds the Henry's Fork in late June and early July isn't so much the Green Drake hatch, although that's a heavy calling card that draws fishermen from all over. What kills it is being the only game in town. Later in the year people scatter to other places: the Madison River, the Yellowstone, Hebgen Lake, and so on. That golden triangle where Idaho, Montana, and Wyoming all come together at Yellowstone Park is where you go when you die if you've been a good boy. It's got everything a fly-fisher could want, including the Henry's Fork, which has its best hatch when most everything else in the way of running water is slow.

Did I say *best* hatch? Let's change that to read "most well-known hatch." The best hatch I've fished so far on the Fork is the Callibaetis mayfly in the middle two weeks of August, which is known, for reasons that are beyond me, as the depths of the off season on that river.

Actually, you're not looking for the hatch at all, but the spinner fall. The duns emerge sporadically, while the spinners fall all together, thousands of them, starting around nine or ten in the morning downstream from Last Chance, in the quietest water.

A.K. and I spent the better part of two weeks there last season with only the occasional side trip up to the Yellowstone River for cutthroats and Hebgen Lake for the "gulpers," big trout who are also eating—loudly—Callibaetis spinners. We stayed in the KOA Campground at Last Chance so long the manager finally asked us to move our tent to another spot. Seems we were killing the grass.

We'd arise around dawn, A.K. happy and energetic, me not *un*happy, but much slower, bolt coffee and breakfast, stop at the cafe for a couple of enormous cinnamon rolls fresh from the oven for lunch, and hit the water a good hour and a half before the hatch.

The first morning we were there early out of enthusiasm and because even the best hatch charts show only average or ideal times and dates. Good thing. If we'd come later, we'd have missed all but the tail end of the little black & white duns. We'd have also missed the young bull moose we spotted several times, always early in the morning, and came to refer to as Bullwinkle. A full grown bull moose is as stately and handsome an animal as any walking the planet, but a young bull, with his little antlers and enormous nose, is, well . . . cute.

The Callibaetis fall would come off more or less on schedule, and last for anywhere from two to four hours. The larger trout seemed ambivalent about the little black & whites, but they were *on* the Callibaetis from the word go. They'd start rising before you noticed the bugs on the water.

The fishing was difficult or, as they say now, "highly technical." The current was slow and smooth, the water was clear, the bugs were small (about a size 16), and the fish were Henry's Fork rainbows who will literally count the number of tails on a mayfly before eating it in slow water like this where they have the time.

The fish were also cruisers, which Mike says is something we fishermen taught them to do. Years ago you could find big rainbows lying in one spot in the current sipping bug after bug. These fish were not always easy to catch, but you could at least show them your fly and be fairly sure they'd seen it.

Mike has seen the change in his years on the river. Now the larger trout will pick a good stretch of current and move up through it lazily, taking a bug here, a bug there, and then one over there, seldom rising in the same place twice in a row. Until you figure it out, it can look like six or eight enormous trout all rising sporadically instead of what it is: one big fish passing through.

It gets more complicated. Sometimes it *is* six or eight fish, and they're all passing through at their own speed, some fast, some slow. Sometimes they seem to work up twenty or thirty yards of stream, then drift back down and do it again. In the slowest water, they'll sometimes noodle around in an area no larger than a small motel room, again, never coming up twice in the same spot.

The worst is the huge trout who works up past you and just keeps going, never to be seen again. You get two or three casts to him, and then you're standing there like you were late for your own wedding and just missed the last bus.

On the other hand, you'll now and then find one who actually *does* stay in one place. In fact, this may be the reason why so many fishermen in recent years have come to love the bank feeders on the Fork. They're just as hard to catch, but at least they'll stay put.

This can rattle you out of the traditional, slow, contemplative pace of fine dry-fly-fishing, but don't let it. As tempting as it is, you won't catch fish by chasing them—at least not very many. It sounds paradoxical, but the way to deal with cruising trout in this situation is to take the pace even slower than usual.

And don't be greedy, either. I've watched many a very good fly-fisher work this slow water and have never seen anyone take more than a few fish in a single session. The trout are hard; many of them are quite big. If you get a few fish in a day, maybe even a 20-incher or better, you've done as well as anyone deserves to do. As A.K. says, the slow water on the Henry's Fork is where you go when you've already caught enough fish to prove whatever it was you had to prove. Now you want to see how good your nerves are.

On that trip, fishing the same spinner fall morning after morning, A.K. and I both landed several 20-inch (or slightly better) trout and hooked and lost at least as many more, if you agree that any trout who takes you into the backing and breaks you off was "at least 20 inches," even if he was only 16.

I'm especially proud of one of mine because I worked on him for three mornings and hooked and lost him twice before finally landing him. He was one of those rare trout who actually stay in one place, in this case, probably because it was such a difficult spot to cast to that he felt secure.

He was one of those unperturbable trout. I'd make a bad cast and he'd go down, but I'd keep my eye on the place and in fifteen minutes or so he'd be back, rising steadily. So *I'd* go back and maybe hook him this time, but get broken off. That would be it for the day, but the next morning, there he'd be, sipping the same flies in the same place again.

Given the time—days, weeks—you will sooner or later catch a fish like this. And you take the time. It can become very important.

On two separate days, the Callibaetis were followed by a good fall of flying ants. Actually, the ants came toward the end of the spinner fall, but they must have been delicious, because every fish in the river switched to them immediately. The first day I didn't have anything in the box that was even close, though I did manage to tempt one nice rainbow with a surgically altered Humpy. That afternoon in camp I tied up a dozen reasonable copies, and so did A.K., who had had two when the fall came on, had lost one, and was not about to go back the next day with a single fly.

As we finished tying, A.K. said, "Well, that takes care of the (deleted) ants," an allusion to Murphy's Law of matching the hatch, which says that tying a good supply of flies to copy an unexpected hatch insures that said hatch will not come off again until you are out of the state.

But, wonder of wonders, it did come off, four days later. Mike had told us the ants were one of the most enigmatic events on the river. "You can fish for a month and not hit it," he said. "You guys were lucky." And that was referring to the first time.

The trout took those ants with as much enthusiasm as I've ever seen Henry's Fork fish exhibit. We caught a bunch, maybe a dozen between us in less than an hour. There have been years when we didn't take a dozen fish in that stretch in two weeks and thought *that* was great.

And that's not even the best part. The best part is, on the entire trip, in the half-mile or so of river that interests us most, we saw as many moose as we did other fishermen. Three each.

On the drive home I said that this had been the season on the Henry's Fork that I'd been paying my dues for all these years, but it was A.K. (as usual) who summed it up properly. The afternoon of the second ant fall as we hiked back to the truck literally whipped from day after day of catching big trout, he said, making the quotation marks in the air with his fingers, "Well, that'll teach us to come in the 'off season.'"

The Henry's Fork is one of those rivers that has been written about and photographed unmercifully. If cameras really did steal souls, the place would be a field by now. It also constitutes one of the great paradoxes in outdoor writing. Editors will say they're sorry, but they just don't need "yet another story on the Henry's Fork." Then, a few months later, yet another story on the Henry's Fork appears in that very magazine. We—readers, writers, and editors alike—just can't leave it alone and are now, in fact, in the final stages of loving it to death. It's not surprising, since Last Chance, Idaho, is, and will probably remain, the spiritual center of the Rocky Mountains. When you pull up to it in your camper, you haven't just gotten there, you have *arrived*. Even to those who fish it regularly, it is "The Henry's Fork," as much an idea as a trout stream. To the rest of us, it's Mecca.

As fed up as I sometimes get with the crowds, I also have to say that, if you love, or even just like, trout rivers, *you have got to see this one*. And once you see it you have to stay long enough or come back often enough to solve at least one or two of its many puzzles. After all, this is not a spectator sport we're talking about.

In all fairness, it might be time for those of us who have fished it some to write our little memoirs and then move on to the Falls, or the Teton or the Bitterroot or one of the other less pounded rivers this part of the world offers, leaving the fabled Fork to the many newcomers who are currently making fly-fishing a "growth industry."

I don't know if I'll be able to do that or not, but it will help to consider that what many of us love about this place is now at least partly an illusion. The photos of the Fork you see in magazines and catalogs typically show one, or at most two, fishermen standing in the otherwise vacant river— blissful loneliness, man and the wilderness and all that. These stark compositions can be hard to come by at times, what with all the people standing around, but, like the big fish, given the time you can get one. The camera doesn't lie, but it can pick its moments.

This, I think, is an acceptable use of poetic license—acceptable because that's how we want to see the place. Crowded or not, it is still the Big, Empty River.

The Fishing Car

W H E N I was a young feller, I thought my Uncle Leonard had invented the concept of the fishing car; the elderly but still serviceable vehicle that was reserved for angling and angling-related activities to the extent that it was kept loaded, like the shotgun behind the kitchen door. But then I thought Leonard had invented a lot of things, some of which have since turned out to be among the oldest jokes in the world. It's understandable, I guess. In matters pertaining to fishing—not to mention farming, guitar playing, and a number of other things—he had the authority that comes from experience; and I was also into a bit of adolescent hero worship.

The idea of the fishing car spoke to me of a way of life. It was the thought that you could be a sportsman in the same way you could be a Baptist or a farmer or a blond; that being a fisherman could be as much a part of your identity as your fingerprints. And I was at the age where I had just started to puzzle over my identity.

The fishing car in those days was the "ambler." It had actually once said "Rambler" in chrome letters on the hood, but a minor run-in with a fence post had resulted in the abbreviated version. Of course, there was no thought of having it fixed.

It was a black station wagon with many thousands of miles on it that somehow always ran—after a little prodding—and that was always stocked with axes, minnow buckets, tackle boxes, rods, etc. The upholstery was ragged, the windshield was pitted, the dashboard was dusty, the tires were fair, and it had an aroma about it of beer, Coke, cleaned fish, wet wool, and a few other things that were hard to place. The exact opposite of that new car smell.

I don't know what ever happened to it, but, by all rights, it should have been bronzed and placed on a pedestal on the banks of a good bass pond somewhere in Indiana.

I spent as much time as I could with Leonard while I was growing up, and much of it passed in the front seat of the ambler following lazy, circuitous routes to one bass pond or another. We drove the dirt roads most of the time. Some were so little used that by midsummer the tall grass growing between the wheel ruts would slap the front bumper. The roads in those rural counties were laid out more or less on grids, and we got to where we were going by starting at a known point and then angling in what seemed like the right direction.

In the course of things we discovered several little towns that were doubtless unknown to the outside world; towns so slowly paced that a dog could safely sleep on the warm pavement of Main Street in the late afternoon, because everyone knew that Butch might be taking a nap in the road in front of the hardware store. Butch himself, a fair-to-middling hunting dog in his younger years, could live to the ripe old age of eighteen or twenty, and when he finally passed away—quietly, in his sleep—the whole town would feel bad about it for a day or two.

Sometimes we'd stop and ask directions, which could be a laborious process. Everyone knew where everything was, but what was County Road 23 to us was usually the Road Out to the Jones Place to everyone else. I never saw Leonard use a store-bought map, but we followed several that were scratched on paper napkins or matchbook covers.

Leonard was a master at navigating in farm country, but we did occasionally get lost. This was known as "taking the scenic route." There were rare times when we never quite got to where we were going, but we always got *somewhere.*

Leonard made a point of appearing confident and in charge, so it was difficult to tell when he knew where he was and when he didn't. There were times when I'd have sworn we were hopelessly lost, but then we'd pull up to an unlocked gate that looked exactly like the last twenty unlocked gates we'd passed, and he would describe the pond that was still out of sight down a two-wheel dirt track: its size, its shape, the muddy bank, the cattails along the east side, everything. Of course, he did have the reputation of knowing where every bass and most of the panfish in three counties lived.

He also knew half the people in the same area, and if he *didn't* know them, he soon would. He was deeply in touch with the interlocking networks of relations, work, church, and grange that tied the farming community together, and all he needed to make a connection was a name off a mailbox.

It was something to see. Leonard would bounce the ambler up a perfectly strange driveway, negotiate through the dogs, find the owner (who was invariably poking at some broken piece of machinery), and deftly establish himself as a neighbor, if not an out-and-out friend of the family. There would then follow an interminable period of fence leaning, gravel kicking, sky squinting, and a rambling philosophical discussion that included everything from the hound dog at your feet to the President of the United States. Of the two, the dog was the more competent.

It took time, but sooner or later we'd end up catching large bass from an obscure pond that hadn't been fished five times in as many years. The farmer always got some cleaned fish out of it, and then we'd pile into the ambler and drive off, waving at a man who was now our friend or who, at the very least, was too polite to say no to a couple of nice enough guys.

Driving home at night it would occur to me that, although life would surely provide some interruptions, there'd be nothing wrong with doing this all the time.

Of all the trips Leonard and I took in that car, the one I remember most clearly was our longest and last. My family had moved to Minnesota, and I hadn't seen Leonard in a while. I was a teenager then, having attained some height and a considerable dose of that quality that was once known as strong-headedness. My mother smiles about those years now, but Dad didn't live quite long enough to see all the humor in it. Maybe strong-headed is too mild a term.

Dad and I did hunt and fish together, though, and that was our one stable point of agreement through some years that could easily have ended in a complete severing of diplomatic relations.

It was Dad who gave me my first view of fly-fishing. I'd read about it in the outdoor magazines and had even once seen a man using what was known back then in the Midwest as a "trout rod." Dad said he didn't know much about it, but that the people who practiced it were the true artists of the sport. Leonard gave me my second view. "Fly-fishermen are a bunch of conceited pricks," he said.

It took me a number of years to realize that both men were right.

You see, Dad was what you'd have to call a gentleman sportsman type. He would never have considered poaching or doing anything out of season; he loved fine tackle and thought it was vastly superior to catch a fish on a lure rather than bait, because this actually involved fooling the game with your skill and cunning. Leonard, on the other hand, fished to catch fish, which he then killed and ate. He respected private property, but he also believed that God had put fish on the earth for all the people, and these two ideas constantly battled for his soul. His gear was wired, glued, and duct-taped together, and he fished with whatever it took, stopping short only of explosives, and then only because they'd have been too loud.

If I'd actually set out to get a perfectly balanced education as a fisherman, I couldn't have chosen two better teachers.

Where was I? Right. The longest and last trip in the ambler.

It so happened that my sister decided to get married one summer not long after we'd moved to Minnesota, a state that was full of lakes which were, in turn, lousy with fish. Weeks before the actual festivities, the family began to gather. By the time Leonard and Aunt Dora arrived, the house was filled with grannies and aunts and mobs of cousins on the way.

Leonard and I got together out in the backyard, where it was quiet, and decided the best thing for us to do was go wet a line somewhere, just to get out from underfoot, you understand. We packed quickly, left quietly, and drove north in the ambler.

We drove for some eighteen or twenty hours, watching the landscape go from fields to scattered groves to coniferous forests and feeling the hot closeness of the summer air become cool and sharply scented with pine. Somewhere along the line we turned off the main highway onto a dirt country road.

Up there the roads were fewer and farther between than in rural Indiana and anything but straight. They didn't seem to go much of anywhere, but all roads go somewhere, and we finally pulled up to a medium-sized lake with tree-lined banks and water lilies as if it had been our destination from the start. We rented a small, rickety cabin that came with an equally small and rickety rowboat. Both leaked, but were thoughtfully equipped with the appropriate tin cans.

In the days that followed, we caught fish.

There were foot-long perch in the little bay right outside the cabin door that came into the boat with the kind of regularity you somehow only remember from long ago. On the first night we sat down to baked beans from a can and a platter of breaded and fried perch fillets from a lake that neither of us had seen or even heard of before. Definitely the way to begin a fishing trip.

We took smallmouth bass from around the rocky points on small floating lures and spoons. They were an olivish-bronze color and jumped the way I would later learn that rainbow trout do.

The northern pike came from deeper water to big, heavy Johnson's Weedless Spoons trailing strips of pickled pork rind. They were my favorites, being large, prehistorically ugly, and—by stretching the imagination some—even a little dangerous. Leonard said the real fight with a big pike began when you got him in the boat. In any case, there were some minor injuries, complete with blood, and I loved it.

During the middle of some days, we drove around the back roads to look at other lakes and talk to sellers of bait and renters of boats, all of whom were getting their share of fish that week. "Getting our share" is one of those wonderful fishing euphemisms that sound promising, but that can mean damn near anything.

As I said, Leonard was a great raconteur of the fence-leaning or one-foot-up-on-the-dock-piling school, and he enjoyed talking and joking with fishermen as much as he liked fishing itself. He was good at it, too. He knew that few fishermen, himself included, would tell a stranger what he needed to know straight out, so he assembled information not so much by the facts as by evaluating the empty space around them. He taught me, for example, not to pay attention to the lures that were well stocked, regardless of how pretty they were or how hard the sales pitch was, but to always ask what had once hung on the empty pegs. The ones that were sold out were the ones that caught fish.

I guess it took me a long time to come to appreciate the charms and real advantages of just *talking* about fishing, looking at water, leaning on things, reading between lines. At the time I was a little impatient. You remember, it was childhood; the days of wooden rowboats when men who didn't know each other could stand and chew the fat for hours. But I knew I'd be doing it myself someday, so I paid attention and mostly kept my mouth shut in the borrowed style of the strong, silent type. The compliment I was being paid was that of being left to myself—of not having to be watched and kept amused. Back home I felt like a man who was being treated like a boy. Out fishing with Leonard, it was the other way around.

Then, as now, these conversations tended to dissolve around late afternoon when the first boils could be seen out along the weed beds. There was a slow, satisfying logic about it all.

I drove the ambler on many of those back roads, not because I was allowed to, as I'd been in the past, but because a fishing partner shares the
driving chores. Never mind that I was too young to have a license.

It wasn't until a few hours before the wedding—not quite the last possible
moment—that we strolled in the back door sublimely unconcerned, wearing clothes we'd fished in for a week and carrying armloads of fillets. The
house was in a uniform state of hysteria: the women were all at a dead run or
off in a corner weeping, while the men were looking mounted in suits that
had last been worn at funerals. I've since come to recognize the pained,
furtive look they wore as symptomatic of the powerful need for a drink.

"It's about time," someone said, and we were grabbed by the ears and
forcibly washed. The story is told that our clothes had to be burned, but
that may be an exaggeration. I've never felt less welcome arriving at an
event I was supposed to attend.

I remember coming downstairs to the kitchen all clean and dressed up
and running into Dad. He'd been stuffed into a tuxedo and was fondling a
big glass of bourbon with a single, lonely ice cube floating in it. We were
alone, but the sound of chattering washed in from the front room.

"Caught some fish," Dad said (not a question).

"Yup," I answered, all puffed up with teenage conceit and vanity.

He raised his glass slightly in a toast and flashed me an evil little grin,
something between envy, pride, and resignation. Now that I think about it,
maybe he *did* see the humor in it now and then, or if not the humor, then
something. Dad always tried to be strict and straitlaced with me, but word
around the family was he'd had his moments as a young man. I remember
wanting to tell him I'd driven the car for hundreds of miles, and then thinking I'd best not push my luck.

I've traveled in a number of fishing cars since then, from a Volkswagen that
must have been a contemporary of the ambler to a gas-guzzling road slug
that blotted out the sun as it passed by. Each has had a certain romance
about it, based not so much on its looks or performance as on what it was,
where it had been, and where it might be going next.

Koke has a station wagon now that will be just fine after a little breaking
in, but he used to own one of the most famous fishing cars in the Rocky
Mountain West. I remember it as a Ford, while A.K. swears it was a Dodge.
Odd. Whatever make it was, it was big and white with a combination boat-
and-rod rack on the roof and the biggest trunk I've ever seen.

Somewhere in this trunk you could find anything any three people would need on a month-long fishing trip, except that you couldn't find anything if you weren't Koke. The stuff was there in layers, like at an archeological dig, and if you were asked to get something ("It's right on top, you can't miss it."), it could take an hour, during which time you'd come across a dozen articles of tackle that had gone out of production twenty years ago. It became a simile, as in, "What have you been doing? This place looks like Koke's trunk."

A.K. himself has a good one now, a vintage Chevrolet pickup with a 400-some cubic inch V-8 and a camper shell. One of the first custom features he installed was an electric lantern hung just inside the back hatch for de-rigging in the dark, something we end up doing on three out of four trips.

On one of our recent expeditions, A.K.'s tent blew down in a wind that was not quite bad enough to make us get our belly boats off the water (which, I think, speaks volumes of ill about the tent), and we ended up sleeping in the truck. It was a pain at the time because all the float tubes, spare waders, fly tying travel kits, spare rods, camp kitchen, and such had to be unloaded in the dark and stowed under tarps, because it was raining as well as blowing. But in the end I think it was fitting. A car that hasn't been slept in on an emergency basis isn't quite broken in.

Then there's my own succession of fishing cars. There was a white International Scout and then a blue and white Scout that had once been a U.S. Mail truck and had the steering wheel on the wrong side. It was a conversation piece, but that's about the best I can say for it. Both cars were tinny, didn't have enough room in the back, and the four-cylinder engines were too weak. Great for delivering mail, but not too hot for fishing.

Why two of them? I'd just given up on the first one as being not enough truck when a guy who owed me $400—and who was not about to get the cash and who was also about to leave town suddenly for some reason—gave me the second one to clear the debt. "Thanks a lot," I said.

People assumed that I loved Scouts because I had a pair of them.

Those were followed by the longest running fishing car to date, a 1966 red Ford three-quarter-ton pickup with a long bed, a big engine, and four-wheel drive. It was a ten-mile-to-the-gallon monster that was, if anything, too much truck rather than too little. Still, I had great luck with it, partly because it was a solid vehicle with lots of spirit and partly because I had aged some by then, learning some lessons in the process. One lesson was that four-wheel drive doesn't mean you can go anywhere, it just means you can get stuck in worse places.

In his formative months, my late bird dog (and I use the term lightly) was left in the cab and, with nothing better to do, ate the seat on the driver's side. "Why didn't you chew up *your* side?" I asked, but he just wagged his tail and smiled, happy to see me. That dog lived for almost sixteen years, but he never got any more considerate.

Once, while hauling a load of firewood out of the National Forest on a muddy road, I skidded sideways against a ponderosa pine tree and bashed in the left door, closing and locking it permanently, but otherwise doing little damage. I didn't really mind having to get in on the wrong side and slide across, although I did tear the back pockets off more than one pair of jeans on the exposed springs. And it wasn't all that pretty when I got it, either, having once been a yard truck at a lumber mill.

You get the picture.

I got so attached to that truck that I honestly cried when it went the way of all flesh, having de-evolved from a powerful, soulful V-8 into a pitiful, wheezing V-6½. I kept the gearshift knob as a souvenir, because even that had a heavy, well-built feel to it. I haven't seen it in a while, though. One of my ex-cats used to like to play with it, so it's probably under the couch now. The cat, Maggie, also had soul. She died a few years ago in a valiant, if misguided, attempt to eat a rattlesnake. The cat got a decent burial, but I don't own enough land, nor the right equipment, to inter a pickup truck.

You may have noticed I have a thing for big American trucks. Some of that is pure genetic patriotism, but there are also some practical considerations.

I buy inexpensive vehicles, for reasons that will become obvious if you ever drop by the place here, and big old American trucks are cheap. They're also well built, heavy, and they're powerful if the rings are still okay. They do burn a lot of gas, but you have to look at that closely. You can buy a $12,000 pickup that gets twenty-three miles to the gallon of no-lead, or you can buy a $1,000 gunboat that gets eight miles to a gallon of regular. Work it out yourself. How many miles do you have to drive to save $11,000 in gas money?

Your big old pickup will also carry a lot of gear and will sleep two comfortably under the basic camper shell. If you ever break down (it's a fair bet you will), you'll open the hood of your venerable machine to find an engine block, valve covers, starter motor, fuel pump, distributor, carburetor . . . you know, the usual parts. If you're a fair-to-middling roadside mechanic with a wrench, screwdriver, a pair of pliers, and maybe a hammer, it will all make a certain sense. The motors in new trucks look like time machines and, anyway, the problem could be a computer malfunction.

If your old truck looks seedy enough, it's also the last one in the parking lot anyone would think of breaking into, which can be a real advantage. On a normal outing, the gear in my truck is worth more than the vehicle itself.

Along those same lines, I was once told by a retired police officer to remove the decals on my back window, you know, the ones that tell the world what organizations I belong to. "All they do is tell the bad guys what kind of merchandise is probably inside," he said.

Something to think about.

The worst is the one that says, "This Vehicle Insured by Smith & Wesson." It doesn't scare anyone, but it tells them there's probably a valuable handgun under the seat.

You get attached to an old heap, but you don't worry about it like you would a shiny new one. I once left the Ford in a bus stop parking lot for three days while I was off fishing the Frying Pan and Roaring Fork rivers with Koke. When I got back, the truck was as I'd left it, except that most of the gas had been siphoned from the tank and the gas cap was missing. On the plus side, it hadn't been broken into or vandalized. I can almost picture the bum standing there thinking, "Well, there's probably nothing in it, and as for smashing it up for kicks, it looks like someone has beat me to it."

I had enough fuel left to get to a town and buy some more, and, since I'd been happily catching trout for three days (during which time I never once stopped to worry about the truck), I decided to feel charitable. It is, after all, easy enough to construct a scenario where some destitute fellow human being is trying to get from point A to point B without enough money for gas, possibly on a very important errand. A job, maybe, or a death in the family or a girlfriend. Something crucial.

And the gas cap? Well, maybe he just dropped it. It was dark and I was tired. I didn't even look.

As an interim measure, I stuck one of those red mechanics' rags where the cap should have gone. It worked fine, and I didn't get a real store-bought gas cap until someone asked me if I'd decided to turn the truck into a Molotov cocktail and go on a suicide mission.

There's just something *about* the older American pickups. They're like model 94 Winchester rifles or Granger fly rods: ordinary and workmanlike, but still classy and dripping with romance. To drive one is to make a statement about enduring values. It's a way of identifying yourself, in this big, sprawling culture of ours, as a guy who occasionally has to haul stuff.

Of course, it's a personal matter, and there is another side to all this. Last winter I jokingly said to a friend of mine—the owner of a new Oriental recreational vehicle—that a real man drives an American pickup. In an impressively level way, he replied that a real man drives whatever he, by God, pleases.

Okay.

The old blue Chevy pickup I have now—referred to in some circles as The Blue Streak and in others as Old Blue—is a serviceable truck, though it has not quite become the cosmic fishing car. These things take time, not to mention the proper accumulation of adventures and mishaps.

It has some streamer flies and a bass bug stuck in the dashboard, which is a nice, homey touch, and is chugging away on its second used engine. It took me through Wyoming, Idaho, and Montana last summer with only one small electrical problem that was easily fixed, though not so easily diagnosed. It's never let me down seriously except for the time it caught fire at the corner of Canyon Boulevard and 28th Street in Boulder, Colorado. During rush hour. I had no idea so many people carried fire extinguishers in their cars.

Still, it's seventeen years old, and to fix everything that is wrong, or about to *go* wrong, would cost too much. So it's on its way out. I'll always fondly remember tying flies on its tailgate, but I can't trust it far from home anymore.

Buying a new (old) pickup is like fishing a new pond that you know nothing about. It could be full of big fish; it could also be full of alkali—not only fishless, but poisoned. Over the years I have learned the following things:

It will be hard to find, but you want one with a bunged up body that's still in working order. Most people are embarrassingly superficial in this regard and will pay more for a smooth body and a good paint job than for a truck that actually runs. Don't even look under the hood, just take it somewhere and have the compression checked. Then tell the guy who's selling it that it looks like hell.

The shape the bed is in will tell you more about a pickup than any other single thing. If the bed is all dented and scratched up, it was a work truck and was probably used hard. Is the tailgate bunged up on the top edge? It means a lot of heavy stuff was loaded and unloaded. Is the tailgate *missing?* Bad sign. So much stuff was loaded that it got in the way and they took it off.

Well, not always. A missing tailgate combined with a clean, almost pristine bed probably means that a camper sat there until very recently.

What you want is a ten- or twelve-year-old pickup that was used recreationally a few times a year by a seventy-five-year-old fisherman who doesn't kick ass like he used to and who does his running around town in his wife's sedan.

With even some of the used trucks now being too tinny and having too many moving parts to be reasonable, I'm beginning to think the answer is to get hold of a good, solid, well-seasoned pickup and commit to whatever it takes to keep it running for the rest of my life. This would solve a number of problems and would also be a big step toward firmly establishing me as an old fart, something I believe to be the secret, lifelong ambition of every serious fisherman.

I'm fully aware that somewhere down the road I'll run head-on into the fact that nothing can or does last forever. That's one of the reasons why I've never tried to find that lake and that cabin up in Minnesota again. You and I both know what has surely happened there by now. It would be like coming on the ambler rotting away in a field somewhere with the windows shot out.

I guess my sister got married okay that summer, although I can't say I actually remember the ceremony. All the fish got eaten, and Leonard and I were eventually forgiven, though I've never been quite sure what for.

When it was all over, I walked Leonard and Aunt Dora out to the fishing car. They were headed back to Indiana, and the ambler didn't look right with suitcases and garment bags in it. Leonard and I ran down some brief, vague plans for future fishing trips, and then, with nothing left to say, they drove off. As it turned out, I would never see the ambler again, and Leonard and I would never fish together again, either, although I didn't know that at the time. You never know those things at the time.

The last time I saw it, the car was still dusty from the trip to the lake. Aunt Dora had wanted to have it washed, but there just wasn't time.

The Purist

W H A T is it about fly-fishing that attracts purists, those people who must engineer a corner of their lives—sometimes a pretty large corner—where things have to be done properly? I'm not sure I know, but whatever it is, it's why the sport can be used to define the very existence of the practitioner. If you're into it long enough, sooner or later someone will say, "He's one of those misanthropic fly-fishing types," and everyone will know what they mean.

I'm not one of those guys who grew up with a fly rod. Instead, I grew up with a bait-casting rod, tackle box, and, yes, a can of worms. It was okay. In fact, it was a hell of a lot of fun, and it worked just fine for me until I came face to face with fly-fishing. That didn't happen until I was in my early twenties.

When my college graduation rolled around, I was working as a plumber's helper in, of all places, Cleveland, Ohio, getting some money up to get the car fixed and head west. I had somehow managed to finish four years at college and still be three credits short of a degree, so I was working days and writing nights on an independent study paper.

It was awful; not the writing or the work, but Cleveland. The only favorable thing I can say about it is that back then you could hear some good music if you wanted to take your life in your hands to go to the clubs. At twenty-one you're more than willing to do that, because it's clear you're immortal.

They say Lake Erie is coming back now and you can even eat the fish you catch from it without fear of brain damage, but in those days it was a fetid, stinking thing that would give you a rash if you even got close to it. In fact, it was along in there somewhere that the Cuyahoga River (a "river" in name only) caught fire and burned for days. I don't know how I ended up there, but I knew I had to get out, and fast, good rhythm and blues or not.

The plumber I was helping was a man named John Gray, and when I announced at the end of one work day that I would be quitting in a week to attend graduation, get my sheepskin, and then leave the state at the greatest possible speed, he asked, "What's your degree in?"

"Philosophy," I answered.

"Well," he said, "I guess you'll be leavin' the plumbing business and hanging your shingle out somewhere."

I never knew if he was kidding or not, but on the long drive across Kansas I considered it. I could hang my diploma on the wall and put a sign out front saying:

PHILOSOPHER
Reasonable rates—no waiting
No question too large
No question too small

I had no idea what to do with my life and it seemed as good as anything. It was also the only thing I was trained for—I hadn't even learned plumbing.

Instead, I ended up working various labor jobs and found that the western U.S. was lousy with bearded young men with college degrees who had also turned their backs on the establishment and were more or less happily driving nails and digging ditches. In the 1960s, many of the crews were made up of quasi-intellectual types, and sometimes we'd spend a few hours at Tom's Tavern after work discussing whether essence precedes existence or vice versa over some cold ones.

In Boulder, Colorado, where I settled after some months of wandering around, there was even a joke about it:

A guy applies for a carpentry job, and when the foreman asks about his education, he says, "I have a master's degree in English literature."

"Sorry, kid," the foreman says. "We're looking for someone with a Ph.D."

I was in sparse touch with my folks then—without much in the way of a permanent address or phone number—and when we did talk they tended to wonder what I'd be doing about a career. No problem. By then it had become clear: I was going to be a writer (a *serious* writer) and an equally serious fly-fisherman, not necessarily in that order. In the meantime, I would work labor by day, play blues guitar by night, think deep thoughts, and, as it turned out, get married and divorced so quickly it would have made my head spin if it hadn't been spinning already. As so often happens, the final dispute wasn't over politics, philosophy, or even faithfulness; it was over brown rice. Macrobiotic or not, I was sick of it.

I saw the whole thing as a revealing detail, an insight, fodder for the great surrealist novel I'd be getting to work on any day now.

Fly-fishing was, of course, perfect. It was solitary, meditative (if not brooding), enigmatic, and properly Bohemian. Going by the stereotype, at least, it was practiced by tweedy, thoughtful types who exuded a low-key but constant literary hum, if for no other reason than that so many good books had been written about the sport.

It was also quite beautiful.

But the best thing was, it led you inexorably to one paradox after another. The idea was to catch fish, but the best writers made it evident that it was perfectly okay not to as long as you failed to catch them with the proper grace and style.

The catch-and-release ethic was just beginning to blossom then, so if you actually did catch a trout, you'd probably release it. The fisheries management logic behind this was flawless, and that's why fly-fishers practiced it—but it's not why they *liked* it.

They liked it for its Zen flavor. Yin and yang—fish and no fish—it's all the same. "Trout" is defined only by the absence of trout surrounding it. Good day or bad, the creel remains empty, except maybe for a couple of beers. It was a kind of poetic game that you could win simply by coming to understand the rules.

I thought of it as a case of personal enlightenment at the time—as you think of everything in the first few years of legal drinking age—but it turned out that thousands of my fellow hippie baby boomers had seen the same light. I'd only been at it for a few years when the late Arnold Gingrich—one of the great old fly-fishing gentlemen—said he no longer had to apologize for the sport; that fully half of the best fly-fishers he knew were under thirty.

The rules.

They came from England, not from Izaak Walton, who was, in fact, a bank-napping bait fisherman, but from Halford and that bunch of chalk-stream types. To them a fly was a dry fly; not only that, it was a *may*fly; not only that, it was cast upstream to rising trout. End of discussion. Anything else is poaching.

There didn't seem to be any reasoning behind this, but remember, it happened in England.

Also in that country, G.E.M. Skues legitimized the wet fly by tying it to imitate a mayfly nymph and calling it that: a nymph.

After trashing our brook trout fisheries along the East Coast, we Americans imported the brown trout from Europe along with the British ethics and techniques that had grown up around that fish.

We also imported English-style naturalism, and the Catskill flytiers began to fashion trout flies on English models that looked like our bugs. They worked, and we still fish many of them.

Somewhere along the line, the naturalists hooked up with the entomologists, and Ernest Schwiebert eventually wrote *Matching the Hatch*. It wasn't the first book on angling entomology, or the last, but it was the one that made its title part of the language. Today you can find fly-fishers who talk about how they've been matching the hatch, but who have never even read the book.

By this time it was permissible, among the intelligentsia at least, to fish with flies imitating any insect, crustacean, bait fish, or whatever that a trout might eat—on or below the surface—with the possible exception of the salmon egg. In fact, studies were quoted to the effect that trout did 80 percent (or some other large percentage, depending on which expert you read) of their feeding under the surface, and the implication was that the smart fisherman—the *effective* fisherman—would fish with nymphs most of the time.

Of course, "nymph" was no longer the broad term that wet fly had once been. Suddenly there were nymphs, larvae, and pupae, depending on the species of bug in question.

Fly-fishing had begun to become scientific, or at least the terminology of science began to sneak into the sport. Most who go after it seriously now know the life cycles of the major trout stream insects and can tell the difference between the various bugs in their various stages. To many the Green Drake is now an Ephemerella grandis, and the Blue-winged Olive is really a Baetis, although I'm told by those who know that the Green Drake could actually be the glacialis, doddsi, hecuba, or the coloradensis. On the other hand, the *Little* Green Drake is almost surely the Ephemerella flavalinea. If you're cool, you'll refer to it as a Flav. Latin slang.

Oddly enough, the scientific Latin is commonly used only on the mayflies. The same fisherman who tells you about the Ephemerella hatch in the afternoon will refer to the caddis that emerge that same evening as big gray ones or little olive ones. Larry Solomon and Eric Leiser made a valiant attempt to change that some years ago with their fine book *The Caddis and the Angler,* but, at least on the waters I fish, caddis flies continue to be described in terms of size and color alone. The few who insist on talking about the Brachycentrus hatch (#16 brown) have to translate for the rest of us. And yes, we're impressed.

The first people I fished with were cowboys. Well, they didn't actually ride horses and punch cows, but they did chew Red Man and they did wear those big hats. Remember, I was still new to the West. They fished with fly rods in small, secluded mountain streams and beaver ponds, and that's what I wanted: breathtaking scenery and trout.

I got both, but I caught my first trout on bait—worms and, in season, grasshoppers. The time came when I was ashamed of that and even lied about it, or at least carefully failed to mention it. Now it doesn't haunt me, I just don't do it anymore. And, actually, a long fly rod is probably the ideal tool for taking trout on bait from small streams. It's a time-honored method among old-timers around here.

My friends in the Stetson hats did occasionally fish flies. They'd carry a ratty handful in something like a Prince Albert tobacco can, things like Black Gnats, Gray Hackle Yellows, Royal Coachmen, and they'd fish them on the surface, "just like you would a live hopper."

Not unimportantly, I managed to lose my virginity by actually catching, handling, admiring, and even eating a few small brook trout.

"So this is trout fishing."

"Yeah, but it's not *fly*-fishing." Even the cowpokes admitted that.

It's not difficult to learn how to fly-fish, by which I mean it *is* difficult, but there are people who can teach you, and there are books, and volumes of magazine articles, and even video tapes. It's now possible to become an expert without ever catching a fish, or at least to sound like an expert.

What's really hard, though, is to get a handle on what the sport is actually about. You arrive at a view by osmosis—by being around fly-fishing and the people who do it—because the values are implied or assumed but seldom flatly stated. There does seem to be a kind of built-in moral tone to it, but mostly we tend to just figure it out as we go along.

There are those who live by the code: "Fly-fishing only." These are the purists who prefer the fly rod because it's poetic, graceful, and old, and also because it's hard to master. In fact, it's *impossible* to master. However good you get, there will always be casts you can't make and fish you can't catch.

The purist fishes exclusively with a fly rod, which means that he owns a spinning rod and sometimes uses it, but he doesn't take it seriously, doesn't talk about it much (is, to tell the truth, a little embarrassed about it), and stores it separately from his fly tackle.

Chances are it's a very good rod.

The snob is exactly like the purist except he doesn't own a spinning rod. He used to, but he gave it away years ago, not wanting to have the filthy thing around the house. Furthermore, anyone who does fish with a spinning rod is sleazy and cheap and his parents probably weren't married. This guy is not nice, or very happy either, and the time will surely come when he gets pretty lonely, too. Snobbery occurs as the result of a logical fallacy. We all want to experience and appreciate something of excellent quality, but it doesn't follow that we're every bit as good as what we do.

Granted, fly-fishing breeds its share of snobs, but so do other disciplines. There were, for instance, a number of them involved in the Spanish Inquisition.

You'd have to say the ultimate purist is the one who fishes only dry flies, with no exceptions. If the fish can't be caught on dries, they can't be caught. I know some people who have flirted with that approach, but none have stayed righteous. All that frenzied activity beneath the surface film was just too tantalizing. I have, however, heard stories and firmly believe such fishermen exist—probably back East somewhere.

I do know lots of people who *prefer* the dry fly, although they'll fish beneath the surface if they have to. A.K. and I are both like that, which is one of several reasons why we get along so well and have fished happily together for so long. We both believe that a 12-inch trout caught on a dry fly is four inches longer than a 12-inch trout caught on a nymph or streamer. It's something many fly-fishermen believe, or feel in their hearts. "And we got 'em on dry flies," they say, as if it couldn't have been any better. Maybe it's a lingering taste of that stern old English tradition. The sport does still have a faint eccentric British aroma to it, although I think I've smelled it less and less in recent years.

Wherever the idea comes from, the dry fly still exerts a kind of tyranny. You can take rising fish fairly on other kinds of flies, but you can't take them *properly* on anything but a dry.

Once A.K. and I were fishing twenty yards apart, in a line with several other fly-fishers who were also evenly spaced, to a fine Pale Morning Dun hatch, and nothing was working. I tried various dry flies (of course), various emergers, and a couple of floating nymphs.

Nothing.

I don't know what everyone else was trying, but every time I glanced up- or downstream, one out of three anglers was rooting around in his fly box. Not a fish had been hooked in nearly an hour.

As the hatch began to peter off and doom was approaching, I tied on a #4 bucktail streamer—a trick, if you want to call it that, that had worked for me before. I slapped it against the bank, twitched it out twice, and had a sweet 16-inch rainbow.

It's what you dream of: not only hooking a nice fish with a large enough audience, but hooking the *only* fish. My shoulders squared. My head swelled. Everyone looked. I knew A.K. was going to deflate me (he considers it his job); I just didn't know how.

He called upstream: "What'd ya get him on?"

"Streamer," I said.

"Shit. If I'd known you was gonna fish bait I wouldn't have brought ya."

I guess the point is, no one really felt that way, but everyone laughed.

The idea of remaining somehow pure—in a largely undefined way—seems to permeate the sport of fly-fishing. The worst you can say about a questionable angling method is, "It's just like bait-fishing," or "Hell, you can do that on a spinning rod."

A.K. and I belong to the fairly small, but still vital, fly-fishing subculture that has settled on split cane rods as unquestionably top drawer, although we are not what you call steadfast about that. We both own some graphite rods and even fish them now and then, usually in situations that demand some kind of thunderstick, like a 10-foot, 8 weight. We have agreed that it's best not to try to defend cane in the company of graphite and neo-space age boron aficionados. Cane rods are just strange (these days) and old. Even the new ones, of which there are plenty, are "old" in a pleasantly kinky way.

It recently occurred to me that I got into cane rods, some years ago now, because almost everyone was impressed by them and, by implication, impressed by their users as well. I've stayed with them partly from habit, partly because I like them, and in *large* part because it now freaks so many people out.

This is what the purist does, be he fly-fisherman, collector of old cars, or whatever: he settles on a time in the past when it (whatever "it" is) was as good as it ever got. He also understands the considerable implications of that. When he says, "They don't make 'em like they used to," he means, "and they could if they wanted to, but they don't, and I don't understand why."

Some fly-fishers try to go back as far as possible in search of some kind of enlightenment. Among them are the people who are buying the pre-split cane style solid greenheart rods now being offered by the Partridge company.

To be completely unspoiled, one might actually have to regress back to silk lines and gut leaders. Silkworm gut is hard to come by now, but I did once try a silk line out of curiosity. It was a 33-yard Hedge "Balanced, anti-fly splash" (whatever that means) line that cast beautifully, but had to be unspooled, dried, and redressed every half-hour. It was authentic as hell, but also a pain. When, during a drying session one August, a bunch of grasshoppers chewed it to pieces while I took a nap, I wasn't all that disappointed.

Purity by nostalgia is an interesting idea, but the logic of it is inescapable. To do it right you'd have to live naked in a cave, hit your trout on the head with rocks, and eat them raw. But, so as not to violate another essential element of the fly-fishing tradition, the rocks would have to be quarried in England and cost $300 each.

Much of the inherent snootiness of fly-fishing begins to dissolve when you cease to specialize in the salmonids; the trout and salmon. Not only is it impossible to keep your nose in the air while fishing for bass or crappies, you're also in another culture where the value system is reversed. In trout fishing you'll find perfectly ordinary people trying to look, act, and sound like Old World sporting gentlemen, while on the bass ponds you'll run into doctors and lawyers making out like they quit school in the fourth grade to go work in the cotton fields. Bass writers even purposefully misspell words, like "hawg," while trout writers only misspell words by accident.

I may have been on the way to being a snob myself at one point. I was catching trout with some regularity on a split cane fly rod using flies I'd tied myself and was pretty self-satisfied. I'd learned just enough entomology to sound bewildering to those who didn't know any at all, and I guess I'll have

to admit to feeling superior to spin fishermen, especially those who refused to be impressed by my language and my tackle.

Then I found out you could catch bass on a fly rod. Well, I guess I actually knew that all along, but when I read Dave Whitlock on the subject, it
sounded neat. It also sounded familiar.

Species-specific trout purist or not, I was raised on bass, panfish, and
pike, and five paragraphs into my first Whitlock article on bass bugging, I
realized I missed them. I also realized the inherent possibilities in this:
more fishing, more tackle, and more language—Southern English rather
than Latin this time.

Back then, fly-fishing in warm water was not popular around here.
Among the fly-casters I hung out with then (some of whom I still fish with)
it was viewed with a kind of patient amusement. I was treated like the one
guy in every crowd of beer drinkers who has a weak bladder.

My friend, Gil Lipp, who had at the time just decided that a nymph
wasn't quite as bad as a live minnow, gave me the nickname that has, unfortunately, stuck for many years now: Grits. It was, of course, an allusion to
Mr. Grits Gresham, one of the great outdoor writers who has become even
more famous recently for his beer commercials on TV. That Gil even knew
who Grits Gresham was revealed something of *his* hidden angling past (and
he a native Colorado boy and all), but I let it pass.

To his credit, Gil soon started coming out with me in April to catch
spawning bluegills, rock bass, pumpkinseeds, and the occasional genuine
largemouth bass. He pointed out that the rivers were in runoff and the dry-
fly fishing for trout was lousy. He also insisted on using a 7½-foot, 4-weight
split cane fly rod that he'd built himself. Intentional or not, that rod turned
out to be an ideal tool for making the contest between fisherman and hand-
sized bluegill a fair one.

At that time, Gil and I, and later A.K., were among the very few I ever
saw waving fly rods on the local warm water ponds. Suddenly the vast majority of our colleagues were spin fishermen, and some of them really knew
their stuff. I learned more from them than they did from me.

I also found that some of them were threading their grape-flavored rubber worms onto single, barbless hooks and were—wonder of wonders—releasing their fish.

Can you beat that?

More and more local fly-fishermen got into warm water—at about the
same rate as its popularity was growing nationally—and it wasn't long before some of them called me to complain about the crimes being committed against the panfish in some local ponds by a small Vietnamese
community. "They're hauling the fish out in buckets," they said, and hoped

that, as the outdoor writer for a local newspaper, I could "write it up, you know, get some action."

After a few phone calls and a little footwork, I came up with the following information:

A. None of these people were willing to risk their pending citizenship by getting busted for anything, least of all poaching fish.

B. They were keeping crappies, bluegills, and bullheads, and a legal combined limit for a family of five consisted of 400 fish, or "buckets" of them, if you prefer.

C. A fisheries biologist said that removing small panfish in those numbers (they kept everything they caught, no matter how small) could only help the overall gamefish population. That's why the limits were so generous in the first place.

D. The Vietnamese turned out to be friendly, polite, and damned good fishermen, putting many of us native Americans to shame on all three accounts.

And E. When you look into a bowl of Vietnamese fish stew, it looks back at you.

The people who called were right to be concerned, and more of us should call someone (even if it's only a reporter) when we think we see something wrong. But in this case it was a misunderstanding. Those guys were trouters who probably couldn't remember the last fish they'd killed.

As I said, things are a little different on warm water.

To some—to me, now—the purity of the sport is found nowhere but in the tackle. Because it's classy, demanding, and fun, you cast flies on a fly line and leader using a fly rod. Putting a fly ahead of a casting bubble on a spinning rod is effective in some situations, but it's not fly-fishing. Nymph fishing with a fly rod and a fly reel loaded with nothing but monofilament line is damned close, but it's not fly-fishing, either. Doing the same thing except with a fly line *is* fly-fishing because that's how I do it, and if it wasn't I'd have to give it up.

See?

Different species of fish in their different waters are all fair game, and each has its charms.

Taking trout on dry flies in flowing water is supreme if only because it's one of the loveliest things you'll ever have a hand in. It's better if the fly copies a real insect, even better if it's one you tied yourself, and better yet if it's one of your own design. Depending on how far you care to take it, it can be better still if you built the rod, tied the leader, and do it in a stream that no one else knows about.

Under some circumstances, one trout may be better than another. In the Mountain West, a cutthroat can be better than anything because it's a native. Same with the brook trout in the East. Rainbows can be better because they fight so nicely, while browns could be better because they're supposed to be smarter. A golden can be better just because it's so outrageous.

Big trout are better than little trout; difficult trout are better than either of the above; and big, difficult trout, well . . .

A huge trout caught on a streamer isn't as good as the same fish on a dry fly except if he's so big he doesn't eat winged insects anymore and so couldn't be caught that way. But then maybe he's in one of those glorious trout streams with 200 pounds of aquatic insects per acre of bottom and *does* still swallow a bug now and then. But then, you can never really be sure of that, can you?

There are very few things in life that are dead center. Three of them are: 1955 Ford pickups, B.B. King, and dry-fly fishing.

It's said that bass are smarter than trout because they'll eat something the like of which they haven't seen all week, "reasoning" that it's food. A trout, the same people say, is selective because he's too dumb to recognize anything but the little tan caddis flies he's eating at the moment as edible.

Whatever. Bass fishing with a fly rod can be delicate, careful stuff at times, but it never loses its inherent clunkiness. With more and more trout-fishers buying bass rods and fishing the ponds, bass flies are getting more realistic. As on the trout streams, fishermen will often answer the question, "What are you using?" by describing the creature they're trying to imitate: frog, leech, mouse, baby muskrat. But even the supposedly accurate patterns retain a bug-eyed goofiness, and those red and white things with the rubber legs that don't look like anything in nature are still much in evidence.

The hotshot, tournament-style bass-fishers use all kinds of electronic fish-finding gear and talk about pH factors, thermoclines, and other technical-sounding stuff. Many even treat their lures with chemical concoctions designed to put fish in a "positive feeding mood." One of the most popular of these is Dr. Juice Fish Scent. Dr. Juice himself is pictured on the label, and he looks like he's been drinking the stuff. He also looks a lot like the poet Allen Ginsberg, but I'm sure that's just a coincidence.

Fly-fishers, on the other hand, tend to retain a pastoral attitude. They cast their deer hair bugs along the weed beds in the evenings with little thought of the water chemistry. "Twitch it once and then just let it sit there," they say. "Drives bass nuts."

Panfish look and act like little bass (they're in the same family, after all) and function as the fish that even serious anglers don't have to take seriously if they don't feel like it. The big ones are not that easy to find, but you can almost always catch the average fish, with a fly rod, without squinting your eyes, grinding your teeth, agonizing over what fly to use, or even thinking very hard. You can get intense about them if you want to, and you'll be rewarded for it, but they can also offer some relief in a discipline where trout, bass, and several other more "respectable" game fish must be taken seriously or not at all.

Panfish are also handsome fish, ranging from the tasteful, almost tweedy crappies to the gaudy pumpkinseeds, and you can keep a large limit of them without feeling the least bit guilty.

Pike are primordial-looking and have a threatening appearance that they can make good on. Their teeth are like needles, their gill covers are like knives, and the spines on their fins are like spikes. Guides often hate them because they lead to injuries, and experienced pike-fishers use long-handled hook disgorgers to handle them.

They're the only freshwater game fish I can think of that were named for a weapon of war.

In the right kind of water at least, the fly rod is as effective as any other kind of tackle, but very few fly patterns have been designed expressly for pike. Most use bass flies even though three or four big pike can shred a deer hair bug down to a bare hook. Real pike flies are usually simple—i.e., easy to replace—and durable. You can make a good one by wiring a strip of screaming yellow rabbit fur, skin and all, to a weighted hook.

Pike can be as low-spirited as largemouth bass in places where they're heavily fished, but the few wild ones I've caught, in the Northwest Territories and, years ago, in northern Minnesota, had the confident aggressiveness of animals that aren't used to being messed with.

Once, in Canada, we were fishing for pike in a narrow channel between two lakes. The place was known to the guides as the Snake River because it looked a little like a river and was full of pike, or "snakes," as they called them with obvious distaste. Both sides of the channel were lined with deep weed beds that could be twenty feet wide. You'd slap a popper on the outside edge, and the stalks would begin to part five feet back as a big pike with blood in his eye charged out. With this kind of warning it was easy to strike too soon and miss the fish, but it didn't matter. Cast the popper back out and he'd come for it again.

We were doing this with fairly light tackle—7-weight fly rods with about 6-pound leader tippets—and the fish could have broken us off easily by simply diving back into the obvious safety of the weeds, as any bass or trout I've ever caught could be expected to do. But not a one did. They fought hard, but they did it out in the open water where they didn't have a chance unless they inadvertently rolled up in your leader and cut it with their sharp gill covers. This is the innocence you see in truly wild things that still think people can be dealt with in the same way as other predators. It's the same mistake once made by the American bison and the passenger pigeon, and, although we were happily catching lots of big fish, it was ever so slightly heartbreaking.

But we *were* catching big fish and it never once occurred to us to reel in and go home. A fisherman's sympathy always comes later, after the fact.

Fly-fishing for trout is poetic; for bass it's somewhat existential; for panfish it's corny, but fun. For pike it's rough and tumble—the branch of the sport that reminds me of stock car racing.

To some, this business of doing things right translates as flying first class, you know, up in the front of the plane where the seats are wider and you get your drinks before the folks back in steerage do. Excuse me, "cocktails." These are the fishermen who make the distinction between drinks and cocktails; between the camp cook and the chef at the lodge. They spend a good deal of money.

There's nothing wrong with this unless, like the snob, having the best gets you to thinking you deserve it.

I have very little experience with this kind of fishing. I'm your standard proletarian, drive all night, sleep in a tent, cook off the tailgate kind of fisherman. For both esthetic and practical reasons, I go in what Thomas McGuane would call the style of the "Old Rugged." It's an important distinction here in the West. According to McGuane, the *New* Rugged consists of working on screenplays so the bank doesn't take the ranch.

The only experience I've had with upper crust fly-fishing was a few years ago at Three Rivers Ranch on the Henry's Fork.

The lodge was old and rustic in a purposeful way. Not phony, just carefully orchestrated. I found it seductively comfortable; a place where you could easily lounge around in leather chairs talking fishing until the wee hours while sipping good whiskey served from an elaborately carved oak bar. Or maybe it was mahogany.

I stayed in a two-bedroom cabin—one of several—that was furnished with antiques, including an ornate potbelly stove with one of those chrome loving cups on top. Plenty of hot water, towels, the beds changed daily, and a chilled bottle of white wine and a bowl of fresh fruit waiting when I checked in.

There was a small Orvis shop on the premises which did not appear to be open to the public.

I fished with two of the guides and found them to be somewhat older than most in the area, at least as good, if not better than average, and noticeably more solicitous to sports.

Now, don't get the idea I paid for this. A full-blown week at Three Rivers would have cost me what I normally spend on a half a year's fishing. I was graciously invited to slip in for a few days before the real paying guests arrived; while the guides were still scoping the rivers and the chef was trying out some new dishes.

I wasn't uncomfortable. In fact, I was more comfortable than I'd ever been before on a fishing trip. It became evident that, given the chance, I could get spoiled easily. Still, I felt vaguely out of my element.

The first day I floated the lower Henry's Fork from Warm River down past Ashton with Dennis Bitton and one of the guides. The fishing was good, but that's not what I recall. We were back in time for drinks and then a fine meal; the kind that comes with several forks, and I learned that, although one doesn't exactly dress for dinner, one at least puts on a clean shirt.

The next afternoon a guide and I ended up on a remote stretch of Robinson Creek—one of the great underrated streams in that part of the country. We slogged down into a steep canyon and caught a few nice brown trout on nymphs. Slow fishing, but good. Then, as evening came on, a hatch of small, wheat-colored caddis flies came off and fish began to rise. I tried a #16 Elk Hair dry which the fish refused, and was just switching to a #18 when my guide came over and said, "I should mention that even if we leave now we'll still be late for cocktails."

In all my years of fishing, no one had ever said anything like that to me before.

I'm one of those fly-fishers who do actually take panfish—bluegills in particular—seriously. I scout their spawning runs in the spring, try my best to plot their population cycles, and otherwise maintain a fascination for them. In recent years I've taken to fishing for them with an 8½-foot, 2-weight graphite rod that I've reserved exclusively for panfish ever since I discovered that I could cast a #6 or #8 popper with it. A quarter-pound bluegill will bend it double, and I once landed a 4-pound bass with it by accident, but that's another story.

I think bluegills are best fished for with long, light rods that let them show off, so when I came across a magazine ad for telescoping crappie rods, I got an idea. These things are 11 to 15 feet long, very whippy, and not all that bad looking. And, the ad said, some are designed to be used with a fly line and bugs. Generically they're crappie rods, but the various models have names like "Bream Buster" and "Perch Jerker." It was too much to resist.

I ordered one straight from Alabama and have been watching the highway for the UPS truck ever since. The man I talked to on the phone couldn't tell me about line weights, but said the rods were real noodly. Maybe I can get away with a 2- or 3-weight line.

When I asked what kind of reel seats the rods had, the guy said, "They don't *have* reel seats, but some people tape reels to the handles."

Fine. Why not?

The Music of the Spheres

IT'S toward the end of May; shirtsleeve warm most days, but still cold—
rather than "cool"—as night comes on. The cottonwoods, willows, and dog-
woods are leafed out and some grasses are up, but it all looks new and almost
edibly tender. The efficient, hard greens of summer are yet to come; it will
happen imperceptibly, but one day there it will be. Great Blue herons fish in
the shallows, and a few Canada geese are still on the nests, though most are
now out on the ponds towing dirty yellow goslings behind them.

You've been fishing the warm water for a month now, having been
skunked, or nearly so, the first few times out. But that's part of it. The
spawning of the bass and panfish starts early. Well, not "early," really; exactly on time, in fact, but sooner in the year than you have ever been able to
get used to.

It's a holdover from childhood, reinforced by outdoor photography and
magazine stories. This kind of fishing is supposed to take place in hot
weather, complete with mosquitos, but when you look at your slides of
past seasons, you see your friends in jackets and wool hats standing among
brown cattails catching bluegills.

The spawning bluegills are easy. They'll hit any wet fly, nymph, or streamer they can get their small mouths around. All you have to do is find them, and that's not too hard, either. They spawn in the same spots season after season, and you've been fishing these ponds for many years.

The largemouth bass are on the beds at about the same time, and, although it's not quite like shooting fish in a barrel as some say, they can be found and they can be caught. There's some debate over the ethics of this. Some say spawning fish should be left alone ("How would *you* like it?"), but you have yet to make your mind up on that one. In a sense it does seem unfair, but then you've been told by warm-water fisheries managers that bass seldom spawn successfully here in Colorado because of the skittish, fitful spring weather. The water warms, but then a cold front comes in and it cools down again. Or it snows, or cold snow-melt water pours in, or something. A change of only a few degrees can, and often does, kill the eggs. Most Colorado bass fisheries are put-and-take in one way or another. The fish are residents of these ponds and plenty wild enough, but few were actually born here.

From a management point of view, it's okay, but usually after a few trips you begin to feel cheap taking them off the beds like that, even though you're releasing them. They fight sluggishly, seeming puzzled, or maybe even resigned, and they don't even hit from aggressiveness so much as from a kind of housecleaning instinct. You cast a fly onto the bed and the fish picks it up to move it out.

Among these bass are some of the biggest examples of the species you'll see all year, but once you've seen a few, it's enough. You return to the bluegills, who nail a fly harder in the spring than at any other time of year, taking them on the 2-weight rod so they can show off. Then you hunt up some pumpkinseeds for no other reason than that they're so pretty. Sometimes they're in with the bluegills, but you know of two places where they'll be off by themselves.

This is all near shore, including the bass, but then you climb into the float tube and go looking for the crappies spawning in deeper water. This is a bit more cerebral, since you're no longer sight-fishing to fish you can clearly see, but working deep, maybe even with a sink-tip line, in up to eight feet of water. The fly is a size 6 Weedless Wooley in bright yellow; a new pattern, but an old idea. "Crappies like yellow," everyone's granddad used to say, and all those grandpas were right. Maybe they were right about a lot of things, but that's the one that has stayed with you.

It's spring and everything is mating. Remember the lady biologist you met out here once who was busy studying the sex habits of the frogs? She explained how the males just jump on anything, trying one thing and then another until something submits. And then she gave you that look that seemed to say, "Just like you, right?"

But forget about sexual tension for the moment. As if there were some justice, the first fishing of the season is predictable and it's here. It's almost as if there were some reward for having come through the winter without wigging out. It was a long winter of working, tying flies and watching crooked and/or stupid politicians on television. At one point you caught yourself feeling sorry for anyone in government who made a practice of telling the truth because there's no good reason to believe him. You found yourself missing Jimmy Carter. Remember that interview?

"What are you going to do now, Mr. President?"

"I think I'm going to learn to be a really good fly-fisherman."

You understood that to be significantly different than just saying, "I'm going to go fishing."

Now, regardless of the placement of the equinox on the calendar, it has become summer. The fish have finished their reproductive business and have moved out of the shallows. They're hungry, and, as luck would have it, lots of things to eat have recently been born.

They'll lurk in the deeper water during the heat of the day, feeding casually as opportunities present themselves. They can be caught then, but it's a lazy, time-consuming kind of fishing. Not bad at all, you understand. In fact, there are days when you're genuinely up for it.

You settle in the belly boat under a wide-brimmed hat. Between the chapeau, full beard, and sunglasses, the only part of your face that's exposed to the sun is your nose, and this you slather with suntan lotion—the waterproof kind. With better than half of you beneath the water line, you'll stay pleasantly cool.

The selection of a streamer takes what would appear, to an observer, to be some thought, but "thought" isn't quite the right word. You gaze into the streamer box, which, because it's early in the season, is still nearly full of flies, looking for some sign. Bright colors with lots of wafting marabou and tinsel to catch the light? Or maybe a more sedate, more lifelike eel or bucktail bait fish pattern? How about the meaty, mechanical-looking weedless crawdad? Maybe the rubber worm copy tied with the six-inch strip of rabbit skin.

There have been days when the right fly seemed to crawl from the box into your hand saying, "I'm the one," and there were days when it was right, but this time none of them speaks. Nothing you know—or suspect—about bass clicks with anything you know about fly tying, so you fall back on "bright day, bright fly." That's something else a lot of grandpas used to say.

You pick a big one because, well, because what the hell? The same reason you used when you chose a small one last time. What you're trying to do is tempt intuition into your corner, even though intuition seems to have stopped off for a few drinks today.

The leader tippet is 2x (6-pound test) just in case. The big bass are rare, but they're here—somewhere. You could reasonably go even heavier, perhaps, but even the 2x muffles the action of the fly. You used a streamer with lots of marabou so that the breathing of the materials might make up for the wire-stiff leader. This is only logic, but it might attract a real insight.

Much is made of logic in fly-fishing these days, especially when it comes to trout, but the bass-fisherman is still often faced with trying to decide whether his fish will eat a red and white thing as opposed to a bright yellow thing when there's no discernible reason why he should bite either.

During the course of fly selection you and your belly boat have drifted out from shore. The light from the blue sky is flat and shadowless, and the surface of the water shows not a single crease from any movement of the air. Still, you have somehow drifted ten feet and would, if you sat perfectly still in the belly boat, apparently end up on the far bank in an hour or so. The pace of fishing at midday is a little quicker than that, but not much.

The cast is made quartering off to the northwest, toward the deeper water. The weighted fly lands with an audible "blip," pulling the leader down with it as it sinks in the clear water. The monofilament leaves the top in jerks as a section of it hangs up on the surface film until the increasing angle of the descending fly pulls it under. You should have thought to rub it with mud while you were still close enough to shore to get a handful. Then again, what's the hurry?

You watch the leader, knowing that a bass will sometimes be taken with curiosity about a slowly sinking fly and hit it. Or maybe—more likely, in fact—a kittenish young panfish with a mouth too small to take the hook will give it a tug. The fruitless noodling of a baby bluegill can affect the leader in the same way as the mouthing of a five-pound bass. The times when you strike and miss, you assume it was the former, but you're never sure.

With the leader sunk almost to the tip of the floating fly line, you begin to paddle the flippers, very slowly. You'll troll down the deep slot at the laziest speed possible; just enough to keep the fly moving. The bottom here is no more than ten feet down, with the weed tops closer yet to the surface. You want the supposedly weedless streamer to go just into the vegetation where a little bait fish would hide. There are no natural contours to the bottom here, just what was left by the steamshovels that took the gravel out decades ago, but there's a kind of logic to that, too. You'll troll about 200 yards down the slot to the south, then back to the north, then take the arm pointing pretty much west, and then back to where you are now. If it takes less than an hour, you're going too fast.

With the sun high and the weather hot, the bass are sulking in the places that are the most comfortable for them. They're waiting for things to be more to their liking and are probably in something of a funk. You try to picture it in terms you can understand. Imagine yourself when you're like that. You will not respond positively to razzle-dazzle, but a needling suggestion—that could work.

Thinking "Slowly," you begin up the pond. There are geese and some coots in the water with you, seemingly unconcerned with your presence as long as you're at a safe distance. The heron was a different story; being one of the spookiest of birds, he heaved off on his great, long wings as soon as you came in sight. That's why waterfowl hunters use copies of them as confidence decoys. Supposedly ducks know that, too.

The original plan for today had been to meet two belly boating friends here at about five in the afternoon for a few hours of bass bugging. It had, however, been one of those late spring/early summer afternoons when warm weather was still a fresh and joyous thing tugging at your mammalian consciousness. The fishing gear had been assembled and loaded in the truck by lunchtime. That left four and a half hours before it would be time to leave. There was plenty of work to do, but with this virulent a case of pond fever, it would have taken you that long to get comfortable in the desk chair.

On the drive out to the ponds, threading the dirt country roads away from the foothills and out onto the flatlands, you decided it would be a good idea to be on the water at something less than the ideal time of day for fishing. Instead of just arriving at the right moment (and congratulating yourself on your exquisite sense of timing) you would be able to watch it evolve from the bright, siesta doldrums of midday to those hours just before and after sunset when the fish, as they say, "move." You tell yourself it will be both educational and spiritually uplifting, as all imaginative excuses for goofing off are.

A few hours after you first stepped into the water, you're back on shore using the belly boat as an easy chair. The chest waders are rolled down below your knees so you can air out a bit. Neoprene waders are great for belly boating—streamlined and comfortable—but you *can* get a little ripe in them. It's suppertime: a half-hour rest break, the high points of which are a sandwich, apple, candy bar, and several long, luxurious slugs of water from the canteen. A cup of coffee would hit the spot, but the truck, with the camp stove and coffee pot, is parked nearly a mile away.

That, in fact, is one of the things that makes this your favorite pond. Of all the odd little bodies of water here, this is the farthest one from where you have to leave the car. It's not unusual to be alone on it, at least during the week, which is considerably more than can be said for what are known as the "front ponds." It's nameless, but you and your friends have come to call it The Bass Pond so as to distinguish it from all the other bass ponds.

Speaking of bass, you managed to take three little ones and one about a foot long while trolling; more than you expected. Then you switched to a size 12 Hares Ear Soft Hackle and took some small bluegills. After that it was break time, so you'd be fresh when your friends arrived. They're due in a half-hour, which means they should have been here by now. Any second now they'll be coming over the rise through the tall grass with float tubes strapped to their backs.

Soon the pond will move into its evening program. The bass and the larger panfish will come out of the deep water to nose into the shallows. This they'll do to the music of the spheres—the turning of the planet that drops the sun, slants the light, cools the water, and brings the fish to the surface. The catching of the first fish of the day on a floating bug is an ordinary, predictable event that still has a certain cosmic significance.

Your friends arrive, talking and waving in anticipation. They can see you came early and have been fishing. They understand and approve of this, calling you a sneaky son of a bitch and accusing you of spooking the pond, before they ask how you did.

"Got a couple," you say in your best understated Gary Cooper drawl, avoiding their eyes so as to give the impression that it was actually more than "a couple," but you're too modest to brag. It's a standard working man's gambit that stops short of actually lying and always works.

Your friends hustle into waders and flippers and string up their fly rods as you casually clip the still wet, plastered streamer from your leader and hang it on the drying patch, threading it deeply into the sheepskin. The only disadvantage to barbless hooks is that they'll sometimes jiggle loose from things like drying patches and hatbands to vanish into that yawning void where lost flies go.

You tell yourself you'll put the streamer back in the box where it belongs as soon as it's completely dry—maybe in an hour or so—while noticing that the drying patch holds at least a dozen flies left over from last season.

From this collection you pick a little pencil popper. It's a size 6, store-bought job with a long, thin, cork body, feather tails, and long rubber legs. The back of it is painted in a kind of frog spot pattern with eyes. You had just about given up on bugs like this, figuring that the fish can't see what's on the top anyway; that it's just a bit of fanciness designed to catch fishermen. But then there was that study, the one that said the bug resting on the surface bent the surface film in toward it, refracting the light so that the fish would see the bottom of the bug as it actually was with the top lying in a sort of halo around it. It could be true, and the bugs *are* real pretty.

This is such a standard bug for you now that you finally broke down and ordered several dozen of them, in assorted fancy color schemes, from the factory where they're made in Ohio. They're hard to find out here in the West. It's considered a panfish bug, but that, it took you almost ten years to realize, is little more than a matter of nomenclature. Bass like them. In fact, they prefer them to the larger bugs so often that you've begun to change your ideas about fly-fishing for largemouths.

The smaller bug is more like what the fish would be eating on a day-to-day basis. We like to think of bass waiting with ominous, predatory composure for the opportunity to eat a muskrat, but they couldn't actually do that, could they? They have to eat what comes along, and this thing splits the difference between damselfly, dragonfly, grasshopper, moth, and baby frog.

Also, you have begun to think, eating these things involves less of a commitment—less of a *decision*—from the bass than attacking a bullfrog or duckling. The fish seem to take them more casually and sooner, too; after less teasing. The biggest bass you've seen caught in this state—about 8 pounds—was taken on a popper a size smaller than the one you've just tied on your leader. It wasn't taken by you, of course, but by a friend you loaned a fly to. Sure, it was your idea and your fly, but *he* caught the big fish. Remember, fairness is a human idea largely unknown in nature.

The three of you waddle down to the water and cast off into the pond in your tubes. It is still what most would call "daytime," but the shadows of the cottonwood grove where the owl lives are leaning into the pond, and, although the air hasn't cooled enough for you to wiggle into the sweater yet, it is about to cool, and that gives you the intellectual equivalent of a slight chill. The social chatter is over now. From here on out, the talk between you will be technical and, with any luck, congratulatory.

When the fleet was launched, you just happened to be in the middle, and your partners now naturally peel off to the left and right, leaving you headed for your favorite weed bed. It angles out from the cattail marsh along a spit of gravelly sand that drops off sharply to what passes here for deep water. The fish like this. They prowl from the dark water up into the cover of the weeds at this time of day without ever having to offend their nocturnal sensibilities.

Did you subconsciously jockey for this position when you started? Did your friends, just as unconsciously, allow you your spot? You'll never know. It just seemed to happen.

It's early yet; not quite dark enough, but the light is bouncing off the water now instead of slicing in and below your dangling butt; the evening has already begun. The fish are hungry, that is, they're *supposed* to be hungry now. Sometimes an evening goes by with no action. You don't know why this happens, although you have determined that it is not, as some say, the phase of the moon.

That determination was made somewhat scientifically, and you're proud of it. Last year you got your hands on a lunar chart, one of those that farmers use. In it you could look up any day of the year and find it to be, for instance, a good day to plant corn, a good day to "kill noxious growths," but a bad day for slaughtering hogs and for fishing.

If accurate, this information could have been invaluable. It could have made you the hottest bass fly-fisher in the county, especially since this down-home, *Farmers' Almanac* style of celestial mysticism is largely out of fashion now.

But how to test it? If you fished only on good days, you would surely prove the theory because you'd catch some fish. It would be the classic self-fulfilling prophecy. Even if you fished on what were supposed to be good, bad, and indifferent days, you could still unconsciously skew the results because, to be honest, you *wanted* to believe it.

What you came up with was this: you just fished as usual, that is, as often as possible, without looking up the days on the chart beforehand. You made a mark on your calendar for every expedition—A+ for a good day of fish catching, A- for a poor day, and a 0 for one that was so-so.

After six weeks of this came the day of revelation. You sat down with the calendar and the moon chart and found, lo and behold, no noticeable correlation. Conclusion: the music of the spheres is still probably real, but it's not a simple melody.

Having approached within casting distance of your weed bed, traveling backwards in the belly boat, you scissor the flippers to achieve a smart about-face and scan the water. It's calm and unbroken, which is okay; the fish won't really be charging around for a little while yet. You cast the bug to within inches of the weeds in front of you, and, before you have a chance to give it the first tantalizing twitch, it goes down in the kind of vigorous but dainty rise peculiar to bluegills. It's a good fish, about the size and shape of your hand, a keeper that puts slightly more than a laughable bend in the bass rod. Nice.

A further advantage of the small bugs is that the good-sized panfish can also take them. You are not one of those fishermen who feel they have to change gears in their emotional transmissions when they go from bluegills to bass. They're members of the same family living together in the same water. Bass will eat bluegills, but adult panfish will also eat newborn bass. One is nothing but a larger or smaller version of the other, and full grown examples of either are completely satisfactory.

With the bluegill released, you cast again, this time farther to the right. There are nearly always bass here, but they are not in predictable spots. There's no sunken stump, deadfall, or other textbook example of where the big one should be hiding. You don't really know how they behave down there below the weed tops, but, in order to give yourself a handle on it, you picture them cruising moodily, sometimes backing into the weeds to lurk. They are a nasty, aggressive fish with a seemingly uncharacteristic shy streak.

The way you move them to a floating bug is by needling. Sure, there are evenings when they'll nail a popper the way that bluegill just did, but those are usually the smaller ones. The big bass are, for reasons that are unclear, considerably more reticent.

It's not unlike playing with a house cat. You know the game, the one with the shoelace. The adolescent cat is easy; flip the lace out onto the floor and she jumps on it. This is so easy, in fact, that it's only fun for a few minutes. The adult cat is a little harder. The string itself isn't enough, it also has to act right. The most difficult is the old cat—the seven-pound, sixteen-year-old spayed calico. Her predatory instincts are intact, but she's seen it all, having killed and eaten, in her time, everything from grasshoppers to baby rabbits. Roll cast the shoelace to where she's sleeping and she will open one eye just wide enough to register her boredom with such a clumsy and obvious ruse.

It can take twenty minutes to get her to bat at the string, and during most of that time the shoelace should lie still on the floor, twitching and crawling just often enough to hold her interest. If you're not up for it, she can wait you out. If you get impatient and wiggle the thing hard right in her face, she'll get up and find a soft place to sleep where she won't be bothered by the likes of you.

Her psychology is as much like that of a big bass as any creature you're likely to meet, and she hits the string in the same way the bass hits the fly: without completely buying the idea that it's real.

The bug has landed on the water with a splat, and the last of the rings it started have dissipated. By tightening the line you're holding in your left hand, you give the fly the subtlest possible jerk—the spark of life.

Was that a slight bulge in the weeds just off to the left? Maybe. There's often no hint at all that a bass is approaching, but sometimes there's just a little bit of one. Without anything you could point to as a clear indication, the surface of the warm water can seem to vibrate before a strike; an effect a musician/fisherman friend once referred to as "basso profundo."

In times past, when the light and the angle were just right, you've seen bass creep to within inches of a floating bug and then hang there looking at it, apparently thinking it over. Admit it. With all the evidence to the contrary, you've come to believe that bass think. What else would they be doing at a time like that?

You've also learned that, as satisfying as it seems at the moment, twitching the bug is the wrong thing to do. At the worst, it will spook the fish and you'll never see him again. At best, it will set off a whole new line of speculation in his chilly little brain. If he's there at all, he'll bite the thing in his own good time. You can't rush him.

You wait for long minutes and nothing happens. Is a fish looking at the fly now or not? How are you supposed to know? You twitch the bug again—tentatively, cautiously—and yes, just the shadow of a wake seems to approach it now. Yes. Maybe. It might have been a ripple from the wind, but there *is* no wind; not a breath of it.

The sky is still blue, but it's darkening. The sun is no longer on the water anywhere on the pond. There's a liquid "whoosh" behind you as a pair of geese land, but you don't look.

No question about it, something is about to happen.

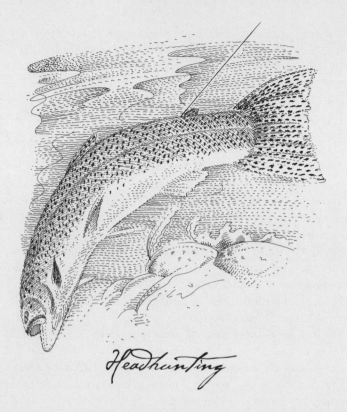

Headhunting

W E all want to catch big fish. That's one of the things nonanglers have straight about us. And the bigger they are, the better we like them. The International Game Fish Association even keeps world records on fish in several categories—including fly rod tippet classes—so we can see how big they get and how big a one can be landed on various strengths of monofilament—presumably for the purposes of comparison. Big fish are old, smart, wily, and secretive, or at least that's how we picture them. They have strong medicine, and, in a satisfyingly primitive way, we feel we can steal their magic by catching them.

But what *is* a big fish?

You can't go by the all tackle world records because those are the largest fish ever caught by sporting means, and it's not wise to adopt a scale that will make your own efforts look paltry. Except for a few real hotshots, world records have little practical meaning.

State records are more useful. You're still looking at monsters, but at least they were caught around home and make some relative sense.

"Relative" is the operative word here, and fly-fishermen are highly adept relativists. In our hands the question ceases to be "What is a big fish?" and becomes "Big compared to what?"

Judging from the stories of fishermen and the claims of guide services, any trout weighing in at 5 pounds is considered big in the overall scheme of things; big in the sense that if you are not impressed by such a fish, you risk being asked just who the hell you think you are anyway.

Using another form of measurement, any trout that's 20 inches from tail to jaw is big, even though he may not weigh 5 pounds. Some use inches, while others prefer pounds. The latter conveys more information. Some fly-fishers split the difference, measuring fish under 20 inches and weighing those above. That's because "18 inches" sounds better than "2½ pounds."

Based on the same stories and claims, a big largemouth bass (or a large bigmouth bass, if you like) will weigh closer to 8 pounds. To most of us who fish for both with a fly rod, a bass is a bigger fish than a trout, even though the world record largemouth at 22 pounds, 4 ounces is seriously outclassed by the world record brown at 35 pounds, 15 ounces and the world record rainbow at 42 pounds, 2 ounces.

For that matter, there are a lot of fly-fishers around who will tell you a brown is a bigger trout than a rainbow. But then, didn't I just say that world records weren't of much use in this context? Right, but how do you expect me to maneuver the discussion away from a 42-pound trout? After all, we're talking about big fish here.

What makes a bass a bigger fish than a trout is average size or, more properly, what is considered a keeper. This is a somewhat dated concept in circles where a keeper is now referred to as a "good fish," but it means the same thing: one you wouldn't be ashamed to bring home *if* you were to bring any home, which, of course, you're not going to do.

Around here a good trout is about a foot long. A good bass is more like 14 or 15 inches. If you wouldn't be happy to catch a dozen of either on a light fly rod, you are definitely out of my league.

"Big" is also a regional concept based on fisheries quality. On the Yellowstone River in Yellowstone Park, a 20-inch cutthroat is a big fish. A 20-inch rainbow from the Henry's Fork is also big, but, although it may be the biggest trout you take in a week's fishing, it's not the biggest one you can hope for.

Hope, as opposed to reasonable expectation, has a lot to do with it. An electro-shocking survey of a modest-sized brown trout creek might reveal the average fish to be 9 inches long, a few odd trout will push up to 15 or 16 inches, and the single old hen brown in the deep hole under the bridge weighs 9 pounds. Hope swims in the deep water in the Bridge Pool, feeding mostly at night. Some refuse to believe it's there. Among the believers are a few who think they've seen it. It's a fish that stands a good chance of dying of old age.

It's hard to argue with the idea that a big fish is the biggest one in the water you're fishing at the moment. In this context, a 14-inch brookie from a little beaver pond at 10,500 feet is the same size as a yard-long rainbow from the Madison River.

Late last summer I was fishing with A.K. and his old fishing buddy from Michigan, Bob Fairchild. We wanted to show Bob some huge Rocky Mountain rainbows, so we went and camped near a famous trout river. For several days, working in fairly crowded conditions, we caught fish that, in the context of this discussion, ranged from good to very good in a river where an 8-pound trout was once caught on a dry fly.

After a few days of this we took an afternoon off to get clear of the crowd. We drove up into the high country and hiked up a diminutive brook trout creek, a lonely little trickle that showed few signs of ever having been fished. It was up in there, a few miles from the truck, that A.K. landed a fat little 13-inch brookie that was clearly the biggest fish of the trip.

This relative-to-the-water-in-question concept gives rise to one of the most common sour-grapisms directed at famous big-fish anglers; you know, the guys with reputations as headhunters who are always pictured with enormous, ugly, dripping fish. "Sure," people say. "If I fished the places he did, I'd catch fish like that, too."

That's at least partly true. Most of us fish for the average fish. We go out during the day to cast poppers for bass, dry flies for trout, or whatever, looking to *catch some fish*. If we go to where the average fish are bigger than they are near home, well . . .

I'm as into this as anyone. I can stay home and fish the St. Vrain and the three forks and sometimes catch "big" 12- to 14-inch trout. No problem. Perfectly satisfactory. I use a light cane rod, tend toward dry flies, and have a fine time.

But then there are the relatively short trips to better Colorado rivers like the South Platte and Frying Pan. According to the last Division of Wildlife study I saw, the average trout in the Pan was 16 inches long, and there were plenty that were bigger. *Much* bigger.

I won't go so far as to say that the Henry's Fork is a better river than the Frying Pan—if for no other reason than that Bill Fitzsimmons, who owns the Taylor Creek fly shop on the banks of the Pan, would drive all the way down here to straighten me out—but I do make the obligatory pilgrimage to Idaho at least once a year. That's simply because fishermen must travel, it's part of the game, and when you go on the road you point your headlights in the direction of larger, rather than smaller, fish.

Being on the move is one of the charms of the sport, but you have to be careful to avoid the "never far enough north" syndrome. My father and I discovered this years ago in Minnesota. We lived in the southern part of the state, but drove north to fish in the summers. Way north, until we were far enough from home to feel the reality of a different place. We wanted to be up there where people went to fish.

Once we stopped in to see a friend of Dad's, only to find that he'd "gone north to fish." Dad turned to me and said, in his best allegorical tone, "Well, I guess you can never get far enough north." Then he gazed wistfully off through the trees in the general direction of the Arctic Circle, picturing his friend "out there" somewhere, standing on the pontoon of a floatplane catching fish. *Big* fish. Bigger than what we were catching, surely. I mean, he was farther north, right?

I remember that as one of those profound moments when you realize not only that your father is actually human, but that even the finest parts of life can hurt you; that it's possible to want too much of what you can't have. Dad died too young, but he was not a tragic character—quite the opposite, in fact. Still, he never did catch *the* big fish, and there came a time when I thought I could see that in his eyes. I'm not saying you shouldn't go. I think you should go as far and as often as you can, just don't go staring off into the trees like that when there are fish to be caught just five minutes down the road.

The other way to catch the big ones is to actually fish for them, which is something most of us don't do. We continue to hope for big fish while fishing for the little ones. Some honestly believe trophies are beyond their talents, but that is true only of the very worst klutzes. Most know how to catch big fish, but are just not up for it.

It's really pretty simple. First you gear up with a stout rod, a heavy leader, and some huge flies. By huge I mean bigger than the biggest ones you have now. Think of a big fish as a human being with a salary in six figures. If you toss a penny on the sidewalk to see what it will attract, you'll get kids and bums. A quarter will get you teenagers and the occasional adult, although the latter will glance around a time or two to make sure no one is looking before he picks it up. A dollar will get you most people, but a twenty-dollar bill will stop a Lincoln Continental in heavy traffic.

Next, find a good piece of water, ideally a lake or reservoir. All things being equal, a good lake will hold bigger fish than a good stream, with very large, productive rivers being the exception. Pick one close to home, because you'll be spending a lot of time there. If you must leave your own neighborhood, take the wall tent, Winnebago, or whatever you have in the way of portable luxury accommodations.

Dress warmly, because you'll be out all night and/or in the worst possible weather. Dead of the night, dark of the moon, and spitting rain is best.

Use a sink-tip or full sinking fly line to get deep and leave the #16 dry flies at home. Not back in the car, I mean at home where you can't get them if you weaken and decide to do a little real fishing, just to break the monotony.

Don't fool around wading and casting from shore. Get into a craft of some kind so you'll be mobile.

Finally, learn to sleep during the day and steel yourself for days, if not weeks, of dredging before you hook *the fish*.

Okay, maybe I'm being a little unfair, but that's how the real head-hunters do it, day in and day out. It's not the only way to catch big fish, but it's how you make a career out of it. I can do it, but only for short stretches and only a few times in a season. Two straight days of kick-ass lunker hunting is about all I can handle, then I'm back to splitting the difference.

Splitting the difference means fishing all day like a gentleman on a good trout stream, taking a break for supper, and then coming back for two hours at night to cast a six-inch-long chipmunk fly to the stickiest logjam in the deepest bend pool in the whole river. Or maybe putting the bluegill rod away at dusk and coming back for a session with a 2/0, goggle-eyed bass bug and a jug of mosquito repellent. It must be done on occasion—especially when the conditions seem to beg for it.

Yet another way involves increasing your odds through precise timing. The prespawning congregation of fat, horney brown trout around the inlet to a lake may only last a week, but you can take your big fish then, and not just one, but several. A locally famous trophy hunter likes to go to the big reservoirs the night before the weekly stocking truck arrives. He says the big browns and rainbows eat the stockers like they were popcorn. They learn the stocking schedules and wait for the trucks.

Of course the hatches are the best; those few, famous, thick hatches and falls of large bugs that move the biggest fish to rise to the surface to dry flies. The most mythical of these is probably the hatch of the huge stoneflies on Montana rivers like the Madison and the Big Hole. The bug is the famous Pteronarcys something-or-other, known also as the giant salmon fly; the two-and-a-half-inch long, orange and black dry fly. Yes, I've seen the bug. In fact, I have one on the desk here in a bottle of formaldehyde. (I got it out to measure it in the interest of accuracy; I was going to say three inches.) Over the years I've hit the ends or the beginnings of this hatch on two rivers in Montana and one in Idaho, but have never seen it in its glory. I've heard the stories, though, from fishermen who are normally calm and droll, guys who shook me by the lapels and swore it was all true, as if they'd just seen Godzilla grazing in a field east of town. "Twenty-four-inch trout on every cast," they said, "cars skidding in squashed bugs on the highway . . ."

Relax. I believe it.

An even more interesting question than "What is a big fish?" or "How do you catch one?" is, "What will you do with it?"

Mounting it seems logical, and there is something smug about having the evidence right there on the wall. Not only that, it gives you a gracious introduction to the story. You don't have to go out of your way to bring it up, you just wait for someone to say, "Jeeze, nice fish," and there's your audience. Anyone who doesn't comment is probably a golfer and wouldn't understand anyway.

I have not been moved to have a fish mounted in recent years, but apparently that wasn't always true. My father swore that when I was just a tyke, no more than this high, I threw a fit because he refused to have a sunfish I'd caught in Wisconsin stuffed. "It wasn't even big enough to eat, and I threw it back," he said. "You raised hell for an hour."

What did I know? It was probably the fourth or fifth fish I'd ever caught and the first that wasn't a bullhead, but at the tender age of no more than five I knew what a mount was and I wanted one.

I still like mounts. I go out of my way to admire them (and not just to be polite, either) and have a special affection for old ratty ones that were caught by someone's daddy—who is now dead—forty years ago when everything, including the fishing, was better than it is now. But I don't have any myself.

There was a time when it was out of the question from an economic standpoint, and I'm not so sure that time has passed. I do now and then have a few extra bucks, but at five to eight dollars an inch, a 24-inch trout is worth two weeks on the road somewhere, during which time one might even catch yet *another* big fish.

I have a few photographs hanging around the place: the 8-pound rainbow from Kipps Lake, a 6-pounder from the nameless lake in Wyoming, etc. The 8-pound trout is my favorite because the photo was taken by Gary

LaFontaine, a big-time famous fisherman whose name drops loudly and who also knows how to make a wide-angle lens add several pounds to an already heavy fish. "Aim his head up toward the camera a little more," he said.

I have so far released all of my truly big fish, unless you count bluegills and crappies, many of which I have fried in beer batter and eaten happily. A.K. killed a 5- or 6-pound brown two years ago, but only because it had taken the streamer deep in the gills and was clearly bleeding to death. It was delicious, by the way. Don't believe what they say about big fish not being good to eat.

I could get all moralistic about this business of not killing large fish, but the fact is, I've just never figured out how big a fish has to be before it absolutely demands to be stuffed. I have also learned that they don't look as big as they really are when they're mounted. You need a real pig to raise discerning eyebrows.

I've only met one fisherman who seemed to have that under control. He asked me, more or less in passing, if I knew where he could catch a 16-inch brook trout. It seemed like a reasonable, but still slightly odd, request, so I asked what he was up to. It seems he already had a rainbow, a brown, a yellowstone cutthroat, a golden, and a grayling—all exactly 16 inches long—mounted on the wall of his den. "Specimens," he said. "Archetypal examples of the trouts (and grayling) of North America, not trophies."

I liked that. It seemed rational, modest, scientific (but not *too* scientific); the well-bred answer to the problem of the trophy. I did actually have a suspicion about where a guy might catch a 16-inch brookie, but all I could bring myself to do was congratulate him on his finely honed aesthetics and wish him well. I'm a sucker for that kind of thing, but I'm not stupid.

So, how big should it be before you mount it? Hard to say. You could devise a rule of thumb, I suppose—if you didn't grunt when you lifted it in the net, it's not big enough—but that may miss the point. Unless you've got a wall full of stuffed fish, it should be a memento of a pinnacle in your angling career, and few of us are willing to admit that we've just caught the biggest fish we'll ever catch. With life as short as it is, that might be a milestone we don't care to pass.

Big fish are what we want, but they're like true love, success, lots of money, or maybe public office: we don't know *why* we want them, but we figure that will take care of itself if we ever connect. It will become obvious, won't it?

Maybe it's the quest that makes sense to us—the fragile balance between reality, possibility, and promise. The fisherman is privileged among human beings as one who can push his expectations with some hope of fulfillment. World peace and universal enlightenment are, I think, beyond us, but a fish that's an inch longer or an ounce heavier than the last one, well, shoot, that could happen.

Yet another problem with really big fish is that once spotted, they can't be hooked; once hooked, they can't be landed. As we all know, it takes tremendous fortitude to come away with anything like a straight face after being taken to the brink and then robbed of the satisfaction. Still, it's illustrative, possibly because it copies life in general so well.

Fly-fishing reveals character, and the bigger the fish the deeper the revelation. A potential wall hanger is not only a horrendous fish, it can also show your partners what you're made of.

Last summer A.K. and I were on our usual jaunt through Idaho and Montana when we hooked up with a gentleman named Bill Crabtree. Bill lives in Texas, but he spends several months in West Yellowstone, Montana, each year—at a place that's been in his family for several generations—to, as he puts it, "just sort of ease out a little, you know?"

One evening, after several days of fishing together, we decided to drive to a pond we knew of to see about getting into a big trout. Enormous fish live in this thing, but it's one of those places where you will probably not hook a fish, and if you do, you probably won't land it because it will be *too* big. For this reason, it's usually deserted, even though it's well known to fishermen in the area.

The main problem with landing the fish—over and above the usual problems one has with big, strong trout—is the weed beds. They're wide and dense and ring the shore, and the gooey, unstable bottom makes wading unfeasible. If you work from shore and get into even a decent fish, he'll take you into the weeds, tangle himself up and break you off. All the big ones have done this a hundred times and are real good at it.

The solution is to fish from a belly boat. That way you stand a better chance of keeping the fish out of the weeds, and, failing that, you can at least go in after him with some hope of coming out again.

You fish a place like this on occasion, not so much to catch trout as to see how much adrenaline you can generate and how much disappointment you can stand. When you're alone you can swear and scream and thrash the water with your flippers when you lose a fish, but in company a modicum of restraint is expected.

It was just coming on evening—the best time—when we arrived at the pond, having hauled our float tubes, flippers, and rods down from the road. The smooth surface of the pond was unbroken by rise or boil, calmly reflecting the darkening sky and a range of mountains, but the knowledge of what swam there made the water seem to tingle with electricity. It was like the peacefulness of a hand grenade from which the pin has just been pulled. We rigged up slowly, with a studied casualness, although our eyes left the water only when necessary.

The first boil was unbelievably large. In most waters you'd assume it was a full-grown beaver, but not here. Here there were no beavers, probably because the trout have eaten them all. It caught us in various states of disarray: Bill and I were sitting on our tubes, half into and half out of our waders with rods still broken down. A.K. was still in hiking boots, but he had already strung up his rod and had a fly tied on—a #14 flying ant like the ones we'd seen on the water. A.K. always strings the rod first and he almost always starts with a dry fly.

He gave Bill and me a questioning glance. I shrugged and heard Bill say, "Hell, why not?"

A.K. worked out some line and cast ahead of the dissipating ripples that indicated the fish's direction. He barely had time to straighten the leader before one of the largest trout I've ever seen in the flesh swallowed the little dry fly with a great slurping and burbling of water.

A.K. set the hook, somewhat gingerly, and the fish shot to the deepest hole in the middle of the pond, tearing 6-weight line from the reel. And there he sat, immovable as a rock the size of a couch. The only sign of life was a petulant thrumming in the line. The fish wasn't scared, he was pissed.

"That was really stupid," A.K. said, half to himself. "Now what am I gonna do?"

Bill and I could think of nothing to say. Stupid, maybe, but there isn't a fisherman alive who wouldn't have cast to that trout from right there on shore. Anyone with the iron will it would have taken to suit up and get into the float tube first would be no fun to fish with.

He thought it over for a minute. It was painfully obvious.

"I'm gonna have to get into my waders and get into the belly boat and get the hell out there," he said. "Someone is gonna have to hold the rod for a minute."

Among fishermen there are moments of unspoken understanding; moments when there is no doubt whatsoever about what is going to happen next. It's enough to make you believe in fate.

A.K. looked over at Bill and me, who were both on our feet by then. Bill threw his hands in the air as if someone had just pointed a .44 magnum at his heart, did a smart about-face and walked off into the sagebrush and cactus. He knew what was about to transpire and he wanted no part of it.

That, of course, left the good old fishing partner.

A.K. gave me a silent look worthy of a Shakespearean actor. It said: this won't work, but it must be tried, and if the fish is lost it will be my own fault; I couldn't possibly blame you—but I will.

I wish I hadn't already put my flippers on, because the gravity of the situation called for something more dignified than for me to waddle over there like a duck and carefully take the rod.

A.K. was into his waders and flippers with one foot in the belly boat when I felt a ponderous wiggle in the line and the fly came loose.

It just came loose, honest.

A.K. froze in the unlikely posture of a man mounting a float tube. Bill was thirty yards out on the prairie, hands in his pockets, looking at the ground like a mourner at a funeral. The shadow of the mountains had swallowed the pond and a songbird twittered in that frantic way they have right at dusk—as if they haven't had enough to eat today and it's going to be a long, cold night.

And then Bill said, "I seen him break it off when you weren't looking."

The loss of a big fish, for whatever reason, reveals character. Much more so than the actual landing of a big fish, which only calls for a modicum of forgivably false humility.

Jay Allman and I were once fishing together on a lake known for its large rainbow trout; fish that were catchable, but that would come a few per day at best. And that's how they were coming to us. They were large enough— 5 pounds and up—that the usual suspicion that there were even larger ones in there was muted. This thought is never absent from the mind of the fisherman, and it is always true, but there are times when it doesn't matter.

We were both in belly boats, and my back was to Jay, but it was one of those clear, calm, profoundly quiet western days, and I could clearly hear the zzzzup of his line as he set the hook and the growl of the reel as the fish bored off almost casually. On this particular lake, the hooking of a fish was an event, so I turned and gave Jay the clenched-fist salute still popular with aging counter-culture types. He returned it with a nod of the head, as his right hand was engaged in palming the reel.

I turned back to the line of cattails in front of me along which the grapefruit-sized head and shoulders of a large trout periodically broke the surface, now here, now there, eating God knew what in no discernible rhythm or pattern. The problem at hand was simply to make a cast that didn't line the fish and spook him. If the fly was the right one and I happened to inadvertently put it in front of him, he might even eat it, at which point it would become an entirely different game that I could also easily lose.

This calls for some concentration.

It was probably five minutes later when I glanced over at Jay. He was playing a fish.

"Another one," I yelled. "Quit showing off."

"Same one," he said, not looking up.

Indeed. For a fly-fisher of Jay's caliber to spend five minutes playing a single trout meant one thing: my presence with the camera would be required. I reeled in and paddled over, harboring visions of a *Sports Afield* cover shot. Blue sky, puffy clouds, red rock hills, big fish. Perfect.

I stopped at a respectful distance to watch. The rod was bent nearly double, the white fly line vanished into a depth of clear water that was hard to judge. And on the end of that line was another nine or ten feet of leader. The fish swam in wide, deep, lazy circles, slowly turning the belly boat with it. Jay was nowhere near panic, nor was he in much control, either.

This was a big, big, big trout.

This was very serious business.

Now Jay adheres to the philosophy of land them or lose them, but don't mess around, so he was playing this fish to what he perceived as the limits of his tackle, trying to get it up off the bottom. It was working, but slowly.

Jay finally pumped the trout up to about six or eight feet, and we both caught a glimpse of him down there. We weren't really surprised at the nearly yard-long form because we'd both already taken some quite large fish there and none of them had been anywhere near this heavy or this tough.

It was about then that the rod went straight; Jay looked shocked for a few seconds, then bowed his head and sat there staring at the patch of orange material on the front of his tube where it says, "Inflate to 1½ psi during use; DO NOT OVERINFLATE" as if pondering the true meaning of the phrase.

After a minute or two of meditation, he looked up, smiled, and said, "Well, let's get another one."

That's all you can do. In fact, it's what you *must* do. It's one of the unwritten laws of the sport. There's obviously nothing to be gained by getting mad at yourself, and no one in his right mind would hold it against the fish.

In Camp

ANOTHER wet, heavy snowfall that will turn to mud in only a day or so. It's almost a good rain, but not quite; a sure sign of spring in Colorado. Every few years, around this time, we'll get a snowstorm with thunder and lightning. If I live to be a hundred I'll never get used to that.

A friend of mine and several of his pals left two days ago on their fifteenth annual Rite of Spring Camping Trip. It's a tradition with them, and they now have volumes of stories about being uncomfortably stranded in various parts of the Mountain West.

They clearly do this on purpose, although it seems to be an unspoken agreement.

Day before yesterday they headed west over one of the passes and into Utah, right into the storm that got here last night or early this morning. Sure, I'm a little worried about him, but not much. He's smart and has a strong survival mentality with the training to back it up. I'd be more worried if he'd gone to New York City for the weekend. And anyway, it's exactly what he wanted: planned hardship in the Canyonlands.

I've never tried to horn in on this yearly campaign against the weather, not because I'm not up for it (really) but because they don't actually *do* anything. They just camp, although I'll grant you that can be a full-time job at this time of year.

My own camping has taken a turn in the last decade or so. I don't just go camping like I once did, at least not very often. What I engage in now is what you might call "base camping," staying out in the woods in order to do something other than just be there. That something is usually fishing.

I do almost all of my base camping with A.K. these days, ever since that first trip to the Henry's Fork when it became evident that we had similar ideas about such things. A fairly high level of agreement in these matters is mandatory. You can go fishing with a guy who has a divergent style of fishing (within reason), but it's pretty hard to live with someone who disagrees with you about how the camp should be run.

Efficiency is our watchword. A fishing camp should function in such a way that the campers can fish rather than hang around doing chores and cooking gourmet meals. It should also go up quickly so you can fish the evening you get where you're going instead of pitching camp and then fishing in the morning.

Our motto is, First Things First.

Most of our camps in recent years have been next to the pickup, so that if the tent is the main lodge, then the camper shell, backed up to face the fire pit, serves as the storage shed. That kind of arrangement can be handy, but if you're not careful it can become *too* handy. With all that room it's tempting to bring all kinds of things you don't really need, even though all they'll do is get in the way. The things you might need, but probably—even hopefully—won't (like the first aid kit and the .357 magnum) are few enough not to be a problem.

We have the tent, sleeping bags, the modest but complete camp kitchen with utensils, Coleman stove, and bottle of whiskey, two coolers (one for beer, one for food), a cardboard box for canned provisions, several tarps, coil of rope, and the odd box containing knives, axes, screwdrivers, etc.

On some trips, especially the shorter ones, we bring a small stack of firewood from home so we don't have to waste time gathering it on the spot, and, of course, we seldom go anywhere for any length of time without the fly tying kits.

The rest of the stuff is fishing gear which, once camp is set up, is stowed at the back of the camper shell for easy access. A.K.'s stuff is on the left and mine is on the right.

All it takes is restraint and a clear vision of the problem at hand, which is to live on-site with as little fuss as possible and to catch fish, or, failing that, to at least give it one hell of a try. We've got it to where it takes no more than forty-five minutes to set up a camp, the only discussion being where the tent goes, and that can often be done with a point from one and a nod from the other. The camps vary some from place to place, but they're all pretty much the same. Coming back to them late in the evening is as familiar as entering your own darkened home at night. But then, what's home but a permanent camp?

This is something we just fell into and have never talked about much. We've never had to. Between us we probably have seventy years of camping experience, which, I like to think, allows us to differentiate between the necessary and the fluffy in terms of both chores and equipment.

Something else we just fell into is A.K. doing all the cooking. That's how it was the first time and how it's been ever since. Maybe it's because we use his kitchen; it's certainly not because he's a better cook.

Let me point out that I don't just lounge around with a mint julep while A.K. is slaving over a hot Coleman. In the morning I've got the sleeping bags aired out, the truck loaded, and lunches made by the time A.K. announces breakfast. In the evenings I've got the waders airing out, drinks made, and the fire going in time to sit and watch the stew come to a final simmer.

And A.K. is actually a pretty good camp cook. At this stage of the game it would be impertinent, if not insulting, for me to offer to take over for him.

If it sounds like there's very little camp lounging and fire-gazing, you're right, but there *is* a little of both. No outdoorsman worthy of the title is immune to the simple charms of camp.

These become apparent after supper with a few drinks around the campfire. Sometimes more than a few drinks. If we're out for a week, there's one night when we settle in and get seriously shit-faced. This usually happens at the end of a supremely good day, but not always. Good day or mediocre (I can't recall anything you could honestly call a "bad" day of fishing), it is a quietly joyous, celebratory drunk, the kind where at some point in the evening you look up at the clear Colorado, Idaho, or Montana sky to find that the satellites are standing still, but the stars are moving.

On normal camp evenings, the day's exploits are gone over in some detail, and philosophical implications surface. One night, after several straight days of sublime fishing on the Henry's Fork, we realized that we'd reached a new height in the area of losing count. Not only had we automatically lost track of the number of trout we'd caught, we suddenly couldn't remember how many times we'd been into the backing that day, something we'd normally keep track of.

At some point the plan for the following day is decided upon. This can be a long, involved sifting of options or it can be as simple as:

"Same place tomorrow?"

"You bet."

Some nights are spent examining questions. Why does the No-hackle mayfly dun pattern so often work better than a sparsely hackled standard fly? The hackle on the standard pattern represents legs, and, as A.K. has pointed out many times, "A mayfly *has* legs, right?"

It's a serious ponderment. I think it bothers him deeply.

Most topics naturally relate to fishing in one way or another, although we do sometimes take a few minutes to solve the world's problems. At night, around a campfire, a few minutes is all it takes.

A much more lengthy and heated discussion is likely to ensue over what the perfect fly rod for a certain stream or lake might be. We both still like to fish split cane rods, but have softened on that a little in recent years. In fact, I'm thinking of buying a 9½-foot, 6-weight graphite rod made by one of the famous manufacturers of such things. It's a fabulous rod, even though it's not made of bamboo. I'll have to get A.K.'s permission to do this, or if not permission, then at least some kind of grudging assent like, "Well, I guess if you want to fish with one of them plastic rods there's nothing I can do to stop you."

However the evening goes, someone is required to mention how great it is to be sitting around in camp, even if it's raining and we haven't caught any fish yet. After the appropriate pause in the conversation someone has to say, "Jeeze, this is great, ain't it?"

Another unspoken rule is that high-tone grammar is to be avoided wherever possible. The last thing you'd ever say in camp is, "That is something up with which I will not put."

There was a time, not all that many years ago, when I was into the classic off-trail backpacking head and thought that anyone who stayed in an official campground was a pussy. The *real* camper strained and sweated his way to the highest, most remote lakes where he caught cutthroat trout at the risk of life and limb. He ate cheap, starchy food, slept on the rocks under the sky, drank bourbon, and stayed up half the night howling at the moon. If he happened to meet a clean-cut hiker, he'd become sullen and dangerous-looking and slink off into the trees muttering about how the goddamned flatlanders ought to stay where they belonged.

Perfection was found only in solitude, with wild trout who had not seen the wader-clad legs of a human in at least a year. And that was not open for discussion.

But then, somewhere around my thirtieth birthday, it did become open for discussion, and I relented. It was as simple as that. Maybe I was getting a little older or something.

There were numbered parking spots with ready-made fire pits. Sometimes there was a faucet with cold water. Sometimes there were even bathrooms. Bathrooms! Well, at least the seats were cold.

"Of course, it's not real camping," I told myself, "but it *is* outside at least, and it's convenient, and it's a hell of a lot cheaper than a room."

And then I began to almost like it.

The campgrounds A.K. and I stay in now are filled mostly with fisherpeople, with the occasional vacationing family or retired couple thrown in for balance. Most lack what you'd call a real community spirit, but they're not unfriendly. There's even a sort of double-edged social hierarchy. The upper crust travels in monstrous Winnebagos or those big, shiny Air Stream trailers that sport, among other things, TV antennae. Sometimes these things travel in herds, and when a caravan of them descends on your campground it is referred to as an "aluminum hatch."

On the other end of the social ladder (not the "bottom," just the other end) are us tent campers. Pioneers. Tough guys. It may be my imagination, but I think we're accorded a certain respect. More than once we've had camper dwellers come over to visit, at which times we adopt the style of the clipped, one-word response.

"You guys fishing?"

"Yup."

"Doing any good?"

"Some."

And so on.

On occasion we hear what almost sounds like an apology.

"I'm not fishing myself this trip. It's"—he looks over his shoulder at Mom cooking dinner and the kids playing frisbee—"it's sort of a family vacation, you know?"

"Yup."

We've never talked about this, either, but I think it's a bit of compromise for A.K., too. Some nights when all the congratulations have been congratulated and the plans have all been made, we tell each other about our great, lonely camps of the past:

A.K. and Bob Fairchild on Hunt Creek back in Michigan. The little stretch of it between private deer camps that no one, and I mean no one, knew about back then. Opening day, cold, frost, or even a skiff of snow. No hatch. And, amazingly, a few brook and brown trout to flies. Not worms—flies. A modest creek with mostly okay fish, but wild, too. Sixteen- to eighteen-inch trout were sometimes caught. Big for Michigan. Hell, big for anywhere. And, naturally, not a soul within miles, not another track from that year on the obscure old logging road. The tall, ancient spruce trees around the fire pit. I've never seen it, but I can see it. I've heard about it a hundred times and could stand to hear about it again. I'm like a little kid with his favorite bedtime story.

"You forgot the part about the big trees, A.K."

"Oh yeah, the big trees, they were enormous . . ."

And some of my own, too:

The time Ed Engle and I stayed in the mountains until the food ran out and then stayed on eating nothing but trout—because the fishing was so good—and finally got so weak we just barely made it back to the car and then drove to the nearest truck stop and ate pancakes and eggs and then hamburgers and didn't even get sick.

Or the time on Goose Creek—also short of food—when we really wanted a trout to eat, but couldn't catch one. I made a fire to cook the last of the rice while Ed went back to the stream. He came back in twenty minutes with a great big trout, a rainbow as I recall. Said he'd been fishing with flies, but then noticed some grasshoppers. Since we were at an awfully high altitude for hoppers, he took it as a sign; caught one; apologized to it; hooked it right on his fly and caught the big trout on the first cast. He said he tried for another fish with another hopper, but didn't get one and knew why.

There was a long silence during which I thought, okay, I'll bite.

"Why?" I asked.

"Because I forgot to apologize to the second grasshopper," he said as if it was obvious.

There's precious little hanging around the tent during daylight hours now, but on trips that stretch to a week or more, the obligatory camp afternoon is observed. This is when fly lines are cleaned and re-dressed, when the leaders are rebuilt, when certain lost items are looked for under the seats of the truck, and the general clutter that results from days of feverish fishing is straightened up.

A trip to the nearest town to do laundry and get supplies will be required.

Chances are flies will need to be tied; either replacements or new brainstorms. Tying in the wind—it's always windy when you try to tie outside—

is feasible as long as you remember to weight down anything you're not holding onto. The flies produced are usable, but typically far short of gorgeous and can be readily identified later as "wind flies."

It's a lazy, pleasant couple of hours that still don't quite amount to goofing off. There are things to be done, even if the pace is slow. Just *sitting around* in camp is about as much fun as watching a bobber.

It occurs to me that it's been two seasons now since I've strapped the stuff on my back, hiked into some lake or stretch of stream in the mountains, and stayed there for a few days. About as long as you've had to make reservations for a wilderness campsite in the area near home where I used to go. I'll now pay good money to sleep in the dirt at a campground, but I find it difficult to make a reservation for an unspecified patch of rocks and pine needles in the wilderness area.

But there are still plenty of places around here where you can roll out your sleeping bag when and where the spirit moves you, and I think I'd better do that again soon. I don't want the sparse, remote camps to become campfire myths about my fading youth. I'm not that old yet.

I think I even know where to do it; it's where the four-wheel-drive track turns away from a certain little stream leaving a long stretch of water that few people fish. I'll bet I can talk A.K. into this with no trouble.

The campgrounds are convenient and comfortable, but I think it's a good idea to get back in the bushes now and then because, for me at least, "back in the bushes" is the real holy ground of this entire endeavor, the famous rivers notwithstanding.

And the fishing can be pretty good, too.

Koke decided to do that a couple of years ago and asked me to go with him. I wanted to, but couldn't for reasons that must have seemed important at the time, but that I can't remember now. What I remember now is wishing I'd gone along.

"Okay," he said, "but act as my check-in."

This is mandatory when you go into the woods alone, or even with a friend, for that matter. Tell someone where you're going and when you'll be back so they can mount the rescue if you *don't* come back.

The story that surfaced later was that Koke had gone into the canyon exactly where he said he was going to. It was a canyon with a little creek in it that held some nice trout, but that was seldom fished because of its ruggedness. He was going to be there for two or maybe three days, and it was on the first day that he tangled up in some rocks and took a very bad fall, the kind where your eyes go dark and your head buzzes. He later quoted himself as thinking, "Please, if anything is broken, let it be the fly rod."

That's pretty serious.

He was sore and bruised, but not mortally wounded, so he stayed and fished, as anyone in his right mind would have done. The weather, he said, was lousy about half of the time, and I remember sitting here in the comfort of the house, taking care of whatever was so important, wishing I was up there sitting in the rain with him.

I was gone when he came through here, but when I got home I found the following note tacked to my front door—the only clean limerick I've ever seen, which I have committed to memory:

Koke has returned from the gorge of St. Vrain
All weary and aching and racked with great pain
But his fond early wishes
Of many great fishes
Were borne out through the sun, wind, and rain

KOKE

Staying in the campgrounds is a little like fishing the Green Drake hatch on the Henry's Fork. You can't let the people get you down. In fact, you have to get into what it is: something of a mob scene with a mob scene's attendant charms.

One evening, in a campground populated by middle-aged fly-fishing types, including me and A.K., a handsome young couple in their early twenties arrived. They pulled in right next to us and so we waved, just to be polite. We were busy at the moment arguing over whether the wings on the flying ant fly pattern should be down or upright and whether they should be made of feathers or waffle-pattern plastic. Very deep stuff.

But the couple bounced over, introduced themselves, and said they were on their honeymoon. For some reason, people who are on their honeymoons want everyone they bump into to know about it.

A.K. nodded sagely, and I said, "Yup."

When they left, A.K. mentioned that the lady was a handsome specimen—something that wasn't lost on our other neighbors, either—and we went back to poking the fire and discussing ants. But you couldn't help but watch from the corner of your eye as they cooked up an intimate little dinner, opened a bottle of wine, and retired to their dome tent.

Now a dome tent, in case you've never noticed, has several tightly stretched panels that act like the speakers on your stereo set. They clearly broadcast whatever noises are being generated inside. There were whispers and giggles and the unmistakable sounds of sleeping bags being unzipped. A dozen fly-fishermen sitting around half a dozen campfires fell silent and listened.

Then A.K. turned to me and said, "I wish they'd get it over with so we could all get some sleep."

Some of our camping equipment goes back a long way, although only a few items go all the way back to the wood, canvas, and leather "conquer the wilderness" style of camping we were both brought up in. Now we're as much into nylon and aluminum as anyone. A.K. even has a new tent, a nice one, too, although it did have to be modified a bit.

The night it blew down in the windstorm and we had to sleep in the truck, he was sorely disappointed in it. The tent itself was okay, but the light aluminum poles were bent and twisted like the wreckage left by the *Hindenburg*.

Luckily that was to have been our last day belly boating the reservoir anyway. The next day we headed over to the Frying Pan River to do what A.K. refers to as "real" fly-fishing in running water. We stopped in Basalt, and A.K. asked around about an electrical supply place. There was one, which was lucky. It's a pretty small town. A.K. had the guy copy the tent poles in steel conduit. The guy was a fisherman and ended up doing it for what must have been no more than the cost of materials.

The new poles are heavy, but that doesn't matter because this is too big a tent to be backpacked anyway. It's a car tent, and with those steel poles the pickup will blow over before the tent comes down again.

I talk about "our" equipment, although most of what we use belongs to A.K. My stuff is mostly for backpacking, although some of it slops over nicely. I don't even own a tent, but then, why should I? A.K. has one

Enough Fish

THE trout were enormous; long, fat, heavy. I couldn't see them at the moment in the dun-colored, predawn light, but they were there. I had seen them twice the day before, and, for once, it was the exactly logical place for them to be: in the deepest hole in the pond, in the thickest, most bug infested vegetation. Oh, they were there all right, at the long end of an easy cast in no more than four or five feet of water.

But maybe I should start a little closer to the beginning.

I'd heard about this place from a friend back in Colorado, a knowledgeable—though amateur—fisheries type who is one of the few fly-fishers I know who actually understands what the biologists tell him. And the ones he knows tell him plenty, knowing he'll use it to his own advantage, but wisely and reasonably.

My friend said he'd seen biologists' reports on the place showing huge brook trout at the top of an incredible food chain measured in tons of insects. Temperature, water chemistry, vegetation; everything was just right.

The ponds were in a mountain valley a good forty miles off the main highway in a little-traveled part of southern Montana. Much of the water in the valley, including two large lakes, was taken up by a waterfowl sanctuary where fishing was not permitted, but around the edge of the refuge were some spring-fed ponds and streams where you *could* fish.

My friend hadn't actually been to the place, so it was a story; one he knew I'd want to hear. I have a thing for ponds and another thing for brook trout. When the two came together in a single spot, he just had to call. Thanks.

I ended up in the neighborhood of those ponds the following August on a long, circuitous trip that replaced the money in my wallet with a stack of nonresident fishing licenses and filled the less than airtight pickup camper with the fine, brown dust of four western states. The one scheduled stop was the Federation of Fly-Fishers Conclave in West Yellowstone, Montana, where I took part in a writer's panel and where my traveling partner, Jim Pruett, also had some business.

The conclave itself was just fine, but there was a slight pall over the proceedings in the form of poor fishing. The water was unusually low and none of the local rivers were much good. That, at least, was my experience and also the general consensus. A famous fisherman snuck out one afternoon to an equally famous river and showed up later at a party in the courtyard of a motel.

"How'd you do?" someone asked.

"Well," he said, as everyone stopped talking in anticipation of the master's pronouncement, "I caught an 18-inch rainbow . . . in 9-inch increments."

Disappointment isn't really the word. Fly-fishermen, a stoic bunch overall, seldom give in to that emotion in public. They either figure it out (keeping it to themselves when they do) or pile into their vehicles and move on. And they do both philosophically.

I asked around about the ponds, trying to do it quietly so as not to tip my hand. To my horror, everyone knew about them. In fact, the third person I asked handed me the current issue of the *West Yellowstone News*. He thought I'd be interested because the cover story dealt with the area I'd been asking about.

I ended up with the typical mesh of conflicting news and advice, mostly from people who knew the place but hadn't fished it in recent years. It was tough. It was easy. Everyone fished it. No one fished it anymore. There were still big fish there. There were no big fish left; they'd all been caught, stuffed, and hung above mantels.

At the end of the conclave, as several hundred fly-fishers were preparing to leave the fly-fishing capital of the Free World for mostly undisclosed points in the further pursuit of trout, Jim and I split up. He was going to meet his brother on the Yellowstone River and I was heading home where, for various reasons, I was already overdue.

Head home indeed, with those ponds only an eighty-mile round trip off the straight shot back to Colorado? Right. The people back home who required my presence would have to buy "car trouble," and they *would* buy it, too. That's one of the advantages of driving a pickup that's older than the oldest dog you ever knew. "I'm surprised you made it back at all," someone would say.

It also just happened that I had a few days left on my Montana license; days of fishing I'd already paid for that would be sinful to waste.

I drove south into that knuckle-shaped end of Idaho and then, somewhere around Henry's Lake, turned northwest onto a dirt road that went, quietly and without fanfare, back into an unpaved corner of Montana. Jim Pruett is one of the best people I've ever traveled with, but, after some weeks, it was not unpleasant to be alone. Fishing is odd in that it's a solitary exercise that's usually practiced in groups. The camaraderie can be the best part, but it's also what sometimes leads to competition and even conceit.

Fishing alone can unmuddy the waters and allow you to return to the society of anglers with the capacity to remove the crap. For instance, A.K., who has been known to fish by himself happily for days on end, once invited someone to go fishing with us.

"Maybe you hadn't noticed," the man said, "but I don't fish with just anyone."

"You know, you're right," A.K. replied. "I *hadn't* noticed."

The road was a good one as dirt roads go, and I could have made good time except that I was apparently passing through open range. There were no signs to that effect, but I was slowed and stopped repeatedly by cattle standing in the way looking at me with that air of calm but uncomprehending proprietorship that has earned them the nickname "slow elk." It was a good sign, though. A sign of very thin traffic.

Part of the story I'd gotten from my friend on the ponds was that they were not heavily fished, and, although they were more widely known about than I was led to believe, I thought it could still be true. They were in a part of the state that the majority of tourists don't bother with and were near—but off the regular routes to—several famous rivers that take the brunt of the fishing pressure.

And they were ponds, after all, something most fly-fishers tend to pass up in favor of flowing water. Granted, rivers have their charms, but so do ponds. They can be isolated, hidden, even forgotten, in a way that can never happen with a stream, and there's the purely practical consideration that, all things being equal, a good pond can grow bigger fish than a good stream.

They can be a different kind of trout, too. Regardless of species, they're often deeper-bodied and rounder than river fish, and, psychologically, they can be more restless and curious. They're cruisers, hunters, not unlike bass.

The valley itself is a wide, flat, mountain-rimmed piece of land at an altitude that was not noted on my map. It felt high, though. The road had pointed gradually but steadily uphill for the last thirty-some miles. The one bit of information that had come up again and again involved some large brook trout that had been there once and might be there still.

I was looking for the Widow's Pool, which is known on maps and signs as Culver Pond. It was named, I was told, for the Widow Culver, although who Mrs. Culver was—or is—and why she has a trout pond named after her I don't know. That's the kind of background information a writer is supposed to jump on, but it seemed to me at the time that the pertinent journalistic facts involved these rumored big trout. And anyway, there was no local library or historical society to consult. In fact, there was little in the valley besides water, sagebrush, and the trumpeter swans for which the refuge had been established.

I found the pond after negotiating several unmarked dirt roads and parked the truck in a spot where others—but not too many others—had parked before. There were small but official-looking signs saying "Culver Pond" and "No Camping"—not a lot of information, but enough.

The pond looked a little questionable at first. It was shallow right where I'd stopped and had what looked like a clay bottom, though the water was spring-clear and there was healthy vegetation. No trout were immediately in evidence.

I was just about to take an inspection walk along the bank when another pickup arrived, this one sporting Montana plates. An older gentleman and an elderly bird dog got out. The former removed a strung-up spinning rod from the bed, glanced at my Colorado license plates, and stalked over to the water. He ignored my friendly wave, rather pointedly I thought.

The dog pissed on the right front tire of my truck and then followed his master at a respectable distance.

I approached slowly. In such situations, one adopts a studied casualness so as not to appear too eager, as if you're wandering around with nothing much in mind. You seldom fool anyone with this, but it has to be done.

By the time I'd ambled over to my colleague's side, he had baited up what looked and smelled like a pickled minnow and had lobbed it expertly out into the pond. I offered the dog my hand. He didn't seem overjoyed at meeting me; I ventured a pat, which he endured but didn't like much. Then, turning to the man, I said, "How ya doin'?"

"Uh," the man said, not looking away from his bobber.

He'd cast to a surprisingly deep hole where the bottom was dark with weeds. As I watched, a large shape materialized down there, and then another, and another. The hole was filled with a good dozen enormous trout—as big as the carp in an old farm bass pond, but *trout*.

I voiced a profanity under my breath, and, although the expression on my friend's face didn't change, his wrinkles grew visibly deeper.

The problem was obvious: I was standing there, complete with out-of-state license plates, in *his* spot, looking at *his* fish. If you're not a fisherman, the magnitude of this seemingly harmless fact will probably escape you.

It would have been useless to ask if he fished here often (though I had the feeling he did), or if the trout were brookies, or if he had ever caught any, or how big they really were. I did what common angling courtesy demanded. I thanked him and said I was going to go find a place to fish.

"Nice talking to you," I added.

I was in the cab of the truck with the motor running when the guy walked up. His face was still stern and his voice was gruff, but he said, "You see that cottonwood tree over there . . . ?" and launched into a clear and detailed set of directions to another good hole in the sprawling pond. "You try it over there," he said. "Maybe you'll get a nice one."

Then he turned and walked off without a nod, a tip of the hat, or anything.

So I followed his directions, which were accurate right down to the bush and fence post. Yes, he fished there often. At this point the dirt road was fifty yards from the water, but I could see the rises on the still surface of the pond. It was midmorning, maybe nine o'clock.

There was nothing man-made in sight except the road itself, not even a faint plume of dust out on the valley floor from another car. That was a good thing for two reasons: I would have the fish all to myself, and there was no one to see me as I doubled my usual rigging-up time by dropping every piece of gear I laid my hands on at least once, including the camera.

Excited? Well, maybe a little.

The bottom was clay, all right, sandy-gray, thick, sucking, claustrophobic clay. It was the kind of goo you stop sinking in tentatively and that leaves you with the feeling you could start again at any second, finally to go out of sight altogether, leaving nothing but a floating hat and an abandoned truck. That's why I didn't wade out as far as I'd have liked to. There were plenty of weeds on the bottom but, for some reason, their root systems gave no support. This is the kind of situation where if you lose your balance you *will* fall in the water, simply because it will take too long to extricate your foot from the muck to take that saving, balancing step backwards.

I was out far enough to see that the trout were rising and boiling along the edge of a dropoff where the shelf of shallow, weedy bottom I was mired in gave way to darker water. There were scattered Callibaetis mayfly duns on the water, about a size 14 or 16.

If I had to have a favorite mayfly, it would be this speckled dun. Mayflies in general seem Victorian, with more parts and more exaggerated proportions than they really need. Add to that the Baroque speckling pattern on the Callibaetis wing, and you have a creature whose beauty goes way beyond mere function. In that way, they're like the trout themselves.

They're a still-water bug, common on many trout lakes, and they hatch in a sporadic, surging way so there's never a uniform number of them on the water. First there's a lot, then there's a few, then there's a whole bunch of them again. It's as if they're trying to confuse the trout so a few of them will get away, and I've heard it said this is exactly what they're up to. It's a survival tactic.

The trout were cruising just below the surface, some of the larger ones leaving wakes. About one in three rose to the surface to take the winged flies—their "glups" were clearly audible in the still air—while the rest boiled under the surface taking emergers. I tied on a #14 Hares Ear Soft Hackle, a kind of universal emerger pattern, thinking, "It can't be this easy, but you have to start somewhere."

It was that easy. On the second crawling retrieve the leader stopped with a good deal of authority, and I set up on what felt like roughly two pounds of fish. The trout stayed in the water, boring instead of jumping. I played him hard and lost him in the thick weeds six feet in front of me.

"Well, of course, you idiot," I thought. "What did you expect?"

With a fresh fly of the same pattern on, I picked out what looked like a sizable fish, cast a few feet ahead of him, and felt the weight on the second slow strip. I played him out in the open water, and when his head came up I skidded him over to the net just like I knew what I was doing.

A brook trout, 14 or 15 inches long, deep-bellied, deeply colored from the rich water and a good diet. Not the mythic wall hanger, but a trout, and a good one.

There followed an hour and a half of steady fishing to cruisers, during which I lost some and landed plenty. Most were respectable keepers at 12 to 14 inches, though I didn't keep any, and a few ran up to 16, 17, and, I believe, 18 inches. I don't usually stop to measure fish in the heat of things, but I was fishing an old Granger 8½-foot, 4-weight cane rod with 56 intermediate wraps from cork to tip, 18 on the butt section. I used the first few of these as a rough scale, but back on the tailgate of the truck with a tape measure, I couldn't remember if the biggest trout had gone nearly to the fourth wrap or just past the third. In the finest angling tradition, I chose the larger number.

Yes sir, an 18-inch brook trout.

It ended as Callibaetis hatches do; petering off, surging back, weaker each time, ending with the odd small fish rising well out of casting range.

It was barely noon, although it seemed like a whole day had gone by, so I made a sandwich, had a warm beer, and then drove around the valley watching the swans and looking at other ponds where no trout rose. My map showed a fair-sized lake at the end of a long, twisting road up the northern slope of hills, so I drove up there and found, lo and behold, a little lodge. There were five or six small cabins and a main building inside of which was a bar and many mounted fish.

By reflex, I sat down and ordered a beer, a cold one this time, from Greg Williams, bartender, manager, head guide, etc., and commenced to learn that in the surrounding lakes, ponds, and streams one could catch rainbows, cutthroats, brook trout, grayling, and lake trout. No, they weren't *all* huge, but the ones hanging on the wall were, and so were the ones held by grinning clients in the regulation collection of snapshots.

Nor was the area fished very heavily, being, as Greg suggested, not quite in synch with the mass mental picture of Idaho/Montana trout fishing with its MacKenzie boats and wide rivers. But those who did fish it were known to come back. The cabins were regularly occupied.

In the fall there was good hunting for elk, deer, and grouse, with bears in evidence.

I went to the bathroom, but couldn't find the light switch. Greg came in behind me and lit an oil lamp. No electricity except for a generator to cool the beer.

The closest phone?

"About fifty miles."

"Sure I'll have another beer," I said, and the plot began to hatch. I'd drive home and pick up a few things—rifle, shotgun, more fishing gear, winter clothes. I'd empty the savings account, rescue the dog from the kennel, and drive back. I could slide in and out of town in early morning so as not to be noticed and as far as anyone would know, I would just not have come back at all. Jim would say he'd seen me last in West Yellowstone.

No one would find me. Not the I.R.S., not my editor at the newspaper, not even A.K. would know where to look. I could send him a farewell post-card, though, with the confidence that he'd smile, burn it in the fireplace and never say a word.

Somewhere in there I switched from beer to coffee so I'd be able to drive, even though there was damned little to run into. Then, without entirely dismissing the plan, but considering the possibility that I'd been on the road a little too long, I drove back to the hole on Culver Pond that held the big trout, all of which had been clearly longer than 18 inches. Much longer.

The old man and the dog were gone, which meant, I suspected, that the fishing was better there in the morning than in the evening. The trout were still there, looming in and out of the weed-shapes; much put-upon trout that would show themselves, but that were not about to do anything stupid.

On a stouter rod and a sink-tip line, I tried the Hares Ear Soft Hackle, then a more accurate mayfly nymph, then a damselfly nymph, then a craw-dad pattern, then three different streamers in panicky succession. With each fly change my stomach clutched a little tighter with a combination of hunger and failure.

After dark, resigned, I drove to the closest turnout that didn't say "No Camping," warmed a can of beans, ate, and slept.

I was back before dawn with a thermos of fresh camp coffee and some two-day-old West Yellowstone doughnuts. I couldn't see the trout for lack of light, but they were there, no doubt about it. They were the kind of fish that are always there; so big and so close to uncatchable they're almost not real.

Standing out there in the cold half darkness it occurred to me that if I left then I could be home in twelve hours, scratching the dog behind the ears, listening to several weeks of tape on the answering machine, and going through a stack of mail looking for checks. I found myself wondering, in a strangely detached way, if I'd be staying or leaving.

Maybe what you ask yourself at a time like this is, "Why am I doing this?"

Challenge? Excitement? Relaxation? Ambition? (or lack of ambition?) To "get away"? To get away from *what?*

Is it all just an excuse to drive hundreds of miles on strange roads, drink, eat poorly, not bathe, and come off generally as some kind of harmless, aging beatnik? And if it is, so what? You couldn't do any of this without the fish, but how large a part do the fish actually play?

More than one outdoor magazine editor will tell you, "We're not too interested in 'why I fish' stories." As I once heard it put, "Our readers already know why *they* fish and they don't much care why *you* do." Based on some years of talking to fishermen, I'd have to admit that's about the size of it.

There's a good deal of latitude in outdoor writing. It's the original gonzo journalism, after all, Dr. Hunter S. Thompson notwithstanding. Another editor once said his magazine seldom accepts fiction, "except what normally occurs in any fishing story." But one thing that doesn't seem to be permissible in angling literature is to just walk away from good fishing for no other reason than that you've had enough.

Is it possible to have caught enough fish, at least for the moment? You know you can't catch them all, and there's no reason why you should want to. A year ago—maybe even to the day—I was standing at another piece of water puzzling over other fish. No, I don't remember the exact situation, but it was August; what else would I have been doing? Given half a break, I'll be doing the same thing somewhere else a year from now, both diminished and enriched by another season. Definitely older, possibly wiser—if I've paid attention.

It was just dawn when I drove off in the general direction of home without so much as having strung up a rod. I was looking forward to the long haul across the expanse of eastern Wyoming, a stretch of country that some have called featureless, but which is, in fact, filled with tranquillity. My only regret was that I wouldn't be able to see the old man's face when he pulled in later that morning to find that the guy from Colorado wasn't fishing his spot.

Sex, Death, and Fly-fishing

Sex, Death, and Fly-fishing

O N a stretch of one of the forks of a small river near where I live in northern Colorado, there is, in the month of July, a fabulous Red Quill spinner fall. As near as I can tell, it consists of at least three different species of these reddish-brown mayflies ranging in size from number 12s down to 16s or 18s. The fall lasts for weeks—sometimes more than a month—on and off, coming and going, overlapping, hardly ever the same twice.

No, I don't know which specific bugs are involved and, at the risk of insulting the entomologists, I'm not sure how much it would matter if I did. When the fall comes off, you fish one of the Red Quill or Rusty Spinner patterns in the appropriate size. When it doesn't come off, knowing the Latin name of the insect that is mysteriously absent lets you piss and moan in a dead language, but otherwise doesn't help much.

And there are plenty of evenings when this thing doesn't work out from a fishing standpoint, even though the bugs are at least in evidence on an almost nightly basis. As spinner falls go, this is the spookiest one I've seen, probably only because I've seen so much of it. Usually it has to do with the weather.

Here on the East Slope of the Rocky Mountains, midsummer is the season for hot, clear, bluebird days punctuated by late afternoon thundershowers. Mayfly spinners—most of them, anyway—like to fall in the evenings when the light is low, and the air is cool and maybe a little damp. That's *a little* damp; a full-fledged rain can put them off, depending on the timing.

If the rain comes early enough in the day, it's over before the spinner fall should happen, and it has actually helped things along by chilling and humidifying the air a little. It's part of the local lore that an early shower can mean a good spinner fall later on.

If a thunderstorm comes late enough, after the flies have already formed up over the stream—and suddenly enough, without announcing itself with too much wind or cool air—it can flush the bugs into the water where the trout can get them.

This can make for some great fishing, provided the rain is heavy enough to knock the flies down, but not so heavy it makes the water too rough for the trout to see them—in which case the fish won't feed on them after all.

When that happens, you race downstream in your rain slicker to where the current pools out at the head of a small canyon reservoir in hopes that when the storm passes, the bugs will be collected down there and the trout will rise to them.

That's assuming the rain doesn't last too long, and doesn't muddy the water so much that the trout, once again, can't see the bugs on the surface of the stream, and, once again, won't eat them.

When the rain comes at its more normal time—a few hours before dusk, before the spinner fall should start—it may cool the air in the canyon *too much,* and cancel the event, although you might just hike up there anyway because some nights the weather clears off, warms up just enough (but not too much), gets very still, and the spinner fall is unusually heavy.

Sometimes.

Not always.

And I am not being sarcastic when I say that trout are known to be particularly fond of spinners.

On rare overcast, drizzly afternoons, the Red Quill dun hatch can last late, and the spinner fall can come early, giving you hours of good fishing with a transition point when both forms of the bug are on the water at once. Many trout can be caught on dry flies then if you're smart enough to notice what's happening with the weather, drop everything at home, and get up there early. Under gray skies and drizzle, dusk is usually too late.

Wet, gloomy summer days are unusual in semiarid Colorado, and this has only happened three times that I know of in something like ten years. I missed it once, although I sure heard about it later from some friends who were there. They caught lots of trout, including some big ones. It was great, they said, in a not so subtle tone of accusation.

The assumption out here is, you should always go fishing, period. If you don't, even for what might appear in other circles to be a good reason, the suspicion is that you are getting uppity or, even worse, lazy. You get some grief for staying home, and when the fishing was great, well . . .

People will forgive you for missing it once or twice, but no more than that.

On other days when I *was* there and ready, the air got too cool, or a stiff breeze came up, or the drizzle got too drizzly, or something. Once it was looking just right until a sheet of hail drew itself across the canyon like a gauze curtain, and my friend Koke Winter and I ended up huddling in the flimsy cover of a juniper tree getting whacked hard by a few less hailstones than if we'd been standing out in the open. A big one got me square on the back of the hand when I reached out to pick a nearly ripe raspberry. By morning I had a bruise the size of a quarter.

It was all over in about twenty minutes, and the evening slid into ideal, textbook conditions—cool, still, dusky, humid—except that not a single swallow flashed in the air over the stream to eat the bugs because there were no flies, and not a single trout rose for the same reason. The sky was clear with stars, the air was freshly washed and thick with clean, organic smells, the reservoir was a dark, disk-shaped mirror. To anyone but a fly-fisherman it would have seemed peaceful and quite pretty.

We figured the hail had killed all the flies and knocked all the trout sense-less, so we went home. Koke doesn't drink anymore, so we couldn't even stop for a beer.

For the absolutely cosmic spinner fall, it seems as though perfect condi-tions have to also be *preceded* by perfect conditions, and I don't know how far back in time this meteorological juggling act has to go. I do know that even a slightly larger dose of what would normally be ideal is deadly. I sup-pose there's a lesson there.

It seems like your best bet for a workmanlike, day-to-day spinner fall is a clear, warm evening with no wind. This kind of conservative weather stops short of being the model of perfection, but it doesn't court disaster either.

The more you fish the more you start seeing these things the way a farmer does; it doesn't have to be great, just, please, don't let it be awful.

On those days you hike up the stream with the last direct rays of sunlight still on the water. This is a shallow, stooped-shouldered, forested canyon with a few rock outcrops at the water, and a few more standing up at the lip. The slope is gentle enough lower down to allow for some patches of wild grass. The stream has a sand and sandstone bottom, so even when it's clear it can seem to have a brownish cast to it. Some evenings it gets amber for a few seconds just before the light goes off it.

A good hundred yards downstream from the riffle we always start at, you can see the swarm of mayflies high in the air above the stream, dipping and climbing, their clear wings flashing. At these times they look like they're spinning, hence the name.

These particular mayflies seem to begin mating about the time the light goes off them. It's not a deep canyon, and it runs roughly east and west, so the sun stays on the water longer than you'd think it should. Not that you're likely to be impatient or anything. The bugs copulate on the wing, and then begin to fall on the water right around dark.

Sometimes, as the insects dip lower and lower over the stream, the odd, eager brown trout will jump out of the water and try to grab one. He seldom gets it. Nine times out of ten this is a little fish and you ignore it, but when it's a big trout you tie on an upright-winged Red Quill and cast it over there.

He almost never takes it. I know this to be true, but I have yet to figure out why. It should work but it doesn't, that's all.

Usually the few trout you see rising sporadically here and there while the spinners are still in the air will be taking ants, beetles, the occasional midge, errant mayfly dun, or caddis fly. Whatever happens to be around, in other words. This is not an especially rich stream, so the fish have learned to eat whatever is there.

On many nights the real spinner fall, and, therefore, the real hot fishing, begins after dark when you can't see what you're doing. You stumble over rocks, wade too deeply and ship water, snag your fly in the bushes, and tie wind knots in your leader that you don't know about until you hear them whistle past your ear. The question then is whether it will be easier to retie the leader or untie the knot, keeping in mind that you can't see what the hell you're doing in either case.

When you do get a good cast on the water, hints as to where your fly is and whether or not a trout has eaten it are sometimes telegraphed back to you in terms of spreading, starlit ripples and/or soft plopping sounds. But they're just hints. You can fish for hours without knowing for sure if you're using the wrong-sized fly, getting a bad drift, or if you're getting strikes you don't know about.

***

There are a few of us who fish this thing regularly, even though the trout aren't normally very big, and even though we often don't catch very many of them. The fact is, we seem to be truly fascinated by it, and I say that based on the evidence.

When we go up there and the spinners aren't happening for some reason, we don't tie on streamers or fish ants to the bank feeders because that might trash the water if the spinners actually do come on later. Nor do we work upstream to fish the pocket water with caddis flies because the spinners might come on while we're gone. We do a lot of standing around with spinner patterns already tied to 5 or 6x tippets, fly rods under our arms, hands in pockets, waiting. Sometimes there's a big beaver to watch, or little brown myotis bats to dodge. It can be nice and peaceful.

I like to think of this spinner fall as one of the great enigmas: the kind of thing that puts all the how-to-do-it fly-fishing writing in its place. If you hit it just right, the problem is not "How to Catch Trout During a Spinner Fall"—that's something you'll do without much trouble at all—but hitting it right is a matter of exquisite timing and some luck. It's the kind of puzzle where the challenge isn't to put the pieces together, but just to locate all the damned pieces in the first place.

We sometimes catch ourselves getting a little conceited as we stand out there in the dark without having landed so much as a single trout between us all evening. I mean, this is the really *difficult* fishing, definitely not for amateurs.

Someone finally says, "I'll tell ya, this isn't something for those guys who have to have 'big fish and lots of 'em,' is it?"

And someone else answers, trying to keep the uncertainty out of his voice, "Nope, it sure isn't."

For the moment at least, we fall into that class of fishermen who fancy themselves to be poet/philosophers, and from that vantage point we manage to pull off one of the neatest tricks in all of sport: the fewer fish we catch the more superior we feel.

Part of the fascination has to do with the mayflies themselves. We fly-fishers have a historic and abiding affection for them, and it's no wonder.

First there's that seemingly magical transformation. The insects spend most of their lives as downright unattractive bugs living under rocks on the stream bottom, but then, one day when all the signals are green, they swim to the surface to emerge as these really pretty flies. Even people who aren't especially interested in bugs will admit that mayflies are quite beautiful, at least after you've explained that they're not some kind of mosquito.

Beauty from ugliness, the sudden freedom of flight after a lifetime under a rock, and all that. It really is something.

These are the mayfly duns, and, as we all know, the ones that aren't eaten up by trout or birds fly to bankside bushes where they soon molt into spinners.

As pretty as the duns are, the spinners are even prettier. Their tails get longer and more graceful, their body colors brighten, and their wings get clear and sparkly. They're lovely, and this seems appropriate to us, because now the bugs' only chores in life are to mate and expire. Scientists call the whole group of mayflies Ephemeridae, from the same Latin that gave us "ephemeral," or "lasting for a brief time; short-lived; transitory." Even "tragic" if you want to stretch it.

We seem to have a real affection for the image of a beautiful insect that only lives for a single day (more or less) and whose only mission is to make love just once. They don't even eat. Poets got off on this as symbolic of the fleeting nature of life, love, and beauty until it became a cliché and had to be dropped or turned into a joke. The last literary reference I saw to it was in an old *Playboy* cartoon that showed a boy mayfly saying to a girl mayfly, "What do you mean, *'not tonight'!?*"

Mayflies and fly-fishing have always been inseparably connected (they're our favorite bug, after all), and that may be one reason why the sport is still seen as contemplative, even now with all our scientific and technical hoopla.

This really is kind of sweet, in a nineteenth-century sort of way, and it's not too difficult to attach religious overtones to it as well, but it's also efficient as all get out in a biological sense. Technically, this behavior is called semelparity, and it is described best by David Quammen in his wonderful book *Natural Acts:* "An animal or plant waits a very long time to breed only once, does so with suicidal strenuosity, and then promptly dies. The act of sexual procreation proves to be ecstatically fatal, fatally ecstatic. And the rest of us are left merely to say: Wow."

Quammen points out that bamboo trees (from which fly rods are made) do it this way, and that salmon (on which fly rods are used) do it this way, too. I think that's interesting. Could there be some wild, metaphysical connection that makes fly-fishing incredibly sexy?

I sincerely hope so.

***

Mayflies mate and die en masse (it's been referred to as an orgy, but never as a mass suicide) probably at least partly for the same reason that large numbers of them hatch all at once: because hungry trout eat great numbers of them at these times and, with lots of the bugs making a break for it at once, some will get away to finish the business. It's a kind of suicidal diversionary tactic, and it works just fine in a system where the individual doesn't count for much.

The spinners mate and lay their eggs a little upstream from where the duns hatched, usually over a riffle, thus ensuring that the new eggs, as they wash downstream, will land on the bottom more or less in the same place the last batch did. If they hadn't always leapfrogged upstream like this; that is, if they'd mated and laid their eggs each season where they'd just hatched, they'd have slid downstream a few yards each year, and by now they'd have washed out to sea and become extinct.

And they don't all hatch or fall on the same day either. These things usually stretch over periods of days or weeks, and may start early one year and late the next as conditions dictate, so that something like a random storm or cold snap won't wipe out an entire population.

Hatches and spinner falls are large links in the general food chain, too. The bugs are regularly eaten by creatures like swallows, nighthawks, bats, and, of course, trout. Having the hatches and falls last for days or weeks ensures that the mayflies will survive into future generations, but it also means that trout and others can make dozens of meals out of them instead of just one.

Once the falls have started there are always a few stray, expired spinners floating in shallow backwaters and stuck to weeds. These are clues. While waiting to see what's going to happen this evening, you can cruise the banks and at least see if there was a good rise the night before when you were somewhere else.

And nothing is wasted either. At the end of the spinner fall the few little dead bodies that aren't eaten by trout end up making a small but real contribution to the decomposing organic matter on the stream bottom that serves as fertilizer for more aquatic vegetation that is grazed upon by later generations of mayfly nymphs that hatch to feed new generations of birds, bats, fish, and so on.

It's nothing short of elegant, and the mayfly/trout connection we flyfishers look so hard for is just a thin slice of it. There are also the game animals that drink from the stream, and the fishing birds that live on young trout, muskrats that eat the aquatic plants, and the swallows that eat the mayflies and live in the cliffs that were excavated by the stream itself.

A good ecologist can put dovetail into dovetail until the whole thing stretches out of sight. We call it an ecosystem now; earlier Americans called it the Sacred Circle. Either way it can make your poor little head swim with a vision of a thing of great size and strength that still depends on the under-pinning of its smallest members.

It's a little harder to place our own role in all this because we're the ones doing the placing, so we naturally want to put ourselves at the top some-how, even though we don't actually fit there. Some say we humans have gotten to be so aberrant now that we don't fit *anywhere* in all this. I don't quite buy that, although it must be admitted that we're not exactly a har-monious species.

This fishing business probably has something to do with play—practic-ing a highly refined food-gathering technique as if it really mattered, even though we don't need the food and will probably release any trout we hap-pen to catch. Play is what puppies do. It looks like good, innocent fun—and it is—but it also develops the predatory skills that will be needed later in life by the serious adult canine. Ever notice how *hard* a puppy can bite?

I don't know exactly what fly-fishing teaches us, but I think it's some-thing we need to know.

A mayfly spinner lies on the surface of the stream in what fishermen call the "spent" position. To picture it accurately, remember that the insect has just had the first and only orgasm of its life and is now, in the natural course of things, dying from it. His body lies flush with the water, wings spread, legs out flat, tails splayed wistfully. Usually he's limp. If he struggles at all, he does it feebly at best. There's probably a silly look on his face, although it's hard to tell with insects.

Now picture seventy-five or a hundred of them lying on the water within casting range of where you're standing. As spinner falls go, this is not a ter-ribly heavy one, though if you hit it right it's plenty heavy enough.

You have to imagine this even on-site because the bugs lying flat on the water are all but impossible to see. Even in good light their clear wings will have faded to nothing more than faint outlines, and the light will probably be turning a dull gray by now. It's very possible to fish a spinner fall suc-cessfully without ever getting a look at the bug you're imitating so carefully. It can become a matter of belief.

What you *will* see, if all is as it should be, are the distinctive rises of brown trout. The spinner rise is lazy, or at least businesslike, because, it's said, the fish "know" that the bugs are spent and won't get away.

There are differences of opinion about what trout know in an intellectual sense, but I have to buy the characterization. A trout feeding on an active insect—say, a mayfly dun, caddis fly, or even an egg-laying spinner fluttering on the surface—is likely to slash at it eagerly, but the same fish will sip the drifting spinners lazily. In slightly faster water, he might show the porpoising, head and tail rise, but that's about as excited as he gets.

This is important. How hard a trout works to get a given bite of food determines how many of those bites he has to take to first get even, and then make a profit, physiologically speaking. This goes right to survival, with no detours for fooling around or showing off.

During a spinner fall the fish will often ease down into the slower water below the riffle, or even to the tail of the pool. Why fight the heavier flows up ahead? The bugs have had it, and they'll be down here where it's easy soon enough.

Of course the trout understand what's going on. It's nothing less than conceited to think we do, but of course they don't.

The last time it all came together for me was two seasons ago. The weather seemed right, and my friend A. K. Best and I had driven past what was an almost sure caddis hatch on a nearby stream to check on the spinners. It was an act of bravado. It felt promising.

We saw the swallows weaving in the air first, and only spotted the bugs when we were at The Spot with the toes of our waders in the water. Even then they were just faint specks that showed up only because they were moving. There were no wings flashing in the last of the sunlight that evening. It was cloudy, cool for summer, threatening rain, but not raining yet.

We had the stream to ourselves because only tough, smart fishermen like us aren't afraid to get wet.

I don't know what A.K. fished with, although I'm sure he announced the pattern with the usual flourish. I tied on a #14 Michigan Chocolate spinner, a fly A.K. had turned me on to years before.

This thing has fine split tails of pale dun hackle fibers, spent hen hackle wings of the same color, and a thinly dubbed, dark brown body. Generally the feather wings of spinner flies are white because that's as close as most tiers feel they can come to clear with natural material, but A.K. had once told me that the pale dun wings become more realistically indistinct in the water than the white ones everyone else uses. This from a man who has been known to stop casting when the trout are biting, catch a natural insect, and float it in a backwater next to his imitation, cackling to himself if he likes what he sees, going silent and thoughtful if he doesn't.

The flies began to fall, and the fish started to feed with just enough light left to see by. It was all strangely matter-of-fact, as things you wait for patiently sometimes are when they finally happen. We picked what we thought were the biggest trout, fished long, thin leaders to mimic the flaccid drift of the spinners, and caught fish until past closing time at Andrea's Cafe.

It was as simple as that.

The Red Quill spinner fall on the North Fork is one of the few things in nature that I feel actually *belongs* to me and a few friends. I don't mean it's a secret. In fact, during the weeks it's on you'll see the odd new face from time to time. Often it's a guy who's well-dressed, well-equipped, and who looks a bit out of place, but he's sniffed this thing out and there he is, ready to catch some trout.

He sometimes picks us out as locals (using the fly-fisherman's innate skill for evaluating fashion and body language) and asks us what the story is on this spinner fall he's heard about.

"Well, some nights it comes off and some nights it doesn't," we say. This sounds pointedly vague and useless and the guy's brow furrows with suspicion. He's no kid. He's been snowed by smart-assed locals before.

I guess we *are* exercising a little home-courtsmanship, but it's basically the truth. That's all we really know about it.

Of course, waiting out there in the dark with the sky full of bats and owls, we sometimes begin asking the great questions that can kill time so nicely: sex, death, and fly-fishing; the meanings of life and sport; are we real participants or just observers, and what kind of difference does it make?

The new face, who may well disappear after a few more nights of this, joins in the conversation, but he remains wary and watchful. If something wonderful isn't about to happen, then why the hell are we all standing around like this?

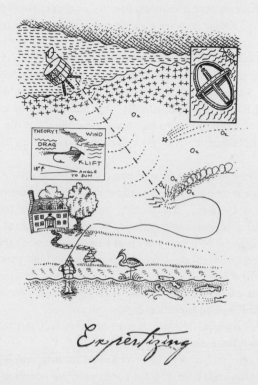

Expertizing

T H E guy called me from his office, or, rather, his secretary called.

"Mr. Gierach?"

"Speaking."

"Please hold for Mr. So-and-So."

And there I was—eight in the morning, conscious, but only halfway through my second cup of coffee, listening to a soulless elevator arrangement of a Beatles tune. And I hadn't recognized the name either. I considered hanging up, but I was curious. If this turns out to be a salesman, I thought, I'm gonna say something really unpleasant about his mother.

But no, when the guy finally came on the line he turned out to be someone who'd read my stories and liked them—clearly a man of taste and breeding, even if his telephone manners weren't great. He told me that he had recently moved to an exclusive, private subdivision that had an equally private trout lake on the property. Very posh, very costly. The lake was filled with huge rainbows, but it had turned out to be a tough, moody body of water, and in the six weeks he'd lived there he hadn't been able to catch any fish. Not one. He found this situation to be unacceptable.

"I'd like to have an expert show me how to get them," he said. It took me a few seconds to realize he wasn't asking me to refer him to an expert: he meant me.

The man didn't exactly sound desperate, but there was a grave edge to his voice as he said that *others* had caught big rainbows from the lake that very summer. Some of the fish had been as heavy as nine pounds. I didn't bother asking him if he'd seen the fish or if the person or persons who caught them would be likely to lie about something like the weight of a large trout. It didn't matter. Nine pounds or only seven and a half, I grasped the problem.

You know how you get a vision of someone over the phone by listening to the voice while staring out the window at a familiar cottonwood tree? I saw the guy as clean-cut, late thirties, with a six-figure income, large wardrobe, and a no-nonsense attitude. It was just a guess, but I also thought he might be someone who had negotiated one of those arrangements—spoken or otherwise—that fishermen sometimes make with their nonangling wives: we live in the country, but not too far from town; you get the big house with the stained glass, I get the private lake (and maybe a new canoe), and we live happily ever after, okay?

I've seen this attempted before. It takes some money and a little slack on both sides, but it has been known to work.

And now there the guy was, six weeks and no fish, and he was calling me. I figured that with a little luck I could save the marriage. Getting on this private lake with all the huge trout in it was a secondary consideration.

So I rose to the occasion, as they say, and suggested that I bring along my friend A.K., whom I accurately (and carefully) represented as "at least the expert I am."

"That'd be just fine," the guy said.

I already knew where the lake was, as do most of us locals. It's behind a formidable-looking fence, on a chunk of real estate between here and town where widely spaced, rambling homes hide modestly behind elaborate but tasteful landscaping and lots of trees. All you can see of the lake from the road is the earthen dike on its east end.

It looks quiet and ordered back in there, and I'm sure one of the selling points has to do with security. Residents get in by punching up a personal code that automatically opens the wrought-iron gate. Guests call the house they're visiting and are buzzed in. Everyone else stays the hell out.

I've never actually been offended by this approach to life—privacy is a valuable commodity, after all—but I'd always gotten a slight James Bond rush when I drove by the place: the feeling that getting into the compound would take either some nicely forged papers or a black sweater and wire cutters, but it would be possible. I'd never tried it either way, but, to be honest, it had crossed my mind. I guess I fished for too long as a kid to ever completely outgrow that sense of challenge that's presented by a fence. And the sturdier the fence, the more it gets you to thinking.

The word around was that the lake was pretty good, but then that's always the word on lakes behind tall fences that no one you know has ever fished.

A.K. and I showed up at the appointed time with the full arsenal loaded in a pickup truck: several fly rods each, light to heavy; a selection of lines, floating to full sinking; all the flies either of us could dig up, which was a lot; plus waders and float tubes. In other words, we were in full fly-fishing SWAT team mode. The iron gate slid aside for us, and a woman who was on her way out gave us a rather cool glance, probably figuring we were there to clean someone's septic tank.

Our host (a clean-cut man in his late thirties) met us at the lake. He had a brand-new Old Town canoe lashed to the roof of his Saab. After the introductions, A.K. and I began to rig up while our host sat down in the shade of a box elder tree and cracked a can of imported beer.

"You're not gonna fish?" A.K. asked.

"Not just yet," the guy answered; "I want to watch the 'experts at work' for a while."

He said that with quotation marks, in the jokingly ironic tone fishermen always employ in situations like this, but he was entirely serious.

The lake covered about ten or fifteen acres, plenty big enough for motorboat traffic, although there was no one on it at the moment. It was gourd-shaped, lying east to west with a southwesterly hook at the inlet end. Lazy hills with ponderosa pine trees sloped down to it on the west side, and some box elders and cottonwoods stood along the little stream that fed it. This was a regulation medium-to-large foothills reservoir gone half wild.

Most of the houses had been built at a respectful distance, so, with a few wooden docks lying out on the water and trees standing right to the shore, it did not look any more civilized than your normal resort lake.

At the moment it was dead calm and smooth, reproducing every nuthatch, pine needle, dock piling, and puffy, white cloud like a reflecting pool. A few odd trout were coming lazily to the surface here and there, making slow, flushing swirls. Not what you could accurately describe as even a sparse rise, just enough activity to illustrate that there were some fish in there.

A.K. and I waded in and began the professional-looking process of scanning the water for insects, finding only the occasional ant, beetle, and soggy box-elder bug. Not much of a rise, nothing much on the water. Ah, science.

Well, maybe later something would happen to give us a bearing, something like a caddis hatch, or a nice mayfly spinner fall. Anything would do; even a migration of water dogs would be better than nothing.

Meanwhile, the guy who'd invited us to come figure it out for him lounged under his tree like someone sitting patiently through the previews waiting for the movie to begin.

I shrugged at A.K. and dug out my you-gotta-start-somewhere fly, a #14 Hares Ear Soft Hackle. When A.K. saw that, he went to his streamer box and got out a big, juicy yellow marabou job. We didn't need a consultation to determine that neither of us knew what to do, but that we sure wouldn't catch anything if we didn't get some hooks in the water.

A.K. began casting to the stream inlet where, maybe, some trout would be lying, breathing the cool, dissolved oxygen and eating a bug now and then if one happened by. I started working the open water along the drop-off shelf where—again, maybe—some trout would be halfheartedly cruising.

It occurred to me that, although A.K. and I do know a little bit about trout fishing, this was a strange lake on a slow day and we were no more or less likely to catch a fish there than anyone else. I was glad I'd told the guy we'd "see what we can do," rather than, "If anybody can catch 'em, we can."

But then, that's one of the cardinal rules of expertizing: always leave the door open and the motor running.

Expertizing means acting like an expert. Not necessarily *being* an expert, mind you, but *acting* like one. There's a difference.

It's something we all slip into from time to time when we realize that we know just a little bit more about fishing than the person we're talking to or, worse yet, that we really don't know any more, but the person is willing, for one reason or another, to believe we do.

The symptoms are painfully obvious. When a question is asked we clear our throats, square our shoulders, glance briefly at the ceiling, and begin with, "Well, now . . ." as if we're consciously pulling our minds down from some great height.

Our answers are laced with complicated qualifications. They ramble, they're never simple. Often they're so obscure they end up being meaningless. But then, if you have to ask the question in the first place you probably won't understand the answer, right?

This is a terribly embarrassing thing to get caught at, but it's still a real temptation, especially for people who are in the business in some way, like guides, tackle shop clerks, manufacturers' reps, and, most notably, outdoor writers.

The writer's problem is compounded by the high regard in which many people hold the written word. "It's true," you'll sometimes hear, "I read it in a book." In some circles this is better than having actually seen it with your own eyes. The assumption is that if you write stories about fishing, you must know more about it than the guy who reads those stories. Of course the truth is, the thing you probably know a little more about isn't fishing, but writing.

And there's no real guarantee of that either.

The fallacy is further complicated by those writers who really *are* experts on the water. I'm talking about the ones who are so legendary now that you don't even have to use their last names. You know, like Lefty, Dave, Lee, and Joan. It's possible to get an article published in a magazine and suddenly find yourself in some very fast company.

At the risk of sounding defensive, there are times when this expert business is actually thrust upon you. I remember the first time someone at a party introduced me as an "expert fly-fisherman," or words to that effect. I'd never fished with the guy, so he didn't know firsthand if I even knew which end of the rod to hold, but I'd written these stories, you see.

Being normal, I said something like, "Aw shucks," and let it go. I wasn't exactly making a bundle writing and I figured a little public stroking amounted to a nontaxable fringe benefit.

It was a mistake.

By the time I finally got around to admitting, "Look, I'm actually just a writer" (or sometimes I'd say "journalist" to make it sound a little more like a real career), the damage had been done.

"What a guy," someone said, "a great fisherman and modest, too."

Then a local Trout Unlimited chapter asked me to give a program at one of their monthly meetings. Flattered, I put together twenty or thirty slides that were more or less in focus and headed down to the hall where, once again, I was introduced in embarrassingly glowing terms by a man wearing an Orvis tweed shooting jacket. I was deeply knowledgeable, he said, smart, cagey, a master fly-fisher. I had never fished with this guy either. I walked to the front of the room and looked out on dozens of familiar faces, fully half of whom knew the same streams I did and could fish circles around me blindfolded. They applauded.

This is much more profound than simple stage fright.

Naturally, the most effective way to expertize isn't to hold forth in front of an audience (unless you actually happen to be a genuine expert) but to do the exact opposite, that is, keep your mouth shut and just assume the pose.

After all, we operate in a deeply traditional sport where there are accepted procedures for such things.

You know the pose. It begins with a sloppy, faded fishing hat with a wide, dark sweat mark, and an old vest, preferably with that gray stain on one of the pockets that dates you back to the days when Gehrke's Gink came in those little plastic tubs that leaked.

Waders, be they canvas or neoprene, must be faded and heavily patched.

It helps to drive around in an old, unwashed pickup truck (this gives the impression that you've been all over hell, mostly on dirt roads), and a beard with some gray in it is a nice touch. Luckily, the gray hairs have appeared naturally at my jowls (prematurely, of course), thus saving me from having to sneak into a beauty parlor in dark glasses to have the thing frosted.

As I said, you'll be keeping your mouth shut as much as possible, but when circumstances force you to speak, say very little and be as vague and enigmatic as possible. If that's hard for you to get a handle on, go down to the video store and rent some old Gary Cooper Westerns.

I've found that it's best to avoid facts and stick with opinions. Facts can be wrong, while the worst thing an opinion can be is weird. For that matter, a few off-center opinions can help to give you that impressive aura of unpredictability.

Try this: after landing several large browns, rub the back of your neck, suggest heading into town for a drink, and add, "Brown trout are a dirty, German fish, but brook trout need clean, clear water." That's a quote from novelist Craig Nova, but you can probably get away with it. Novelists— who, after all, are paid to have weird opinions—are almost always better to quote than straight fishing writers.

If you're trying for that aged, weathered effect that can be so convincing, slip a few dated words and phrases into your conversation. Refer to polarized fish finders as "smoked glasses," 7x monofilament as "fine gut," and remember that all cutthroats, regardless of race, are "Rocky Mountain speckled trout."

Note: you have to be at least forty to pull this off; fifty is better.

When theorizing is unavoidable, insist on doing it after the fact. Never predict how you'll do, but be prepared to explain later in great detail why you didn't catch fish, being careful to lay it on something that no one else was paying attention to, like the ozone content of the air or electromagnetic interference from satellites.

And never fall into that statistical macho trap that's so prevalent in fly-fishing these days. If you keep score, you can be beaten, but if you refuse to compete you can leave the impression that you have long since risen above that kind of crap. When someone says to you, "I caught forty-eight trout and ten of them were twenty inches or better. How'd you do?" say, "Yeah, we got some. Couple nice ones, too."

Another nice touch is to be much more excited about the blue herons and sandhill cranes you saw than about whatever fish you caught. This leaves the impression that catching trout is so easy for you it's a foregone conclusion. You hardly even notice it anymore.

Fish alone as much as possible. When you're with a group, wander slowly down to a bend in the river and then vanish into the trees. Don't come back for hours.

When you do return, remember that you are blissed out with solitude and a little distracted.

"Catch any fish?" they'll ask.

"Hm? Fish?" you say. "Oh yes, now that you mention it I *did* catch some fish."

When you're fishing within sight of other people, try to project a kind of aloof stillness. Spend long periods of time studying the water without casting. Find some rising trout, watch them carefully for twenty minutes, and then walk away, muttering to yourself, "Too small" or maybe, "Too easy."

Now sooner or later you'll catch a big trout in front of witnesses—if you put in enough time it's almost unavoidable—but remember that an expert remains cool and detached at all times; no whooping or hollering. Total ecstasy is expressed by allowing that, yes, it's a pretty good fish. The natural inference is that you've caught bigger ones, and lots of them.

The fact is, if you've been fishing for a number of years, and look it, people will assume you know what you're doing. All you have to do is keep from proving them wrong.

I'd advise against it, but if you really do want to set yourself up as an expert, all you have to do is stop talking about how you catch fish and begin referring to your "system." It works every time. And, as a well-known (and genuine) fly-fishing expert once told me, "Be damned careful what you say for fear of being believed. If you say you can catch more trout if you fish with your whanger hanging out, somebody will try it."

I rest my case.

A.K. and I fished our brains out on that private lake. We worked the inlet stream with wet flies and streamers. We fished large and small nymphs in the deep water over the drop-off using sinking lines. Then we cast to the shallow littoral shelves, then fished ants, beetles, and hoppers against the banks. I paddled the float tube into the deepest water I could find and trolled a big brown leech pattern. Then I switched to a bright yellow one thinking I could pull it out by catching a walleye.

Every fifteen or twenty minutes a heavy fish would wallow at the surface, always in a different place. Always in a different *kind* of place.

We tried everything we should have tried, but it was clear the real problem was simply how to put a single fly in front of a single fish on a big pond where precious few trout were showing themselves. It probably wouldn't have mattered much what fly it was, although I guess we'll never know for sure.

As any expert will tell you, this kind of thing happens from time to time.

After a number of passes by his shade tree, we finally convinced our host to get in his canoe and fish. That was right after we'd explained to him that the water was too warm, the sun was too bright, the barometer was too high, the air was too still, the moon was in the wrong phase, and there wasn't enough insect activity to really move the trout.

First the guy apologized for stringing up a spinning rod, saying he wasn't a good enough fly caster yet, but that he'd been taking lessons. Then he started casting a small, gold spinner in the general direction of the drop-off and retrieving it at a rate I'd have said was way too fast. I was going to say something about that, but decided against it, and it was a good thing because no more than ten minutes later he hooked a big rainbow that he played and landed beautifully, using a stern, but gentle hand. If it wasn't an honest twenty inches long, it was at least nineteen—a fat, handsome lake fish that any regular old blue-collar fisherman would be proud of.

It was also *the* fish of the day.

We went on casting until dark without another strike, and then the guy said something about being late for supper. There was no indication that anything normal, like a hot evening rise, was shaping up. Our host didn't offer to let us stay on without him, probably because fishing guests are required to be in the company of someone who belongs there.

When we left, the guy actually apologized for his trout, apparently convinced it had been an accident of some kind, and also still apparently convinced that A.K. and I were a lot better at this than he was. We had, after all, claimed to be experts, or at least we hadn't denied it.

Back at the front gate, I inspected the Touch-Tones and electric eyes, and I now think I know how an enterprising poacher could open the thing if he wanted to sneak in some night. Night fishing under the dark of the moon was the answer, we'd decided. Not that I'd actually do such a thing; it was just curiosity—a residual habit left over from a misspent youth.

I'd Fish Anyone's St. Vrain

A couple of years ago, just before leaving on what was shaping up, via long-distance telephone, to be a wild, rambling trip through Idaho and Montana, I told A.K. about a little stream a man had said he'd take me to—that is, if I could "spare a day amidst all the razzle-dazzle I had planned." Without mentioning its name, the guy had described it as a fair-to-middling creek that didn't hold any real big trout, but he said it was close to his home, real pretty, not too well known, and that he fished it a lot.

"It won't knock your socks off," he'd said, "but I think you'll enjoy it."

There *was* considerable razzle-dazzle planned, and the trip had taken on a life of its own with what was beginning to look like expeditionary proportions. In the end there were airplanes and rented cars, motels, lodges, guides, mackenzie boats, nearly as many big trout as the scheme had called for, a little bit of whooping it up, and a teeth-grinding ride from Bozeman to Island Park in a fast convertible with wire wheels and a Fuzz Buster.

And then there was going to be a day on this quiet little creek the name of which I would learn when I got there, if I decided to go. It sounded vaguely like the kind of fishing I claim to enjoy most.

A.K. wasn't coming along on this one, which seemed odd, but I was calling him out of habit every time a new piece of the itinerary began to solidify.

"Sounds like the St. Vrain," I said, and he replied, "I'd do it if I were you. I'd fish anyone's St. Vrain."

Most of the fishermen I know—even those who think of themselves as Sportsmen with a capital S—have a creek like this somewhere in their lives. It's not big, it's not great, it's not famous, certainly it's not fashionable, and therein lies its charm. It's an ordinary, run-of-the-mill trout stream where fly-fishing can be a casual affair rather than having to be a balls-to-the-wall adventure all the time. It's the place where, for once, you are *not* the tourist.

Even the guy in Idaho, who lives within day-trip range of some of the best trout rivers in North America, has this little creek tucked away somewhere. He can't brag about it in the usual extravagant terms, but he still likes to show it off to, as he put it, "the right people."

You naturally take that the way it was meant—as a combination involved compliment and fair warning.

My little creek is the St. Vrain. I've lived within sight of it for a long time now, and, even though people keep asking me why I don't move someplace where the fishing is better, like Montana, I'll probably live here unless (or until) it gets too crowded up in this end of the country. And that could happen, though it's not something I care to think about.

One reason I probably won't move is that I'm easily spoiled. There's no telling what kind of unyielding snot I'd become if my home water was the Madison.

I'd have to say that I more or less blundered into this situation, largely because I already knew the stream, and the property was cheap, but then I've apparently "blundered" into a number of things that have worked out rather well in the end, leaving me with the suspicion that there aren't as many legitimate accidents in life as there sometimes appear to be. That kind of thinking can get too new-age (and too easy) but it's still tantalizing: the thought that you have ended up exactly where you're supposed to be, and so maybe you can relax.

Granted, that's easier in some places than in others.

Profound relaxation kicks in when you find yourself able to satisfy one of your more acute cravings, like, for instance, the need to fly-fish for trout in a stream just about any time the mood strikes, and to occasionally even have some success at it.

Somehow it's most meaningful if this craving we're talking about has no practical reasons attached to it. Trout fishing where you return everything you catch to the water is a good example of that. Sex with careful birth control would be another.

The day I moved into this house on the creek—well, across the highway from the creek, actually, although it sounds better the other way—I knew that, in time, I would become deeply familiar with it, and that a lot of good things would flow from that. I had already invented a life for myself as a free-lance writer and trout bum—the bohemian equivalent of a country gentleman. By "invented" I mean that the blueprints were all drawn up, it was just a matter of actually building the thing using the materials at hand.

I was living with a girl then, and, if I'd been paying attention, I'd have noticed that her blueprints were a little different from mine, and also that this novel I'd written myself into had a hero who was single. But life is complex, and you can't keep an eye on everything. I say now that she and I were married. That's not technically correct, but I'll stand by it. When the lady moves out and you end up talking to her lawyer, you were married, papers or not.

I could also say she thought I spent too much time fishing, and that I sold too few stories for too little money. That wouldn't be entirely correct either, but it would be close enough.

For the first few seasons I fished the creek almost every day that I wasn't working or fishing somewhere else. I'll say, as humbly as possible, that I came to know it as well as anyone did. And it wasn't all that easy either. It's a small brown trout stream that does get fished some, and browns get funny about that. Even the little ones.

I really did come to know a few trout by their first names, as they say, caught some of them more than once, and felt bad when in early summer one of them was replaced in his usual lie by a different, smaller fish. That almost surely meant the bigger trout had died, and all I'd ever know for sure about that was, in most cases, I wasn't the one who killed him.

It was in the third or fourth season that I was sitting here at the desk trying to write a magazine story about how to do something or other with dry flies. I was straining to describe, both accurately and prettily, how the cast went, and then the drift, and then, if it all went well, how the fish would take said fly on said drift in said type of current. I was ripping pages out of the typewriter, wadding them up, and tossing them on the floor for the cat to play with.

Then I thought, What's wrong with you? Go across the street and *look at it.* That's what Al McClane would do.

I got the rod I kept by the front door, crossed the road in front of the house, walked up to the headgate, got in, waded up to a curl of current next to an exposed tree root, tied on the fly from the article, made the cast, and caught the ten-inch brown that I knew lived there.

Yes. Fantastic. It actually works. I was back at the desk typing in five minutes, my felt soles leaving temporary damp footprints on the rug.

The girl was gone by then. She'd have wanted me to leave my wet hip boots on the porch, I wouldn't have seen the necessity of that, and a distraction would have begun to take shape. Contrary to what some of my friends think, it's not marriage I'm against, it's just that maze of distractions that makes you feel like you're walking in knee-deep syrup.

So, of course, the arm has to go like this, and the fly lands like that, and there's the way the little bulging strip of water where the fish is has almost the same gnarly grain as the root of the black locust tree. Maybe it wasn't *War and Peace,* but I was getting words down on paper that might sell. With all the windows open on the hot, semiarid Colorado summer, the footprints would dry in an hour.

It was a moment when I realized I had something I'd always wanted, and, furthermore, that it had turned out to be something worth wanting for a change. Jesus Christ, was I happy.

Lately I haven't been fishing the creek as much as I used to. I'm not tired of it, I think it's just like that point you reach in a comfortable love affair where it's okay if you don't get it on every single night.

A number of things have happened since I've lived here.

There have been some fish kills. Some were the natural results of low water and rough winters, while the worst, of course, were human caused. The stream survived both kinds rather nicely in the end, both with and without help.

There were some seasons of environmental activism practiced at a level that can't be sustained forever without cracking up, which is a whole other story.

There were the special regulations that came, and then went, because the Division of Wildlife didn't think the creek was good enough to be included in the Gold Medal Fisheries program. And then *that* turned out to be okay because the annoying crowds of fishermen left as soon as the signs came down.

There was the staggeringly expensive Trout Unlimited-planned/Division of Wildlife-sponsored habitat improvement project with its attendant, hands-on lessons in hydrology, and the renaming of Walsh Pond as Walsh Riffle after a single high runoff. Trout streams have minds of their own, and I don't just mean that the trout can be snooty.

There was the spring when everyone got scared because the runoff was so high anyway, and then it started to rain in the high country up the drainage. It looked as if a flood was in the works.

Driving home from bluegill fishing one evening I came to a road block on Highway 36. The creek, normally about fifteen feet down there, was so swollen you couldn't have floated a #16 Adams under the bridge. The official opinion was, the bridge wasn't safe to drive across. It did seem to be vibrating a bit.

The cop wanted me to go around, and I said I lived right over there and was, by God, going to go home to check things out. It turned into something of a discussion and he asked me if I wanted to get my ass arrested. Without thinking, I took a step forward and asked the officer which side of the bridge he wanted to try to do that on.

He relented, which was nice of him, and let me cross at my own risk. I said I was sorry, which I was. Just in kind of a bad mood, you know? I think my house is about to wash away and I don't have flood insurance.

The story got around, as stories will, but in the end it only seemed to help my standing with a certain segment of the community. Maybe I had these literary presumptions, maybe my fishing tackle was too fancy, but anyone willing to duke it out with the police for no good reason must be a regular guy after all.

There's something about seeing a normally sleepy little creek swell up to within inches of bursting its banks like that. It seems to indicate that even long-term appearances can't be trusted. You spend a strangely pleasant all-nighter sitting on the railroad tracks with some neighbors drinking beer, watching what you can see of the water in the darkness, checking the level of it with a flashlight, reexamining how good an idea it is to live this close to a trout stream.

Later you wonder how the fish fared in all that. I mean, it was thick as stew, and tree trunks were floating in it. In the end there were some minor structural changes in the banks. Your house is still there, so now you can selfishly worry about the poor little trouts.

Still later, when the water has dropped and cleared, you find that they're right there as they always were—about the right number of fish, and in all the right places.

It might passingly occur to you, while changing dry flies, that you know how to catch these creatures in certain proscribed situations, but there's a hell of a lot more that you'll never understand. A.K., on the other hand, exhibits no surprise whatsoever. He releases the fish he's just landed and says, "Look, if high runoffs killed the trout in streams like this, by now there wouldn't *be* trout in streams like this, right?"

You can be amazed by it or not, it's up to you.

I don't fish the St. Vrain quite as often as I used to, or quite as hard either. After a number of seasons and lots and lots of brown trout, I've started to get distracted by things. Birds mostly, but other things, too.

Since I've lived here I have identified, in a loosely delineated piece of real estate that is seldom out of sight of the creek, exactly sixty-nine species of bird. The interesting part of that is, only one of those—the varied thrush—was of any real surprise to the ornithological types, and those people can get excited, let me tell you. All the rest belong here.

I've become a fairly serious birder myself now, complete with four guidebooks, a good pair of field glasses, and a fourteen-dollar-a-week feeding habit.

No, I won't list the birds for you. I was tempted there for a minute, but no. Not all sixty-nine.

I'll list the mammals, though: we have mule deer, elk (once in a blue moon), mountain lion, coyote, red fox, beaver, muskrat, fox squirrel, short-tailed weasel, yellowbelly marmot, raccoon, rock squirrel, prairie dog, Colorado chipmunk, porcupine, cottontail rabbit, black-tailed jackrabbit, and assorted, unspecified mice and voles that amount to generic owl food.

The great horned owls that are the most common along the creek eat their catch, and then regurgitate "owl balls": round, plum-sized gobs of hair and bone that look a lot like turds, but that technically are not. An owl will often do that day after day from the same roost, leaving a pile of balls on the ground. You find the spot when, one afternoon, you notice a bunch of magpies scolding an owl. You can break the balls open and see what the owl has been eating by the little skulls and teeth inside. It's fascinating, although I guess you actually have to be there to appreciate it.

This is not something you get into every day, certainly not when the fish are biting. More to the point, it's something I don't seem to have the time for anywhere else.

Of trout stream insects we have nineteen and counting, mostly known by the common names and hook sizes, but with some Latin by way of my friend Ken Iwamasa. Fly patterns are carried to imitate most of them.

For spiders and other terrestrial bugs I don't have a reliable count because I can't swear to the absolute accuracy of some of my identifications, and, frankly, don't look at them that closely if fish aren't eating them. There are lots of them, though, and I have gone to the trouble of keying out such terrestrial oddities as the Gila grasshopper.

A Gila grasshopper is flightless, and, as the name implies, is striped head to butt in alternating orange and black like the famous lizard. Preliminary chumming experiments indicate that brown trout don't care for them, and probably don't even know what they are. It's just as well. It wouldn't be an easy fly to tie.

Way up in the rocks where fishermen seldom go you can find what the field guide tells me is probably a lesser earless lizard. A big brown would probably eat one of these, but I don't know how it would get in the water.

Closer to the stream there are beautiful brownish-orange and green-striped plains garter snakes, gopher snakes—whose defense mechanism is to look like a rattler—and, of course, the impressive prairie rattlesnake itself.

I've always like rattlesnakes for some reason, although I've never lost my respect for them and have, a time or two, killed them when they were coiled belligerently next to my front porch steps. Maybe to make up for that, I also once saved one.

I was walking over an irrigation headgate on the way to fish the Cement Plant run, when I noticed a nice big rattler struggling against the current where the main channel sluices off into the ditch. I don't know how long he'd been stuck in there, but he seemed very tired, and looked as if he would drown pretty soon. On about every third pathetic wiggle, his head would go under.

After deciding against using the bamboo fly rod, I found a good, long stick and fished him out. He lay there on the ground in loose coils for a few minutes, and then crawled off stiffly.

The guy I was fishing with didn't say much, but the look of horror on his face was clear enough. He didn't approve. I didn't know him very well, and never fished with him again after that, but he was surely the one who started the story that this crazy guy who lived by the creek was planting rattlesnakes down there to guard his favorite fishing spots.

When that tale came back to me a few weeks later I said, "Yeah, I know that guy. He's nuts." If someone wants to spread it around that your home water is dangerous to fish, you probably aren't required to go out of your way to correct the impression.

Botany is one of my many weak areas, but I'll say there are no fewer than eight species of tree along the lower stretch of creek, most deciduous, but with some ponderosa pine and juniper. There are also yucca and prickly pear cactus, plus who knows how many molds, mosses, shrubs, vines, weeds, grasses, herbs, grains, berries, wildflowers, and mushrooms. I suppose I could learn and list everything, but at some level that begins to seem pointless. Let's just say the soil is rich, black river bottom, and there's plenty of water, so it's very lush close to the creek.

Most of the exposed rock is, I believe, sandstone, and much of it is covered with various lichens. All I know about lichens is the folklore. The flaky black stuff is supposedly edible (I've never tried it) and the orange stuff is supposed to have an affinity for the urine of large game animals.

After a hard frost has made them wrinkly, the hips from the wild rose bushes make good tea. Lots of vitamin C. Good for colds. Lace it with Wild Turkey or Dickel.

There are chokecherries that can be made into a painfully tart jelly, or, better yet, mixed with something sweeter, like the raspberries.

Some springs I've found wild asparagus, thanks to the late, great Euell Gibbons, although usually I overlook it until it gets too big and woody to eat.

And, naturally, there are fish: dace, some suckers, lots of brown trout, the occasional rainbow, and once a single, confused-looking little bluegill. This, in fact, is the one advantage the fly caster has over your regulation binocular-toting, pith-helmeted amateur naturalist. Those guys never see the fish.

Yes, I have kept some notes, although it turns out that they're not very neat, and weren't all that easy to locate, having been scribbled on odd pieces of paper and stuck in various guidebooks.

I have lots of field guides, have taken to reading David Quammen religiously, and am slowly coming to appreciate the diversity of a single strip of riparian habitat by keeping rough lists in the old style. When it comes to naturalism, I stopped somewhere in the nineteenth century, back when some anthropomorphism was still allowed and the observer didn't have to remain completely objective.

And, of course, when someone with a real science background puts me on the spot I can say, "Gimme a break, I'm just a fly-fisherman."

I have learned a number of things about fly-fishing for trout here, too: the kind of sly, unlikely sort of things you learn when it doesn't matter if you catch anything today or not because you have all the time in the world. When you have the luxury of time you never have to decide if you're goofing off, or actually waiting the fish out. The results will be about the same.

These things—call them tactics or approaches—work on other streams, too, but never quite as well.

Watching birds and doing autopsies on owl balls notwithstanding, I *do* still know where some fish are, including some obscure spots hidden in between the obvious ones that any competent fly-fisher would wade right to on his first visit. Sometimes the reason why a trout is there becomes clear once you've hooked or seen him. Sometimes not. Nor are they entirely dependable.

Still, places like that accrete over the years, and finally begin to illustrate the stream's particular style. They don't quite fit together into a theory, but they end up heightening that sense you occasionally get that translates as, "I know where a trout is."

If anything, A.K. is a little better at this than I am, at least on some days.

I didn't meet A.K. on the creek, nor did I introduce him to it—that would have been too perfect—but we've fished it together steadily for years through thick and thin, so that now it's our standard point of reference. Either of us knows precisely what the other means when a creek is described as "St. Vrain-like" or "twice the size of the St. Vrain" or "a little better than" or "not quite as good as."

"Like the St. Vrain, only with cutthroats" was a particularly good one.

And it's clear what "someone's St. Vrain" is, too. It's a stream you've heard of only in passing, if at all, where the fishing is easygoing—if not actually easy—and where the guy who's showing you around may seem to be ignoring the fishing while pointing out things like an otherwise ordinary-looking boulder where once, on a chilly September morning five years ago, a mountain lion materialized for a few seconds and then vanished like smoke.

This is a stream with what novelist Tom McGuane calls a "neutral reputation." There are some trout in it, you'll learn if you ask, and yes, people do fish it, but that's about it. If it was a real good one, you'd have heard of it, wouldn't you?

All over the West you see these things on maps and drive over them on two-lane concrete bridges. Generic trout streams that vanish too quickly in the rearview mirror. Somewhere there's a guy—more likely a handful of guys—who know as much as anyone about each of them.

I know from experience that showing someone the very boulder on which the lion was sighted is ridiculously anticlimactic, but it's still somehow unavoidable. The right people try to be courteous. They'll direct their attention to this gray rock, say, "Far out," and mean it as much as possible under the circumstances. After all, you can't expect someone to mess his waders over something that happened five years ago.

The same people will try to appreciate your vision of the place, even on days when the fishing is a little slow in the run where, you tell them, you once caught twenty-five browns without moving a step or changing flies. One of the nice things about being a local is that people are virtually required to believe what you say, if only because you were there and they weren't.

I know the St. Vrain is lousy with trout, even when, on the face of it, there's no reason to think that, so I catch myself saying what old-timers have said for generations: "Ooooh, they're in there."

Some years ago my teenaged nephew, Dan, was having some trouble, and he came out here to Colorado to visit his crazy uncle John, and to sort of work things out for himself. I was happy to do it. It had been done for me. This is what black sheep uncles are for, especially those who live on trout streams.

If the truth was known, this had been part of the original blueprint: to fish, write, live by the creek, and at around forty to have become the kind of man who'd have the proper distance on trouble.

Dan and I talked a little, mostly we fished, which is what he wanted to do. I was careful not to interrogate him because that had been done to me, too, and I didn't care for it. I thought, How bad could it be if the kid understands that he should go trout fishing and cool out?

The St. Vrain was being difficult then, and I suggested that we go find some easier fishing. But Dan didn't want that. He wanted the hard fishing, he liked it: was, in fact, fascinated by it. "This is radical," he said.

But he died anyway, not too long after that. Suicide. I had honestly thought everything was going to be okay.

Charley George used to fish the St. Vrain, and he's gone, too. Natural causes. Out in San Francisco where I had lost track of him. When I heard the news the first thing I said was, "I thought he was still in Arizona."

You always have to bring it back to yourself somehow.

Charley was a fine, good-humored minimalist poet. Not the kind who says very little, but the kind who says so much so well in so little space it leaves you giddy. His author's bio reads: "Charley George: writes for hire, fishes for trout, remains in debt."

See what I mean?

***

Dead friends and all the other accumulations. More than time, trout caught, or detailed lists, they're what make you an old-timer on a piece of water. More even than actually being old, or being able to remember when the fishing was better. They may also be why the old-timer isn't giggling happily every time you see him. You think he's a little dinged out, and maybe he is. He's carrying a fly rod, but he's just standing around smoking, or back in the trees watching birds. Maybe fishing has made the guy a little crazy. Maybe this is the one who plants the rattlesnakes.

Put him on a different stream and he'll seem perfectly normal.

Yes, I did fish the little creek with the man in Idaho. As he'd promised, it was small, pretty, fair to middling, and so on. The kind of unassuming little trout stream you wouldn't go to fish if you weren't damned near there already. It was a pleasant break toward the end of a trip that was, perhaps, a little on the frantic side.

I caught a few small trout from spots where, I was assured, other fishermen before me had caught more, and was shown where the elk came down every year, as well as the exact spot where my host had once dropped a five-point bull with a single, brilliant shot.

But I guess that doesn't make for much of a story.

Neither Snow, nor Rain, nor Gloom of Night . . .

A.K. and I were camped on Roy Palm's place, with the tent pitched on a flat, grassy spot about halfway between his house and his stretch of the Frying Pan River. Roy had recently cleaned things up, so there was a big bulldozed pile of brush and tree limbs nearby that we were raiding nightly for firewood. After the first day, Roy's three retrievers, Tucker, Teal, and Rowly, had moved in with us. They'd be waiting predictably at the tent when we got back from fishing the evening rise. We liked the dogs' company and didn't mind the extra warmth at night either. This was a cold camp in late October.

It wasn't the last fishing trip of the year, but it was late enough that this was probably the last camp. So, largely to celebrate that, one night I handed A.K. the fresh pint of Southern Comfort I had stashed in my flytying kit. Sensing the gravity of the occasion, he removed the lid, tossed it into the fire, and we settled down to get ripped.

We do this once or twice a season and, although it's not as socially acceptable as it once was, I still feel it's perfectly all right. If you tend toward the urge to get in the pickup and drive to town looking for a fight, you shouldn't get drunk. But if, in the tradition of the sporting gentleman, you poke the fire, theorize, simplify, rant, preach, confess, and fall asleep, then you should if you want to.

The occasional peaceful bender in a solitary fishing camp is therapeutic, and I won't apologize for it. With the fresh air, cold water, and exercise, the hangovers aren't even too bad.

The confessions usually start about the time the Southern Comfort level has sunk below the riverboat on the label, and it never ceases to amaze me what a long and complicated past your average human being carries around. A.K. and I don't exactly "interface emotionally" or "share our feelings." In fact, we both tend to hold the midwestern stoic view that genuine problems are solved with action, not pissing and moaning. If you run around sharing your feelings too much, you'll eventually arrive at a place where you're not only still screwed up, but now everyone knows about it, too.

What A.K. and I do is just talk. We've been doing this for quite a while, and we now know things about each other that are none of *our* business, let alone yours.

It progressed, as it usually does on this high country river, to the point where we were sprawled next to the fire gazing at the stars, talking about how someday we should learn a little astronomy. Above the Frying Pan at night are the clearest sky and the brightest, most tightly packed stars I've ever seen, and I've been considerably higher.

In altitude, that is.

It was right after A.K. observed that a watched pot *does* boil, it just takes awhile, that I noticed the three faint dots next to the big star to the right of the moon. They were there in peripheral vision, but not straight on. I figured it was a mild hallucination, but when I mentioned it anyway, A.K. lurched to his feet and went to get the binoculars.

We learned later that this was Jupiter and three of its moons, an astonishingly rare sight to see with nothing but field glasses. This was one of the things Galileo saw through his telescope that led him to say publicly that those lights in the sky weren't holes poked in the roof by God, but other worlds. That got him in a lot of trouble with the Church, but he was still right.

At the time, we only knew it was a bad sign to be able to see something out in the universe that clearly from the bank of a trout stream. We'd come for the last of the Blue-winged Olive hatch, and what we'd hoped for was a falling barometer, low ceiling, and some wet, cold misery because that's when the Olive hatches are at their best.

Instead we'd had day after day of blue sky and sun, and night after night of stars. Colorado Indian summer. We'd caught some trout in the late afternoons by sheer persistence and it had been good—not to mention comfortable—but we were hoping for the hardship of cosmic weather and a great hatch to spice up the last of the season. There were good reasons why we both should have gotten back home to take care of some things, but we'd stayed on trying to wait out this disgustingly beautiful weather.

A brilliantly clear sky for three or four nights in a row meant stalled high pressure. It was beautiful—we aren't so gung ho that we're immune to that—but it did not bode well for the fishing.

The night of Jupiter's moons we almost went to sleep on the sobering thought that the weather was going to stay nice—and we couldn't just camp there waiting it out forever. But A.K., hopeful and drunk, pointed out that there would be more fishing yet this season; that if we were just patient we'd get dumped upon and frozen sooner or later.

Comforted by that, we shooed the dogs off our sleeping bags and turned in.

Weather is the key to fly-fishing. Foul weather, usually: imitation commando wool sweaters, hooded rain slickers, wool hats, fingerless gloves, long johns, wet cameras, wet camps, cold food, shots of whiskey for the illusion of warmth. It seems to have some weird connection to that good old Protestant ethic wherein anything that's easy or that feels good is sinful. You can catch trout on a warm, pretty day, of course, but you'll probably catch more if you suffer. In a strange, masochistic way, it only seems right.

Blue-winged Olives are the epitome of this. They're the only mayflies I'm familiar with that hatch predictably at least twice a year, in the spring and fall. Around here that's April and again in October, or maybe March and November in an unusual season. Whatever, the weather is likely to be dismal, and the bugs seem to love it. So much so that a sunny day can actually put a hatch off, although in practice nice weather is more likely to just reduce the duration and the number of bugs. There will be fishing, and it will be perfectly okay, but it's not the *great* fishing.

Ideal Blue-winged Olive weather is the kind that comes with the large, symmetrical movements of the big spring and fall storms. In April it may well be the first dump that's rain instead of snow, in October it's likely to be the other way around. Either way it will be damp, chilly, overcast, and generally grim.

At first there will be wind as the low pressure moves in. If you're on the river you'll probably fish, but the wind chill will ice up the guides on your rod and sandpaper your face and hands. A little of that goes a long way.

With luck, the front will move in and sit, the wind will die, and a thin drizzle will fall straight down, just heavily enough to take the sheen off the surface of the water. Then the mayflies hatch, typically in the late afternoon, and the trout rise up to eat them. This is not sporadic feeding, this is the main event.

A good Olive hatch exhibits one of those neat fits you now and then see in nature and sport. The bugs prefer to hatch in the same nasty weather that makes their wings dry slowly, which keeps them on the water and available to the trout longer. The trout, normally shy of bright light, seem to be more confident about rising to the surface on a dark, overcast day. It's carnage, but since our sympathies are with the fish it's also pretty.

And there you are. You're wet, you're miserable, you're catching trout, the stream isn't crowded, and you feel as if this is some kind of secret thing, as if this is what really happens out here when no one is around.

Accepted fly-fishing lore says the size 16 or 18 Blue-winged Olive that appears twice or sometimes three times a year is probably a Baetis, a small mayfly that produces multiple broods. The *little* Olive—about a size 22—is probably a Pseudocloeon.

Probably, I said.

Some of us use the Latin in the interest of entomological accuracy—not to mention showing off—but we still manage to turn it into a kind of slang. If you consult even a popular entomology book, you'll find that the #22 Blue-winged Olive could be a Pseudocloeon, Cloeon, or Neocloeon—probably one of the ten "more important" of these species, but not necessarily. The same kind of thing is true of the Baetis. In *Hatches* by Caucci and Nastasi, the authors point out that there are twenty different mayflies known as Blue-winged Olives.

To the authors' credit, they leave it to the reader to decide if this makes any difference.

I hold that it doesn't. In the field you fish the same patterns, in different sizes, on a long, light tippet and a dead drift, preferably in the rain.

The insect itself looks delicate to some, but I see it as compact and sturdy, like a Jack Russell terrier. Little, yes, but anything but fragile. The bugs' coloring is dull, chilly-looking, and vaguely military: a cross between faded olive drab and battleship gray. In the air, a Blue-winged Olive vanishes as soon as he's above the trees and against the gray sky. I think his coloration is weather-specific camouflage, although I can't cite chapter and verse for that. It's my own idea. A bug that hatches on gray days and stands a good chance of being eaten by a trout before he can get airborne would be wise to be gray himself on the off chance that it might make a slight difference.

Foul weather. The worst A.K. and I ever fish in on purpose is in January and February. This is accomplished with a fly rod in flowing water, but I don't see it as entirely real fishing. That is, if it were all like this, I might consider changing sports. It's just that a few rivers are open, the season here doesn't close, and so *it can be done.* It's a haunting possibility in a part of the season that seems to demand celebration.

After all, the arrival of the new year is the fisherman's holiday. Not Christmas. Christmas—even in the crass way it's observed now—is still a necessarily public display for family and society, and every real fisherman is essentially an anarchist. He may be faithful and law-abiding, but he still views those entanglements with some justifiable suspicion. He wants to be out when everyone else is in. Eventually I think he comes to crave loneliness.

A "real" fisherman is one who thinks like I do. There are more of us around than you might suspect.

The fisherman feels more comfortable with New Year's because, even though it misses the actual winter solstice by more than a week when placed at January 1, it is still essentially astronomical in nature, and has the flavor about it of a great, cyclic movement so silent and portentous you could miss it altogether if some TV weatherman didn't point out the longest night of the year.

Also, the need for a new fishing license surfaces, and one cold morning, you realize that you have not caught a single fish "this year."

Sometime before Christmas I go over to Ted's Hardware to get a brand-new, unwrinkled, resident small game hunting and fishing license. It's made of a wonderful kind of thin, silky, waterproof paper that won't tear. Flytier John Betts makes wings for caddis flies out of the same stuff.

I buy the license early so I won't forget later, and so there won't be a single minute when I couldn't be afield and legal with a rod or gun if I felt like it. I like to get the very first license from the very first book—numero uno—because I think it must be lucky, but usually someone beats me to it. I once thought about having Ted save it for me, but you can't cheat luck. It might appear to work at the moment, but later it will turn on you in some particularly spooky way, and it's best not to mess with that.

Also, Ted might think I was getting strange on him, and how one is viewed at the hardware store is not inconsequential around here.

Then, come New Year's Eve, I'll tip one to the instant when last year's license expires and this year's kicks in. This is symbolic of the actual new year: that moment when the sun appears to freeze in the sky over the Tropic of Capricorn, and then starts plodding its way north again. That's the kind of subtle event a fisherman can get his teeth into.

Then, sometime in the first weeks of the fresh year, A.K. and I go out and try to catch a couple of trout. We do this as though it were an observance.

The first trout of the year: it *seems* as if it should mean something, so we try to accomplish the feat with bamboo rods, in a river, with flies. Preferably dry flies. For some reason that I'd be hard pressed to explain rationally, a nymph is okay, but ice fishing doesn't count.

Usually by the time this rolls around there has been very little, if any, fishing for a couple of months. September, of course, was glorious—typically the best dry fly fishing of the year; October held on for a couple of weeks, but the high-altitude lakes and streams were off from the cold, if not actually frozen over, and the ones down lower were getting moody.

The Blue-winged Olives happened at least once, either on the Frying Pan or the South Platte: a dank, hideous day of wild fishing at the end of which we wring out clothing, drive to a bar, and sit in a corner steaming, sipping coffee, looking mean and crazy.

Fishermen openly enjoy being thought of as crazy.

And there was the hunting. Deer, maybe a trip for upland birds, and rabbits, which are my favorites because they're so much like trout. The bunny season is long; the hunting casual; you can use something like a Ted Hatfield small-bore flintlock rifle—the firearm equivalent of a bamboo fly rod; and there are days when you get some and days when you don't. Mostly it's that: the lack of pressure when compared to big game. No one ever comes over to your table at the cafe to ask, "Get your rabbit yet?"

By this time A.K. has gotten pretty easy to find. He has settled into his basement shop to mass-produce flies. More and more these days, they're big-ticket tarpon and billfish patterns. The radio is tuned to a jazz station, the perpetual coffeepot is on, the perpetual pipe is smoldering, and he's going through feathers at about the same rate as if he were manufacturing pillows.

And I more or less settle into my own office to write, although my weekly outdoor page at the newspaper forces me out now and then so I'll have something to write *about*. The old "I remember what my daddy taught me when I was nine years old" stuff fills in gaps in the winter, but it soon wears thin.

This is not bad at all, especially in cold weather. A long time ago Charles Waterman said that writing about the outdoor sports gets to be more fun than actually doing them. Well, not always, but I see now that he's basically correct.

It was also a while ago that Nick Lyons said it's good for the soul to have a closed season on fishing. Same idea, different angle. Not fishing for a while gives you a perspective on the sport that being in the thick of it never will. You remember things—good, solid, revealing things—that might otherwise have drifted on downstream and gone out of sight forever.

More recently, Nick wrote from New York to say he still believes that, but added, "The closed part doesn't have to be *so* long, does it?"

Colorado once had a closed season, but no more. Now you can fish any day of the year you can stand to be out. I don't know why that is, and I've never asked. It seems like such a reasonable, tolerant, hands-off sort of policy that it may have been a mistake, and I'd hate to inadvertently call it to anyone's attention.

So it's the new year, easily two and a half to three months till the beginnings of the thaw, but still—by the grace of the powers that be—time to catch the first trout.

This can seem unlikely. By January there is usually snow on the ground even at the lower altitudes, and in the mountains you need skis or snowshoes to get around. It's cold. It's around then that my plumbing typically freezes up, along with the pipes in a number of other old houses along the north, south, and main branches of the creek where, on clear nights, the coldest air settles like doom. I find myself thinking, This is water—the same stuff trout live in—and I can't even get it from the well to the kitchen faucet, let alone the extra eighteen feet to the bathroom.

But then I walk over to the creek to fetch the water that will let me flush the pot. The Island Pool is frozen bank to bank, but below it there's enough open current to dip the bucket into. And this is just a freestone stream, in low flow and unfishable now. The tailwaters will be open, and trout will be feeding. I can picture it. All we need is a day when the air temperature is high enough to keep the line from freezing in the guides.

The thing is, it's easy to pass on winter fishing. You have to summon a little basic courage to do it. You'll be cold, and your pack will be heavy from all the survival junk you'd be stupid not to bring along. But you have to do it because not doing it means you've gotten tired or lazy or too busy, all of which are bad signs.

Once you're past the inertia, a kind of optimism takes over. The odds are against it, but it might be great. It's been great in the past. And, good or bad, it will be exclusive, even on a river that's usually crowded. You think, Any idiot can fish in the summer.

A.K. and I begin turning to the weather maps in our morning newspapers where we pay special attention to the coasts of Oregon and Washington that get first what we usually get a few days later. And we watch the five-day forecasts on the tube, the ones with the adorable little smiling suns and frowning clouds. These are presided over by painfully clean-cut announcers who make the now-common assumption that getting to work on time, and to the ski slopes on the weekends, is the moral goal of the universe, and that the respiration of the planet where we all evolved is just a periodic inconvenience.

We don't want the bright winter thaw, we want the *end* of the thaw, the day when the barometer starts to drop and the sky gets ash-colored. Even if nothing else happens, the fishing can be good. Often it only involves drifting tiny midge larva flies painstakingly on the bottoms of the deepest pools and getting the odd, lazy strike. Sometimes there'll be a decent midge hatch and we can fish little dry flies. And sometimes there will be the elusive third Blue-winged Olive hatch that I've never seen on a freestone stream, but have occasionally stumbled upon on tailwaters. Until the moment I see them I think mayflies would be as unlikely in the middle of winter as butterflies or mosquitoes.

That's the gamble on timing.

We do it every year, because sooner or later there's the day that comes every few seasons when we drive to the river on a gloomy, threatening morning and land thirty trout on dry flies, just like that.

We hike out in a bitter wind and drive slowly back home in the blizzard to arrive home very late. Wives and girlfriends have seen the snow, have heard the travelers' advisories, and have worried enough that they're mad when we finally get in. No motherly smiles. We are idiots, they say. Later, when it becomes obvious that we're not even sorry, we may become reckless, thoughtless bastards.

We're not sorry because the beauty of this kind of fishing is found exactly in its unpleasantness and its appearance of risk. It leaves you tired and a little distant.

It was in April of last year that A.K. and I decided to tumble for all the publicity and drive over to Utah to fish the famous Green River. A few days before we left I called our guide, Dennis Breer, and learned that the Blue-winged Olives were hatching nicely. When I called A.K. to tell him that, he said, "Did you hear the weather report? They say it's going to be 'unsettled.'"

That's what it was. The first afternoon, after checking in with Dennis and setting the tent up in a nearby campground that, miraculously, still had some usable firewood lying around in it, we put in a couple of hours right below the dam, mostly within sight of the paved boat ramp. It had been a lukewarm, sunny day, but the light went off the water early down in the canyon, and as soon as that happened the trout started hitting. We caught some. Not a lot, but plenty for the first two hours on a brand-new river.

The next day we floated from the dam to Little Hole, and the day after that from Little Hole down to Indian Crossing. For the first float the canyon is steep, sparsely wooded in ponderosa and juniper, and the rocks are brilliantly red: the Flaming Gorge. Down lower it opens up a bit, shades from iron oxide red to a more sandy color, and there are sage and yucca on the hillsides. Somewhere in there it goes from mostly rainbows and cutthroats to mostly *browns* and cutthroats—an unusual mix of fish that made the river seem more exotic.

There was a high patchy overcast in the sky above much of the trip, the cool beginnings of a large, slow-moving front coming in from the northwest. Sometimes it would clear and get warm enough to shed a sweater, sometimes it would drizzle enough to require a slicker. Twice there was enough rain and lightning to drive us off the water into the shelter of the cliffs. The fishing came and went in classic response to the weather: the nastier it was the better it was.

It was on the Green that I made what was, for me, at least, a new observation. I knew that Blue-winged Olives seem to like to hatch in the afternoons, but it had never before occurred to me that it's also in the afternoons that the storms build. I would prefer not to believe that this is just a coincidence.

Over the years I've asked a number of fisheries biologists about the connection between weather and fishing. I've learned surprisingly little, but here it is:

All freshwater game fish are photosensitive to some degree, preferring low light to bright, direct sunlight. There may be some genetic predisposition to this, but it's probably learned behavior for the most part. Bright light means exposure to predators, while darkness or shade means safety. In some extreme cases—like brown trout or largemouth bass living in heavily fished waters—the fish can become entirely nocturnal.

Low light in the daytime comes from deep water, shady banks, structures like bridges and docks, and, best of all, lousy weather.

Rain, drizzle, sleet, snow, and wind accomplish the same thing: they texture the surface of the water, lowering visibility, and making the fish feel safer.

Of course it's not quite that simple. Too much rain or snow at the wrong time of year can lower the water temperature and put the fish off. Most of the trouts become sluggish and pouty in water that gets below about 45 degrees. It's entirely possible to have too much of a good thing, especially early and late in the season.

Fine, that part of it makes perfect sense. Fish, especially trout, like crappy weather for largely understandable reasons, but fisherpeople have this mystical streak that searches for deeper meanings and hidden connections.

The barometer is a kind of icon to some fishermen. Given a choice, they'll sit home when it's high and call in sick to work when it starts to fall. The scientists have told me that trout do have sensitive lateral lines that doubtless perceive subtle changes in pressure— and it's known that air pushes on water. Okay, but they say that a trout swimming from two feet of water to three feet experiences a much greater change in pressure than he'd feel from the wildest imaginable change in the holy barometer. It's not the barometer at all, they say, it's the gray sky, wind, drizzle, and such that come with low pressure. The barometer business is probably nothing but an old husbands' tale, they tell me.

I guess I don't believe that, especially since I could swear I've seen trout begin to feed furiously *as* the barometer was dropping, and *before* the sky clouded up or the rain started to fall. I can't shake the feeling that they know.

Look at it this way. We humans, especially those who live in cities, are constantly victimized by sudden and vast changes in everything from noise levels to the particulate content of the air, but we still somehow manage to react radically to the subtlest of signals, like a passing whiff of a familiar perfume or an offhand comment in a peaceful conversation that might just have been an insult.

A pair of fishermen camped along a trout stream might even decide to get shit-faced on a clear night because they feel instinctively that tomorrow's fishing will be a little slow, so a hangover won't hurt anything.

More than once it's occurred to me that I should stop talking to scientists if I'm not going to believe what they tell me.

We caught a lot of trout in two days of floating the Green with Dennis, and we found him to be a fine, mellow guide. Even that early in the season the river was a little crowded with boats, but when we'd come to a jam we'd either pull over and let everyone else go by, or row on down to some fresh water. "Plenty of river here," Dennis would say. "Plenty of fish for everyone."

We fished Blue-winged Olive dries and emergers during the afternoon hatches, and nymphs and streamers to fill in the blanks. The weather was better than it could have been, but it was still bad enough for good fishing, and we never got so cold that we had to beach the mackenzie boat and start a fire, never got so wet that our clothes didn't pretty much dry out overnight.

When we pulled in at the take-out spot on the evening of the second day, it had begun to rain lightly. By morning the canyon was socked in with one of those wet, cold, smoky-looking western storms that sift clouds down into the tops of the trees. The weather map in the local newspaper showed the front sliding gradually east into Colorado, just beginning to swallow up the Frying Pan River.

We broke camp and stopped to tell Dennis we were heading for the Pan. He couldn't understand it. "Fish here," he said, "it'll be great. You can hike down the canyon and wade. Why drive all the way over there?"

It was hard to explain. We had caught lots of trout, including some real big ones, and had seen roughly sixteen miles of gorgeous western river canyon from the luxurious vantage point of a slow-drifting, old-style wooden mack boat. There were wondrous things yet to see: more river on downstream where, rumor had it, fewer fishermen went and the browns were even bigger. Later there might be a hatch of acacia bugs or a migration of strange Mormon crickets that would run across the surface of the river and die by the thousands in the mouths of huge trout.

You have to be careful of greed on a good, new river. You can beat yourself up and finally limp away still without having had enough.

And then there was this weather, a flat, wet, low-pressure storm stalled there on the Green, but also over a familiar river six hours south and east. When it looks as if it's going to be absolutely, horribly wonderful, you want to be on water you know so you can take full advantage of it.

As I said, I don't think Dennis ever quite understood. Maybe he thought we were scared to stay and fish in the rain.

We called ahead and Roy said we could camp on his place again if we wanted to. It was raining when we got there. The dogs were glad to see us, but they were also wet, so we wouldn't let them in the tent. They slunk back to the barn, puzzled and offended, still carrying the sticks they'd expected us to throw for them.

Some other fly-fishermen were on to this, too, but there weren't crowds of them, as there often are on the Pan in more hospitable weather. A few other fishermen are okay. In fact, when you're out there suffering together, a nice feeling of camaraderie develops. You wave at each other, stop to talk more freely. No one actually says it, but you all feel as if you're among the precious few who know how it is and aren't being wimps about it.

We started fishing in the flats below the dam where the big rainbows are known to lie. This is the top end of the catch-and-release area, a spot that, at many times of the year, is too packed with fishermen to even bother with. There were two guys downstream at the bend pool, and one above carefully working the bank. Before the day was out we would run up there to watch him land a nine-pound rainbow.

Plenty of river, plenty of fish for everyone.

The trout were supposed to be eating shrimp then, and shrimp patterns worked. Not beautifully—hardly anything works "beautifully" in an established catch-and-release area—but the right-sized fly drifted in the right way through the perfect spot would draw a strike. It might take fifteen or twenty casts and two fly changes to a fish you could see. If you couldn't see the fish, but believed one was there, it could take longer.

That afternoon we each landed a couple of the square, chunky rainbows the Pan has gotten famous for in recent years. These fish are big, but not pretty. They resemble slabs of bacon, and that's how some of them fight, too, but they're impressive as hell, all the more so for being so ugly.

They're not easy to land either. These fish fight with their weight, which is considerable, and that is often enough. I hooked one that ran me a good hundred yards downstream, right past the two fishermen down there. The fish gained line on me the whole way and broke off as he went around the bend.

"Probably foul hooked," one of the guys said, which was meant as either sour grapes or consolation, I couldn't tell which.

"Yeah, probably," I said.

I didn't take many photos for fear of drowning a perfectly good Pentax K-1000, but I have one from that first afternoon of A.K. holding his big landing net out toward the camera with a trout in it so big the head sticks out on one side and the tail flops out on the other. He's wearing so many layers of wool and chamois that his rain slicker looks like a sausage. His hood is pulled almost closed, leaving just enough room for him to see out and to get the pipe into his mouth. You can just see the top row of teeth from what must be a dazed grin. Apparently it wasn't raining too hard at the moment because he has the pipe upright and it still seems to be lit.

The first night was wet and cold. We stayed in our waders and slickers to cook supper, and then ate in the tent. It was too nasty for evening fire sitting, too wet for a fire, and there was no wood anyway. Roy had done something with the brush pile.

The following day we caught more big fish, and that night we huddled in the tent discussing possible designs for a tarp arrangement off the back of the camper shell on the pickup that would let us cook out of the rain. We also noted that the tent was taking on a little water.

On the morning of the third day we drove into Basalt for breakfast at the cafe rather than face the dripping camp kitchen. This is a trout town, so they know what fishermen are. There were no weird looks, and no unnecessary conversation either. Waitresses in Basalt know that fishermen who look as bad as we did are best left to mutter among themselves.

Breakfast was reviving—pancakes, sausages, lots of coffee—and we set out on what had become the daily schedule only an hour or so late. First to the flats to nymph for hogs, then a lunch break in the steaming cab of the truck with soggy sandwiches and thermos coffee, then to the stretch above the Picnic Hole for the Blue-winged Olive hatch.

The day was hours old before either of us noticed that we were alone. An empty river in a storm is sublime enough; when it's one that is normally crowded it also has some of the poignancy of a deserted city street on a November morning.

A.K. was working the long run just below the concrete bridge, and I was above it, casting to rising trout in the big pool there. The mayflies were coming off well, and fish were lined up, rising steadily and in a quick, efficient rhythm. It was almost easy.

A pelting rain was falling, giving the river a rough slate finish that the trout could just see the bugs through. It was lovely. Fishermen can get nearly religious about the texture of water.

There were lots of mayflies, and very few bugs were getting off the surface. Many were, in fact, smashed flat and nearly drowned. I was fishing a damp no-hackle dun that was floating on its side just like the naturals. The fish loved it.

I'd landed half a dozen good rainbows—and I knew A.K. had done about the same downstream, judging from the muffled whooping I'd heard from that direction—when I saw the big head coming up over near the far bank. This was a very large fish, lying in a large fish spot: a willow-lined eddy where the stream flows backward for ten or fifteen feet. He seemed to be standing on his tail, bobbing up to take a mayfly every four or five seconds.

I caught him. I simply crossed over the bridge, found a good casting position, made a single decent cast, and hooked the fish. He bored for the bottom a few times, and when he went for the main current I had just enough of my wits about me to splash out there (nearly going in) and pull on him in the exact direction he wanted to go. Feeling that pressure, he instinctively swam against it, as any of *us* would do in a moment of panic, and turned back into the slow water where I was able to land him. I'll say he was a thick twenty-four or -five inches and an honest five pounds.

Yes, it was a brilliant job of fish playing. Thank you very much.

The clouds were low enough that I couldn't see the lip of the canyon, only where the red cliffs, now more of an antique rust color, dissolved. The rocks were wet and shiny, with rainwater running over them, sometimes in flat sheets, sometimes in little eroding streams that you could somehow hear over the noise of the rain and the river. The stream itself made the usual slurping sound of current with overtones of the rain sizzling on its surface. Now and then a rock would come loose and fall with a clacking sound. All this had the effect of silence.

I was wet to the skin, wearing as much of my second change of clothing as I could get on. Later, in a warmer, friendlier place, I would find that my body was as pale and wrinkled as a dead fish. When I sat down on the bank and leaned against a rock, I squished inside the rubber suit. I felt cold. I felt as if I had perhaps gone slightly mad. I felt as if I'd just discovered North America and wasn't going to tell anyone about it.

A.K. came crashing down to the stream through the willows and said, "The hatch is over, let's go sit in the truck and warm up." It sounded like a very sane suggestion.

There had been no other fishermen, and all day only two or three cars had passed on the road, but as we climbed out of the river a guy in some kind of a sports car pulled up. He rolled his window down two inches and said through the crack, "Getting any big fish?"

"I just landed a five-pound rainbow on a number eighteen dry fly," I said.

"No no," he said, "I mean *really big* fish."

The guy was young, well dressed, dry, warm, and sitting in a sports car with the heater going.

"You're an asshole," I said.

A.K. agreed. Only an asshole would insult a wet fisherman's trout.

It seemed over, so we drove slowly back to camp. On the outside the tent was sagging pitifully. Inside our sleeping bags and pads were floating in four inches of standing rainwater. The air had cooled enough that our breath was condensing into thin clouds.

The dogs had run out when we pulled in and were now standing there watching us expectantly. Suddenly I couldn't remember how many days we'd been out. Seven maybe.

"A.K.," I said, "I think I wanna go home."

Guiding and Being Guided

LET'S get one thing straight right off the bat: I'm not a fishing guide. Never have been. Never will be. I don't enjoy it very much, and I'm not especially good at it. Most of the times I've tried guiding were when I weakened and gave in to flattery and/or the need for some fast money—two of the forces in nature that will make a person with a normally accurate self-image try to be something he's not, at least for a couple of days.

It hasn't been all bad, but I think I've done just enough of it now to get a feel for what it's like, and to know that I don't want to do it anymore.

The last time was one of the worst. A friend of mine who runs a combination guide service/fly-fishing school was short a hand one week, and in a serious bind with a big-tipping regular party due to show up in a couple of days. This was a somewhat trying bunch, he said, but still valuable, repeat customers. Would I please fill in? He'd pay me well, and consider it a personal favor if I'd help him out.

Okay, okay. If the truth were known, I sort of owed this guy a favor. It had also been awhile since I'd done any guiding. I knew I'd given it up, but didn't remember why quite vividly enough.

As I said, this was a guide service *and* school. I'm not much better at teaching fly-fishing than I am at guiding—I'm always saying encouraging, diplomatic things like, "No, you idiot, not like that, like this!"—but it was only for a few days. How bad could it be?

The sports in question were well-to-do professional people, most on the long end of middle age, who got together every summer for a few days of fly-fishing. I never determined exactly how many there were in the group because they were always getting split up this way and that among the staff, but I know there were no less than eight or nine of them. In other words, way too many for any kind of reasonable fishing trip.

They'd been doing this for a number of years, long enough for some personal traditions to develop, like the big fish fry on the last night.

A couple of days every season, and that's it. In one sense, they'd all been fly-fishing for years (that's what they'd tell you if you asked) but in another, much more meaningful sense, they had about a month's worth of experience between them. But then, they didn't *need* experience because they'd engaged a guide, you see.

The problem—both mine and theirs, but mostly mine—was that these people naturally wanted to catch some trout, but honestly didn't have any idea of how to go about it. Ten minutes after I'd met them, I, their steely-eyed, mountain man guide, had some doubts as to whether it was in the cards for them.

This is not a professional attitude. The Professional Attitude fairly reeks of confidence, enthusiasm, and rural good cheer.

I was sorry I'd taken it on, but there I was, so I waded in. I did, after all, know a little something about this.

For instance, you always start off calling your clients Mr. or Ms. So-and-So, although it's part of the implied social contract that they'll instruct you to drop that before the introductory handshake is released. A guide once told me, "If you say, 'Good morning, Mr. Smith,' and Mr. Smith doesn't say, 'Please, call me Bob,' it's gonna be a long day."

With this group it was "Mr." all around. That's how they wanted it. It's what they were used to. Nobody wanted to be "Bob" to the help.

It's probably best not to ask what people do for a living. They may have traveled a long way to forget about all that, and, if not, they'll tell you all about it soon enough.

These guys never told me anything, probably because a fishing guide wouldn't have understood it, but I gathered from the conversation that it had something to do with small pieces of paper and large amounts of money.

You should also try to find out, politely, just how good your sports are at

fly-fishing. You'll find that out soon enough, too, but it might help you decide where to take them.

The good ones will be modest—"Oh, I guess I do okay"—and a few duf-
fers will lie to you as if you weren't going to see just how good or bad they
are within the hour.

I also know that in the course of things it's acceptable to deliver short,
bright, good-natured lectures on natural history, even with an environmental twist if you can keep from getting too strident, but you should refrain
from arguing politics. If the client brings the subject up you can respond if,
and *only* if, you agree. Even then, it's best to steer things in another direction. Most of us get mad when we think about politics, and angry people
don't fish well. I know, I've tried it.

And you must always bear in mind what your assigned role is. You're an
employee, though part of your job is to appear not to be an employee at all,
but rather a sort of hybrid valet and fishing buddy. You are in charge and re-
sponsible if something goes wrong, otherwise the client is in charge.

You must also remember that you are not fishing, and I mean that literally and figuratively. If you carry a rod at all, it's used only for the occasional
purpose of demonstration or, in a pinch, to search out fish or find the right
fly. The client is fishing, *you* are guiding.

It's required that you at least smile at all jokes, even those involving
members of ethnic groups in woodpiles.

And make no mistake about it: whatever the sport says, however realistic he seems, he expects you to make him catch fish. Lots of them. Big
ones, too. He may or may not be willing to help you out with this.

As David Quammen said, the job demands "the humility of a chauffeur
and the complacence of a pimp." If you decide to be a guide, I think you
should do it for reasons other than that you love fishing.

With this particular bunch, I was guiding *and* teaching the basics of fly-
fishing to a group who claimed to already know this stuff. Teaching is hard
enough on the lawn with willing pupils. Trying to do it on a trout stream
with fish rising and the pressure on is about as overwhelming as giving
someone his or her first driving lesson in rush-hour traffic.

Furthermore, part of the job was to do this while staying out of the way
and out of the conversation like a good waiter. This was, apparently, something of a reunion as well as a fishing trip, and everyone had a lot of catching up to do. For instance, since they'd seen each other last, most had
gotten fax machines.

Then we'd arrive at the stream, the chatter would stop, and they'd all turn and look at me expectantly, as if to say, "All right, we're all ready to catch a fish now, if you please."

Yet another problem was that these people wanted to keep fish for the big fry on Saturday night, to which I was invited, of course. But the school was very catch-and-release oriented, which meant that this particular batch of people didn't fit into the usual program, and couldn't be taken to the usual spots. Naturally, the usual spots were the ones I knew the best. They were also where most of the trout lived.

It also meant that the single fish—large or small—couldn't be made into the genuine victory it should be for a beginner. There were mouths to feed, there was a working body count.

The first two days went well enough, considering the circumstances. That is, not many trout were caught, but no one drowned and I didn't get mad so you could tell. We broke the mob up among some of the other guides whenever possible, but I never had fewer than four people, and the most any of them knew about fishing was that you had to hold the fat end of the rod.

A few things began to come back to me, like that old guys can't wade like younger guys, and that even younger guys can't wade very well when they only do it a few days every year. The bottom of a trout stream isn't much like a sidewalk. Even on a relatively small stream I had to physically place these people in their casting positions, and then come back to lead them out when they wanted to move, which was often. If one of them didn't hook a fish in five minutes it was because I hadn't put him in the right spot.

I also remembered that you shouldn't spread inexperienced sports out too much along the stream because, what with the more or less constant attention they all require, you'll end up jogging twenty miles by lunchtime— over boulders, in waders.

Basically, these men were the worst kind of clients you could have: the kind real guides must have nightmares about. Simply put, they couldn't fish, didn't care to learn, but still expected to catch trout without trying.

They wouldn't even make a stab at casting to the spots I pointed out, nor would they pay attention to any of my attempts at casting instruction because, as any of them would point out, while peeling tangled fly line from their hats, they already knew how to cast. In fact, they ignored just about all my suggestions, which got gradually more forceful as time went on.

One guy insisted on fishing a size 8 Rat-faced McDougal through a hatch of #16 cream-colored caddis flies because he had once caught a fish on this very fly. And the fly looked it.

Naturally, I had to tie it to his leader for him.

At every break they'd all gather around the brand-new Styrofoam cooler that was supposed to be filling up with trout for the much discussed gala fish fry, which, I began to realize, was the real reason for the trip. By lunchtime on the second day we had five or six pitiful little rainbows and one ten-inch brown. They wanted many more fish; I wasn't too pleased with those we had already.

When the man who seemed to be the spiritual leader of the group asked me where all the trout were, not to mention the big ones, I admitted that they were mostly in the catch-and-release area where we couldn't go because we were killing fish.

That was a mistake. If I hadn't said anything they never would have known.

"I'll tell you what," he said, "why don't you take us there, just so we can land a few nice ones before it's all over."

"Well," I said, "I didn't say you could catch them, just that they were in there."

This amounted to insubordination, and I could tell the guy didn't appreciate it, but I couldn't help myself. A real guide would have thought that, but he wouldn't have said it.

So, against my advice and better judgment, we ended up in the catch-and-release area where my troop continued to cast like bored children— fishing the wrong places with the wrong flies—and failed to catch trout that were noticeably larger than the ones they had failed to catch earlier. Now and then one of them would glance at me as if to say, "Well . . . aren't you going to *do* something?" and I'd look back as if to say, "What more *can* I do?"

Mostly I was hoping no one I knew would see me.

But even no-kill water breeds its share of stupid fish, and the leader managed to hook a nice one on his enormous Rat-faced McDougal, which pleased him immensely because it seemed to be proof that I'd been wrong about that. I ran downstream to help him land it, but he wanted to do it himself. I have to admit, he managed it rather smoothly, using my net.

It was a lovely, deep-bodied female rainbow of about sixteen inches with a forest green back, ink-black pepper spots all over, and the bright red stripe down its side that marks a wild fish. She was lovely, a real knockout.

"I'm going to keep this one," he announced, reaching for his aluminum stringer.

"Ah, look," I said, "as I mentioned before, this is a catch-and-release area, so you *can't* keep the fish. It would be illegal."

He looked down at the trout. He was holding it way too tightly. This was a man who had grown used to getting what he wanted, a man for whom the rules ought to move aside of their own accord.

"Come on," he said, "what would really happen if I kept it?"

I considered that. It was pretty obvious.

"What would happen is, your guide would drive into town, turn you in to the ranger, and you'd get your sorry ass busted."

That was either the wrong thing to say, or exactly the right thing. I still don't honestly know, but I *do* know why I don't guide anymore.

When I said I knew something about this, I meant the easy stuff, the etiquette and the posture. That is, under pressure I was able to look and act like a guide. On the water, where it counts, I always prayed for a moderately competent fisherman, half a break from the trout, and then just tried to be a decent caddie, but there is much more to it than that.

For instance, a good guide not only knows how to fish, he is also able to translate that information quickly into terms that are available to all manner of people. Those are two very distinct skills, especially considering the variety of clients you deal with.

You'll get fishermen who don't have a clue; others who *do* have a clue, but little else; all the way up to guys who are so good you wonder why they wasted money on a guide in the first place.

The very best client to have is a jolly, flamboyant tipper who's just happy to be out of the office and who doesn't much care if he catches a trout or not. The second best, and the most fun, is the one who actually knows how to fish. Chances are you won't see many of either in a season.

The thing I always had the most trouble figuring out was the appropriate level at which to intrude. Some people want to be led by the hand through the entire operation, and be complimented profusely even on their mistakes, as in, "Hey, I've seen people hook their ears a lot more often than you do." That's dreary work, but at least you know what's expected of you. On the other end of the scale is the guy who is alone with his muse even in a crowd.

This guy wants to locate his own fish, select his own flies, tie his own knots, and land and release his own trout. He's into solitude, so he isn't up for much conversation, he's noticed the scenery, thank you, and he already knows the names of all the birds. He must want you there because he hired you, but it never becomes clear what the hell you're supposed to do. Just stand there and hold the sandwiches, I guess. After a while you're tempted to go back to the truck and take a nap, but, if nothing else, you understand that you're not being paid to sleep.

You have your professional pride. The only thing worse than having a client get skunked is drowning him or getting him eaten by a bear, but if you flutter around and talk too much, you're intrusive: a pain in the neck. If you hang back too much, you're lazy and/or incompetent. To be good you have to do it just right. With any luck, the sport will at least give you a hint.

In recent seasons—luckily, for everyone concerned—I've spent more time as the client, and the one thing that doing a little bit of guiding in the past has taught me is how to be guided.

A lot of it has to do with getting things straight, most of which can be done in advance. Do you want to be pampered or worked? Be honest. Do you want to catch lots of fish, or do you want to go for the few hogs? You probably won't get it both ways. Be up front about it, and then let your guide locate the balance point between what you want and what you can fairly expect.

If you just want to see the river and catch some fish, fine. If you do have something special in mind, tell the guide, especially if you feel strongly about it. He may be good, but he's not psychic.

"If I can't catch 'em on dry flies I don't want to fish," you say.

"You gotta use nymphs here," the guide replies.

Maybe that's true and maybe it's not, and maybe you're some kind of stuck-up purist who'll never be happy. Whatever, this is not your guide. Maybe it's not even your river.

There will be times when you have to consciously put yourself in a guide's hands: to accept his guidance. The better you are at fly-fishing (or the better you think you are) the harder this is, so the trick is to overcome your ego. Okay, you know rivers, but this is a new one with its own little idiosyncrasies, and maybe you don't actually know everything.

It was like that when A.K. and I fished with Russ Kipp on the Beaverhead in Montana a few years ago. In the stretch we floated, the river is deep, fast, and narrow, with tight, overhanging willows along most of the banks. It's not exactly like a tunnel because you can see the sky. It's more like a deep, green ditch with a river in the bottom of it. The evening before we went out Russ told us what it would be like:

The rubber raft will be moving quickly in the main current. The trout will be tight to the banks, under the willows. You get one cast per spot at close range, so it's going to be fast and furious. Russ told us to dig out our

heaviest rods and overline them by one size so they'd load up with very little line in the air. There would be none of this namby-pamby false casting.
Leaders should be short, level, and heavy, both to handle big browns in fast
current and to get streamers back from the willows.

It doesn't matter how accurate a caster you are, you will hang up in the
brush, and there will be no going back for flies or slowing down while you
tie on a new one.

"This is what we call 'Montana-crude' fly-fishing," Russ said.

The locally accepted streamer pattern was a huge, heavy thing with lots
of rubber hackle called a French Tickler. A properly tied French Tickler
casts like a banana, sinks like a stone, and is deadly to fish who bite it and to
fishermen who get hit with one.

So early the next morning we began shooting down the river, with Russ
at the oars slowing the drift as much as he could, and calling out the spots
along each bank as they came up. "Nice eddy on the left, under the branch,
ahead of the rock . . ." You'd get one cast, which had to be accurate, a second for the fly to sink, another second or two for a twitch, and then you
were into either a fish or the next cast.

When a fly hooked brush, Russ would yell "Down!" and everyone would
duck as the stuck fisherman pointed his rod straight at the snag and the
weight of the raft broke it loose. It was pretty menacing, even if all that
came back was the leader.

Russ said it was a little slow, but we caught enough fish, and each one
gave us a nip-and-tuck fight right to the net, if we could get him that far.

I remember focused concentration and a sore casting arm. What I don't
remember, unfortunately, is much about how the river looked while we
were on it. All I really saw of it was a rolling close-up showing a band of water and a band of brush, now and then punctuated by the yellow flash of a
brown trout.

Scenery aside, it was great, one of the wildest days of fishing we've
ever had. We still talk about it when the fishing gets intense, "Remember
the Beaverhead?" The point is, without a guide who knew how it worked,
we'd have peered down that tunnel of brush and fast water, shrugged,
and driven on to the next river. If nothing else, we needed his boat just to
get in there.

Now and then you'll hire a guide and that's about all you'll get: a boat and
someone to row it.

Three years ago a few of us took a two-day float down a big Colorado trout river that had what Ed Engle calls a high remoteness factor. In this one stretch it flows through a deep, sheer-sided gorge, complete with some horrifying rapids. In a section that takes two days to float, there are only a handful of places where a fisherman on foot—or maybe on horseback—can get down into it to fish some pitifully small pieces of water that are isolated by vertical rock walls and deep water on both ends.

It's a good trout river, fished almost exclusively from big, inflatable rafts.

The man we floated it with was a fine river runner, a big, strapping oarsman who digs rapids and who is, without doubt, the captain of the ship. You wear your flotation vest, and it's buckled all the way to the top, never mind how hot it is. When he says, "Sit down and grab hold of something," you do it without asking why. It will become obvious in a matter of seconds.

But all he knew about fishing was that the trout are in the river somewhere, and people with rods and funny hats sometimes catch them. When he advertised guided fishing trips, he meant that he'd run you down the river, and if you wanted to fish on the way, then that was okay with him.

I had my first suspicions at the put-in point while we were waiting for some other parties to get going.

"So," I said, "what are you getting them on?"

"Well," he answered, "flies, I guess, or some guys use spinners."

"I see. It's browns and rainbows, isn't it?"

"I think so," he said, and then called down to another guide who was getting his party situated. "Browns and rainbows in here, right?"

It wasn't bad. In fact, it was fun to take charge of the boat for a change, and to air out every fisherman's fantasy, the one where you know more than the guide. At first we made suggestions: "Think you could get a little closer to the bank through here?" but gradually we became more assured and the suggestions became orders: "Okay, get us into that backwater over there."

Fly patterns and tactics we had to figure out for ourselves, but that was fun, too. The more you do for yourself, the more credit you can take if you connect with some trout.

When we'd come around a bend in the gorge and an ominous rumbling would begin to build in the air, command of the ship would instantly revert to the guide.

"Reel in and grab something," he'd say. "This one is called 'The Grim Reaper,' class-five rapids." This was his thing, and he loved it.

At a time like that it's perfectly acceptable that the man on the oars knows more about white water than he does about fishing.

*＊＊

I think what a good guide does is to somehow gain purchase on the situation almost immediately, and then, with a touch so light it's imperceptible, he steers things right. When it works it's a wonderful thing to behold. In the end, the client feels as if he did it all himself because, except for a gentle nudge here and there, he did. I can't be any more specific than that. If I could, I'd be able to do it myself. The best I can do is appreciate it.

There are fishermen who don't care to use guides. Some say that being guided cheats them out of that sense of exploration and discovery. Others just don't like to shell out the money, although they'll mine all the free information they can at the local fly shop.

A lawyer friend of mine is adamant. "I won't pay for guides or hookers," he says. "There are some things a man should arrange for himself."

A friend of mine who does walk-and-wade guiding trips on a very good trout river once told me a story about "the old man." He showed up at the fly shop one day in a long, black limo, driven by a tall, dark chauffeur who opened the door, tipped his cap, nodded when spoken to, never let anything like an expression brighten his face, and never spoke. Not exactly sinister, but a little spooky.

Everyone in the shop went to the windows to gawk. "Who is this?" someone asked.

The old man himself was seriously old, approaching ancient, easily into his seventies or better, but who can really tell? You certainly don't ask. My friend described him as small, frail, shaky, walking slowly and breathing shallowly.

What the guy wanted was to catch a twenty-inch rainbow on a dry fly, and to that specific end he had arrived on a fine stream during the Green Drake hatch. In the right place and at the right time, in other words, which at least gives you a leg up on the dreaded Client with the Special Goal in Mind.

My friend, always the professional, said, "Yes sir, I'll do my best," while thinking, Christ, I hope he lives through the day.

It doesn't happen often, but clients do just drop dead now and then.

The old man got into his waders by himself, slowly. They were good canvas waders, worn, but with no patches. A guy who arrives on the river in a limousine would not have his waders patched. At the first sign of a leak he'd have the butler phone Orvis to order a new pair. Custom fitted, of course. They'd have his measurements on file.

The rod was a light bamboo, handmade by a famous rod maker who is no longer with us. It was in a leather-covered rod tube with a brass name-plate on it. My friend didn't recognize the name, but thought maybe he should. When someone shows up in a big, black Lincoln with tinted windows, you can't help wondering, along with the crowd back in the shop, "Who the hell *is* this, anyway?" A financier? Spy? Gangster?

The man spoke very little. He wasn't sullen, he wasn't stuck up, and he wasn't dingy. He just didn't seem to have a whole lot to say.

My friend took the man to the quietest water he could think of where the big mayflies would still be hatching, and tied the locally approved Green Drake dry fly to the man's leader because he made no move to do it himself. The man nodded his thanks, and then tested the knot.

The hatch came off well that day, and trout rose eagerly, although, as usual, they were careful and picky, needing a good drift before they'd strike.

The old guy, my friend said, was a wonderful caster of that gracious, Old World, wood rod style where the elbow is kept at the side, as if you were holding a Bible under your arm. It was slow, graceful, effortless, and accurate: the kind of casting you don't see anymore.

And yes, the old man caught fish. As it turned out, he was very good at this.

By the time the hatch was about to peter off, the man had landed a number of nice trout—had, in fact, put in a very respectable day—but the twenty-incher on the dry fly had eluded him. Nothing was said, but my friend hadn't forgotten about that, and something in the old man's bearing indicated that he hadn't forgotten either.

Up to now, the guide had done little more than watch and occasionally change a fly, but now he spoke up.

"Right over there," he said, pointing, "far bank, in the little curl of current just up from the bridge, see the big head coming up?"

The old man looked at the spot until the trout rose again, nodded, and began wading toward the main current. The cast would have to be across and downstream into slack water. To get the right drift, the caster would have to be standing in some pretty fast, deep current. My friend didn't feel that he should take the man by the arm, so he waded in next to him on the downstream side so he could at least grab him if he went in. This guy was as dry and brittle as old newspaper; in fast current he could dissolve.

The man wobbled precariously a few times, but he stayed upright and got to where he had to be.

The first cast was brilliant, the drift flawless, and the fish took so slowly and casually it would have broken your heart if you'd seen it. The old man set the hook just right—not too soon, not too late, not too hard.

This was the twenty-inch rainbow on a dry fly. In fact, it was more like a twenty-four-incher.

The fight was long, and not what you'd call one-sided, but it came to a point where the big, strong trout was below the bridge and the frail old fisherman was above, with some deep, treacherous wading in between where the current sluiced between the pilings.

The old man started under the bridge, shuffling, leaning into the current, and the guide said, "Uh, listen, would you like me to run down there and net him for you?"

"What I'd like," the old man said, "is for you to keep your goddamned hands off my fish."

"Yes sir," my friend said.

Whoever this guy was, he was definitely someone you'd call "sir."

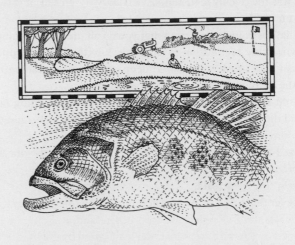

The Chairman's Bass

THIS happened roughly twenty years ago, give or take a season. I suppose I could figure it out exactly, but it doesn't really matter. Let's just say it
was in the old days.

I was in my early twenties, living on the outskirts of Boulder, Colorado,
in a place that had once been a tourist motel, but was by then rented dirt
cheap by the month. It was a pretty place, in an Appalachian sort of way:
apparently handmade from smooth river rocks and cement, not up to
building code in any number of ways, and having seen plenty of better days.
Even when new it would have been considered, at best, rustic.

In the custom of the times, those of us who lived in the seven old units
fell into a kind of loose communal situation. We shared a vegetable garden
out back, fed each other's dogs, took messages for each other on the pay
phone out in the dirt courtyard, and operated a primitive form of the car
pool whereby the person whose vehicle happened to be running that week
was the chauffeur.

There was an open field to the south, a ranch pasture to the east, another field to the west, and a modest creek lined with stately old cotton-

woods flowing by to the north. It may have been just barely in, or just barely past, the city limits.

The creek was just a little too far from the foothills to be very good, but there were sometimes trout in it in the spring and early summer that had washed down from upstream plantings, and we were not above harvesting and eating some of them. The same went for the fox squirrels up in the trees and the cottontail rabbits on the ground. In season, of course.

These were the beginnings of a kind of subsistence period, during which I ("we," that is, it was always "we") lived what seemed like a simple, marginally self-sufficient life while waiting for the sick, evil society out there to spontaneously restructure itself in our image.

Maybe you remember that late sixties version of the hopeful innocence of youth where the future was so shaky it was exciting. We were more than a little naive, but life wasn't bad.

The place is gone now, as are just about all the cheap places to live in Boulder. It was condemned and torn down, and then the town crept out and sucked up the vacant lot that was left behind by the bulldozers. Where my old black-and-tan coon hound was buried, there is now either a four-lane highway or parking lot for an office building. I can't locate the exact spot any more than I can tell you exactly what year it was. As I said, it was the old days.

I had a respectable job then mowing the rough at a golf course. At five-thirty on Monday morning I'd start at point A, pulling a gang of mowers behind an old but serviceable John Deere tractor. I'd mow through Saturday, have Sunday off, and, if it all went according to schedule, I'd start back at point A on Monday and do it all over again. Endlessly, at the minimum wage.

It was okay. At the time I was either a Zen Buddhist or an existentialist, I forget which, and I was off early enough in the day to fish the afternoons and evenings.

There were the usual ponds scattered around the course, and, having a thing for water, I'd always manage to take my scheduled and unscheduled breaks next to them. I'd noticed some little bluegills in these things from time to time, and even a couple of small bass, but had never given the ponds much serious thought because I didn't like where they were.

I've never cared for the game of golf, or mowed grass for that matter, especially when I had to mow it. I thought then (and still do) that fishing should be done in places that are, if not actually wild, then at least unmanicured. I could fish other warm-water ponds that were nearby, and a lot more pleasant, too, so the fish at the golf course were nothing more than a mildly interesting curiosity.

Then, one early morning when I was having a bit of trouble getting wired up for a whole day of mowing, I stopped not ten minutes into the shift to watch a particularly handsome blue heron wading the pond out by the back fence, and saw the boil of an enormous largemouth bass. And I mean enormous.

You know how that is. Even in water you take seriously, you somehow don't want to believe it. Half of your mind says That had to be a big bass, and the other half replies, No, it had to be a carp, or maybe a muskrat. It was just too *big*. These were just water traps, after all.

The evidence itself is gone in a matter of a few seconds, so you're left trying to make the final determination based on the notoriously faulty short-term memory of a fisherman.

It made the diagnostic chugging sound of a bass, right? And what you saw of the back was bass green instead of carp yellow, right?

You understand I had to know for sure, so I pulled my rig over to where the angle of the light and the view seemed about right, and feigned a mechanical problem with one of the mowers.

The foreman was a Republican with eyes like a hawk, and he was of the opinion that everyone in the world except him was lazy and good for nothing, especially guys whose hair was a little on the long side. Still, the machinery was old, and as long as you had a wrench in your hand there wasn't much he could say. I would always have just gotten the thing tightened back up about the time he was a hundred yards away.

By the time I had the whole gang of mowers adjusted properly—and the foreman's pickup was just leaving the shop in my direction—I had managed to see the fish a few times; never very well, but enough to know that it was, in fact, a largemouth bass, easily eight pounds, maybe pushing ten.

Okay, fine. Now back to work. The foreman stopped his pickup as I climbed onto the tractor seat. He sat there glaring at me, gunning the engine.

Now the sighting of a big fish is the sort of thing that can gnaw on you, especially when you're doing a repetitive job outside in hot weather with no one to talk to for hours at a time. However long you fish, you never get over the astonishment of spotting the game, and thinking, Oh, shit, *there he is!*

I couldn't help mulling it over, and later that day I almost piled into a tree while mowing around the next pond because I was watching the water instead of where I was going. There wasn't so much as a single sign of life in that one, but then it was the middle of a summer day when small ponds snooze.

I figured I hadn't seen that bass before because he was largely nocturnal, and I had never been at that particular pond quite that early in the morning before. What I'd seen were probably the last, half-interested pickings of a whole night of feeding. The fish *had* seemed sort of apathetic, as if he was already full, but still going through the motions.

I can't say the golf course started to look like a prettier place to fish, but I ended up wanting that bass.

When I punched out at the end of the day I asked the foreman, as casually as possible, if anyone ever fished the ponds. Just curious, you know?

"You seen one of the chairman's bass, didn't ya?" he said.

I felt as if I'd been caught poaching already, but I asked him to explain that, which he did briefly and pointedly.

"The chairman of the board put them fish in there, and him and his friends are the only ones who can fish here, understand?"

"You bet," I said, realizing that I'd made the mistake of tipping my hand.

The foreman and I never did get to be what you'd call pals.

Maybe that's why I never got around to catching that bass: because the jig was already up. I can remember some of the things I did, or decided not to do, twenty years ago, but not always what my reasoning was like.

I do remember planning it, though.

I'd go over the back fence at two in the morning—or maybe three—at a spot that was only thirty yards or so from the pond across open ground. I'd have to stay low, but once at the water my silhouette would be camouflaged by trees.

My truck would be parked a half mile away with the hood up so any passing police would take it for an abandoned vehicle. That would be believable. The thing looked like an abandoned vehicle even when I was driving it.

I only owned a few fly rods then, but there was an old taped-together fiberglass eight-footer fitted with a worn-out reel that could be expendable if worse came to worst and I had to chuck it in the bushes.

I'd have one size 2 deer hair mouse tied to a level thirty-pound test leader. No fly changes, no long, sporting fight. This was going to be a quick, well-planned assassination.

It never occurred to me that I wouldn't be able to get this bass. The fish was fat, pampered, indifferent, and, most importantly, undisturbed. The chairman might cast a spoon in there two or three times a year, but he would be an aging dilettante who would not fish long, hard, well, or even at the right time of day. I knew that with the certainty of youth.

That fish was stupid, and he was mine for the taking.

I hadn't planned a crime since I was ten years old and a couple of us laid out what we thought would be a neat bank job. There was one difference: at ten you know you won't really do it, at twenty-something, you're not so sure.

But I didn't do it, as I mentioned, and as you probably guessed from the fact that I'm even relating all this. I wish I could say I arrived at my current opinion on such things then, but those developments are usually more gradual. At that time I think I assumed that any American capitalist with the title "chairman" preceding his name was a fascist lackey who didn't deserve a ten-pound bass. Game fish to the people. Now I think anyone with the foresight to surreptitiously put some bass in ponds that he alone is likely to fish is probably a guy I could get along with, and who is, therefore, someone who might invite me to come right in through the front gate to fish if he was cajoled in the proper way.

And if that sounds too noble, then, yes, I was afraid of getting caught, too. Okay?

Private water. It's always bluer and deeper, with bigger, dumber fish. That's one of the myths you live by as a fisherman, and it's a fair enough bet.

It's also a fair bet that the higher the fence and the more menacing the signs, the better the fishing would be if you could get on. A terse KEEP OUT on three strands of barbed wire is one thing, while TRESPASSERS WILL BE PROSE-CUTED TO THE FULLEST EXTENT OF THE LAW on chain link is quite another, "fullest" (rather than just "full") being the kind of overstatement a lawyer would use.

You see, there's some subliminal manipulation going on here.

There are lots of different styles. Some landowners prefer the warning followed with "by order of the sheriff of such-and-such county." That has an officious look and ring to it, while a hand-painted NO FISHING, DON'T EVEN ASK is more down-home serious and probably more immediately dangerous.

I'll point out that only that last one actually prohibits asking permission, although some of the others hint pretty strongly at the answer you'll get.

In some places you need a translator. Up in Montana they often post property by painting orange stripes on the fence poles. My friend Dave Carty says that if the paint is faded, it means "I'm not as upset about this as I was a couple of years ago. Maybe we can discuss it," while a fresh coat of fluorescent paint indicates that there is a .270 trained on your temple at this very moment. Don't make no sudden movements, and do not come up to the house.

There are different styles of what we'll call management, too. Sometimes access, even to very good water, is surprisingly negotiable. "Hi," you say—if you can locate the owner—"can we fish here?" and the possibility exists that he'll say, "Yeah, okay, just close the gates behind you."

"Really?" you say. "Jeeze, thanks."

That sort of thing still happens. I make it work—or maybe I should say it *just works* through the grace of the gods—a couple of times every season. Of course, it's part of the implied contract that I don't tell you where.

Let's just say there's a gorgeous bass and panfish pond hereabouts that I can get on if I go with the guy who actually has permission to fish there. This is absolutely mythical private water in which both species of fish are twice the size of the ones you'll catch in the nearby public ponds, and so easy to fool you really can get weary of it after a while. By prior agreement, we keep nothing. Whatever thinning the populations need is done by the owner.

Going in secondhand, on someone else's coattails, involves the kind of clumsy scheduling arrangements that prevent you from spontaneously deciding that today would be a good day to fool around with some three-quarter-pound panfish, or maybe that you'd like to fish there by yourself for a change. With that in mind, I've toyed with the idea of asking for permission myself. I'll have to sit down and quietly work that one out sometime. Without being able to quite put my finger on the principle, it sounds vaguely unethical.

It was on the coattails of Jackson Streit, a fishing guide in Breckenridge, Colorado, that I got onto a fine stretch of river that's owned by a seriously private fishing club. The showpiece here is brown trout of tremendous size that move up from a reservoir downstream in the fall to spawn. As I recall, the club rules said you couldn't keep one under twenty-five inches, or something like that. You get the idea.

It can get spotty—these are brown trout, after all—and the very best of it is seasonal, but it can be so good you get casual about it.

The day we fished it I watched Jackson hook a huge brown that had chased his streamer to within inches of the bank we were standing on before striking. When he felt the hook, the fish jumped once and landed with a dull plop on the sand at our feet. There he lay, dead still, gazing into the cloudy sky, lost and amazed in the wrong element. Jackson calmly reached down, unhooked the fish, and nudged him back into the stream.

The trout was, I'd guess, twenty-two inches long, not even a keeper, and the whole drama had taken five seconds. No photos, no backslapping.

"The trick," Jackson said, "is to land them quickly."

***

A few years ago in Montana, A.K. and I fell in with a guy named Bill Crab-tree. Crabtree spends his summers in and around West Yellowstone and is what you'd have to call a seasonal local. He's one of those rare guys who fishes long, hard, and very well, but who never seems to get either grim or fanatical about it.

In a few short days of fishing with him we'd learned the simple truth that if we went where he went and did what he did, we'd catch fish, so when he asked us one morning if we'd like to go see about some rainbow/cutthroat hybrids in a little lake he knew about, A.K. said, "Lead on."

The lake was owned by a mummified widower cowboy who was at least a hundred years old, who lived in a house of roughly the same vintage that you'd swear was abandoned, even when you were standing on the front porch. Absolutely authentic, and in the middle of nowhere, too. The lake was not visible from the road.

There were the usual curt introductions, followed by the regulation half hour of shit-kicking, scratching, and inquiring after the health of the cattle and the relatives. Bill said that, naturally, we wouldn't be keeping any fish, to which the cowboy replied "Yup" as if he'd heard this before, and be-lieved it, but still didn't understand it.

A.K. and I stood around trying not to seem too impatient, and when the money for the privilege of fishing there finally changed hands, it was so quick and subtle it could have been a street corner drug deal.

As we were turning to go the cowboy said, "By the way, if you catch that big one, kill him for me, will you? He's been eating up too many of the smaller trout and I'd like him outta there."

"Uh, how big is the 'big one'?" I asked. (The obvious question.)

"Last time I seen him, maybe thirty inches. You'll recognize him."

Not all private water is fabulous, but, as I said, it can be a fair bet—some-thing worth looking into.

There are those who enjoy the commercial fish-for-pay places, like Armstrong's and Nelson's spring creeks in Montana, for their ambience of exclusivity and privilege. I don't have a lot of experience with joints like that, but they're really not bad as a change of pace, as long as you under-stand that you're buying "good fishing" rather than actually purchasing trout. You know the fish are there (you've been hearing about them for years), you know it won't be crowded, and you know you can get on be-

cause you have, of all things, a reservation. Because of the relatively stable nature of spring creeks, the fishing will be as predictable as it's likely
to get, and the money (I think the average is about thirty dollars per rod,
per day) isn't bad.

Incidentally, it's referred to as "renting a rod on the creek" but the fee is
for simple access. There's a story about a dude who showed up, paid his
money, and then asked, "Okay, where's my fishing pole?"

"You're supposed to bring your own," he was told.

Back when I was contemplating poaching the chairman's bass I had
never paid to fish and figured I never would. Fishing that wasn't free may or
may not have been a fascist plot to enslave the masses, but it violated my
personal aesthetic and so I had a rule against it.

I guess I was still working out the morality of coveting my neighbor's
bass.

The personal rules aren't as strict now, and I'll pay for it when I have the
money to spare and when I think it's worth it. I've never done the two big
spring creeks—Nelson's and Armstrong's—because they're booked too far
in advance, and I just never seem to know what I'll be up to that far in the
future.

I've done DePey's (pronounced "DeePews") spring creek and it was
great: a small, weed-choked stream full of trout, funky fisherman's shack
with a picture window, wood stove and fly-tying desk, and a genuine
river keeper named Robert Auger who seemed to enjoy his work immensely. It's a lesser-known creek in the same beautiful Yellowstone Valley with Nelson's and Armstrong's. There are Russell Chatham landscapes
everywhere you look, and you can get on the water sooner than two
years from now.

It was completely satisfactory, but I know I'll never make a habit of it.
I'm not exactly sure why.

Deciding how you feel about this inevitably leads you to wonder, Why
do I do this in the first place? and I'm not sure about that either, although
it's a fair, if self-indulgent, question.

I guess I don't know why I fish in any really definitive sense. I've written
a couple of books about the whys of it, and it occurs to me now that I fish,
in part, so I can write books like that. If nothing else, it beats mowing the
rough at the golf course.

And then there's the mythology of it, which is considerable. The fisherman is "out there" looking around, figuring it out, restless, and mobile, and
he knows about these places, you see. Places you and I *don't* know about,
and couldn't get on if we did. The fisherman is plugged in somehow.

Like Dave Carty in Bozeman, Montana. Dave has only lived there for a few years, but he's already developed an enviable network of places to fish and hunt. He's a relentless scouter and talker who can get on all kinds of private land without paying for it, unless you count the odd bottle of whiskey and the Christmas cards.

Unlike Bill Crabtree, Carty *is* a little feverish about it, but he's also young, and he has such a shameless good time at it that it's not only okay, it's infectious. Driving off in his camper before dawn some morning—seventy miles an hour on a back road, honking at the deer—the conversation will go dead for a few minutes, and Dave can be heard muttering, "Fish an' hunt, hunt an' fish . . ."

And then he's back: "We'll hit that stretch on So-and-So's place, and if it's not happening there we can drive up to the such-and-such ranch, or maybe old what's-his-name will let us on if he's home. Hey, did I remember to buy gas last night?"

Maybe what I'm saying is, private water can be wonderful, poaching is unacceptable, and paying for it is too easy. These things need to be done correctly.

One of my clearest memories from childhood is of prowling around midwestern backroads with my uncle Leonard asking people if we could fish, and getting answers in the affirmative as often as not, plus maybe something like, "And bring me a couple of fish if you get any."

In each particular case it was because we either knew the guy already, or we asked politely and looked harmless enough, or the man was having a decent day and felt generous, or, perhaps, that he could stand some fish for the table, but didn't have the time to go get them himself.

In a general sense, it *was* because he didn't have the time himself. These guys were farmers, not sport fishermen, and, although farming when I was a kid wasn't the desperate enterprise it is now, it was still a damned hard job that required long hours and a sharp eye for not wasting anything. There was fishing because there had to be water for the stock, and once there was a pond full of water, well, you might as well make use of it and toss some fish in. If you didn't already know how it worked, the county extension agent would line it up for you: a few basic, easy-to-meet physical requirements, plus X pounds of bluegills and X pounds of bass per surface acre and you were in business.

Now they'd call it an ancillary use of an existing resource, which is just newspeak for common sense.

It was all private, but it seems to have been arranged so that there were obvious, even intentional, chinks in the armor. This was in the old days, too, when it was not yet generally accepted that any courteous stranger could be a serial killer.

Part of the implied social contract went like this: if the guy says no, you say "thanks, anyway" and move on. He doesn't owe you an explanation. It's his pond, and they're his fish, just like that big, beautiful bass, like it or not, belonged to the chairman.

Rivers

HENRY'S Fork of the Snake: It's the second week in August, the middle of the so-called off season here, and there's almost no one around, even though the Callibaetis mayflies are falling on the water down by Osborn Bridge every morning around nine o'clock. This event, someone decided without consulting you, is not considered to be one of the better hatches on this river, and so, for the moment at least, the mob has departed.

More than anything, it's strange. The K.O.A. Campground in Last Chance is all but deserted; the famous Green Drake water upstream from the Railroad Ranch is empty except for that one gull that's always perched on Bird Rock; guides are working other rivers; fly shop owners are drinking coffee and waiting patiently for the September crowds.

This is a big river, but not an intimidating one. In the flats above the bridge it's wide, slow, sleepy-looking, and eminently wadable in most spots, with waist-deep water and a hard sand bottom. You get dunked only when you get too casual, or too engrossed, and simply walk into a channel. This happens more often than you'd think.

Right through here the river splits into three channels. The land is flat, but mountains are visible in every direction that affords a view. To the east you can see all the way to the Red Mountains in Yellowstone Park across an open sagebrush meadow where sandhill cranes strut. To the west the pine forest comes right down to the water and leans in on the bends.

This is navigable water, the bottom end of a good float through the Railroad Ranch stretch, but on this trip you haven't seen a boat in days, and only a few other wading fishermen who looked dwarfed by the scenery.

It's more than strange, it's eerie. A famous river, a clockwork spinner fall, big trout rising under overcast skies that make them confident and casual, and only three other fishermen in the last five days. Granted, the afternoons and evenings have been a little slow—caddis hatches have been off and the hoppers aren't really doing it—but what do you want, nonstop action? "No," your partner admits as you sit in camp one day, tying up more Speckled Spinners to replace the ones you've left in fish, "I guess that's not what I really want after all."

The guy at the fly shop, who has plenty to time to talk right now, says, "Sure, there are more rising fish at other times of year, but there are more rising fish *per fisherman* now. You guys are probably doing this exactly right."

Dropping the "probably," you let that ring in your head: "You guys are doing this exactly right."

Frying Pan: Basalt, Colorado, qualifies as a bona fide trout town because, for a population of less than a thousand people, it has two fly shops and a sporting goods store, and because when you walk down Main Street in neoprene waders no one asks you if those are some kind of ski pants. That kind of thing will sometimes happen up the road in Aspen.

You don't spend much time in town because you're always busy fishing the Frying Pan River, but after many seasons you've come to know the place a little, largely through trips in from the campground for supplies, and the occasional cafe breakfast or celebratory dinner and drinks.

The Pan is a quick, jumbled river in a steep, bright, rufous-colored canyon with lots of trees. On a clear day it's red, green, and ice-water blue. In the fourteen miles from Ruedi Dam to the confluence with the Roaring Fork, you'll find every kind of water you'd ever want to fish. The trout are very big.

In February you check into a motel, using as an excuse the fact that the Little Maud Campground up by the dam is closed for the winter, but secretly relieved to have a warm, dry place to sleep after those cold days on the river. The woman behind the desk tells you, without being asked, that the river is fishing well and they're getting them on midges. This kind of information gets around on a daily basis; it's part of the mass consciousness of the town.

The desk clerk may or may not be a fisherperson—may or may not, in fact, have a clear mental picture of what the hell a midge even is—but the report will be accurate.

"Exactly *where* are they getting them on midges?" you ask.

South Platte River, Colorado: It is a promisingly warm April night. You sit at the flytying desk faced with a small pile of #18 dry fly hooks and a much larger pile of materials in natural dun and shades of dyed olive. To your right, next to the cup of coffee, sits a fly box that has been nearly picked clean by the Blue-winged Olive hatch on the South Platte—last fall's hatch, and the one that is going on right now, the one you fished three days ago and will drive down to hit again tomorrow morning.

When you think "Platte" you picture the first clear view of the river from the trail: the shot nearly straight down into the glassy Ice Box Pool with the huge gray boulders at its head looking like, as Dave Taylor of Trout Unlimited says, "elephants on a skating rink." In the right light you can see the trout stacked in there. Lots of them. Big ones. They're either rising to some tiny hatch or nymphing. They look easy, but they are not.

You're not thinking of the fish you caught the other day, but the ones you didn't, especially the one in the backwater under the big, flat rock decorated with the stripes of high-water marks. He wouldn't even look at the Olive Dun Quill, then glanced at the no-hackle and the Paradun, seemed to actually sniff at the floating nymph, and then just dissolved away, leaving the last of the hatch to a smaller trout.

Under the fly-fisher's kinky, existential scoring system, a fish like that cancels out dozens that were hooked and landed.

Maybe a quill-bodied no-hackle, or a trailing husk, upright-winged emerger, or perhaps a split-winged dry fly with a parachute hackle tied underneath the body. It's late, and a full night's sleep would feel good in the morning, but what you really need is something just a little bit different than all the Blue-winged Olives that rainbow has already seen.

Gunnison River, Colorado: You are lying under a juniper tree in an unzipped down sleeping bag in the Gunnison Gorge, one day out on the float trip. Already you're used to feeling closed in by the high canyon walls. Even now, in low late summer flow, this is a big river in a small space. In most places there is no way out except impossibly straight up toward the slot of blue sky or on downriver the way you're going. In a very palpable way, there is noplace else, just this. To get the same isolation on flat ground you'd have to go north until you hit tundra.

The night is warm, the moon is up, and there are only a few mosquitoes. From the absence of grunts and rustles in the other bags scattered around, you guess that the rest of the party is asleep.

Except for Tom Austin, that is. As we were all drifting away from the fire, looking for a spot to lie down on that was level and free of ants, Tom was stringing up a rod and tying on an enormous rabbit hair sculpin. You sensed that the head guide was not entirely happy about that, although he knew enough not to say anything discouraging to a guy who is Going Night Fishing in a big way.

Guides are like mother ducks: they like to have everyone accounted for at all times.

So maybe you're not the only one lying awake listening to the river, waiting for footsteps to come up out of it. Go to sleep, you tell yourself; if he gets one on that huge streamer, he'll wake you up and tell you all about it.

Roaring Fork of the Colorado: You're fishing a golden stone-fly nymph in that deep plunge pool at the head of the long run, the one that takes six split shot to get to the bottom of, even now when the water is low. It has been a slow day, with nothing but whitefish so far, and you find yourself wishing once again that you were one of those guys who know the Roaring Fork; who know, for instance, where the big trout are.

Then you tell yourself that whitefish are better than no fish at all, that they are perfectly honorable when caught on flies, which is true enough, and you begin to fish a little more casually. It's not always going to be like the cover of a glossy magazine, right?

The river here seems bigger than it is because it tugs at you so insistently. This water falls a long way from the headwaters down to the Colorado River. It seems to be in a hurry to get there; things happen quickly, and there are a lot of places it won't let you go. They don't call it the Roaring Fork for nothing.

You've fished this stretch maybe twenty times over the years and have never even tried to get to the other side. The other side, of course, looks pretty damned good.

The next strike doesn't crank you up too much until you feel the weight. In fact, that throbbing could be nothing but the current working against a snagged leader. But then there is the unmistakable shaking of a big head down there.

Oh, shit.

The fish turns, heads down into the run where the water gets white, staying deep. You feel the leader ticking and bumping against all kinds of junk on the bottom, and then you're standing there like an idiot holding a slack line.

Surely it was just another whitefish—a big mother, sure, but still just a whitefish.

Green River, Utah: Little two-lane Highway 6 out of Golden to I-70 West, and then halfway across Colorado on four lanes at high speeds in the general direction of Utah. North at the town of Rifle (after a stop to fill the thermos) and up to Meeker where you turn west again along the White River. Coming down out of the Flattops onto rolling high plains, the river here is wide, muddy, and full of carp. With those flat, lava mountains to the east, you are suddenly in unexplored territory, sitting up a little straighter on the truck seat.

At this moment in your life you have only heard of the Green where it's a fast, cold stream in the tall canyon under the dam. They say it's like so many other trout rivers you'll probably know what to do, but it's still going to be a new one.

You know vaguely that farther down the land folds open, and the stream gets wider and warmer until eventually it becomes a high desert river that has unearthed many fossils. Maybe there are big brown trout down there, and maybe not. Certainly there are rattlesnakes. The downriver reports have been secondhand, conflicting and tantalizing. Someday you may have to go look at that, too (on a long drive your mind spreads in this kind of widening circle), but right now it's off your personal map, so it might as well be filled with perpetual fog and monsters.

Coming up on Dinosaur, Colorado—just minutes from the Utah border—you stop for some pop and a look under the hood of the truck. It's running okay at cruising speeds, but is stalling when you slow down. Nothing is obviously amiss, but then neither of you is what could be called a mechanic.

The decision is obvious: if it cruises okay, then let's cruise. If it stalls when you slow down, then don't slow down.

At the junction of Highways 40 and 64 stands a snarling green plaster dinosaur in need of paint. Heat is rippling in the air, so you can't quite focus on it. The day has shaped up prickly hot, sage-scented, and a little dusty, even without wind, and you would feel depressingly far from any trout except for the Uinta Mountains standing on the western horizon. Down here the white stuff is alkali. Up ahead it's snow.

Bitterroot River, Montana: The guy at the fly shop, standing under a sign that reads BITTERROOT TROUT DON'T SPEAK LATIN, said you only need one fly, an Ugly Radimus. "Well, then, what are all these other flies for?" you asked, pointing at the bins of hoppers, mayflies, and caddis patterns. The answer was vague, something to do with tourists and hedged bets.

So the four of you hit the river armed with several dozen Ugly Radimuses (or is it "Radimi"?) and, sure enough, the fish like them, at least for a while. When the Red Quill hatch comes off, the fish, not surprisingly, want a Red Quill, size 14, but after that it's the Radimus again, in the fast water and along the banks.

Okay, it's the only fly you need *between hatches*. Fair enough.

You're high up on the Bitterroot's main branch, above the last bridge where boats put in, just below the confluence of the East and West forks. These are almost the headwaters, the place where the Bitterroot Range of mountains comes south, jogs north, then swings south again, surrounding you in a rough, three-sided bowl that the river flows out of going north. There's no one around.

The river is fast here, running only in the deepest channel in the fast spots, and then spreading out in the riffles, but you can see from the wide streambed where it gets a lot bigger in the spring.

Right through here it seems to be full of rainbows and cutthroats all the way from fifteen inches to little finger-sized ones with parr marks. This is exactly the spot where what you'd call a mountain stream becomes what you'd call a river.

Later in the afternoon you meet another fisherman. He's crouching on a glistening white stretch of exposed sand and round, bleached river rocks examining a bear track. "Is that a grizzly?" he asks, and you say, "Too small, probably a black."

From that he takes you to be a local, and asks what kind of cutthroats these are. "West slope," you say, having learned that just this morning.

Then he looks at the fly in your hook keeper and says, "Now, is that an Ugly Radimus or a Madam X?"

"Don't know for sure," you say, "we don't get that technical around here."

Yellowstone River: After your first day on the Yellowstone at Buffalo Ford, you find that you have been infested with buffalo mites. It's not a pleasant experience, but, it occurs to you, it is a singular distinction in this day and age. A.K. leans over, sniffs at your shirt, and says, "Well, the bugs made an honest mistake. You smell like a bison in rut."

Just a few miles downstream from its source at Yellowstone Lake, the river here is already wide, deep, big, and western. Fishermen work it close to the banks because that's about all you can do. Luckily, that's also where the fish are. The Ford is the only place around here where man or beast can cross. Sometimes the man will have a little trouble with the current.

It's a toss-up which you were more impressed with, the pretty cutthroats or the buffalo, although it's the latter that are statistically more dangerous than the grizzly bears. That's because they stand around looking prehistoric but peaceful, and people think they can pet them, or put their kids on their backs for pictures. Nine times out of ten, they're dead wrong about that.

At one of the usual buffalo traffic jams, tourist after tourist, each with an Instamatic camera, gets too close, and a harried ranger yells at them. Another ranger comes over to your car and asks if you've seen a guy he's looking for, a guy who, according to amazed witnesses, jumped on a bull buffalo, rode him fifty yards across a meadow, and then stepped off neatly to scattered applause.

"That's a real no-no," the ranger says.

You haven't seen him, but you'll look. The guy was described as weighing two hundred pounds, wearing a denim jacket with the sleeves cut off, and riding a Harley.

"If we spot him," you say, "we'll grab him for you."

Wyoming

M Y old Courtland landing net, the one I carried on fishing trips for years, is now lying somewhere in the upper North Platte River Valley in southern Wyoming. With any luck, it's been picked up by another fisherman and is now in use, though probably it's waterlogged and rotting on the bottom of the pond. That is, I think that's where it ended up. When something is lost you're never exactly sure where it is or it wouldn't really be lost, right?

By way of consolation, a friend told me that if you go off and leave something behind, it means you have a serious need to go back to the place where you left it. Not to find the thing in question, mind you. We're talking mystical reasons here, some form of spiritual gravity.

Okay, fine, I'm not immune to cosmic influences, but I don't like losing things. Gear is expendable, but it should be used up and thrown away, not left behind by accident.

And I still needed a net. I have a spare, but it's one of those little bitty ones that were fashionable a few years ago; you know, the ones that were light and easy to handle, but too small for any fish that actually required a net to land.

The trip I'd just come back from had firmly reminded me that there are times when a guy needs a nice, big net, so I drove into the Front Range Angler fly shop in Boulder to buy a new one.

"New net, eh?"

"Yeah, lost the old one in Wyoming."

"I'll bet there's a story there."

"No story. I just lost my fucking net, okay?"

The new one is a big, wide-mouthed Broden made of zebra wood and ash. It's very pretty, and a little on the expensive side, but what the hell. I always wanted a Broden, so I wrote it off as a case of forced upgrading, and made a vow to try and hold on to it.

Losing the net on that trip was appropriate, I guess, because Wyoming fits into my personal mythology as the kind of place that can swallow things up without a trace—single engine airplanes, pickup trucks, people, landing nets, you name it. The very sound of the words "lost in Wyoming" have a doomed ring to them, as if the thing in question wouldn't be any more irretrievable if it were on the dark side of the moon.

Many of my friends and I have a way of neglecting Wyoming. When you live in Northern Colorado, Wyoming can become nothing more than that big flat thing you have to drive across to get to Idaho and Montana. North to south, it's roughly ten hours tall. For reasons I've never been able to determine, it can be an hour longer on the way back. Either way, it's a grind.

I've been on many drives like that over the years. The ones where you ride silently through that long stretch where no radio stations reach—silently because you're hours into the trip and have already talked everything out at least once. No music, no conversation. You gaze through the windshield in a kind of trance until finally your passenger points out the window, and says with genuine excitement, "Look, a tree!"

That's in vehicles of the old school with nothing but a radio. More recently I've made the trek armed with a tape deck, and now Wyoming has much to do with traveling at high speeds listening to rock and roll at equally high volumes to cut through the shrieking of the wind.

Depending on the company, that is. If I'm with Jim Pruett it might be reggae, or Paul Winter space jazz. The latter I find a bit too cerebral for the excessive speeds you reach on those long straight highways, and the album recorded in the Taj Mahal has parts in it that sound like a loose bearing in the water pump.

In the back of one's mind there is always the creeping horror of blowing a water pump seventy-five miles out of Rock Springs.

Sure, I know there are mountains and rivers up there—I've seen them from a distance, and even been in them a time or two—but the parts you have to gut your way across are the archetypal wide-open spaces with horizon-to-horizon sagebrush relieved only by the receding ribbon of highway under you and the occasional lonesome cow.

Not that I'm exactly complaining. I still prefer the folded geography of mountains, or at least the shelter of trees, but, after over twenty years of living in the West, I've come to appreciate the plains. Too much of it can give you the prairie madness, but in small doses it's good for you. It's an acquired taste.

Not long ago the state of Wyoming announced that it wanted to attract some artists and writers to give the place a little more of a cultural ambience. It was a great deal for thoughtful types, they said. Cheap living, few distractions, and lots of peace and quiet.

That's for sure.

I thought of that the morning of the day the net turned up missing, while gazing out through the open door of an outhouse at a neatly framed piece of Wyoming. The scene was downright Oriental in its simplicity: bluish-gray sky, greenish-gray sage, and a gopher. No snowcapped mountains, no sentimental pines. It was refreshing.

I had tried to paint years ago in the Midwest, but it didn't work out, and I ended up a writer instead. Looking back on it I think it was the preponderance of objects in any given composition. Too much stuff, too many brushstrokes, at a time when I wanted simplicity. Painting hadn't occurred to me in a long time, but there, in that part of Wyoming where daily life goes on just a peg or two above sensory deprivation, I think I could do it. And I'd save a bundle on art supplies, too.

It was an idle thought at dawn, a time when there were fish to be caught.

I was up there with my friend Jay Allman, fishing a working ranch where he and a handful of others lease the fishing rights to several fine prairie ponds. Jay is the owner of Trout Traps, Ltd., the float tube manufacturers. I guess he'd qualify as an executive, though you wouldn't pick him out of a crowd as such in his cowboy hat and T-shirt.

Jay refers to the ranch as the Official Trout Traps Belly Boat Field Testing Facility. The Branch Office consists of a small, somewhat battered trailer with a propane stove, but no electricity, and an outhouse with an uncluttered view and several .30 caliber bullet holes in it. Plugging crappers is considered a respectable sport here in the West—with a year-around open season. Spend enough time on the plains and you'll begin to see the charm of it.

The trailer sits on the banks of the largest pond—more of a lake, really—

with the trailers of a few other lessors in sight. Most of them are bigger and prettier than Jay's, including a couple of shiny Air Streams, but Jay is not the kind of guy to squander a lot of money on something so basic as shelter. An aluminum rowboat with trolling motor is tied up three steps from the front door. This is no-frills country living at its best.

The ponds are very rich, but deceptively plain-looking. At first glance they look like they should hold bass and bluegills, if anything at all, but no. It's trout. Big trout.

Jay says the quality of the ponds has to do in part with the sagebrush depositing calcium in the soil that then leaches into the water to beef up the chemistry. If you're not already familiar with the place, I can't begin to tell you how much sage there is in Wyoming.

The ponds are thick with vegetation, and, because they are cool, but lying in the relatively low band of high plains habitat, they carry a diverse mix of aquatic food forms, all in large populations. There are scuds so thick you have to wash them from your waders when you come out of the water; warm-water creatures like damsel and dragonflies; and cold-water ones like various mayflies and caddis. The picture you get of the trout in ponds like these is that they could never really be hungry. They have the freshwater shrimp to graze on more or less constantly, and they seem to suck up the other bugs more for variety than anything else. If they're not lazy, they are certainly contented.

The centerpiece hatch is the ubiquitous monster prairie lake caddis, a wheat-colored bug about an inch and a half long that lives in every good prairie lake or pond I've ever fished. It's the still-water equivalent of the great western stone fly, though it's not nearly as well known.

This had started out as a desperation fishing trip, one that had fallen through a time or two already that summer, but that we both felt we needed badly. Like most executive types, Jay works way too long and hard for his own good. Like many writers, I don't work nearly as hard as I claim to, but still somehow manage to suffer from periods of seemingly job-related burnout. Jay needed to get back to his ponds, and had been trying to do so for the better part of a month. I felt I needed to accomplish a little stress management, and also wanted to see if half of what he'd said about this place was true.

Finally there was the phone call:

"Meet me at seven Tuesday morning. I am getting the hell out of here."

I was typing. A deadline was coming up.

"I'll be there," I said.

Tuesday had a lot to do with high speeds and Led Zeppelin ("Stairway to Heaven" is still a great song), and I was scribbling in one of the notebooks the newspaper gives me that say NEWS—PROFESSIONAL REPORTER'S NOTEBOOK. Yes, that's a little pompous, but they're free. Still, we were at the ranch, unpacked and rigged up, long before the evening rise on the big pond. I felt fresh, but wobbly, as if we'd stopped too quickly. Wyoming is not nearly so formidable when it's where you're going.

Late that afternoon we putted across the pond in the boat to fish by wading the far shore. My first trout, a little ten-inch brown, hooked himself as I was impatiently stripping in a bad cast for another try. This doesn't quite qualify as catching a fish by mistake—I mean, you *are* fishing, after all—but it's not what you'd call a fine job of trout angling either.

Jay had suggested streamers until things picked up, so I'd tied on an all-purpose olive-colored Weedless Wooly, and was practicing my distance cast. I'm not too bad at this as long as real tournament ranges aren't called for, but when I haven't been on still water for a while it takes me a good twenty minutes to work into it.

For that matter, it can take me a little while to get into just plain fishing itself when things back in the world have been hectic. My pace is wrong, and there are all these things in my head, including the lead guitar part from a certain Led Zeppelin tune.

Working on the long cast is a good beginning. With all that line in the air you have to tell yourself, Sloooooow down on the backcast. What's the rush? Dad used to ask me that when I was a teenager. "What's the rush?" It's as fair a question now as it was then, and it always seems to come in his tone of honest curiosity. Like if there was a good reason, then okay.

And don't put your shoulder into a distance cast, you think. You've been doing this long enough to know it's not a matter of brute force. This expensive bamboo fly rod with the nickel silver fittings is here to work, you are here to orchestrate.

Jay, of course, was casting beautifully right off the bat in that crisp, businesslike way that graphite rod fishermen have. And this after checking in at the factory that morning, and then driving for five hours in a souped-up Blazer, screaming snatches of conversation over a howling electric guitar. But then, he's in a different line of work.

In a technical sense, the cast is the soul of fly-fishing. When you have it down, you're there. In a nontechnical sense, you can then begin to consider where "there" is.

In this case, it was the valley of the North Platte River: the thin strip of riparian habitat along the stream itself, with high plains on either side of that, and the beginnings of forested foothills beyond *that*. The ponds were in the open, low-lying dishes tucked into miles and miles of sage, but from just about any of them you could spot hills and some trees if you started to get a little agoraphobic. Farther to the west are the Sierra Madre Mountains, to the east the Medicine Bows. It's classic western ranchland—prairie with water—and mercifully far from the interstate highways.

Jay had told me how good this water was, and I believed him without reservation. We have one of those unspoken treaties that would go something like, "I'm too good a fisherman to lie, and you're too good to believe me anyway." Still, the first night at a new place breeds misgivings. With coaching, you know what to expect, but in another just as real way, you have no *idea* what to expect. At first the big pond lay there, glassy and ordinary-looking, except that this was known to be fine trout water. The effect is not unlike seeing a sports car crouched under a canvas tarp.

The first few trout were small, and came from the weedy shallows on our side of the drop-off. I'd released my first one with some impatience, but by the time I hooked the second the cast was working more smoothly, and I took a minute to look at him. A foot long, nicely colored, healthy, little teeth, staring eye: a regulation, pan-sized brown trout, but, nonetheless, a new fish from new water. And you can't have big trout without some little ones.

Not long after the sun went off the pond, the first boils appeared predictably over the deeper water, and I experienced that psychological squaring of the shoulders—the old, "Okay, here we go, better evaluate the situation."

The specks in the air, on closer inspection, turned out to be gangly, long-legged midges looking like mosquitoes, but without the little hypodermic syringes. The slightly larger check marks on the surface were Callibaetis mayfly duns with the particular mottled markings on the wings that would key them out—if one cared to go through that agony rather than fish—as one of the twenty-some species of this bug.

And the caddis were just caddis, big enough to pick out clearly even at some distance. They were also what the fish were eating.

I'd tied up some of these large bugs with quill wings and sparse hackles for still water, but it had turned out that they didn't float well. Fly tying lesson #248: a size 6 dry fly can't be dressed as lightly, relative to hook size, as a size 14. There's too much steel in the hook, too much weight for the surface tension.

Then again, these things would float for a cast or two if you didn't skate them, and once under the surface they made a fair emerger. Lesson #249: don't throw the flies away too soon.

After a dozen or so casts with the caddis, I snapped the fly off in a fish that left a loud, flushing boil behind it, the kind of cold-water shark that forces the smaller fish to feed shyly somewhere else, giving the impression that there *are* no little fish. I nicked two more very large trout, but lost them, and finally retrieved the fly and sharpened the hook. Then I popped the fly off in a fourth trout by setting up entirely too hard on the strike.

I was getting pretty excited, which is something you don't actually have to do. When fishing writers describe the circus atmosphere of a good rise, they are mostly putting their own emotions onto the trout. You don't have to be cold-blooded to be a good fly-fisherman, but there are times when you need to remain calm. It sometimes works to just watch for a few minutes, perhaps breathing deeply and slowly at the same time.

Okay, in reality, trout weighing several pounds eating large flies is a perfectly ordinary circumstance here. It probably happened last night, it will just as probably happen tomorrow night, and after you've packed up and left, too. It's business as usual.

Since I'd looked last the sky had gotten purple. A great blue heron was flapping slowly off to the west, long neck tucked up, legs trailing behind him sentimentally. Nothing out of the ordinary.

I retied the leader with a heavier tippet, knotted on a new fly, and methodically sharpened the hook to a needle point. Okay. Then I looked up to see that the bugs were gone and the rise was over, just like that. That purring, splashing sound was Jay reeling in and wading back toward the boat.

The next morning we loaded the belly boats into the truck, and drove back up the road a mile to Jay's favorite pond. It was a small one, the kind where fishing from a float tube gives you a feeling of omnipotence. It was kidney-shaped, deep in the middle, and had a mucky bottom with lots of weeds. There were stands of cattails along the inside curve of the bank, and a long inlet arm snaking off to the south. Along the north end was a muddy slide where the cattle waded in to drink. All in all it was your standard stock pond, except that a little after dawn there were big trout charging around in it, leaving their wakes and swirls on the surface.

That morning Jay had said that if there were damselfly nymphs in the water to use my best copy, otherwise use a leech.

"How about the big caddis?" I asked, always wanting to fish the dry fly.

"Maybe tonight," Jay said, slamming the truck a little too quickly over the washed-out clay road leading to the pond.

Wild stories and predictions are what you usually hear on the way to someone's favorite water. Jay said very little, but was clearly in a big hurry to get there. There was no rock and roll now, though. Now it was just grinding gears and meadowlarks.

Ten feet into the shallow end of the pond, I looked down and saw the pale green, inch-long damsel nymphs in the water. Herds of them were migrating to the weeds where they could crawl out and hatch into flies. Some were climbing onto the float tube with me. They were all action, wiggling frantically, and making as much headway side to side as forward, sort of like a chubby old house cat trying to run.

It was too shallow yet to use the flippers properly, so I was pushing with my heels, kicking up billows of mud, and tying on a damsel fly nymph.

My damsel nymph is pretty basic for this day and age: thin-bodied with a wisp of marabou at the tail, bluish-green pheasant hackle, and—the one concession to snazziness—black painted bead chain eyeballs that are so easy I couldn't resist. People have sometimes admired them, which is often as good a reason as any for tying a particular pattern. They also work, which is the other reason.

Jay paddled to the deep water, while I worked out along the weed beds. Neither spot was any better than the other, he said. It soon became obvious that damsel nymphs were boiling up out of every inch of bottom, and the trout were everywhere, feeding actively, but languidly, as if, sure, this is great, but we're sort of used to it, you know?

Jay and I were both into fish within a few minutes, and it was hot. The strikes were nearly always the same: a dull thud in the rod as the fly just stopped in the water, then an almost audible thrumming in the line as it went tight, and vibrated from the wrist out. Then, after what seemed like a second or two of indecision on the part of the fish, the no-nonsense run began, during which you had better not have line tangled around your flippers.

Some fish bored deeply, others jumped. A few were so big and portly they tried to jump, but couldn't, and ended up wallowing almost pitifully on the surface.

We must have taken a dozen trout each that morning, all rainbows. None were under eighteen inches, none that we landed were over twenty-two. I took some color photographs. The fish we managed to break off may have been bigger yet (as you automatically assume) or the results of operator error, or maybe strained and weakened tippet knots. Let's say they were bigger. Let's say that especially because Jay had caught, earlier that year from the same pond, a seven-pound brook trout, one of only a handful of brookies that had survived a planting some years ago.

Seven pounds is a hell of a big trout, let alone a brook trout. As firm and healthy as those rainbows were, the biggest ones we caught that morning still only weighed five, tops.

Did I say "only"? You know what I mean.

It had been furious at first, and had then petered off in roughly fifteen-minute increments until the strikes were noticeably few and far between, our arms were sore from fighting fish, and you'd have to look for quite a while to find a damsel in the water. At about ten o'clock Jay switched from a damsel to his secret leech pattern, and began trolling the deep trough.

I took a shore break. A belly boat is probably the most comfortable thing to fish from, with the possible exception of a lawn chair, but it's still good to get out after a few hours, especially when you forgot to pee before you got in that morning.

And so we fell into the program. The damsels in the early mornings were like clockwork, always there, and always good. From ten o'clock to about noon you could pound up a few more trout on leech patterns. Then, in the late afternoon, *something* would happen. It was never quite the same twice, but the fish would feed, and after a while you could figure it out.

Of course, if so much as a single big caddis showed itself, there was no guessing. That was the one bug that every piece of trout water seems to have: the one the fish will eat, whatever else they may or may not be doing. It was the mythical sure thing, and we had it covered. We'd captured a few naturals the first night and I had copied them at the portable fly-tying kit using light wire hooks and lots and lots of ginger hackle to stand them up on the water.

In fact, we had it *all* covered for once—hatches, flies, timing, place—and the fish were all big. It does sometimes happen that way.

The hot afternoons were down time. There were naps—some planned, some inadvertent—and I made entries in the notebook that seemed at the time to have something to do with the story I was supposed to be working on. It wasn't the story itself, nor quite an outline, nor all of it even on the subject at hand, for that matter. During the all-nighter I'd pull back home to get the thing out on time I would discard page after page of it, wondering vaguely what the hell I'd meant by this or that. This mess is what a writer is usually talking about when he refers to his precious "notes."

These were long, slow, hypnotic breaks with the craziness of some very fast fishing just over with, and more of it coming up in the evening, as soon as the sunlight slanted and the air began to cool off again. I'd lounge on a flat spot between the truck and the pond, using the beached float tube as an easy chair, notebook on knee, pen in one hand, can of lukewarm beer in the other. If pressed, I could say I was working, but I'd catch myself thinking, for instance, that it was going to be good to see Susan when I got back. Not aching to go home or anything, just thinking how it would definitely be okay when I *did* get back. I mean, you do have to go home sometime, right?

Regardless of what you've heard, it's entirely permissible to miss the girlfriend while on a fishing trip, especially between hatches, but you do have to watch it when you have a pen in your hand. If you're not careful, all your sunsets will be orgasmic, and all your trout will be pulsing and throbbing.

One afternoon we drove into town for a good meal. Not that we were exactly starving, but we'd been putting away convenience store camp food that does little more than keep you going. Jay had set the tone the first night with a frozen pizza cooked in the propane oven. It was okay, although gnawing it off the charred cardboard was a chore.

Town was Encampment, Wyoming, on the small river of the same name. Downtown consisted of a general store, the Bear Trap Cafe, the Mangy Moose Tavern, and very little else. Over prime rib at the Bear Trap I asked Jay about the Encampment, and it turned out to be yet another in a growing list of little streams a guy really ought to get around to fishing sometime. There are so many little streams, so many cafes. Some days it's almost too much to contemplate.

"I've heard there are trout in it," he said; "I guess it can be pretty good."

The waitress came over to ask how the food was. "Great," we said, which was not an overstatement.

"I'll tell him you said he was a pretty good cook for poor white trash," she said, nodding toward the kitchen door. I smiled, thinking she was surely kidding.

"Leroy!" she yelled. "These guys say you're a good cook for white trash."

I stopped chewing. Jay glanced around to check the location of all the exits.

Leroy, all 250 pounds of him, came to the kitchen door, gave us a blank stare, and winked at the woman.

Local humor.

***

That was the evening the net disappeared. I had an especially big rainbow right in front of the tube—twenty-two inches easy, maybe twenty-four, a glorious, side-of-bacon-sized trout—and when I reached smoothly for the net where it should have been fastened to the D ring on my right, it just wasn't there.

I'd never landed a trout that big by hand before. It wasn't easy.

This was a wooden net and should have just been floating out there somewhere, but it was gone. I looked for a long time while Jay caught fish, occasionally saying things over his shoulder like, "Maybe it's still in the truck," to which I'd answer, "No, I just had the damned thing ten minutes ago."

The night was warm and still, stars were out, coyotes were yipping close by. My net was lost in Wyoming.

That was the one night when the trout got a little spooky and leader shy for some reason. This naturally calls for lighter tippets and smaller flies— the standard trout technician countermove. Fine, but these were very large trout, and as I rerigged with a smaller fly and thinner monofilament, I realized that this would make the fish easier to hook, but also harder to land, so that the closer I got to success, the closer I also got to failure.

An interesting thought. Also an apparent dead end.

As I mentioned, the trailer didn't have electricity, but Jay is a bit of a gadget freak and had a tiny, battery-operated television set in there. We turned it on that night to catch the news.

The picture was grainy and the sound was poor, but we could make out that a large building somewhere had fallen on a whole bunch of people, killing most of them. It occurred to me that, out here, things the size of a K-Mart could fall out of the sky all week, and probably not kill anything but a few prairie dogs.

So there was more trouble out in the world, which we could have guessed, but probably could have lived without hearing about. Frankly, it was hard to feel too sorry about it. This stuff happens all the time, and it's become a survival skill to avoid letting your heart break every single time.

The guy doing the southern Wyoming weather report didn't seem too sorry either. He came on right after the film of this horrible accident and said that weather prediction up there is easy. "It'll either be too hot, too cold, or too windy tomorrow, ha, ha."

***

Back in Encampment, Jay had made a phone call, and so had I. It became obvious that we were leaving the next day, but not before fishing those damsel flies one more time. In the past few days I had landed more twenty-inch and bigger trout than in the two or three previous seasons combined. Still, a few more wouldn't hurt.

I didn't waste any valuable time looking for the net again. I'd be pissed off enough about that later to snap at the guy at the fly shop, but at the moment the trout would be biting. I had two of the damsel nymphs left, and, if those got lost, a couple of small olive leeches that should work. I knew what should work now.

It was the kind of morning I'd come to expect. I even learned how to hand-land the big, slimy fish with a little bit of style; came out of the damsel hatch with one fly left; switched confidently to the leech and kept catching fish. Put simply, I was happy.

We'd agreed to leave around noon, at the beginning of the long dead stretch that would last until evening. It wasn't that long a trip home from here. We'd be back about the time the rise began. I knew how it all worked now, and that's as good a time as any to go.

Even Brook Trout
Get the Blues

The Family Pool

THE Family Pool is in the Cheesman Canyon stretch of the South Platte River in Colorado. This is an old favorite fishing spot of mine—the pool in particular and the canyon in general—so I naturally thought about trying to disguise it here. That sort of thing is entirely permissible when writing about fishing as long as you don't get too cute or too superior about it.

I considered it, but then realized that in this case I didn't have to worry about revealing the spot. After all, this particular section of the Platte is a kind of showpiece trout river. It has been designated by the Division of Wildlife as a Gold Medal stream, and by the U.S. Fish & Wildlife Service as an irreplaceable, class 1 fishery; it is the state's oldest and best-known catch-and-release area (to hold up your end of an angling conversation in Colorado you have to have fished it), and the fight over the proposed Two Forks Dam project has brought it to regional, if not national, attention.

In old newspapers you can find photos of various dignitaries and celebrities who have fished the canyon or, more likely, the water below it that's easier to get to. President Bush has never fished it, but I know he's been invited.

Some years ago a friend of mine sent an article on Cheesman Canyon to a national outdoor magazine and the editor wrote back, "Christ! Don't you guys in Colorado fish anywhere else?"

In other words, it's a famous river, and I guess I'd have trouble referring to it as "a pretty good trout stream somewhere in the Rockies" with a straight face.

In a part of the country known for pretty canyons, Cheesman is an unusually handsome one. It's steep sided, narrow, deep and raw looking, with sparse stands of spruce and pine where it isn't littered with fabulously huge, lichen-covered granite boulders that have come loose and plowed their way down from the canyon walls.

I have never gotten used to the size of these rocks. You're supposed to feel insignificant when you look at something like the night sky, but what does it for me is something more immediate, like a lopsided pile of five boulders, each one bigger than my house.

The stream stair-steps down through this in riffles and smooth, green pools, making some of the most luxurious pocket water you'll ever see. A series of fishermen's trails now run the length of it, but there are places where the footing is skimpy and dizzying, especially in those spots where the trail leads you high above the river and the gravelly scree that passes for soil wants to crumble away under your feet.

From those vantage points—on days when the light is good and the wind is down—you can usually spot fish in the pools, although you learn that when conditions are such that you can see them, they are damned hard to catch.

The Family Pool itself is near the bottom of the canyon. When you hike in on the Gill Trail and begin to work your way upstream, it's about the sixth obviously good hole you come to. I could tell you to look for the big rock, but that probably wouldn't help much.

I don't know for sure how it got its name, but I have a theory: The pool isn't properly a pool at all like some of the other placid holes in the canyon, but more of a braided run at the end of a long riffle. Trout feed well in the faster water there, and the current helps to mask flies that are a little too big, not to mention slightly sloppy casts and drifts that are less than absolutely perfect. When you're standing on the trail above it, the Family Pool is one of the places where you usually *can't* spot trout, even on a bright, calm day. Relatively speaking, it's an easy spot to fish, and I think people used to bring their families there so the kids could catch something.

That would have been in the old days when you could kill trout. It's rare to see a family in the canyon anymore. Now it's mostly serious grown men dressed from the better catalogs.

It would also have been in the old days that you could have legitimately called the Family Pool—or any other spot in the canyon—"easy." Even before the no-kill rule, a lot of canyon regulars released all their trout, and the fishing got progressively more difficult in the years after the regulations went on, finally leveling out at what I guess must be the upper intelligence level of your average trout. You can still catch them—and sometimes you can do very well because there are a lot of fish in there—but you cannot make many mistakes. The fishing has been described as "highly technical," and beginning fly fishers have been heard to say they don't think they're ready for the canyon yet.

I know what they mean by that because I wasn't ready the first time, either. I had more or less learned to catch trout with a fly rod, and had reached that first plateau where you begin to think, This is not as hard as some people make it out to be. Then, after the first few times I sauntered into the canyon—the picture of confidence with store-bought flies and freshly patched waders—I had to admit that maybe it could be pretty damned hard after all, and frustrating, too, because the fish were big and you really wanted them.

I stayed with it, though, and eventually started to catch trout there. I had to because it's a rite of passage. Around here, if you don't crack the canyon, it will be said that you never really got serious about fly-fishing. My first few trout in the canyon were from the Family Pool, up at the head of it in the fast water where a good old Adams dry fly would pass for the more accurate Blue-winged Olive mayfly dun I later learned to use in the slower water.

I guess the Family Pool was the first spot in the canyon where some of my friends and I actually gained some purchase on what was then the hardest trout fishing we'd ever tried to do. It was also the first place we learned to put a name to. A passing fisherman told us what it was called back when there were few enough other anglers that you could stop and talk to them.

We got into the small, entomologically accurate fly patterns everyone said you needed (nothing bigger than a size 18) and began carrying boxes of tiny nymphs, floating nymphs, emergers, thorax duns, stillborns, no-hackles, parachutes, and so on.

Those of us who weren't into it already took up fly tying because we couldn't afford to buy all this stuff. Then we began to argue about whether the trailing nymphal husk on an emerger pattern should be wood duck flank or dun hackle tip. We also worked on our casting a little bit and began carrying spools of 7x tippet material.

This is where we began to realize that successful trout fishing isn't a matter of brute force or even persistence, but something more like infiltration. Technique is part of it, but so is keeping your head straight and your touch light. We were proud of our successes and became philosophical about them. This was about the time when we all started saying "Fishing is like life," which of course it is.

For years we'd head to the Family Pool first because—if things were right and no one was on the water ahead of us—it was usually good for a couple of fish. Hooking a few right off the bat would wire us up for the rest of the day and we'd eventually wander off to other spots that we came to know as The Wigwam Pool, The Ice Box, The Channels, The Flats, The Spring Hole, The Chute, The Holy Water—and to a few other places that I really *am not* going to tell you about.

Still, when A.K. or Ed or Jim Pruett or I would go down there in separate cars, all we'd ever have to say was, "I'll meet you on the river," without having to specify the Family Pool.

Another nice thing about the Family Pool is that it fishes pretty well in most stream flows, except for the very highest when it becomes the Family Rapids. There are a lot of spots in the canyon that fish nicely in one kind of flow, but not so well in others. I don't have a problem with that. In fact, it's fun to be able to look at how high the river is and sort of figure where you might be able to catch some fish. But it's also handy to know of a place that will probably be good no matter what—as long as you can get to where you have to be on it.

When you come into the canyon you are on the north side of the river, but if you want to fish the Family Pool you need to be on the south bank. Trust me on this, I've tried it both ways. On the north bank you are standing among the fish and it just won't work.

In normal flows, there are two places to cross the river in this stretch; one below the pool and one above. When the river is running high, it's best to try crossing at the wide riffle upstream. A good wading staff helps. I learned one spring, after nearly drowning, that if the wading is too tense there, then the pool is too high to fish well anyway.

And when the Family Pool is too high to be good, you probably should have gone to a different river or maybe to a farm pond for some bluegills.

I know that I first fished the canyon in 1974 because that was three seasons before the catch-and-release regulations went on. That would be eighteen years, two wives and six jobs ago now. Technically, this makes me a veteran: a guy who remembers it from "before"—the main difference between then and now being the number of people. You naturally enjoy this old-timer status, and glorifying the old days a bit seems unavoidable. I do remember when there were more 18- and 20-inch trout in there, but, honestly, there was never a time when they were *all* 20 inches.

The size of the trout and their numbers have fluctuated over the years and there have actually been some poor to mediocre seasons, although, to be fair, even then the trout in Cheesman Canyon are a little bigger and some prettier than most around here.

There are those who say the decline had to do with poaching, while others claim it was the fault of the people at the Denver Water Board who do damaging things with the stream flows at crucial times of year. When we're not trying to address them politically, some of us think of the Water Board as a malevolent natural force—the modern equivalent of evil spirits.

The fisheries biologists I've talked to aren't sure, but they won't rule out the stresses on the fish from continuous, heavy fishing pressure or even natural population cycles. Or, for that matter, all of the above plus some other things we don't know about.

The last time I was down there it seemed to me there were fewer trout than in recent years, but some of them were bigger. And so it goes.

A lot of new fishermen began to show up when the no-kill rule went on, and we learned, along with the Division of Wildlife, that enlightened regulations can be even more glamorous than good fishing. In this context, there are two extreme kinds of anglers. Some just don't fish a place until it becomes fashionable, while a few others slink away the minute it does. In the long run, there are always more of the former than the latter.

Most of my friends and I fall somewhere in the middle. We bitch about the crowds and have taken to fishing the canyon on weekdays at weird times of the year, but we keep going back, even though now there are people on the water we don't recognize—not so much the individuals as the type.

For instance, there are the guys who carry those pocket counters in their vests. Ask one of them "Are you doing any good?" and he'll whip the thing out and say, "I have taken 27 fish since nine this morning. That would be an average of 6.75 trout per hour."

"Ah . . ." you say, for lack of a better response.

When we started fishing the canyon together, my friends and I saw the catch-and-release business as more mysticism than game management—an attitude that I know aggrieves some fisheries biologists who just don't see the religious implications of it. And there was also something in there about an enlightened lack of competitiveness that would eventually lead us into harmony with ourselves and the environment. We gave this some thought at the time, or at least we directed a lot of talk at it.

Eventually that mellowed to the kind of perspective the Division of Wildlife guys might agree with. You hike in and fish hard and as well as you can. At the end of the day when you climb out of the canyon, you're refreshed from the "quality Colorado outdoor sports experience," but you're empty-handed, however well you did. Having to release any trout you catch means—in an odd sort of way—that it doesn't matter if you catch any or not.

But of course it *does* matter if you catch fish or not. It's a paradox, and as any fisherman knows, one good paradox can cancel out hours of idealistic wrangling.

You can get better at fishing as time goes by (simply getting better is probably the ultimate goal of the sport), but there's a moment when your ideas about it set up and become more or less permanent. Then you spend the rest of your active life trying to balance the way things should be with the way they are. Maybe it has more to do with your age than anything else. I know a number of people whose thoughts on sport solidified—for better or worse—in their early to mid-thirties, and that was that.

I think my own glowing vision took shape sometime after I began to catch trout on dry flies in the Family Pool on a fairly regular basis and felt ready for more difficult water and a bamboo fly rod. On film that vision would resemble a trout-fishing documentary starring Thomas McGuane, written by Russell Chatham and directed by Akira Kurosawa. You're not aware of this kind of thing when it happens, but in retrospect you come to know that it occurred while you were knee-deep in a certain pool on a certain river in September of 1979. You were fishing a #18 Blue-winged Olive emerger on a 5-weight fly rod that you no longer own.

So the Family Pool has become a kind of focal point for some of us. In a way it reveals more about our feelings for all this than water we fish more often because it's always an event. The place is only a two-hour drive and then a short hike from here, but weeks and even months go by when we don't get down there. Still, this is the best trout water any of us fish on a regular basis. It's a treat; a homecoming; also a trip where you take one of your very best bamboo fly rods. When we fish it we're on our best behavior—that is, we're about as serious, careful and patient as we ever get.

It also comes up in conversation a lot. On a cool, overcast day in March, someone is likely to say out of the blue, "This would be a good time to be fishing the Family Pool," and then someone else will pick it up. "The flow will be about 300 cubic feet" (probably lower, actually, but we're fantasizing now) "and a midge hatch will be on. Or maybe the mayflies are starting." There's a moment of silence then as we all visualize it. This exchange usually takes place in town, although it's even been known to happen on another trout stream if the fishing is slow.

Don't get me wrong, the fishing can be slow in the Family Pool, too. Because of the crowds in the summer, we now fish it mostly in what some think of as the off season—roughly from October to late March or early April—which would include the late and the early Blue-winged Olive hatches, with midges in between. It can be cold then, and there's an ancient stone fire ring on the south bank where—I like to think—generations of fishermen have built willow-twig fires for warmth and coffee while waiting for the trout to start rising. The fishing can be surprisingly good between fall and spring, but the hatches can be spotty, and patience is often called for.

I also like to think that if this old, blackened fire ring wasn't already there when we discovered the place, we'd have built one ourselves. This is a good pool that's worth waiting out, and it's also a friendly, domestic sort of spot that encourages coffee breaks, conversation and the occasional deep thought.

I think it was there that I finally decided to quit smoking, even though I know I'll always dearly love the drug, and even though I didn't tackle the job that very day. It wasn't the constant harping from the Surgeon General that did it, or the pointed suggestions of friends, or even the fact that the whole culture is encouraging tobacco heads to kick. The fact is, I've never responded well to criticism. The more people told me I shouldn't do it, the more I thought, It's a free country, I'll smoke if I want to.

What it was, finally, was the realization that I am a plodding worker and a slow learner and it's going to take a long life for me to enjoy the few things I'll ever figure out. That, I suppose, is the kind of thing that comes to you on the bank of a difficult, but familiar trout stream—not to get sentimental about it or anything.

And there's been some serious talk around that fire, too. Up until recently a lot of it had been about the proposed Two Forks Dam project that, if built, would have flooded much of the river. Not long ago the Environmental Protection Agency, after many delays, finally came out with a final veto of the project. Oddly enough, those of us who had opposed the thing for years didn't buy champagne and celebrate. I think we were a little numb, feeling less like we'd won a battle and more like we'd just narrowly escaped getting hit by a truck.

So lately the talk has been turning to how good it is to have the canyon back. (It did seem for a while as if we'd already lost it.) Of course it doesn't stop there. There seems to be an unlimited supply of persistent, hard-hearted bureaucrats out there, and the pouting water providers who've been deprived of their project are now saying the new dams that will have to be built will cause even more environmental damage than Two Forks would have. It's an undisguised threat that, I suppose, sets the tone for the next fight.

But until that fight shapes up, we can't seem to leave Two Forks alone. The party line had been to defend the canyon and the miles of water below as pristine wilderness, although water providers who did their home-work—not to mention habitual devil's advocates like Ed—pointed out that the fishery in question is actually somewhat artificial.

Releases from the existing dam at the head of the canyon keep water tem-peratures more or less uniform and create a tailwater fishery, or a kind of man-made spring creek. Wasn't it a little paradoxical to have been fighting to save a stretch of river from a dam when said river was *created* by a dam?

Well, no, I'd tell Engle. A thing's origin in the past (going on a century in the past in this case) doesn't have anything to do with its quality in the pres-ent. And the sketchy historical info indicates this was a pretty good fishing stream even before Cheesman Dam, although it was cutthroats then instead of browns and rainbows. And the canyon still *looks* exactly like it has for a million years.

Goddammit, Ed, I know you agree with me on this!

But to Ed, arguing is a sport, sometimes even a contact sport, and to an outside observer our friendship would look like a running rhubarb that's been going on for almost twenty years now. The point he's making is valid, though: Isn't it interesting that the logic you apply to the opposition is abrupt and unforgiving, while the reasoning for your own position is fluid, creative and finds room for infinite subtleties?

About then someone sees a trout rise—or thinks he does—and everyone watches the water. Sure enough, a couple of fish have begun working down in the tail of the pool. Okay, who's going to try for them first? And what do you suppose they're feeding on?

No one goes out of his way to make this point, but it's another good one: You must be an environmental activist at some level—there's no way around it that'll still let you live with yourself—but you should never get so grim about it that you stop enjoying what you're supposed to be fighting for. Even if you lose in the end and some consortium of bastards dams the river, it won't be because you didn't speak up. And for the moment at least, you are still living in the good old days.

***

I moved west in the late 1960s and have lived around Colorado ever since. Montana, with bigger rivers, fewer people and harder winters, beckons occasionally, but I guess I like it here well enough. For some reason, I finally settled on the outskirts of Lyons, a town that's roughly the same size as the little Illinois burg where I was born.

Small towns are all the same. I lived here a long time before there were any signs of acceptance, and when they came they were not in the form of a parade down Main Street. Some people tentatively called me by name or ventured "How's it going?" Being a small-town boy, I knew enough not to actually tell them, but to say, "Oh, just barely gettin' by," to which they'd reply, "Well, that's about all you can expect," and I'd say, "Yup." So now I'm a local.

A friend once told me that I'm ahead of my time here, that is, I'm stuck in the sixties, but Lyons is stuck in the fifties.

I think all I had in mind at first was to get out of the hot, sticky, crowded Midwest and become the kind of guy who knew the names of the pools on a great trout stream, knew the hatches and fly patterns, knew where to find dry wood for a fire on a cold day and otherwise just felt at home. And if that stream wasn't 100 percent natural, then I'd know of some that were.

From that standpoint, I can say that my life has been an unqualified success. I guess I've gotten used to it all by now—even gotten blasé about some things—but, luckily, I still get knocked out by where I am on a pretty regular basis.

Sometimes it happens when I just walk out my front door at home to go look in the mailbox. There'll be traffic on the road out front, but there are some pretty foothills to the south and west that are a hell of a lot farther away than they look. I've lived here long enough to be able to calculate, or at least come to grips with, the distances. Even though I'm down in the mouth of a little valley here, I can see farther than I ever could in Illinois or Minnesota or Ohio.

I'm not too far from a good-sized town, but there are things that make me feel nicely removed: the hills, the eagles in the air and the fact that when I make the last turn west heading up to my house, the sandstone ridges do something to the public radio station I listen to that makes Vivaldi's *Four Seasons* sound like it was being played on kazoos.

And, not incidentally, there's a little creek across the road with some brown trout in it. These are not the most gorgeous hills or the most magnificent creek in the Rocky Mountains, but they are nonetheless *in the Rocky*

Mountains, and if you were born a midwesterner you'll never outgrow the idea that this is exotic stuff.

Something like a sense of place kicked in when I moved here, and I realized that I felt genuinely comfortable for the first time in my life. The air was clear and dry enough; the rocks and trees were the right color; the water was as cold as I thought it should be. Maybe this was profound, or maybe it was just the result of watching too many western movies as a kid. Whatever, it has never worn off.

Not everything that's happened to me out here has been wonderful, but even when things were grim, the scenery was still gorgeous and the fishing was good. There was always the consolation that I was a boy from the Midwest who had infiltrated a new environment—creating only a few ripples in the process—and learned to be at home in the Rocky Mountains. So whatever unpleasant crap was happening to me, I knew it could have been worse—I mean, I could have been poor and troubled in Cleveland.

If I haven't become a genuine westerner, I at least now hold some of the appropriate opinions. I think my part of the country is being used as a nuclear waste dumping colony by the East, and if we were smart, all of us west of the Mississippi would secede.

And when a book reviewer refers to Tom McGuane as "a Marlboro man with a taste for quiche," I see it as typical Eastern Seaboard myopia, as if brilliant novels written by someone from the Rocky Mountains—or anywhere outside of New York City—somehow violate a law of nature.

Interestingly, many of the people I fish with now are also transplanted midwesterners, and I think we all get into this to some degree. After all, life is going to be the way it is no matter what, but we live in a place we like now and that means a lot to those of us who appreciate countryside.

Even after quite a few years of fishing the Family Pool, someone is bound to poke the fire during a lull in the conversation and say, as if he'd just noticed, "Shore is purty here, ain't it?"

Relatives back home tell me I speak like that now—with a western accent—although I can't hear it myself. To me it sounds perfectly normal.

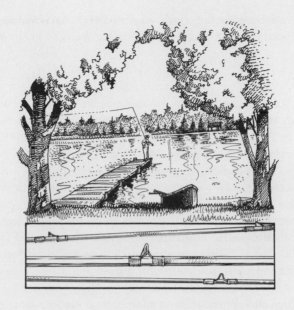

Bamboo

STEVE Binder is the most dedicated bamboo rod collector I know. For a while he said he honestly didn't know how many rods he owned, then, not long ago, he said he realized that was some kind of avoidance tactic, so he counted them. At the time there were around fifty. He hasn't fished all of them because they're coming in too fast, but he's working on it. I've never been out with him when he didn't have a trunkful of rod cases, and I'm not sure I've ever seen him fish the same rod twice, although one gets confused in this blur of varnished bamboo.

Steve is the kind of fisherman who'll ask, "If you could only have fifteen rods, what would they be?"

He told me he got into this not to amass a world-class collection or to make a profit (although a profit can be made if you know what you're doing) but just to learn about the rods because he liked them and was curious and had the money to buy them.

I believe that. I've only known Steve for a few years, but he seems like the type who'll dig into something that strikes his fancy and come out a few seasons later somewhere between a topflight amateur and a pro, just for the sheer hell of doing it.

I once suggested that to his wife, Sharon, and she said I had no idea how true that was. There's probably a story there. Probably none of my business.

Last July Steve invited me up to his cabin at the Kenosha Trout Club for what sounded like a theme fishing trip. Bobby Summers, the famous rod maker from Traverse City, Michigan, was flying out to fish with Steve, and they'd decided to make it a party. Two other well-known rod makers, Charlie Jenkins and my friend Mike Clark, were going to show up, as well as me and Bill Vidall, not collectors in Steve's league, but definitely accumulators and users of bamboo rods.

I try never to pass up a chance to fish this great private lake from the comfort of Steve's old but posh cabin, and I figured I could pick up all kinds of esoteric, inside stuff about bamboo fly rods if I could just keep my mouth shut and listen. It sounded like a good group—if a little too big—and, yes, it also sounded pretty high tone.

There's an atmosphere of classy sport around Binder's cabin that I find hard to resist. It's not just the lake full of brook trout. Steve has set this thing up so that everything exudes either quality or the proper amount of funk, from the food and booze to the art on the walls to the surprisingly comfortable rocking chairs built like wood-and-gut snowshoes. Naturally, there's no telephone. Bamboo rods—reeking of tradition as they do now—fit right into that.

A.K. was invited, but, because of unspecified prior commitments, he would have time either for the Trout Club or the Green Drake hatch on the Frying Pan River, but not both. He would have loved to immerse himself in bamboo rods, talk and brook trout at a classy cabin in the woods for a few days, but, typically, he was more jazzed about dry fly fishing on the Pan, sleeping in his tent and eating canned Dinty Moore stew with hickory salt.

As I said, the prior commitments were not explained. In this group, the assumption is you'll go. If you can't, no one asks why for fear the reason would seem too trivial.

So it was decided that A.K. would go camp on the Pan at our usual spot behind Roy Palm's place in about a week, and I and anyone else who wanted to would join him after we finished at the lake.

Then we decided none of this would be right if Ed wasn't there, so he agreed to drive up from Palmer Lake and meet us on the Pan on or about a certain day.

Steve's son Cass would probably show up at some point, and it wasn't clear how much of this he, Vidall, Charlie or Mike would be in on. I tried to keep it all straight for a while, then decided I wasn't in charge, so I didn't have to worry about it.

Finally, A.K. called Roy over on the Pan to ask if he minded having a slightly larger mob than usual camping on his property. No, A.K. said, we didn't know exactly how many, but this was beginning to look like the trip that takes on a life of its own. Roy said he understood, having been on a few like that himself.

I talked to some friends who bring in my mail and feed my cats while I'm gone; said I didn't know exactly when I'd be back. That was okay, they said, "We aren't going anywhere for a while."

I filled the saddle tanks on the pickup with 32 gallons of gas, strapped the canvas canoe on the roof, threw in the float tube just in case, and checked the camper for the tents, tarps, camp stove, coolers, food boxes, water jugs and such that are always supposed to be in there, ready to go. Then came waders, flies, fly-tying kit, reels, and five or six of my best bamboo rods.

I had discussed which rods I should bring with A.K. like a schoolgirl deciding on what dress to wear to the dance. A.K., always the pragmatist, said, "Bring the rods you'll use and then throw in a couple of pretty ones."

I met Binder and Bob Summers at the cabin. Actually, they passed me a few miles from the dirt road turnoff and I chased them the rest of the way. I'd been driving slowly, enjoying the kind of dreaminess I get into now at the beginning of long trips with no clear end.

I met Summers as he held the gate open for me at the club. Steve set about the practiced ritual of opening up the cabin, while Bob and I unloaded gear. At some point cold beers appeared. Then Mike Clark's big white fishing van with the belly boat rack on top eased down the drive. There were more introductions, more beers and more people trickled in. As fishing expeditions go, the atmosphere was more social and less, shall we say, "businesslike" than I'm used to. Still, it wasn't long before rods were strung, canoes were launched and fish were caught.

And then Steve was firing up this thing that looks like a cross between a propane tank and a jet engine and cooking his famous Cajun blackened steaks. Until I met Binder, I didn't like blackened food—I thought Cajuns were an unfortunate race of people who couldn't sing and couldn't cook— but Steve is one of the few who can burn the meat just right.

For the next few days some people came and went—Cass showed up late, Charlie Jenkins had to leave early, etc.—and we fished with, cast and talked about bamboo rods, sometimes far into the night. I don't know how many rods were there. Charlie, typically modest, showed up with two of his, and he'd have only brought one to fish with if Steve hadn't wanted to look at the other one.

Summers, out of his Michigan element and not knowing what to expect, had brought a pretty good stack of his rods, from short and light to long and heavy.

Mike Clark was also well represented. He had a couple of his own rods, Binder had one and I had two. If I remember right, Vidall ordered a rod from Mike on, or just after, this trip.

And there were some Grangers, Heddons, Winstons, Leonards, a Pezon et Mechelle, a Thomas & Thomas, a couple of Dickersons, and I don't know what all else. A rod would come out of its tube to be admired, and then we'd all naturally have to go down to the dock and try it. All of us, that is, who hadn't wandered off to catch brook trout.

Then another rod would be brought out for comparison, which would remind someone of another rod he'd brought, and so on into the afternoon. There were graceful, demanding parabolics; delicate, weightless midges; crisp dry fly rods; thunderstick western wind rods.

As you might expect, the three rod makers were thoughtful casters. They'd false cast a new rod tentatively, cocking their heads as they felt it load, then watching the loop over their right shoulders, not forcing themselves on it, but waiting for the rod to show them what it wanted, then saying something like, "Uh-huh," or maybe, "Ah."

Every now and then trout would start rising within range of the dock and someone might think to tie on a fly.

When one of the guys who'd gone off to fish wandered back to the cabin, someone would say, "Did you get a chance to cast Mike's eight-and-a-half-foot six-weight?" and the whole thing would start all over again. There were rods lying in canoes, on the dock, on the picnic table, propped against trees, and hung on the inside and outside rod racks at the cabin. Somehow, none got stepped on.

One of Charlie's rods, a 7-foot 3-weight, was the very one that had come in second in some kind of bamboo rod competition that was held by the Anglers Club of New York a few years ago. I tried it out on the dock. It was a sweet rod in every way, and I'm sure it and Charlie deserved the honor, but I, for one, would never be able to judge an event like that: objectively rating one good rod above another, and then telling other people what I'd decided as if that actually meant something.

Rods are like books. I can usually tell quality from junk, but the idea of rightness is harder to pin down and impossible to defend. For instance, if you happen to like John Updike's novels better than those of Jim Harrison, as some deluded easterners do, what could I possibly say to make you feel otherwise?

I did eavesdrop on the three rod makers a few times and, after talking with Mike off and on for quite a few years, I should have known what to expect. Aside from sheer castability and workmanship, Binder comes at rods in terms of their history and collectible status, while I think more about warmth and tradition, but the rod makers talked about glues and varnishes, planes and forms and milling machines and heat treating and where to get good stripping guides: the nuts and bolts of it that, I have to admit, don't interest me all that much.

The secrets I had envisioned learning boiled down to one: that these guys were simply working craftsmen with an abiding interest in the details of their jobs. They're not gurus, and they seem a little puzzled by the fishermen who want them to be.

It actually seems like a fair division of labor. Those of us who use bamboo rods—sometimes spending more than we can afford to get them—formulate the poetry and the romance, while the makers simply work to build the best fishing poles they're capable of.

When things got too technical, I'd go out and catch brookies. The fish have their moments there, but mostly they are friendly, easy trout that will bop a weighted Hare's Ear nymph or Elk Hair Caddis dry fly that's fished with any attention at all.

I've never done as well there as Mike did one afternoon when he stood in one spot down at the outlet and caught no less than forty trout, but I was doing well enough that I found myself airing out rods I'd brought to show off rather than to fish, just to remember how they felt with a trout on.

We ate well at the cabin: steaks, spaghetti, hot green chili and, one day, an incredible mess of brook trout. The club's management strategy had recently turned from numbers of fish to trophy size, and to that end they wanted the larger brookies thinned out heavily. So one morning we all dutifully set out to kill lunch. I'm an advocate of catch-and-release fishing (about 98 percent, as Mike says) but I've found that in recent years I'm more and more delighted by an excuse to kill and eat wild fish. They're just so damned good and, yes, they're noticeably better when caught on a bamboo rod.

The trout were butterfly filleted, slathered with butter and herbs, quickly grilled and served with beer and potato salad. I don't know how many fish there were, but they stuffed seven grown men to the point where we were all staring at the last two saying, "No, go ahead."

One night, to get a taste of local society, we drove to a roadhouse not far down the highway that's patronized mostly by people driving large, black motorcycles. It was a cozy, friendly place with a resident Doberman who seemed to recognize the smell of fishermen. On the only other automobile in the parking lot, there was a MADD (Mothers Against Drunk Drivers) bumper sticker. Inside, the bartender was wearing a DAMM (Drunks Against Mad Mothers) T-shirt. The food was great.

The next afternoon we pulled into Roy's place on the Frying Pan. Some people had dropped off in the days we were at the cabin, and when the trip finally shifted into Phase Two it was down to Binder, Summers and me in two vehicles.

A.K.'s camp was set up when we arrived. It was typically snug and efficient: fire, shelter, light, food and a cooler of Coors Light laid out more or less in order, designed for quick escapes in the mornings and lounging in the evenings. A.K. himself was off fishing.

Ed wandered in later that day, and by the time we headed out to fish the evening hatch there were four pickup trucks parked as discreetly as possible back in the trees, a circle of tents facing a fire pit, A.K.'s elaborate camp kitchen, which is known locally as "the A.K. Box," a folding camp table compliments of Binder, aluminum lawn chairs, a stack of firewood covered with a tarp and, of course, Roy's dogs.

There's always a changing roster of retrievers here, Chesapeakes, usually, and they always move right in to the current fishing camp. This time it was our old friend Teal—now semiretired and a little gimpy—and an adolescent Chesie named Gus. Gus didn't understand what was going on, but he seemed eager to learn.

When Roy came home from his fly shop down in Basalt, he wandered out to say hello and said it looked like a tribe of Gypsies had moved in on him. I don't know exactly how he meant that, but I liked the sound of it.

The fact is, enough visitors camp here in a given year that Roy recently erected a palatial outhouse. Before the cement stoop was dry, he scratched "Dedicated to friends and fishermen" in it with a stick. It occurred to me that this might just be self-defense against having God knows how many visiting fishermen shitting God knows where around the place all summer, but I finally decided it was just one more example of Roy's considerable class and generosity.

The running bamboo rod discussion had actually begun to peter out over the last couple of days—it's a bottomless subject, but it's possible to get numb, and there are, after all, fish to be caught. But then that first evening on the Pan, with some new people, and some new rods, it started up again, and Roy, who I'd never seen fishing anything but a graphite, went up to the house and came back with a lovely little 7½-foot Gary Howells, so as not to be outdone.

The whole bamboo rod business can get pretty complicated. Among the old rods there are legitimate museum pieces; a whole range of collectibles from rods by acknowledged masters like Payne, Garrison and Gillum down through many other individual makers; to Leonards, which, for some reason, seem to be in a high-priced class by themselves; to the good production rods like the Heddons and Grangers; merely decent production rods like South Bends and Shakespeares; real antiques; some curiosities and some out-and-out junk.

Among the new rods are those made by companies like R. L. Winston, Orvis and Thomas & Thomas; rods built by dozens of independent makers now working around the country—ranging from famous masters to unknown hobbyists—and some imports.

And then there are obscure models, special models, limited editions, one-of-a-kind custom rods perhaps built for celebrities, rods made by one company but with another company's name on them, vintage nameless rods of various quality made by who knows who, the T&T rod built for the prime minister of Australia and so on. As I said, it's a bottomless subject.

Somewhere in there you cross the fuzzy line between fishing rods and collector's items, and that's what clouds things up. That and money. I hesitate to get into actual figures because they change constantly, but I'm the one who brought it up, so here goes.

For between $700 to $1,600 you can get, at this writing, all kinds of new and used production rods, new and used contemporary handmade rods and a fair range of collectibles. Some of the rods in this group will increase in value sooner and more spectacularly than others. Damned few will lose their value, assuming they don't get slammed in car doors.

There are some good, usable fly rods for less than that, although many of the old, quality production rods that were once affordable are being sucked into the vacuum left by the top-of-the-line collectibles, some of which are now going for five figures.

Discussions of money are unavoidable when it comes to bamboo rods because they *are* expensive and there are precious few real bargains left. A good, usable bamboo fly rod will now cost you between twice and five times the price of a top-quality graphite, and therein lies much of the mystique.

In some circles, how little you paid for a rod is a matter of status. In other circles it's how *much*. I've been told of bragging matches where one collector says, "I fish my $3,000 Payne," and another counters, "Well, *I* fish my $6,000 Garrison. So there."

If by "fish" they mean they took it to a nearby stream once and caught a few little trout just to see what all the fuss over Payne and Garrison was about, okay. Anyone would do that. But if they mean they threw it in the pickup and took off for a couple of weeks in Idaho, I don't know if I believe it, or if I'm impressed.

It's like the guy who made the news a few years ago for paying half a million dollars for a bottle of wine at auction. "What are you going to do with it?" the reporters asked. "I'm gonna drink it," he answered.

One hopes, depending on one's opinion of the idle rich, that it was either damned good or that it had turned to vinegar.

I guess the collecting end of bamboo rods interests me because I have the same morbid fascination everyone has with rare old items costing large amounts of money, and because some of the used rods I bought to fish with not too many years ago are now beginning to appear in the rod lists well out of my price range. But I really just like to fish them, and so I wish they weren't so expensive.

Then again, you have to look at that from the proper perspective. Let's say a good rod maker builds you a handmade bamboo fly rod for $800—a more or less reasonable price these days. He's probably put about forty hours into it; his raw materials and parts are expensive and sometimes hard to find; he's got tools and machines to buy and maintain; rent on the shop; plus all the odds and ends that accumulate in a small business, like stationery, business cards, brochures, advertising, shipping and whatever else. Not to mention screwed-up blanks that get broken up and tossed in the wood stove, bad checks and the years he probably spent learning how to do this, during which he didn't make a penny and spent at least a small bundle to get set up.

In the end, you're looking at a highly skilled, self-employed craftsman who's pulling down $8 or $10 an hour at best, which, to me, does not seem unreasonable.

To put it another way, it's your lawyer and your doctor who drive BMWs and vacation in the Bahamas, not your rod maker.

I picked a lot of this up from hanging out with Mike. I met him years ago when he was just starting to make bamboo rods. He was working nights and weekends in a friend's wood stove–heated garage, hand-planing rods and financing the whole thing by operating heavy equipment. He reminded me of some starving artists and writers I've known.

I'll spare you the full-length sob story. It's enough to say he worked long and hard, burned up a lot of unsuccessful blanks in the stove, spent his rare days off fishing prototype rods to see how they acted and didn't start selling rods until they were good, even though people had begun to pester him, and even though he probably could have used the money. I got the third one he made for sale, a few years later I got a second one and now he's making me that 7 foot 9 incher.

For a long time Mike was an unusual rod maker in that he only did custom work—no standard models. He'd work out length, line weight and action with each new customer, and then he'd ask the guy what kind of reel seat, spacer and color of wraps he wanted; whether the hardware should be blued or shiny; whether he wanted a hand-rubbed tung oil or a varnish finish and so on. In the end, no two rods were alike. This cost Mike more in time and materials, so his profit margin was lower, but he said it was more fun that way.

Mike still does mostly custom work, but he has finally allowed himself to develop a handful of more or less standard models, if only because so many people have asked him to reproduce certain rods. I'm proud to say some of those were first made for me and A.K. It's not that we had much to do with their design, but we did ask Mike to build them.

Because so many of Mike's rods are unique (and because he's getting to be well known), some collectors are already interested in him. In the grand scheme of things, his prices are still reasonable, but the day will probably come when he joins those few contemporary rod makers whose rods are collector's items before the varnish is dry. When that time comes he may be able to drop another new engine in the van.

One evening on the Frying Pan, A.K. said it was a relief to be in a group where no one was asking, as some people do, "Why do you guys fish those old wood rods?"

I knew what he meant, but I actually like it when people ask that. Fishermen are usually fairly crazy, and their main goal in life is to grow up to be even crazier yet, so when one of these nuts walks up to me and asks why the hell I'm doing what I'm doing, I feel like I'm really out there—well on my way to becoming the cosmic old fart.

But the social implications are a side benefit. The fact is, when compared to graphite, bamboo is better in every way for the kind of fishing I do, that is, casting at normal ranges with light- to medium-weight rods for trout, bass and panfish.

A bamboo rod loads more naturally and reacts more organically to the whims of the caster. It's also more forgiving than graphite, so in the end it's much easier to cast well if you're not an expert. People worry about the slight extra weight, but all that does is make the rod work more while you work less so that, even though a comparable graphite is lighter, I find it more tiring to cast. And I'd hate to hear what our forefathers—who fished 10-foot solid greenheart rods weighing a couple of pounds—would say to all this whining over a couple of ounces.

I find that a good bamboo rod will mend line with more authority, cushion light tippets better and play fish with more stubborn guts than any graphite I've tried.

For sheer sensuality of casting and for fishing that requires some subtlety, a good bamboo rod is simply the superior instrument, so it doesn't really bother me that it costs several times what a graphite does, because it's several times better.

Not that I'm what you'd call a stickler for quality in general. In fact, my life tends to operate on the "good enough" principle most of the time, but fly-fishing is what I love the most and have stayed with the longest, so it seems logical to do it with the finest tools I can afford—or not afford, as the case may be. The fact that my house, clothes, pickup and such don't live up to that model only seems to make the rods stand out more brilliantly by comparison.

And they are just plain beautiful, which I think is why collectors have glommed onto them while pretty much ignoring rods made from other materials, however old or historically interesting they might be.

I've considered getting into collecting as such myself, and after talking about it with Binder for a couple of years, I can see how it might be fun: buying some rods that aren't too pricey right now—but that I've guessed will evolve into the next generation of Gillums and Garrisons—and just stashing them away for ten years to see if I guessed right.

I mentioned that to Ed one afternoon while we were sitting around drinking coffee, and he asked me if I really wanted to get into taking great fly rods out of circulation and hiding them until they were worth so much no one would ever fish them again.

Ed does that. He's an intellectual saboteur who will make you examine your own thinking with a critical eye whether you want to or not.

Ed and I do have somewhat different visions of the world. I once told him that if I couldn't fish with fine tackle, I might not fish at all. He said he'd fish if they made it illegal and he had to do it at night with a pitchfork. Be that as it may, I still usually find his logic inescapable.

We talked about it for quite a while, getting into things like how human beings attribute value, the morality of turning a profit through inaction, what you're really doing when you take something that could be part of your real life and turn it into a monument, etc., and Ed finally convinced me—or helped me to convince myself—that I should simply buy the rods I wanted to fish if I could afford them, and if they ended up worth a fortune someday it would give my surviving relatives a nice surprise.

And it isn't all about money, either. There's a lot of good, honest nostalgia connected to bamboo rods. Mike Sinclair once showed me a sweet old 10-foot Orvis rod from about 1890. It was a handsome rod with a sheet cork grip, red intermediate wraps, sliding band reel seat with a maple spacer, but the best thing about it was, it had old, dried trout scales stuck in the varnish on the butt section. You've got to think these are from trout caught on a hot day a hundred years ago, and if you're like me, that makes your mind go all soft and gooey.

I used my 8½-foot 5-weight Clark most of those days on the Frying Pan—it's still my favorite fly rod—but I did break out the old San Francisco Winston for a day, and when we hiked up to some beaver ponds to catch cutthroats, I took the 7½-foot Thomas & Thomas Special Trouter.

Summers fished various Summers rods that Binder was drooling over, Ed fished a sweet old Granger Favorite, Binder fished God knows what all, and A.K. alternated between his workhorse 6-weight Clark and his magnificent prototype Heddon President—a rod he keeps talking about retiring, but that he's fished enough that it's had to be refinished twice.

There was some snazzy lumber around, but now we were really *fishing*. We all happened to be doing it with bamboo rods, but that was no longer the point. Binder said later he'd felt the gears shift that first day on the Pan when he asked A.K. if he wanted to try a certain rod, and A.K. said, "Maybe later, right now the fish are biting."

Steve finally decided he had business to take care of (a bad bamboo rod habit takes capital to support) and Summers had a plane back to Michigan to catch, so they left first. A.K. got to thinking about all the fly orders he had to tie and left a day or two later.

Ed and I stayed on a while longer, but the fishing was so good we were running out of things to prove, so when we came to the end of the groceries it seemed like it was probably time to go. We stopped in Basalt for breakfast before we drove our separate ways, and I got a *Rocky Mountain News* from the machine in front of the cafe, more to find out what day it was than anything else. The headline said that the invasion of Kuwait by Iraq would probably cause an increase in gas prices.

"What invasion?" I said.

"I don't know," Ed answered, "but welcome back to civilization."

I know it bothered A.K. not to be among the last to leave, but he'd finally located a pod of fish he couldn't catch, and that, after days of fabulous dry fly fishing, seemed to satisfy him somehow.

These trout were in a tight little backwater against a steep, moss-covered shale cliff miles downstream from the head of the Green Drake hatch. It was one of the prettiest and most difficult spots I've ever seen on a trout stream. The current you had to cast across was fast and too wide to reach over. The current you had to get a drift in was braided and flowing pretty quickly in the other direction. The right cast put an S curve in the line with one belly upstream in the main current and the other upstream in the opposite direction on the far side of the stream with enough snap in the delivery to pile the leader for a drag-free drift of maybe 6 inches.

The trout were big, some of the biggest we'd seen. They were rising happily to Pale Morning Duns, nosing up into the current and then dropping back, never in the same exact spot for more than a few seconds at a time.

If you've been toying with the idea of getting a bamboo fly rod, watching A.K. cast will push you over the edge. I've seen it happen. On a lawn or casting pool he looks like anyone else who's a pretty good fly caster, or only slightly better because of that fluid, almost relaxed pace bamboo trains you into. But on the water, with rising trout and conflicting currents . . . Well, it's just something you have to see.

He never did hook one of those fish, although he did miss a strike or two. He spent hours at that pool, taking a break to fish easier water only to rest it. When we first found this place, A.K. was using either the Heddon or his 7½-foot 5-weight Clark, I don't remember. When we went back the next day, he switched to the 8½-foot 6-weight Clark. You could say the spot captured his attention. He said it called for a rod with some reach and, once a fish was hooked in that fast water, some authority.

A.K. manages to have more fun than any fisherman I've ever known. Here's a guy who's fished for God knows how many years in Michigan, the Mountain West and a handful of exotic locations. He's one of the top professional fly tiers in the country, author of one of the best fly-tying books ever written and owner of a pile of fine bamboo fly rods, all of which get used.

Still, every fish he hooks might as well be his first, and every fish he can't catch is some kind of profound joke. Once in a while he'll say "Shit!" when he misses a strike, but nine times out of ten he'll laugh out loud.

That's what he did when he finally reeled in and walked away from that pool, knowing he'd be breaking camp in the morning—he laughed, said, "Well, that was fun," and wiped off his rod with a bandanna because one never puts a bamboo rod back in the case wet.

On our last day, Ed took up A.K.'s position at the pool and, after several hours of trying, caught one of those big trout. It was as simple as that, as amazing things always are when they finally happen, although catching a trout that A.K. couldn't get is not something that happens every day. It was a brown, 19 inches, Ed guessed, and he usually guesses small.

When I got home I called A.K. and told him about it.

"Good," he said, "good for Ed. What rod was he using?"

Montana

I ' v e spent a good deal of time in Montana over the years, but, as any of my friends from up there will tell you, I'm still a tourist from Colorado: a guy who drives up to the Big Sky Country when the fishing is good, but who spends his winters safely at home, in the balmy climate of the foothills 700-and-some miles to the south.

They'll say "balmy" because when it's 25 below zero here—as it occasionally is—it's 50 below in Montana. Of course with the windchill factor, that would be more like minus 80. If it snows 3 feet here on the Platte River drainage, you can bet they got 10 feet in the Absaroka Mountains, or at least that's what they'll claim.

My friend James Goossen wrote from Billings last winter saying it was so cold he saw a lawyer with his hands in his own pockets.

This "ours is bigger than yours" business is the kind of thing Texans used to pull until everyone got sick of it, but in this case it *is* true for the most part. Montana is bigger, emptier and less civilized than Colorado. At last count, there were fewer people in the whole state of Montana than there are in the city of Denver (a favorite statistic of Montanans and Montanalovers alike). Consequently, the place is richer in fish, game and open land. It's also tougher to make a living there, and, yes, the winters can be horrendous. Having spent some of my boyhood in Minnesota (which is roughly level with Montana on the map), I understand that living through bad winters is a justifiable point of pride.

There's a mythology in operation here, and most Montana writers have gotten around to authoring the "I Was There When the Big One Blew In" story; you know, the one about that first monstrous blast of winter coming in from Canada: the storm that shows us who's boss. These things usually read like notes from the edge of the world. They're all similar, and they're almost always good.

I guess I'd always been a little envious of that—it's hard not to envy those Montana writers in any event—but now, after this last trip in the final week of October, I finally qualify.

I'd been hunting with Dave Carty, and it had been one of those brilliant trips. We'd shot many Hungarian partridge over Fancy the pointer in the fields around Bozeman and Livingston—with one especially fine day almost in the foothills of the Crazy Mountains—then we'd gone up along the Madison River with Poke the springer to get some ruffed grouse out of the places where the aspen and spruce came together.

(Yes, it probably goes without saying that the upland bird hunting in Montana is better than it is in Colorado.)

And then, flushed with sport and intrigued by variety, we headed up to the country around Denton, where Dave said we might be able to get into a few pheasants.

The pheasant cover was mostly along the Judith River, and Dave had permission to hunt on a ranch up there. There were also some Hungarian partridge on some local farms that, of course, Dave also had access to. We were in Dave's pickup camper with provisions, spare clothes, guns, maps and both dogs. The camper is a little oversized for the truck, so it wobbles from side to side like a Gypsy wagon.

We drove up from Bozeman and went to the wheat field first, just to get a few birds to start this leg of the trip off right. This was the place where Dave said he'd had his best Hun hunting that season. The weather was cool, crisp and bright: good for walking, but Dave said he wished it was wetter. Fancy doesn't scent the birds as well when it's dry.

No more than twenty steps into the field we jumped a small covey of partridge. They flushed in front of the dog rather than holding for the point, and they were well out of range.

We followed the birds for an hour or so, flushing them out of range and then chasing them down again until they started to get tired. This is strenuous work, and later Dave told me I'd held up well. He used to live in Colorado himself, but he's been in Montana long enough now to have taken on some of the native characteristics. What he meant was, I'd done okay for a guy from the banana belt of the Rocky Mountains. He'd have expected even less of me if I'd been from, say, New Jersey.

Dave was surprised that the birds were so spooky. In an accusatory tone, he suggested that maybe the farmer was letting someone else hunt on his land. Dave has many widely scattered places to hunt. That way the shooting is more natural, and, although he kills a lot of birds, he never takes too many from a single covey.

Finally the birds flushed over a low rise, and when we came over the top, a single got up. I missed it. We found that the birds had split up into singles that got up one at a time. Dave says this is standard practice for quail, but unusual for Huns.

We worked the field carefully, and Fancy did well. Dave shot two birds, I shot one.

While all this was going on, a breeze had come up, and it was a cold, steady one: the kind of autumn wind that cancels out the warmth of the light and then makes the sun itself seem chilly. I thought it was blowing out of the northwest, but I couldn't be sure. Back home the mountains are orderly and lie north to south. Up there the ranges are scattered all over the place, so I can't always tell where I am. From the high spot in that field I knew you could see the Judith Mountains, the Little Belt Mountains and the Big Snowys, but I couldn't tell which was which without the map.

I could have asked Dave, but didn't. For one thing, it didn't much matter. The pertinent bit of information here was that a big front was coming in quickly—any idiot could see that. For another, no true outdoorsman wants to have to turn to the guy next to him, point vaguely toward a distant cloud bank and ask, "Uh, is that north?"

As we worked those single birds with the dog, the breeze turned to an outright wind with moisture in it. The temperature dropped and there were visible slivers of snow in the air half an hour before the bank of smooth, charcoal gray clouds finally turned the sky dark. Disoriented or not, I could tell this was the kind of storm that comes from the north, down out of Canada. I did recall from the map that there was no range of mountains between us and the Canadian border, and at a time like this, "Canada" forms up in the mind as a dusty stubble field between you and the Arctic Circle.

We headed back to the camper for more clothes and wool hats. A blow like this can mean the end of it for a while, so we weren't anxious to stop hunting, even though exposed skin was beginning to sting.

Poke was locked up in his kennel. He whimpered joyfully because he thought we'd come back to get him, then he cried pitifully when he saw that we hadn't. Out there on that open, windy dirt road, he sounded pretty goddamned mournful.

We decided on one last, quick swing, and the last covey got up out of range again, with the wind, and were gone like missiles. The air was thick with snow then, and we couldn't see where they went. I remember thinking that, in the hand, a Hungarian partridge is a fat little bird covered with great fly-tying material that does not look very aerodynamic. Without much discussion we groped our way back to the truck and lurched off through the snow in what Dave said he thought was the general direction of Denton.

You know Denton: it's out in the middle of the open hay fields along the Judith. This is hunting rather than fishing country, although that, I suppose, is an out-of-stater's perspective. I've actually been told that there are plenty of trout in the streams out there for those who know when and how to fish them, it's just not the "high-fashion razzle-dazzle you tourists are looking for."

Anyway, Denton: It's about 7 miles up the county road from Coffee Break. There's a two-block, mostly one-story main street, much of which was clearly built before World War II. The same goes for most of the houses, of which there aren't many. This is an eminently practical town where you don't blow a lot of time and money building new stuff as long as the old stuff is still serviceable. There's no fly shop and whatever basic items a guy might need in the way of sporting goods can be picked up at the hardware store. Naturally, the tallest building is the grain elevator.

We had supper at the cafe (chicken-fried steak with gravy, canned vegetables, homemade rolls) and then parked the camper along the railroad tracks out by the grain elevator. This is the kind of informal industrial park that is technically private, but that's far enough out of everyone's way that you can probably camp for the night undisturbed. The local policeman may rattle your door at three in the morning because the camper isn't a familiar one, but he may not make you move, especially in a snowstorm.

It was stinging cold by then, with snow falling steadily in a high wind, and ten minutes into the settling-in process we learned that the camper's heater didn't work, even though, Dave assured me, it had worked fine just two weeks ago. After finding and studying the directions and then attempting a field repair, we lit the burners on the propane stove to take some of the chill off. It was better than nothing.

We slept that night with one burner turned to low and a couple of vents open for fresh air. The camper rocked like a boat in the wind, and snow rasped on the windward side. The small windows got milky with ice inside and out. Luckily Dave had brought both dogs, so we didn't have to fight over who got to sleep with a warm puppy. I got Poke, the temperamental genius who snores.

We'd had a few beers that evening, so naturally I had to get up in the middle of the night to relieve myself. I was barefoot and I wasn't thinking, so when I stepped outside the bottoms of my feet stuck to the steel tailgate of the truck like a wet tongue to a pump handle. I could picture being found just after dawn, half naked, frozen solid in an undignified pose. I began to empathize with cattle that freeze in their pastures on nights like this. There would be a moment of enormous helplessness, during which you would go ahead and pee anyway—one last, completely practical act before death set in. But then my feet began to come loose and it appeared that I would live through the night after all.

I had just enough of my wits about me to glance over at the town. Nothing moved and no lights were on. It's quite possible that many doors were unlocked. I could easily see from one end of it to the other through the snow. The geometric lines of the buildings were softened by the shapes of cottonwood trees in the yards, and it looked no more out of place on the northern prairie than a collection of magpie nests.

By six the next morning the wind had calmed and the air was cold enough to freeze my breath in my beard when I peeked outside. The sky was still low and gray, but it had stopped snowing. Smoke was coming from some chimneys, and plumes of exhaust marked a few pickups that were warming up.

We decided to bundle up and hunt, but when we found that the truck's engine wouldn't turn over we figured we'd better walk into town for a strategy session over coffee and pancakes. The dogs, assuming we were leaving them to starve and freeze, whined horribly. Hunting dogs who aren't hunting are pretty miserable anyway, and for some reason they always think the worst of you when things get a little grim.

We hiked over to the same joint where we'd had supper. It had been pretty good and it also seemed to be the only cafe in town. A dozen trucks were parked in front of the place, but otherwise the main street was empty.

We'd no sooner sat down and ordered breakfast than an old feller at the counter said, with an air of unquestionable authority, "Two degrees this morning." A dozen large men in coveralls and baseball caps nodded silently over their coffee. Either this guy was always right, or they'd all looked at their own thermometers. Every thermometer in town would have come from the hardware store across the street, so there'd be very little variation between them. It was 2 degrees out, no doubt about that.

Then the man said, looking at us, "You boys are hunting." Native Montanans don't inflect much, so a question sounds like a statement.

"Yes," I said, "birds."

"I was here before these birds was," the old man said, gazing out through the frosty window as if he could still see it like it used to be. Presumably the skyline of Denton would have been about the same back then. I thought of asking, "You mean these birds in particular, or the species?" but I knew what he meant and it's probably best not to be a smart ass with someone you don't know.

Turns out he didn't much care for the Huns or the pheasants ("chinks") because they were both introduced species and he thought they'd gotten together and run off most of the sharp-tailed grouse ("prairie chickens," locally). He knew we weren't after the chickens because that season was closed.

Of the grouse he said, "I used to shoot five a day behind where the bank is now." After a sip of coffee he added, "I was here before the bank, too."

The bank itself looked none too new. It was the kind of place that might once have been knocked off by armed men in fedoras driving touring cars.

The first newspaper I'd seen in a week was a thin one from Great Falls. It said that the presidential campaign was as nasty as ever, but that the whales trapped in the ice off Alaska had been saved. The cafe was warm and steamy enough that the newspaper was limp.

On the way back to the truck we stopped at some kind of machine shop with an OPEN sign in the window and asked a total stranger if we could get a jump. "Sure," the guy said, "take my car. The keys are in it. Cables in the trunk." There was only the one car.

Later I would have time to be amazed that this guy would just give his car to a pair of scruffy-looking hunters he'd never seen before—that kind of thing really doesn't happen much back home—but at the time it didn't seem too unusual.

I never did figure out what kind of shop it was, and I didn't give it a lot of thought because we were off to start the vehicle, chip the frozen dog water dish from the floor of the camper, and find some pheasants. There was no sign on the place, but I guess everyone in town already knew what it was, so they didn't need one. Denton is the kind of place where you don't make a big deal out of what should be obvious.

As it turned out, we would not get skunked that day. Dave would bag a couple of partridge in a stretch of sagebrush where we didn't expect to find them. When they flushed, I stood there marveling that the birds were in that kind of cover, while Dave, working on instinct, executed a nice double. Eventually, I made a nice shot on a high-speed cottontail. We would only see three cock pheasants in range: Dave missed one out along the river, and the other two were in a front yard in Denton, right next to some dead flowers in a white-painted tractor tire.

It was all winding down anyway. The following day I would get on a plane in Bozeman and fly back to Colorado. I had a bunch of frozen birds in my luggage—insulated with dirty laundry; I had staked out two small, obscure trout streams to try next summer; and I had been there when the Big One blew in. To tell you the truth, it was no bigger than the ones we have back home.

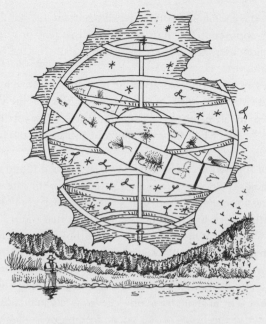

A Year in the Life

A few nights ago, February 13 to be exact, A.K. and I were driving back from our third trip this month to the South Platte River. It had been a cold, breezy day on the water, so when we finally broke down the fly rods and pulled off our waders, it felt good to get out of the wind and warm up in the cab of A.K.'s pickup. Say what you like about big, old American trucks, they have seats like couches and great heaters.

It felt so good, in fact, that as we drove up the canyon to where we catch the highway at the town of Pine, we began to get a little drowsy from the combination of warmth and weariness. This called for coffee and maybe a Snickers bar, but we didn't stop at the first little store, because by dark on most days the coffee there has turned lukewarm and sour. Instead we went 10 miles on down the road to the place where the coffee would be more or less fresh and where I could put real milk in mine instead of that white, powdered stuff. Being traditional field sportsmen, we understand these intricacies of survival.

The conversation picked up after that, and we began to congratulate ourselves on how close we'd come to hitting it the way we wanted to. February is when the good midge hatches usually start on the Platte. That's the *good* ones, as opposed to the thin, spotty ones that may or may not come off through midwinter. Around here, February usually has the first real dry fly fishing of the year.

The midges aren't as predictable as the Blue-winged Olive mayflies that come on in late March or April, but the expectation is definitely there. You can hit a decent midge hatch in December or January, but you'll consider it a tremendous break, while the same thing in February—though it's only slightly less rare—seems only right.

On each of the two previous trips down there we'd found a few trout feeding sporadically on the surface for a short time in the afternoons. Not what you'd call a proper rise, but, still, a handful of fish coming to the surface to eat little bugs with wings on them—a clue that the real hatch was building up. We'd caught most of our few trout those days on nymphs, but A.K., through persistence, had managed to hook a few on dry flies. Nymph fishing is okay—its saving grace being that it's difficult—but when you're doing it while waiting for a hatch to start it can begin to drag a little.

This last time—from about noon on—the trout had been nosing up into the faster water at the heads of the pools, feeding on midge pupae, and every time the wind would go down for a few minutes, they'd rise to the surface.

It was the wind that finally did it to us. It wasn't quite too strong for fly casting, but it ruffled the water enough that the trout couldn't see the size 24 midge flies on the surface, either ours or the real ones.

How many variables are there to hitting good dry fly fishing in the off season? Dozens at least, from great astronomical considerations down to the moods, currents and wind riffles in a stretch of river no larger than a bathtub. To guess only one thing wrong is a sort of victory. We'd caught a few fish as it was, but if it had been a calm day, we'd have hammered them. Or, so as not to sound too confident, we'd have had the opportunity to hammer them. Catching big, smart trout on tiny flies and 7x tippets in low, clear, cold water is not what you could call a foregone conclusion.

We planned the next trip for the following week, Wednesday or Thursday, when the front that caused today's wind was past and the next one would be somewhere between approaching and settled in.

Like all fly fishermen, we hate wind, but we also know that when you're trying to fish the hatches you have to court it. The best dry fly fishing seems to be on gray, wet, clammy days when the barometer is either low or dropping. You want it calm for all kinds of reasons—so you can see the rises, so the fish can see the bugs on the surface, so casting is easier, so you don't die from the windchill—but you also know the proper weather is the kind that *makes* wind.

Perfection in weather is hard to come by here in the Rocky Mountains, but the perfect days do materialize; days when a slow-moving or even a rare stationary low pressure system sets up over the river and, for a few precious hours, doesn't blow or clear but just squats there, dark, cold and drizzly. Eventually you come to believe in the old fishermen's weather mythology, because days like that are always good. You can never really count on them, but you know they'll happen if, as A.K. says, you go out often enough, always carry a rain slicker and learn to cast in the wind.

After enough trout fishing you develop a specialized perspective that some see as gloomy. On a bright, bluebird afternoon in April, someone will say, "Isn't it a nice day?" and you'll answer, "Humph."

So we talked and drove and sipped coffee and, somewhere around the Turkey Creek turnoff, A.K. made the annual announcement. "Well," he said, "I guess the fishing season has started."

Since you can fish legally all year here in Colorado, the beginning of the season is a personal matter, and figuring out when it is means you've learned something fundamental about how (and maybe even why) you fish. A.K. and I fish together for a lot of reasons, but mainly because we've arrived at this kind of thing together and now agree that the fishing season begins at that instant when catching trout on dry flies becomes more likely than unlikely.

This usually happens in February, but it's not a date you can mark on a calendar. It slides around from year to year. Still, when one of us declares the season open, the other no longer feels moved to point out that it never closed or that we've actually been fishing off and on for a couple of months.

It's just communication between friends, which, with time, evolves into a form of shorthand. If we're on the stream one afternoon and A.K. says to me, "It'll get darker sooner the longer we wait," I'm likely to say, "Yeah, I see what you mean."

So, although it's possible to fish hard right through the middle of winter, A.K. and I usually settle on going out a few times in late November, December and January to catch some fish as a kind of observance of the fact that it can be done. Usually we fish with fly rods in what open water there is, sometimes we noodle some trout or perch through holes in the ice, but mostly we take what amounts to a little less than three months off. A.K. ties flies for sale, I tie some flies for my own use and write. We go out when there's a break in the weather and/or when the shack nasties get too bad.

But there's something resembling a work ethic in sport, and when you decide the season has begun, things change.

If you miss the midge hatch in December or January, you recall the times when you hit it in the past, agree it was just nice to get out, and pretty much bag it. The season is on when you spend the drive home talking about *why* you didn't hit it this time and, more to the point, how conditions could shape up better in the next couple of days.

Your work habits begin to suffer, and you go down to the store to buy a big box of plastic bags and six cans of dolphin-free tuna because suddenly you're making a lot of sandwiches.

There was a time when former wives and some friends would start rolling their eyes at this point, but I've noticed that, over the years, city folk with no poetry in their souls have largely dropped out of my life of their own accord, so now there is little or no eye rolling to deal with. It's just fishing season. The most natural thing in the world.

Another thing that happens is, you begin to look ahead meaningfully rather than theoretically. When I say I tie flies through the winter, I mean I do it casually until about mid-February, all the while telling myself I really should get it in gear because the season is coming sooner than it seems. That's usually just enough tying to get me geared up for the minute #20 through #26 midges I suddenly realize I don't have enough of.

Naturally the little flies are the hardest, so the casual practice time is crucial. A.K. doesn't experience this—being a professional fly tier and all—but if you take a few months off from tying and fishing, your fingers turn to hams at about the same rate the wading muscles in your legs go soft.

A.K. has several midge patterns of his own design that work well for him and his customers. I end up copying a lot of what A.K. does—and I have been known to use his patterns—but my favorite midge is still the good old Kimball's Emerger. A.K. doesn't like this fly because it's ugly. I either think it's handsome enough or I like it precisely *because* it's ugly, but it catches fish anyway. Something like that.

This is a hackleless fly pattern, but I tried adding a sparse hackle to it this year to make it float better and land upright more dependably. A.K. thought that was a good idea when I told him about it. "It might make the thing a little prettier," he said.

That comment almost stopped me. When you get into fixing things that aren't broke, you can run afoul of the Law of Unforeseen Consequences. After all, I thought, tying hackle on a fly that works well enough without it might be like putting flying buttresses on an outhouse.

So I tied a half dozen with hackle that I'll try on the next hatch. If they don't work, I'll give them away and forget about it. If they do work, I'll tie a few more in different sizes and colors, but I won't throw the hackleless versions away, because they *have* worked and will again when the occasion arises.

That's why we carry so many flies: so that when what should work doesn't we have plans B through, say, E to resort to rather than just giving up. You *will* give up from time to time through the season, but it should always be by choice—because you're tired, or you've already caught enough fish, or you've been fairly beaten. You should avoid having to give up because there's nothing left to try.

All fly fishers carry as many patterns as they can, but we dry fly fishers are the worst. For one thing, our fly boxes don't reflect what you could call the reality of the sport, that is, that trout do the vast majority of their feeding under the surface on nymphs, larvae, pupae, crustaceans and other yucky-looking forms of aquatic life. If practicality was the issue, a guy would carry boxes and boxes of nymphs and a few well-chosen dry flies for the odd hatch.

But we dry fly types do it the other way around. We carry five or six boxes of floating patterns—those pretty, clear plastic boxes with the pool-table green felt bottoms—and maybe one old blue plastic case full of nymphs.

Bill Kelly, aka "Catskill Bill," a fisherman from Sullivan County, New York, calls dry fly fishers "10 percenters," based on the premise that trout do only 10 percent of their feeding on floating flies. I don't know exactly where that figure came from, but it's widely accepted and I like it well enough that I may start using it as a motto. I don't know if they still do it, but back in the 1960s, members of the Hell's Angels started proudly wearing "1%" patches after someone said in print that it was only one percent of the bikers that gave the rest a bad name.

Ten percent actually seems about right when you think about it; an appropriately slim chance for success in a sport like this. Fly-fishing in America still has a rural, Protestant flavor to it, and most of us live with the ideas that failure is the natural outcome of any human endeavor and that anything that's too easy isn't as good for the soul as it could be.

***

It's only February, but we're already talking about what happens after we
hit the midge hatch on the Platte. The probability that we *won't* hit it seems
low. We'll just keep driving down there. Fishing season is on.

After the midges should come the early Blue-winged Olives. Probably
the little #22s first, and then the #18s, with that almost inevitable day when
the midges will hatch in the morning and the Olives will come off in the afternoon. If we take a long shore lunch complete with a fire and coffee, we
could spend a whole day without ever defiling our leaders with lead
weights and sinking flies.

We'll try to hit this early on the Platte and maybe a little later over on the
Frying Pan, a trip that will involve the first tent camp of the year. If the
Olives run long enough on the Pan, we might try to combine that with
what Roy Palm calls the Mother's Day Caddis Hatch on the Roaring Fork.
This is a hatch we've never seen, but Roy knows it well and he has a boat.

Somewhere in there we'll doubtless hear from some frantic fisherman
that the stoneflies are on somewhere—probably the Fork or the Colorado—and we'll probably go at least once and just miss it. A year wouldn't
seem complete without blowing at least one stonefly hatch.

From then on the dry fly fishing should pick up. There will be little early
brown stoneflies, followed by little yellow stoneflies, with the many
species of caddis beginning to emerge as the weather warms.

Midges will hold on in some of the tailwater rivers, and they'll be important throughout the whole short high-country lake season. Some of those
lakes will also produce great hatches and spinner falls of Callibaetis
mayflies—Speckled Duns and Speckled Spinners—although there's no
telling when that'll happen. There are about sixty good mountain trout
lakes in the national forest, wilderness area and national park that form our
home range, and the only thing you can be sure of is that sometime between the first week in July and the middle of September the Speckled
Duns will hatch on about half of them.

There will be the little Pale Morning Dun mayflies in there somewhere—
at different times on different rivers—plus the tiny Trike duns and spinners,
various species of mayfly lumped together as Red Quills, a #14 yellow
mayfly locally called a Sulpher (although I'm told eastern fly fishers would
disagree with that) and, of course, the Green Drakes.

You can pretty much plan on the Green Drake hatch on the Frying Pan,
where I've seen it last as long as six or even eight weeks. It's less predictable and shorter on the Roaring Fork and maddeningly sporadic on

some smaller streams I know of. On some of the creeks you'll find them in two sizes, not unlike the Blue-winged Olives. The entomologists say it's the *Ephemerella grandis* and the *E. flavilinia*, but I prefer to think of them as the #10 and the #14.

Late in the Pan hatch there's a darker bug that some call a color phase of the regular Green Drake, others call a Slatewing Drake or a Great Red Quill, and that a few snoots insist on calling an *Ephemerella coloradensis.* Some years ago A.K. and I spent a long time trying to figure out what this bug was before we realized we didn't really care. All you have to do is tie a handful of your Drakes in a sort of negative mode: a reddish body with a green rib instead of a greenish olive body with a reddish brown rib.

After the Drake hatch on the Frying Pan and some other rivers, the hatches will come full circle and you get the late Blue-winged Olives and midges. It's almost like early spring again. Even the weather is about the same.

Last year we had one of our best weeks on the Frying Pan, the kind of trip a dry fly fisher just has to talk about.

The river was supposedly in a slump that summer, after getting famous in previous years for its artificially inflated trout. It seems the Division of Wildlife had planted some deep-dwelling freshwater shrimp in Ruedi Reservoir to feed the lake trout. This was a species of little crustaceans that lived at such dark depths they were clear. No body color at all.

But Ruedi is a bottom-draw dam—which accounts for the great tailwater fishery in the river below it—and the shrimp began to peter out into the stream. Naturally, the trout ate them, and in a few seasons the upper river was full of huge rainbows so fat and ugly they were almost obscene.

Just as naturally, fly fishermen came from all over to catch these things, local fly tiers went half mad trying to tie a clear scud pattern, and, from the point of view of those of us who have fished there for a long time, things generally went to hell for a while.

But then the scuds finally all flushed out of the dam, and one year the enormous, ugly trout were just gone. Word got out among the yuppies that the Frying Pan was in the shit hole, and they all blasted off for the next hog factory on the agenda.

Panic had set in, although all that had really happened was the Pan was pretty much its old self again: a beautiful little river with its usual astonishing dry fly hatches and lots of pretty, healthy, normal-looking trout. There weren't as many 20-inch-plus fish as there once were, but the accepted local wisdom was that, now that those nasty old hogs were out of there, the younger fish would fill in that slot in a season or two.

We were there in that week when July turns into August and the Green Drake hatch is still below the catch-and-release stretch up under the dam. There were some fishermen working the hatch, but not too many, and they all tended to cluster at the advancing head of it, so we'd just fall in behind this small mob and have all kinds of water to ourselves.

We would have figured that out for ourselves eventually, but we didn't have to. That first day I'd asked Roy down at the Frying Pan Anglers shop in Basalt where the Drakes were coming off. He said to look for a bunch of guides and sports and then fish a mile downstream. "The sport is the guy fishing," Roy said. "The guide is the one in the fluorescent hat standing next to him, pointing at the water."

In the afternoons, just as the Drakes were beginning to thin out, the Pale Morning Duns would come on. The fly that worked was a thing Roy and A.K. designed and that A.K. ties for the shop. It's like a Ginger Quill, except the wings are lighter, the hackle is yellower and there's a subtle pinkish color to the quill body. Roy calls it a Frying Pan Special.

Many of the fishermen on the river have now taken to calling Pale Morning Duns "PMDs," which I don't like because it reduces poetry to a set of initials and leaves the impression that these guys are in too much of a hurry to wrap their mouths around a pretty, Old World phrase. I guess it's better than the scientific terminology, though. Now and then you'll still meet one of those bug men who see you examining a natural fly and wade over wearing the dour expression of a fly fisherman about to speak Latin.

We fished for days. I forget how many, but no one wanted it to end. Every night in camp we congratulated ourselves for staying on the old water while the fickle headhunters had moved on, and wondered if this could last into next season.

We were catching trout every day, lots of them, and all on dry flies. There were as many as five of us fishing together at times, but we never felt crowded and I don't think anyone ever tied on a nymph. When the dry flies weren't on, we just didn't fish. Consequently, the camp was neater than usual.

For my caddis flies, I usually try to tie Elk Hair, spent, low water and skittering versions in dark and pale colors, all of which I could get in a single box if it wasn't for the giant lake caddis patterns that take up so much room. For the small stoneflies I use something that closely resembles the Len Wright Skittering Caddis fly.

For small mayflies I try for regular hackled flies, parachutes, thorax ties and no-hackles, often in both dubbed body and quill body versions. The Callibaetis dun can be copied nicely with either the A.K. Best Olive Dun Quill or the standard Blue-winged Olive (not to mention the good old Adams) in sizes 14 and 16, but I like to tie a special pattern with mottled gray partridge wings to mimic the speckled wings of the naturals.

The bigger mayflies usually pass with collar-hackled and parachute styles, although that apparent lack of confusion is usually made up for with color variations.

The midge selection is built around the Kimball's Emerger, with various trailing-husk and winged, hackled flies in different colors and sizes from 20 to 26.

Mayfly spinners are dubbed-body and quill-body flies with whole feather, clipped hackle or poly wings. A Red Quill Spinner in the right size could pass for just about any spent mayfly, but I like to have Chocolate, Ginger Quill, Pale Morning Dun, Callibaetis and tiny black and white spinners, too.

Then there are the Royal Wulffs, plus some buoyant-as-cork Royal Humpies and a couple of other white-winged flies for fast water, and the Adams dry in sizes 12 through 20—just because pure imitation isn't always the answer.

I'm not a real nut for terrestrials, but I like to have some black and cinnamon ants, flying ants, beetles, grasshoppers and crickets. Sometimes— rarely—there are actual falls of terrestrial bugs, but mostly they're good search patterns to work in the dead times between the morning and evening hatches in summer. This is when most fishermen will fish nymphs in the deep water, but A.K. and I feel that terrestrial dry flies are *fished,* while nymphs are usually *resorted to.*

We both carry emerger patterns to cover some of the mayfly hatches, and we have more or less worked out the touchy matter of definition here. That is, a dry fly not only floats on the surface of the water, it also has wings of some kind. Hackle is preferred, but technically optional. If it floats but doesn't have wings, it's a greased nymph.

We settled on this to put an end to those long theological discussions that would ensue if I caught eight trout on a floating nymph and A.K. landed six on a righteous dry fly.

The way it stands now, he would have done better than I did, number of trout notwithstanding. And if we're in the same situation and I put split shot on my leader and dredge up a hog brown from deep water, A.K. will be sympathetic. "It's a great fish," he'll say. "Too bad you didn't catch it properly."

***

This extends into the fly tying as well. We try to tie good-looking nymphs with the right materials, but when it comes right down to it, the wing case and shell back on a dark stone nymph can be any old feather dyed black, while the wing on a dry cricket really should be natural crow—black, yes, but with those subtle, purple, wasplike undertones.

Where this idealism comes from I can't exactly say, especially since we do fish nymphs and wet flies when that's what it takes and, for that matter, one of my favorite flies of all time is the Hare's Ear Soft Hackle, an ancient wet fly pattern that, as near as I can tell, harks back to the days when most fishermen thought of a dry fly as one you couldn't get to sink right.

There have been days when we just walked around during the dead times, dry flies tied to our leaders, looking for the odd rising trout in a backwater and waiting for the hatch to come off, but just as often we fish nymphs when that's all there is to do, and we do it more or less happily.

I guess what I'm saying is, we consider ourselves to be dry fly purists, but if you watched us fish on any given day, you might not be able to tell. It's more along the lines of an interior landscape.

It's also interesting that the dry fly ethic applies to trout and maybe grayling in flowing water, that it's less important on lakes and ponds, and that for other species of fish it dissolves altogether.

Maybe it's because we've both been at this for quite a while now, and started back when artfulness still outweighed practicality. The winged insects trout rise to—and the flies tied to imitate them—*are* lovely for the most part. Mayflies look like sailboats or angels; midges are delicate; caddis flies are quick and almost mechanical and crane flies look like miniature flying bicycles. The giant stoneflies are horrible up close, but in the air they look like armored hummingbirds. The underwater stages of these insects, however, all look like either worms or cockroaches.

It could be as simple as that: prettiness, plus the smaller chance of success that makes this a sport in the first place. Or maybe we just read too many of those old books where the authors said they'd rather fish chicken guts off a dock than tie on a wet fly, or words to that effect. We were young and impressionable once, you know.

And I think this thing we have for bamboo fly rods has something to do with it, too. It seems a shame to use a fine, handmade casting tool to lob a weighted, short-line nymph rig 10 feet when you could do the same thing just as well with a broomstick.

That might be why streamers are a kind of sidebar to all this—almost a separate discipline. Streamers sink, but you still *cast* them.

I guess we'd be hopeless snobs if it wasn't for that work ethic I mentioned. You fish as if how you go about it matters deeply, but you can't forget that it matters for unimportant reasons. It's not like religion. You're not trying to be saved through good works, nor are you looking to bring down the infidels. There's nothing like logic to this; nothing you could use in an argument and no reason to argue except for fun. It's just something we like to do: a habit, like wiping your hands on your pants.

I was fishing the Platte River with Ed once when a nymph fisherman waded past and said to him, "I guess you're gonna fish dry flies whether the trout want 'em or not, huh," and Ed said that was about the size of it. End of debate.

It seems to me that dry fly fishing is a lot like writing. There's room for great artfulness (not to mention the constant danger of self-indulgence), but in the end it's usually best when it's hard nosed: Start at the beginning, say what you have to say, and stop when you come to the end. The paragraph that begins "And so, as the sun sinks slowly in the west . . ." should always be deleted. There are even deadlines. A good mayfly hatch will probably only last a couple of hours, so you do the best you can in the time you have.

I ran that analogy past A.K. one day on a river somewhere. We hadn't seen a rise for hours and we were just standing around talking and waiting for the hatch to start. He said it sounded good, but he thought I was spending too much time thinking. "Maybe you should tie on a nymph and catch a couple of fish," he said.

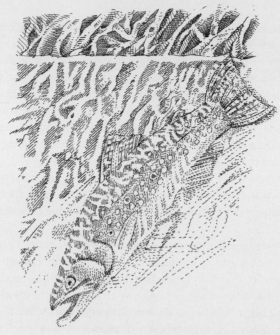

Even Brook Trout Get the Blues

FISHING is a collection of instants: moments when it either comes together with amazing perfection or goes horribly wrong. Never mind the vast silences between those times when something actually happens. Sure, the long, dead times set the tone, but you usually forget about them even as they're happening, or file them under some broad heading like "dues paid."

The hours of driving or hiking and then not catching fish once you're there are like the blank paper in Taoist paintings meant to suggest fog, out of which comes a single tree and half a bridge made more poignant by all that empty space.

Or maybe fishing is more like poetry: a different, more organic way of putting things together—very likely a superior way—that goes light on rules. There's really only one supreme rule in fishing. Namely, don't get too sappy about it or people will think you're a cream puff.

When it's all said and done, I think brook trout are my favorite fish, if only because good ones are so unlikely out here in the West—"good" meaning "big," of course, the complicated philosophy of aesthetics notwithstanding.

Brookies were originally introduced into the Rocky Mountains back around the turn of the century on the premise that more fish would naturally be better than fewer fish. That seemed reasonable at the time, but it turned out that brook trout outcompeted our native cutthroats for food and spawning habitat, and some biologists now trace the decline of many cutthroat fisheries to the introduction of brookies. In some places brook trout have been poisoned out so cutthroats could be reintroduced.

Brook trout also have very loose spawning requirements, so they tend to overpopulate, stretch the food supply and become stunted, sort of like bluegills in a pond with no bass to eat up most of the little ones. The fact that brookies seldom live past four years also helps keep them small, and it doesn't help that they're now mostly found in the backcountry where life for a trout is hard anyway.

The introduction of brook trout here is now seen by some fish culturists as a classic example of doing the right thing in the wrong way, a good-hearted mistake.

In his definitive *Standard Fishing Encyclopedia,* Al McClane says brook trout do fine in their native range—roughly from Georgia to the Arctic Circle and as far west as Michigan—but in general they do not introduce well. And, he goes on, "Large brook trout occur in the same regions where they existed millions of years ago—with very few exceptions."

Naturally, it's those few exceptions that interest fishermen most.

Brookies have an odd, contradictory status with western fly fishermen. We like them, but we think of them as little, which puts them in a whole different category. They're fun, they're pretty, but no one wants to hang a stuffed 8-inch fish over the mantel, or brag that he could have, but he turned it loose. Even the name "brookie" is diminutive.

We also tend to consider them easy, so we can't even agonize over fly patterns like we do—and want to do—when we're engaged in the more profound business of stalking big trout. If you hold to the full mythology of the sport, brookies and bluegills are the only two fish you can legitimately expect to catch on poorly tied #10 Taiwanese McGintys from Kmart.

But we do like them because they fill a need. In fact, they may actually embody the complete aesthetic of the sport: Fly fishermen have an investment in being serious while at the same time not actually taking it all seriously, so we like these little fish precisely because they're little and easy, even though as a rule we're into trout that are large and difficult.

However, because they're usually small, a big one is noticeably more mythological than a big rainbow, brown or cutthroat, so when a brook trout reaches a certain size we can get more excited, walk farther, stay out later and tie more flies than we did when we were just being serious. See?

Around here, the rare large brook trout occasionally comes from water where it doesn't belong—out of nowhere, in other words. You'll go into a bait shop or marina at a big reservoir and there on the wall, among all the huge stuffed rainbows, browns, pike and lake trout, will be a 3- or 4-pound brookie on a plaque. It'll be half to a quarter the size of any of the other fish, but big for a brook trout—well worth mounting.

Oddly enough, it doesn't look small by comparison, but stands out as something even more outrageous than the 20-pound Mackinaw right next to it. Maybe it's just the broad orange stripe at the belly, green back, white fin margins, yellow spots mixed with red dots haloed in blue. Brook trout are gorgeous, and taxidermists paint them up like neon signs.

This fish was caught accidentally by a troller, or maybe by a kid casting spinners off the bank for stocked rainbows. Whoever hooked it, it was probably the last thing he expected.

Brookies themselves are seldom stocked anymore, so how this one got in there is a mystery. The standard explanation is that it was born high up in a feeder creek, washed down in the spring runoff, somehow escaped being eaten by the big fish in the reservoir and then spent its short life growing to great size.

Or maybe there really is a small population of them hanging on in there from the old days. That would be plausible, since the big, shallow, fishy western reservoirs are something like the lakes in the brook trout's home range, where some of the really big ones come from. There's lots of room, lots of food and lots of big, predatory fish to keep their numbers in check, so the relatively few that survive can grow large.

You'll hear other theories, but the upshot is always the same: It's a fluke. There may be a few more, but it's not like you can expect to catch them. Big brookies are the exact opposite of the eager, easy little ones. As they become great, they tend to sink from sight.

Several years ago, Jay Allman and I were fishing some spring-fed prairie ponds in southern Wyoming, where the trout were gigantic. These were perfect stock tanks: secluded, private, water chemistry like champagne, forests of weeds, vast herds of bugs. No way they could have been any better. The ponds were full of rainbows that ran from a fat 18 or 20 inches on up to fish we couldn't land on good, stout tackle under favorable conditions.

But in the pond we spent the most time on there was supposed to be this giant brook trout. That is to say, Jay said he'd caught it once, either earlier that year or the season before, I don't remember which. He said it had come from the little inlet arm, that it had taken a leech pattern and that it weighed around 7 pounds.

He'd released it, so it was *supposed* to still be in there—even bigger now, you automatically think. Just the one, as far as he knew. Why and how? Who knew. Washed down out of the Medicine Bows one spring, or dumped in by one of the men who shared the lease, or dropped by a clumsy osprey. Who cares?

There's a significant difference between the big trout story and the actual report, but when the guy in the next float tube caught the fish and can point to the spot, you'd have to be the ultimate cynic not to buy it.

We never caught the fish or even saw it, but several times a day one or the other of us would paddle slowly up to that little inlet and fish it with the fly that was currently working. Not a fresh fly, but a used one all gooed up with rainbow slime so it wouldn't smell of human.

One can only wonder about some of the hogs we lost. They were almost certainly big bows because they fought that way—the few seconds of throbbing when you set the hook, the fast run that could backspool a reel with the drag set too light, then the not quite audible "ping" as the leader broke—but you can't be sure. I have no idea how a 7-pound brookie fights, and when it's between one kind of trout and another, guessing what you had on that then broke off is like calling a coin toss and then losing the quarter.

I don't know about Jay, but I caught more sheer tonnage of trout in a few days on that pond than I would land over the rest of the season. They were all rainbows, but I remember the place now as the little spring pond where there's supposed to be a big brook trout. Sure, it could have died of old age by now, or been caught and kept by someone else, but no fisherman ever really believes that.

It was the same story when Gary LaFontaine and I fished on the Blackfeet Indian Reservation in northern Montana five or six years ago. Rich prairie lakes, big rainbows and rumors of leviathan brook trout.

"Where?" we'd say, and we'd get a different lake from everyone we asked, not to mention a different weight—8, 9, 12 pounds. There weren't many of them, though, everyone agreed on that.

That was the trip where it rained constantly. It was early in the year, cold, bitter, and the harder it rained, the better the fishing got. We didn't catch a lot of trout, but it seemed like each one was bigger than the last. But no brook trout, not even little ones. Maybe we were on the right lakes and maybe we weren't. There was no way to tell.

One day we stopped at a hardware store in Browning. To make conversation, I asked the guy behind the counter how long it was going to keep raining. He said he didn't know, but the old man on the front porch could tell us.

So we asked. What the hell. The old man looked at the sky, held up one hand with the fingers spread and said, "It gonna rain five days."

It did, of course, but he could have heard that on the radio.

Out here, at least, that's how it is with big brook trout. They're supposed to be there, but you don't catch them, and you finally pack up and leave with the feeling that something unusual has happened.

Brook trout sometimes crop up in the work of certain observant writers whose books have "trees in them," as Stephen Bodio says. I like to think this is a bit of literary resonance that's missed by readers who know only that a brookie is a kind of fish.

In Jim Harrison's novella *Brown Dog,* his main character says, of Michigan and, incidentally, of fishermen, "There is something in the air up here that makes us lie a lot. For instance, if you catch three brook trout you say you caught fifteen, and if you caught fifteen you say you caught three."

That's exactly how I am with beaver ponds. There's a moment in the life of the right beaver pond—a moment that lasts maybe a season or two— when it will have big brook trout in it.

You start with a small, Spartan stream up in the mountains. It holds a few brook trout, but the conditions are marginal, so the fish seldom get very big. A 9- or 10-incher is a whopper, and there aren't very many of them. For that matter, there may not be a whole lot of fish total—large or small—and, considering the brookie's tendency to overpopulate, that shows you how tough things are.

But when a family of beavers erects a new dam, the neighborhood improves overnight. There's deep water for cover and protection from winterkill, more insect habitat and a spike of nutrients from all the flooded vegetation. The few brookies lucky enough to find themselves in there have it wired, and they'll grow relatively large.

I'm told that in flatter parts of the country beaver ponds can be large enough to float a canoe and they can last a long time, but out here they're usually small and have short life spans. After a few spring floods they may silt in, and in a really good flood the dam may blow out. In my experience the overpopulation business begins to kick in about the time the habitat has begun to degrade, and the whole thing can happen in as little as five or six seasons, with the fourth or fifth summer producing the biggest brook trout. By the time a beaver pond appears on the latest USGS map, the big trout are probably gone. You can miss it, but if you manage to see it, it's a little like watching geology happen.

Seizing the moment on beaver ponds means a lot of walking and exploring. You need to check known beaver meadows for new ponds every few years and try to remember what you found so you can come back at the right time. You also have to make a guess at where the pond is in the process.

A brand-new dam with green sticks in it and a few little trout in the pond can mean a wait of three or four seasons, which can strain the memory down the road. "Okay, was that two years ago now, or three? And, come to think of it, which creek was that?" All of a sudden the mountains, which you'd begun to think were getting a little crowded with tourists, seem vast and trackless again.

I don't do it, but a guy should probably keep a journal on this, complete with map references. You never make notes on the map itself because people might *see* your maps. As it is, I spend a lot of time catching little fish, and I find it's possible to lose my concentration, ending up with the gnawing suspicion that up one of several little mountain creeks there's a beaver pond that should be about ready. Naturally, this means more walking, but if I start to worry about my memory, I can console myself by thinking, Well, at least I can still hike.

I feel I understand the process, but I tend to scout beaver ponds when I'm in the right mood, or when the fishing elsewhere is poor, or, rarely, when the fishing is so good I feel I can take a break and walk up some little creek just to see what's there. I do understand it, but when I find a hot beaver pond, the best I can call it is informed luck.

And if I catch fifteen big fish I say I caught three little ones.

I've seen the same kind of cycle happen in mountain lakes, although here it's less predictable and not even guaranteed to come off at all. A few years ago I was grouse hunting with James Goossen and his Lab Max the Wonder Dog. As so often happens, we'd walked many miles and found no grouse. It was a cold October day; calm, with a light snow falling. I decided we should go look at a nearby lake because I was losing heart and because the moment you give up without actually going home is often precisely when you find birds.

This was a small, rugged lake near timberline that was known to have some little brookies in it. I hadn't fished it in several years and didn't know anyone who had. When you find a lake full of 6- to 8-inch brookies, you tend to write it off. I'd have come back to check it out if they'd been baby cutthroats, but little brook trout don't instill much faith.

The lake was slate gray and dead calm, so we could see the rises from a good distance. Even from a couple hundred yards the fish looked pretty good, and up close the boils were impressive. It can be hard to accurately tell fish size from the rises, but you could see these weren't tiny trout.

James asked Max not to get in the lake, and we walked down the bank trying to get the dull light at an angle that would let us see into the water. The fish were feeding on a good midge hatch and some of them were wallowing close to the surface, with their dorsals and tails showing. It was still hard to tell their exact size—you need a fish in the hand for that—but I guessed them at around a foot long with a few pushing 14 or 15 inches. There weren't many fish, just a small pod of them feeding along the east bank.

I couldn't actually see that they were brook trout, and I suppose the Division of Wildlife could have dumped some cutthroats in there. Still, there were brookies a few years ago, and if the lake had been restocked I'd probably have heard about it. Clearly a working theory was needed.

All I could figure was that the lake had winter-killed a few seasons ago, pruning off most of the fish and leaving a few survivors with more than their usual share of food and room, starting a fresh cycle at some indeterminate point in the past. I'm told that can happen.

But "why" wasn't the problem. The problem was, there were good fish rising, but it was late in the year for high lake fishing. Already there was a skin of ice on the shady side of the lake. This could well be the last hatch until spring. It was late in the afternoon—about time to start heading back—I was standing there with a double-barreled shotgun and the nearest fly rod was 30 miles away, most of it on bad roads. I really wanted to see one of those fish, and it struck me that some of the closest ones were just about in range.

It was one of those irretrievable moments, and I asked James, in what I hoped was a casual tone of voice, "Do you think Max would retrieve a trout if I shot one? Hypothetically, that is."

"Hard to say," James said suspiciously, adding, "and I'm pretty sure that's illegal."

Right. If it wasn't illegal it should have been, so I decided against it. I'd gone for many years without shooting a trout, and I guess I wasn't ready to start.

In the grand scheme of things, those weren't big brookies, they were "good ones." Still, around here a 14- to 16-inch brook trout is about the best you can expect, and even then you're pushing the limits of probability, so I'd have to say they were big enough. I've caught a handful of 16-inch brook trout hereabouts—at least half of them in a private pond A.K. and I were invited to fish last fall—and I watched Mike Clark take an honest, measured 20-inch brookie through the ice from a lake where, the summer before, I'd taken a single 17-incher.

These are all exceptions, which explains all the whooping and yelling and snapping of photographs.

If you want to really "get into" big brookies, as they say, your best bet would be to fly up to the Hudson-Ungava Bay region of Labrador, one of those places McClane was talking about where big brookies have existed for millions of years and, by all accounts, still do.

Or maybe you'd try the Nipigon River in Ontario where the world record brookie (14 pounds 8 ounces) was caught. That happened way back in 1916, but the fishing is still supposed to be great.

I talked to a guy who'd been up there once. He usually has a lot to say about fishing, but when I asked him if it was worth going he said, "Yes."

Are the brook trout as big as they say?

"Yes."

When a normally talkative fisherman changes his tone like that, something intense is in the works. Maybe it was so good the poor guy was still stunned six years later.

I may yet go up there because there's part of me that thinks the big brook trout should be at the end of a long journey into the fish's home range, culminating in a trip in a single-engine plane with pontoons and then maybe in a wooden boat poled by an Indian guide. In a way it would only be right: back to the source and all that.

I've done things like that before and they've usually worked out well. The fishing wasn't always as easy as I thought it would be, but it was dependable. The big ones were in there, the guide at least had a clue and sooner or later you'd probably get one. Maybe even a couple.

I've now and then wondered if the safari is an adventurous, stand-up way to attack the problem, or the dilettante's way out of many long walks and fishless days. I've never made up my mind on that, so I guess I'll have to keep trying it both ways. One thing I *have* learned is that failure is harder or easier to swallow depending on what you have invested: three thousand dollars, or five bucks' worth of gas and a cheese sandwich.

Then there's another part of me that thinks the big one should come from my own backyard if that's humanly possible. After all, a 20-inch brook trout in Colorado would be the fish of a lifetime. It was for Mike, and it would have been for me, too—even through the ice on a hand line. But if I went to Labrador with half a dozen fly rods and *didn't* catch 20 inchers, I'd have to fight the idea that it was a bum trip.

In fishing there's a fine line between the impossible and the merely unlikely, the point being to reach as far as you can without actually losing your grip. I know there are a handful of monster brook trout in Colorado, and I also know the best way to catch one is to take up trolling for Mackinaws in the mountain reservoirs and hope for the best.

But, although there are no clear rules, these things should be gone about properly or not at all, and when you're thinking in terms of small waters and a bamboo fly rod, it's a different game. When you're looking for something that might be there but probably isn't, the practical edge is off and you know you're on a more philosophical errand.

When A.K. and I go out for brookies we usually figure 9 inches is good enough, measured from the tip of the thumb to the tip of the little finger with your hand spread as wide as it will go. Usually we release these and anything else we catch, but if there are a lot of them and we decide on a trout dinner, four fish of that size will just fit in my square cast-iron frying pan.

I guess I've accepted A.K.'s view of brook trout from his days in Michigan, where they're native and also the official state fish. There the brookie is the backwoodsman's trout: maybe not big, but wild, pretty, dependable and good enough to eat to make up for the size.

And they're seen as easy, *in a way.* That is, put a reasonable fly in front of one of these fish and he'll probably take. Okay, but the best ones live in creeks flowing under impenetrable willow tunnels in remote, boggy, bug-infested, quicksandy swamps. Whenever you talk about brook trout, there always seems to be a "yes, but . . ." in there somewhere.

Apparently, the Rocky Mountains are steeper, but otherwise easier to walk than much of Michigan. A.K. tells me overgrown western beaver meadows are nothing compared to Michigan cedar swamps, but he allows the former are still plenty hard to get around in; and large brookies are about as rare here as in Michigan.

Sure, there could be a big one—if that wasn't in the back of your mind somewhere you might not even go—but there probably isn't. Mostly we think in terms of exercise and scenery. Sometimes you have to walk a long way to get to the lakes and streams where brook trout live, and those places are always quiet and pretty.

We use bamboo rods, but sometimes not our very best ones because it's possible to fall, and that's how you break a tip. Then again, great rods are meant to be used, so the choice can be agonizing. Something like a 7½-foot 4-weight is about right because it will let small fish show off well. And if it happens to be somewhat old and maybe have silk wraps, so much the better.

We may cut the fly selection back to a box of drys and a few nymphs, leaving room in the vest for sandwiches, canteen and rain jacket, but we use the good flies, no seconds. A.K., who won't fish with a fly he hasn't tied himself, will tell you he doesn't *have* any seconds.

The fine tackle is part of it for us. For one thing, it helps us prop up the idea that we're a class act, you know, sportsmen of such stature that we can walk a long way and slog through lots of underbrush without caring that the trout aren't big. Of course we go to that trouble because the odd brookie *is* big, but it takes sensitive men like us to appreciate the delicacy of that paradox.

We have found some good brook trout out in those beaver meadows, sometimes in a big, new pond on the main stream, but just as often hidden in some surprising little corner. There'll be a deep slot in an old side channel with the soil held in place by aspen roots, and just enough current and food to grow a decent fish.

Or maybe it's a shady plunge pool holding out below an all but wrecked old dam where you hear falling water to your right when you know the stream is on the left. That is, it's on your left now. Beaver meadows seep and change and move around inside themselves, so what you hear is a remnant of what was the main channel maybe ten or fifteen years ago.

A nice-sized brook trout in a place like that constitutes one of those quintessential fishing moments. Here's a fish that isn't supposed to be there in the first place and isn't supposed to get big, but things have gotten right and stayed that way for just long enough, and here you come following the sound of water in what might be that trout's last season.

This will be a tough spot, so you might not be able to catch the fish. If you do manage it, you'll probably release him because he seemed happy in there, or let's just say he was exactly as he should have been, given the conditions. I don't think trout actually get happy the way we do. Whatever, you don't want to be the one to bring this to an end unless the moment has clearly lasted too long.

That can happen. A.K. once caught a 16-inch brook trout from the last deep corner of what had once been a big, sprawling pond. We were working up the creek looking for new dams and this was a place I wouldn't have bothered to cast to, but A.K. has a way of sniffing these things out.

When I saw the bow in his rod and the splash of the fish, I trotted over with the camera, but before A.K. even landed the trout we could see it was old and weak and skinny. It was an honest 16 inches—we measured it—but a third of its length and most of its girth was a big, hook-jawed head. The body was so thin you could see its ribs. The fish may not have actually been dying at that very moment, but its future sure looked bleak. The pond had gotten too small and there just wasn't enough food.

A.K. killed it, not so much to eat—although he did that and said it was good—but to put it out of its misery.

We could have felt bad about this, but we didn't. It was just mortality, pure and simple, and I think that's one of the reasons why we like to wander around in the mountains with expensive fly rods: to get a taste of things the way they really are, minus the usual crap. You'll hear people say that birth is a miracle and death is a tragedy, but a sportsman eventually comes to see that anything that happens every day is just plain ordinary. Life is just life, and even brook trout get the blues. The trick is to not get too bent out of shape about it.

A.K. strung the skinny old fish on a willow stick, held it up proudly and said, "This is why we measure 'em in inches instead of pounds."

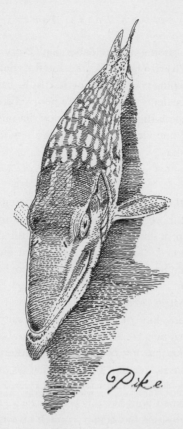

Pike.

NORTHERN pike fishing is something that gets hold of me when things start seeming too normal. There's a whole esoteric universe of pike fishing, complete with famous Norwegian pike anglers and often-told apocryphal stories, but to a fly fisherman with the usual thing for trout, it's a kind of sporting backwater, which is the kind of thing I need.

I think I fish, in part, because it's an antisocial, bohemian business that, when gone about properly, puts you forever outside the mainstream culture without actually landing you in an institution. It's a nice position. No one considers you to be dangerous, but very little is expected of you.

Okay, fine, but then you wake up one morning to find that three-quarters of your friends are also trout fishermen and they don't think you're strange at all. For instance, whatever odd thing I may have once done on a trout stream, you can be sure Koke Winter did something even odder back in 1958. When you're up against masters, you can't win.

So I go pike fishing because they're a wonderful sport fish, because I remember them fondly from childhood, because there's a whole new mythology to learn, but probably *really* because A.K., Koke and a bunch of other people don't understand what I see in it.

That's not to say I'm any good as a pike fisherman. Every time I try it again I get a fish or two and learn a little bit more about it, but as it stands now I feel as though I'm catching pike like a tourist, that is, based on good advice, but still largely by accident. I know that's a poor substitute for real skill. Skill in fishing is a nebulous thing based largely on seasoned intuition, perhaps informed by a little knowledge, but catching a few fish now and then doesn't mean you have it.

I'd been building up to pike this year because I'd completely missed last season almost without noticing. I was too busy with trout, bass and panfish in the spring, and then with trout and hunting in the fall—the two times of year when the pike fishing is best. But Ed Engle and I talked about it off and on over the winter, and when he called to say the pike were biting at a big lake we know of, I was ready.

Psychologically ready, that is, jazzed on early spring and prepared to turn last winter's talk into some kind of action. I never actually pack until I get the frantic phone call that says Ed, or someone he knows down there, has caught pike or seen them moving or has favorably interpreted some string of natural omens or has just caught a case of what Ed calls "the boogies."

Ed is a great partner on expeditions like this because he's a tenacious researcher. It seems that pike fishing has begun to catch on with some Colorado fly fishers. It's happened quietly, behind the scenes, and there's no danger that pike will replace trout as the coolest possible fish, but now it's to the point where there are accepted fly patterns, standard ways of rigging leaders and so on. Ed had sniffed this stuff out and he fed it to me over the phone, piece by piece.

When he and I first tried pike fishing with a fly rod years ago, all we knew was that we needed big flies and pretty stout tackle, something to let us mimic what we once did with plugs and level-wind bait-casting rigs. So we used our bass rods and some oversized trout streamers, the kind of setup we'd seen in articles about trolling for landlocked salmon. As trout purists, we applied the usual chauvinism: They eat minnows, so you use some old minnow imitation. They're northern pike, how smart could they be?

This worked well to a degree. That is, we caught some fish, but not any more than the trout fishermen on the same water were catching by accident, which was naturally unacceptable, even though we had a few small fish to show. We kept some that Ed's wife, Monica, turned into pike amandine. The fish's stomachs were full of crawdads, which shot the minnow theory all to hell.

Pike are delicious, by the way, and eating them is not something you'll get much grief about. Even the pike fishers believe that in the waters where these fish live there are plenty of them, and although your typical fly fisherman may not understand the attraction, he'll congratulate you on your stringer of pike because he thinks they're nasty, trout-eating vermin.

There's a case for that. I once spoke to the fisheries biologist who first brought northern pike to Colorado back in the 1950s. They were used to clean the rough fish out of some cool-water lakes but, like terrorist bombs, they couldn't be aimed. At one reservoir they ate all the suckers one year, all the dace the next and finished off the trout in the third season.

"Pike will eat anything," the biologist said, "they're great."

This season was the one where Ed decided to get serious about it—and when Ed gets serious, something memorable usually happens—so I happily went along for the ride. Being guided through something by an old friend is nearly as good as learning it for yourself.

The day we arrived at the reservoir, the wind was blowing hard and there were whitecaps on the water. Trout fishers don't like it like this, but it's supposed to be good for pike. The standard theory on this is that the wave action stirs up the insects and crustaceans on the bottom, which are fed upon by little fish, which are, in turn, eaten by big, hungry pike.

Northern pike spawn in the shallows in the spring, and then later, with the spawn over and the water still cool, they'll feed close to shore. They're a cool-water fish, though, so they'll typically retreat to deeper water during the summer. Then, in the fall, they'll move into the shallows again where a fly caster can get at them.

The most commonly used pike rig involves a heavy fly rod—a long 8- or 9-weight—and a 50-pound-test monofilament shock tippet in front of whatever you want the actual breaking strength of your leader to be. This is a saltwater-style rig that's seldom seen, or needed, on fresh water. You can land a big pike on a lighter leader, but the pike's sharp teeth are less likely to cut the 50 pound. Some fly fishermen even use wire leaders, but those are awful to cast.

At the terminal end of the leader you tie in a small metal snap. This serves two purposes: It allows the fly to work a little more naturally in the water, and it saves you from having to tie improved clinches in that fat, stiff mono or, worse yet, learn a new knot.

The most popular patterns for pike are what are called "Bunny Flies." A typical Bunny Fly is tied on a large, saltwater hook, usually with big, bead chain eyes to add a little weight. A long tail of dyed rabbit fur (on the skin) is tied on, and ahead of that another strip of fur is wrapped on the hook shank Palmer hackle–style.

Yes, they are very quick and easy to tie. And, no, they don't quite qualify as bait, if only because the rabbit skin is tanned.

The most effective colors seem to be all black, black and red, and red and yellow. You can actually buy these things in some fly shops now, which wasn't the case just a few years ago, when pike fly fishers were apparently on their own.

The fishing itself is rather simple. You want extensive shallows with a nearby drop-off, and you want to cast into the chop, which naturally means casting into the wind. You wade out into thigh- to waist-deep water and stroll slowly down the bank, casting as you go. At least that's what you do if you don't have some other idea.

To a trout fisherman who's been trained to read water, identify bugs and strategize constantly, it seems way too random. The fish are cruising and so are the fishermen. Sooner or later one may bump into the other, although in my experience, you're about as likely to step on a pike as you are to hook one.

Still, I'm told this cast-and-walk thing is standard procedure on the large, dish-shaped, largely structureless western reservoirs where, at best, you may have some vague clue, such as that the west side of the lake is better than the east. There are those who are a little more attuned to the subtleties of the sport, but I am not among them.

So you walk and cast into the wind. Now and then you stop and stretch your casting arm, which is getting sore. Casting a big fly on a heavy rod into a moderate gale is not something your muscles get used to out here.

Ed told me which turnout to head for. He'd been here a few times before this season and he felt he knew where the spot was. As we drove around the shore, I was surprised at how few people there were. This was a time of year when trout could be caught, although it was far from the best time, and the bright, windy weather was wrong. It was the height of the pike fishing, however, but even at that there were only half a dozen other fishermen on the whole, enormous body of water.

This kind of fishing is getting a little more popular, as I said, but there are still very few fly rod pike specialists around. One of them was clearly out there on the water, though. We couldn't tell which of the tiny wading dots in the distance he was, but we could spot his car. It was a clean, late-model four-wheel-drive wagon with a Colorado vanity plate on it that read ESOX. I didn't know what it meant, but Ed, with his science background, told me the Latin name for northern pike was *Esox lucius*.

I've been told you can no longer get vanity plates that say anything even vaguely resembling TROUT, BASS, FLYROD, or anything else that obvious, because they've all long since been taken. But I'll bet this guy had no trouble with ESOX, except that down at the license bureau, where they try not to let you sneak by with something dirty, someone may have wondered if maybe this was Lithuanian slang for oral sex or some such thing.

Ed and I rigged up on the open tailgate. We were a little sheltered from the wind, but I still had to chase a sock across the road before I could get into my waders. Walking down to the water, the lines slapped our rods. Remember, wind is good, I thought.

I had tied some all-black bunny flies because I already had the black rabbit and figured the color couldn't make that much difference, but Ed suggested I try one of his red-and-yellow ones. He said that with the clear water and strong sun, the bright fly would probably be better. And anyway, the last few times this was the fly that had produced the best.

"We haven't really hammered them yet," he said, "but we have gotten some."

I envied him for the insight, as I tend to envy any fisherman who seems to know what he's doing.

We waded into the water then, about two long casts apart, and started slowly down the bank, heading roughly west. The bottom slopes gently here, so from waist-deep water you could cast out toward the middle of the lake on one side and back toward shore on the other. They say neither direction is regularly better than the other, but on days like this when the waves are rolling in well, the big pike often lurk closer to shore than you'd imagine.

There was also the possibility of a trout. They're in this lake, and pike fly fishers sometimes catch stupendously big ones by accident. For that matter, the trout fishers now and then inadvertently hang a pike when they're fishing something big enough, like a #2 Woolly Bugger, for browns, but even a medium-sized northern will often snap the leader smartly.

A trout fanatic I know said that's just as well, since many of his colleagues aren't into pike and don't know what to do with one when they get it. One poor innocent even tried to hand land one by its lower lip like you would a bass. He was rushed the 60 miles or so to the nearest emergency room to get sewed up, ruining a day of fishing for the poor guy who had to drive him.

There is a mythology to pike fishing, much of which has to do with bleeding wounds on dumb fishermen.

We fished down the bank together. Ed was ahead of me, so I was casting to water he'd already worked, but that didn't matter. If they were there, the fish would be cruising and hunting, so it was just as likely that one would move in behind Ed as that he'd get to them first.

We worked down this bank for, I'd guess, two hours.

The waves I was standing in seemed high. Their troughs would drop down below my butt and their crests would sometimes ship over the tops of my chest waders. One would roll through gracefully and lift the weight off my feet. Then the next would come and slap me hard. Balance had to be paid attention to. I felt like I was being shoved around.

I'd have been wet from spray, except that the wind we were facing into was cool, dry and dehydrating. The sun was bright, but it felt cool, too, or at the most lukewarm. I began to feel like I was drying out. My skin felt papery, my mouth chalky. I had a canteen in my day pack, but getting it out would involve wading to shore, and this is a persistent kind of fishing where you think twice about breaking your rhythm.

And I guess there was the suspicion that, since I had no clear idea what I was doing, maybe a little hardship would turn my luck. Wasn't it John McDonald who pointed out that the whole concept that fishing should be fun is a fairly new idea? So suffer a little. I don't really believe it, the evidence is against it, but maybe there's an intelligence out here that will take pity on me. You know, give me a fish just for having faith.

This is probably where religion came from in the first place. I can picture someone back in prehistory up against a difficult practical problem thinking, There must be something out there to help me if only because I need help so badly. In the heat of the moment, it wouldn't seem unreasonable.

I began to cast automatically while watching a mountain range to the west. In that dry, clean, windy air it seemed like it was right there, an easy hike away, or no more than a fifteen-minute drive, but I knew that it was behind—way behind—that hospital emergency room that was 60 miles off.

My mind had begun to wander. When the fishing is like this I begin to think, not cogitate or ponder, just think, about, you know, things. A day or two after I got back from this trip Susan asked me, casually, "Do you ever think about me when you're fishing?"

"Sure," I said. This is the correct answer, true or not, although it just happens to *be* true in this case.

"I don't mean just when you're out, but when you're actually fishing."

"Absolutely," I said.

***

And so this is how it goes. You wade down the bank, casting. Eventually the pickup is a yellow dot back on the horizon, at which point you turn around and fish back. Then, after a cup of coffee and a candy bar, you start again at the same place, heading off in the same direction because this is supposed to be the good bank, and because it could all have changed. While you were peeling your Snickers bar, the wolf pack of big pike could have moved in. You'd never know the way you might with trout. There'd be no dainty rises speckling the surface, no lazy tailing, even if the water was still enough for you to see such things.

If you were in the wrong mood you could begin to see this as drudgery, but in the right mood it's more like a cross between meditation and casting practice. This fishing is slow, so you can't stay keyed up. You have to trust your reflexes to set up on the occasional strike.

I got a bump hours into it, that live jerk that can't be bottom or a wave or anything but a fish. My reflexes seemed to work. That is, without having to think about it I hauled on the rod to set the hook, so when the fish turned out not to be on, it couldn't have been my fault. Right?

The lake seemed enormous, oceanic. It even smelled like an ocean; not the salt, but the decomposition, the rafts of rotting vegetation washed up on shore and the inevitable dead fish the gulls and ravens pick at. I'm used to small water—creeks, rivers, farm ponds, little mountain trout lakes. This thing was measured in miles. I knew it to be full of fish, but in two or three hours I had come upon one willing pike. I was hungry and, now that I thought about it, a little tired. It occurred to me that nothing in life vanishes as irretrievably as a lost fish.

The pike may in fact have moved in, because it wasn't long after that that Ed got a good take. I heard him say something—one of those single-syllable exclamations fishermen use, not quite a word, but a little more than a grunt—and when I looked up, he was setting the hook. He set it hard three or four times to make sure. Since not much was happening, I waded over to watch.

At first there was just weight and throbbing on the rod; that preliminary phase where the fish begins to figure out that he's having some kind of difficulty and the fisherman tries to determine how excited he should be.

The pike made a halfhearted run out into deep water, taking some line, and then Ed reeled it back in without much of a fight. This could have been a modest fish, or a hog that just hadn't gotten cranked up yet. Sometimes a big fish will seem more annoyed than anything. If you're lucky, he won't panic until he's gotten a little tired out and it's too late.

There was another run, and then Ed brought the fish back a bit closer than he had the first time. When Ed saw it, he took a step back and said, in a perfectly level, conversational tone, "It's a mother." Ed seems a little bit excited most of the time, but when there's reason to be excited, he tends to become calm.

Ed fought the fish for a while, and I figured it was a pretty good one because he was being more careful than usual, but otherwise it was hard to tell. When I finally saw the pike, my first thought was to get out of the water. It looked like a green log, and when it bored off on another run the flick of its tail threw water 2 feet in the air.

The fish is still in the water and you're not the one playing it, so the realization comes upon you slowly. No telling just how big it is, but big. Oh boy, you think, don't freak out. Don't start yelling instructions, you know it doesn't help.

You like to have an audience when a huge fish is landed, but in this case I think we were both glad no one was around. There are some odd mechanical aspects to this kind of fishing. The well-equipped pike fisher carries a gaff, long-handled hook disgorgers, jaw spreaders and a short, weighted club that a gangster would call a sap, but that a fisherman calls a priest. Unhooking a big pike is a little like changing the spark plugs in the truck with the motor running.

Ed had some pike tools, but neither of us was very experienced at this, and the fish honestly scared the hell out of both of us. A pike is a fabulously ugly fish. The body is a kind of military green, snaky but, on a big one, also obscenely fat, like a python that's just eaten. The mouth is like a leather duck bill with many teeth, the eyes are nasty and hooded, and, once you get hold of it, the fish turns out to be chillingly slimy, with clear goo looping off of it like snot.

Bluegills are precious, trout pretty, bass handsome, but a pike is in an entirely different class. You have to love them not in spite of the fact that they're hideous, but because of it.

Ed did a workmanlike job of gaffing the thing, but then, after looking around to make sure no one was watching, we dragged it up on the beach and beat it to death with a rock. We didn't want to have to touch it until we knew it was dead.

It taped out at 40 inches. Around here, any pike over 30 is considered trophy size.

We decided we had to know what it weighed, so we dragged the thing up to the truck and drove to Chaparral Park Mobile Fishing Tackle, a combination trailer park, grocery store and fishing shop that had the closest scale.

Dave and Barb were happy to weigh the fish. It went 18.7 pounds on a reg-
istered scale. One hell of a nice pike, they both said.

Then Dave got out a Polaroid and took Ed's picture, or, rather, a picture
of the fish incidentally being held by Ed. There's a difference. This they
tacked on the wall along with maybe a hundred other snapshots of people
holding fish. Although Ed's pike was one of the largest there, it still seemed
to shrink amidst all those other little color photos.

There was fresh coffee on, good, strong, free fisherman's coffee that
took two spoons of powdered nondairy creamer without changing color.
Barb began mopping the pike slime off the linoleum floor, and Dave said,
"Yeah, a guy could slip in that and break his fuckin' neck." The excitement
had subsided.

Then we went fishing again, and as we got back into the grinding pace
of it, the big fish began to fade for me, except for the knowledge that a big
fish had been caught, which could mean . . . Well, you know.

I began to see that no great epiphany was at hand for me, although this
would all go on file, and maybe someday my personal pike lore would build
up to where I could look at some big, featureless bowl of stored irrigation
water and think, Yes, this looks right, probably without entirely understanding what looks right *about* it.

Not too much later I did hook a pike. It was just as it should be. The fish
thumped the fly hard, I set up, and he bored off slowly, but with great de-
liberation. I knew he was no 40 inches, but he was going to be a good
enough fish. I played him into knee-deep water and hand landed him gingerly, grabbing him behind the head, careful not to get into the sharp gill
covers. A good fish, but not big enough to require the gaff.

He measured 27 inches, which is a nice-sounding number to a trout
fisher, although it's only a fair-sized pike, especially in light of Ed's earlier
performance.

Ed admired my fish. "Good one," he said. "Healthy, pretty, nice size,
and," he added, alluding to Ernest Hemingway as he sometimes does, "it
showed courage."

Okay, fine, the guy who caught the enormous fish does have one wise-
crack coming, and I could see that Ed deserved the big one. He'd done his
homework, he'd come up here several times before to scout it out and he'd
even bought a gaff and a jaw spreader. It made the kind of sense you'd expect to see if there was some justice in the world. I guess I hated him for it.

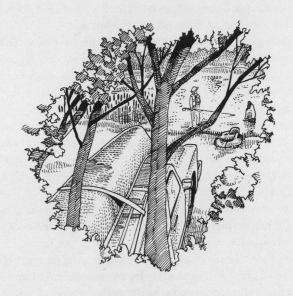

The New Pond

O N E thing you'll notice about fishermen is that—in the time-honored tradition of humans everywhere—they never seem to be able to get enough. Once an angler has become serious about the sport (and "serious" is the word that's used) he'll never again own enough tackle or have enough time to use it. And his nonangling friends and family may never again entirely recognize him, either.

The same thing goes for places to fish. We all say the good fishing waters are fewer now because of development, irrigation, pollution and/or excessive angling pressure. That's absolutely true, but, by the same token, there are still so many good places to fish that if a guy in, say, his mid-thirties was to quit his job and start right now, he couldn't hit them all before his legs gave out.

I've met a couple of people who actually *are* trying to hit them all, or at least come as close as possible. They seem deliriously happy one day and a little despondent the next—pretty much like the rest of us, except with better tans.

If you can afford to be a jet-setter, you'll fish in all the famous, fashion-

able places with the best tackle and the canniest guides, and the exceptionally hip will have fished these spots for at least a year before they were
splashed all over the magazines. If you're more blue collar, you'll have a network of good local spots (many of which you'll keep quiet about) and you
may put together the trip of a lifetime once or twice each season. Either
way, you'll never quite be satisfied.

And that goes for the tools of the trade as well. Once something clicks
and you have become a fisherman, you'll likely embark on the search for
the perfect rod—which, naturally, must be fitted with the perfect reel,
upon which must be spooled the perfect line. If you ever achieve that in
graphite, you'll immediately begin wondering why some people prefer
split bamboo.

At some point you'll probably begin tying your own flies because it's
cheaper in the long run and because the ones in the stores, though often
close, just aren't quite as good as they could be.

Whatever you start with—bass and panfish, trout and grayling—you'll
eventually begin wondering about other fish. Maybe salt water will beckon
if there's time, although there may not *be* time.

A friend will call with an unusual plan of some kind. He'll say, "I don't
know if you'd be interested, but—" and you'll interrupt, saying, "If it
swims, I'm at least curious."

So you diversify, learning, in the process, that the perfect pike rod is not
necessarily the perfect bass rod, and so it goes. Eventually this can become
what looks like a life's work.

I don't see this as greed or fanaticism. I prefer to think of it as just a
healthy sense of adventure, complete with all the profound notions that
can go along with that: intellectual curiosity, the role of humans in the environment, life, death, sport, gourmet food, peace of mind, whatever.
Fishing is a silent, often solitary business. You're bound to start thinking.

So when a guy says something apparently harmless like, "Look, you're
worried? You're hassled? You're fighting with your friends? Go fishing," he
may already have begun to radicalize your consciousness. You go out there
and try to insinuate yourself into the natural scheme of things by fooling a
couple of fish, and the first thing you learn is just how far you get by being
pushy and impatient.

You can study, upgrade your gear, carry more flies and try to achieve
greater finesse overall, but it only begins to work when you finally slow
your pace and take things as they come, which may be right now, in a day
or so or, rarely, never.

Aha! you think.

Back home you may begin to see that human activity is the only thing in nature that doesn't seem to happen in its own sweet time, which is the real reason you have more fun fishing than you do working. You'll probably become something of an environmentalist—possibly even a radical one—although in other areas of life you may be able to take things a little easier now.

Aha! again.

This perspective on things can change you irreparably. If it comes to you early enough in life, it can save you from ever becoming what they call "normal."

When I was a boy, a kid who would rather fish than play football or speed in a car was a dork. Now he's considered a dweeb—roughly the same thing. It's a burden at the time, but it's possible that said kid will grow into one of those rare adults who can distinguish between the things in life that can be controlled and those that can't; who can perceive mistakes as natural phenomena and who can just generally remain calm: a person who, if pressed, will tell you that the universe may or may not have meaning, but it sure seems to have a sense of humor.

This is, I believe, a profitable, comforting and accurate worldview that, among other things, makes you want to spend a lot of time fishing, not, as Robert Traver pointed out, because it's so important, but because everything else we do is equally *un*important.

As I said, this is profound, but only if that's the way you want it to be. In other words, the guy who says he fishes because it chills him out and because he just likes, say, trout, is not necessarily wrong or dull. One of the things you do out there with a rod in your hand is confront yourself, and if that confrontation isn't a big, cosmic deal, so much the better.

I was getting ready to leave for a fishing trip recently—packing in the afternoon to leave that evening—when Larry called to see if I wanted to go with him and Steve Peterson to fish a certain private bass pond, one I'd heard about and had wanted to get on for some time. He wanted to leave in twenty minutes.

Larry is an expert at wangling himself (and friends, if they're lucky) into secret, private fishing spots, but he's not one to give you a lot of notice. To fish with Larry, you have to be in a more or less constant state of alert. It also helps if you don't have a regular job.

Larry is this way because *he* doesn't have a regular job. When asked what he does for a living, he'll usually be vague. When someone asks me, I say he's a blacksmith who makes beautiful Damascus steel knives, and I may add that he sort of buys, sells, trades, fixes and/or redesigns things. No, I can't be more specific. Things. Anything. Another way to put it is that he's self-employed. In any event, when he feels like going fishing, he usually just goes and the first you hear of it is when he's standing on your front porch in his waders. Sometimes he'll stop to make a quick phone call.

I explained that I was supposed to meet Ed in Palmer Lake that evening for a quick getaway the next morning and was going to try and get a little work done in the meantime.

"So," Larry said, ignoring the mention of work, "we'll go a little early and you can drive your own car. You can leave for Palmer Lake from the pond. The most you'll be is a little late."

Sure, of course, makes sense.

Then I felt this cold nose on my elbow. "Ah, but I'm dog-sitting and the dog's owner won't be out to pick her up until later this afternoon."

"So," Larry said, "leave the door unlocked for your friend. That's a coal black, ninety-pound German shepherd. No one is going to break in."

If this was one of those Walt Disney morality play cartoons, I'd be Goofy and Larry would be the little guy with horns and a pitchfork whispering in my ear, "Forget about what you're supposed to be doing. Go fishing."

I went. I was packed anyway except for a few odds and ends and, after all, this was a *new pond*. I'm not out to hit every good fishing spot in the United States, but I do plan to make a dent—and the bigger the dent, the better.

The pond was a little over an hour's drive east of Interstate 25, the line that, in my personal cartographic system, officially separates the foothills of the Rockies from the Great Plains. More than that I cannot say. Larry led the way in his silver Cadillac while Steve and I followed in my pickup, with the canoe strapped on top. Larry drove slowly (for him) so that, with the pedal right to the floor, I was able to keep up. Steve and I had only the vaguest idea where we were going.

We pulled off the highway at one of those little towns that isn't really a town anymore, even though its dot and name are still on the map. Millie's Cafe, the Feed and Hardware and the few other once-friendly mom-and-pop operations on what was formerly a cottonwood-shaded main street were vacant and filled with nesting sparrows. One or two of the houses looked like they might still be lived in. What's there now by way of a business district is a joint baking in the sun out by the highway, selling gas, beer, pop, junk food and maps: the bare essentials needed to keep strangers moving through.

I do patronize these places—one occasionally needs a microwaved hot dog or a Coke for sustenance—but I hate to see a place go to seed when what it gets replaced with is of lesser quality by far. Millie's may once have served the cosmic chicken-fried steak, but now I'll never know.

To be fair, the new joint serves a predictable hot dog and the pop *is* cold as advertised. The kid behind the counter seems a little stoned. Maybe he is, or maybe he's just feeling the normal effects of working a boring job for minimum wage.

I guess I'd been in one of those moods lately: you know, the kind where you don't feel very pleased about things, but can't quite put your finger on why, although deep down you know it's just the residual existential nervousness that comes from trying to make a living and reading too many newspapers.

When I'm at home, my morning ritual involves heading down to Andrea's Cafe, where I swill coffee and devour a newspaper pretty much cover to cover, skipping the business and sports sections. I see this as a kind of civic duty—trying to keep up, trying not to be ignorant—but so many things are always going wrong, and they're such big things.

This kind of brooding may not be entirely good for me. I once overheard a waitress down there saying, "When John comes in in the morning, I put a cup of coffee on the corner of the table and push it over to him with a broomstick."

I'd recently told a friend that I'd resolved to only get pissed off at those things about which I could conceivably do something. "Good idea," he said, and it was, but I hadn't actually managed it yet.

On the other hand, when you're on your way to a new, possibly great pond, these little moments of nostalgia and self-doubt are short-lived. When you're fishing, you just want to find this particular pond and then catch that specific bass. For a time you stop worrying about what you'll want next.

We got our cold Cokes, and Larry's Cadillac spewed gravel as he left the parking lot. Driving only 10 or 15 miles per hour over the speed limit had made him a little twitchy. To stay in the spirit of things—and to illustrate that my old pickup isn't exactly a dog—I spewed a little gravel myself following him. If there had been anyone left in town, they would probably have disapproved.

It took a while to locate the place and a while longer to get on the pond. There was the man and his wife to meet, a neat country spread to be admired, dogs to pet (one with a sore ear), weather to be discussed: the usual obligatory pleasantries you engage in while trying not to seem too anxious. The owner would like to have shown us his pond personally, but he couldn't. Too busy, he said. I told him I knew what he meant.

The pond, when we finally got on it, was beautiful. It was big and rambling, amoeboid shaped, lying in a natural swale out of sight of the road, with old cottonwoods along the north bank and a cattail marsh lining an arm pointing southwest. The water was matted with duckweed and there was bleached, flooded timber for the bass to hide in. Two boats were pulled up on shore: a canoe in good repair and an apparently well-used duck boat. The owner was a hunter (his house was filled with the mounted heads of animals, but no fish), so I guessed there were more ducks shot here than there were bass caught. A promising speculation.

A flock of a dozen white pelicans flushed when we drove up, and they wheeled overhead a few times before heading north where, presumably, there was another pond. The herons and coots stayed put, however, apparently willing to share the water with us as long as we behaved. We got into belly boats, struggled out through the weeds and began to fish.

And we caught some: a number of decent bass (one of Steve's was the best at, let's say, 4 pounds) as well as some very respectable bluegills. There are bigger bass in there, according to Larry, who knows the pond and who is seldom wrong about these things, but you hardly ever catch the biggest ones on the first trip, and on those rare occasions when you do, it doesn't seem quite fair.

Then too, we had arrived in midafternoon and we all knew that, regardless of how hard we fished, the hot two hours would be either side of dusk. I'm surprised we caught as many fish as we did.

I knew I wouldn't stay for the main event because that would mean I'd pull in at Ed and Monica's house at three in the morning. We planned to leave for the lake at five, and the fact that I hadn't had any sleep wouldn't mitigate that. So I was sight-seeing and fishing out of curiosity—taking it easy. That night I told Ed that I had stopped to "look at" a new pond, and he knew what I meant.

So we fished the pond for a couple of hours and, although it was a new one to me, I found it completely recognizable. Sure, every bass pond has its own little quirks, and if it's a good one these are worth learning, but on another level this was just "warm water." The fish were where they should have been for the most part, and they bit the flies that should have worked.

I don't mean I wasn't enjoying it. In fact, this feeling of recognition made me enjoy it more than usual. Sometimes fishing is nothing more than the process of airing out the modest skills you've developed over the years, not so much to catch fish as to just go through the familiar, comforting motions. I knew I was fishing at the wrong time of day and, after struggling through the duckweed in the belly boat for a while, I knew I should have used the canoe instead. But this was one of those days when the pressure was off; when knowing what you're doing wrong is almost as good as doing it right.

Steve and Larry stayed until past dark (and did well, I heard later), but I had this appointment with Ed, who'd be wondering where I was. I was also a couple of strange dirt roads from the highway. I figured I'd recognize my way back in daylight, but probably not in the dark.

As I walked back to the pickup from the far end of the pond, it occurred to me that the truck looked pretty good parked out there in the short grass and the slanting, yellow light, its camper shell full of gear, the canoe on top, the bug-spattered windshield. I also noticed it was beginning to take on that squashed, rounded look pickups get with age and use, as if, left to their own devices, they'd eventually evolve into De Sotos.

Maybe it was the idea of having just fished and wanting to leave early so I could fish some more someplace else, but I thought, If I passed this truck on the road, I'd wave.

It also occurred to me, for some reason, that I now had just about everything I'd wanted when I was fourteen years old and was just starting to hang out with the men I admired and wanted to be like. I was all grown up, even to the point of having some gray hair in the beard. I had moved west, where I had a little place outside of town close to a decent trout stream. I had become a pretty good fisherman—maybe not an expert, but one who had seen enough bass ponds that a strange new one had a comfortable, homey feel to it. And I lived in a world that, although far from perfect, was still filled with new secret fishing spots just waiting to be discovered.

I even had a girlfriend with a great figure—something else I aspired to at the tender age of fourteen, if memory serves me.

(You're right, I should also mention that she's witty, intelligent, an accomplished reporter, reviewer and the business editor of a newspaper, but what we're doing here is looking back into the mind of a fairly typical fourteen-year-old boy in 1959. Okay?)

The fact that all this didn't make me as giddy as I thought it would then was also okay. You're bound to register a little damage over time, losing some of your innocence in the process, but with luck you replace it with what, at certain moments, feels a little like the beginnings of wisdom.

I remember that, as a boy, the men seemed glad and competent in the field, but there was also sometimes a kind of subdued melancholy about them, too. I didn't understand that as a kid, but I do now. Some of those grown-ups gave me what I thought was a hard time then, but by the time I was thirty I'd forgiven most of them, and now, in my forties, I'm beginning to see it's not up to me to forgive anybody for anything. It turned out that life was both more and less serious than they told me it was, but they were just figuring that out for themselves, and how do you get that across to a teenager who just wants to chase girls and catch fish?

Anyway, somewhere in the past, based on the little I knew for sure, I had fastened on the perfect life as one based on art and sport, plus a few other things like love, friendship, pretty country and good food. Given a loose enough definition of art, that's what I had. I didn't get too tangled up in my childhood, though, because I had places to go, more fish to catch and maybe fifteen minutes of daylight in which to find the highway again. I could only spare a minute or two to realize I was happy.

Before I got behind the wheel, I turned to wave at Steve and Larry, but they were out of sight behind some trees. So I stood on the gas and put up a cloud of dust as I left. I thought it was the kind of signal they'd understand.

Dances with Trout

Quitting Early

T H E deal was this: Most of the river was private through this stretch, or, I should say, the surrounding land was private, since Montana's enlightened Stream Access Law allows you to walk and fish on any river as long as you stay below the high-water line.

Still, some of this water would have involved a really long, hard hike from the nearest public access except that one landowner allows fishermen to park and get in on his land for a fee of three dollars. You have to know where the turnoff is, but once you get down to the river there's a large, hand-painted sign that explains the procedure in detail, complete with some interesting spelling errors.

You get an envelope from an old, tin tackle box on a stump, stick three dollars in it, write your license number on the outside and put it in the slot on a large, handmade strongbox that's too big and heavy to steal.

There's no one around, it's an honor system, but before you even think of not doing it, you come to the part of the instructions saying that nonpayers will be banned. Actually it says, "NONE PAYERS WILL BE BAND," which somehow makes the point with even more authority.

There were some other fishermen rigging up there, and one of them came over and asked me if it was true what he'd heard about the old man who owned the place: that he'd drive down from the hills in the evening, check the envelopes against the license plates and go after cheaters with a shotgun.

"You bet," I said, although I'd never met the old man or even heard the story before. Everywhere you go in the Rocky Mountain West you'll hear tales of crazy old landowners with guns. More of them are true than you might suspect.

My partner and I had floated a different stretch of the same river with a guide that morning. We'd caught lots of trout and then had a great, leisurely meal at a little roadhouse nearby where it was okay to wear waders inside but, "please, no cleats." Before our guide headed back to town, he told us about the strongbox, the three dollars and all; said we should fish there as long as we were this close and asked me not to write about where it was. So I haven't. Okay, Tom?

He said, "You want to fish river-left this evening and river-right if you go back there in the morning." River-left is to your left as you look down-stream, which is how Mackenzie boat guides view the world. It would also be the shady bank at that time of day.

You had your choice of sides because there was a rickety old one-lane wooden bridge down there. The river was way too wide, deep and fast to wade across.

Lunch was long and slow, as I said, but we were still at the bridge with our three dollars paid by early afternoon. Our guide had blasted back to town in what seemed like a big hurry. Some of these guys tow their Mackenzie boats faster than I'd drive a Porsche on those twisty, two-lane roads, but you hardly ever see them in a ditch, so they must know what they're doing.

This was in mid-August. The day was hot and bright, and it was going to be quite a few hours before evening when things should pick up. So we rigged up slowly to kill time: stretching leaders, checking perfectly good knots, adjusting reel drags that didn't need adjusting, carefully smoothing every last wrinkle out of the wader socks and drinking our canteens dry; hydrating, so we wouldn't have to carry water.

We even stopped and talked to another fisherman who was mad because he hadn't been able to get any good pancakes. He'd eaten breakfast in a dozen cafes and restaurants around there, but the pancakes were always too thick and fluffy. "Now any good pancake," he said, "is thin and firm, right?"

We listened to this guy for longer than we normally would have, but even at that, we were on the river by three o'clock and it would probably be seven or later before anything really happened.

The fishing was refreshingly slow-paced after the frantic morning in the Mack boat. We split up and worked the pocket water near shore, pretty much ignoring the great, roaring main channel out in the middle. I was using a size sixteen dry caddis fly with a little Hares Ear nymph on a short dropper, a rig I like because you seem to be casting a dry fly like a proper sporting gentleman, even though you're hooking most of your trout on the nymph.

I also like it because it goes against the still popular myth that the only way to catch trout in these big, western rivers is to dredge the bottom with a huge weighted stonefly.

The fishing was slow, but it felt good to be wading in cold water under a hot sun, and now and then—maybe once every half hour—you'd hook a nice, fat rainbow that just couldn't wait for the evening hatch. It was dreamy enough to stop and look at the birds and maybe scan the hillsides for game, but you'd get just enough strikes to keep your mind from wandering to far-off things like home, work and the future. This is probably how a grazing deer feels: happily lazy, but still alert and in the moment.

Things did pick up a little toward evening. A few caddis flies began to come off and some trout started rising. When I finally broke the nymph off on a fish, I clipped the rest of the dropper off and fished with the dry fly alone. When I lost the little Elk Hair Caddis to another trout, I tied a fresh fly onto a new, slightly heavier tippet, squared my shoulders, readjusted my hat and got serious for a while.

This is exactly how a summer day on a big, western river is supposed to go: hot fishing in the morning, petering off to a midday during which you can either pound up the odd trout if you want to or take a nap, then slipping into an evening rise that will likely last until past dark.

By the time the sun was completely off the river, I'd landed half a dozen good trout on the fresh caddis fly, including two rainbows that would have gone around sixteen inches. I'd started the morning with a couple of good fish on a dry fly, so this seemed to be an appropriate place to quit. When I released that last big trout I remember thinking the first one I'd caught that day had been thirteen or fourteen hours before and that I'd lost track of them in between. I also remember being a little tired.

Sure, the fish would keep feeding and there'd be enough light to see my caddis fly for another half hour or so. For that matter, with stars and a quarter moon, a guy could tie on a #10 Royal Wulff and go on for half the night, but toward the end of a long day that's gone well I now often ask myself things like, Just how many fish do you have to catch?

No, I'm not always this laid back, but we'd been out for several days, so the initial adrenaline rush had subsided. I've always enjoyed that moment on a trip when the long haul comes into view—plenty of water to fish, plenty of time—and it no longer feels like a suicide mission.

I got up on a faint fisherman's trail winding through the sage and headed back. When I passed my partner I yelled down to him, "I'll see you at the truck."

"They're really rising down here," he said.

Back at the parking lot I set up the camp stove on the tailgate and made coffee. There'd been six or eight trucks and jeeps there when we went out, now there were three. Right next to me the guy who'd asked me about the landowner there hours before was pulling off his neoprene waders and wringing out his wet long johns and socks. He sniffed his underwear tentatively and said, half to me, half to himself, "Can't tell if this is river water or condensation."

He seemed pensive, as though he was coming to the realization many of us have reached over the last few years, namely that neoprenes—expensive waders that make you wet whether they leak or not—are probably an elaborate practical joke.

"Got time for some coffee?" I asked.

"I'll have a beer," he said, reaching for his cooler, "but I sure as hell have time. The guy I'm with will probably be out there till midnight."

I said, "Yeah, my partner will be out late, too, if only because he knows I quit early."

The guy laughed knowingly at that, and then we ran through the usual fisherman's business. First things first: How'd you do today? (We'd both lost count of trout caught and were satisfied.) Where else have you been in the last few days? How was the fishing? What flies did you use? How do you like that rod? And, by the way, what's your name?

Shortly after dark two guys came off the water, derigged quickly and without much comment and drove off in the third pickup. Half a mile down the dirt track they turned left onto the county road, in the direction of that little roadhouse. I caught myself wondering what time they stopped serving burgers there and fought the impulse to look at my watch. Checking the time when the time doesn't matter always makes me feel compulsive.

The river had gotten louder—as rivers do on those clear, western nights—and we watched what we could see of it for a while without talking. What we could see was a wide black stripe in a bumpy gray landscape.

There are times when I really enjoy that: coming back a little early, getting out of the waders, brewing coffee, unwinding and knowing that my friend is still out there in the dark somewhere, probably—presumably— landing a few more trout. It's like figuring the bats must be out because of the time of day and the season, even though you can't actually see them.

I knew what he'd say when he finally dragged in. He'd have hammered them, big ones, starting ten minutes after I left. (That might sound suspicious, but it would be true—the big trout really do move after dark, and the guys who stay late on the water usually get some.) He'd tell me this in a slightly accusatory tone because my quitting early would have offended him in some way. In the final analysis, he thinks I lack a certain grim determination when it comes to trout fishing.

And he's right, I do. In fact, it took me a long time to get to where I could fish as if it mattered, but not as if I was at war with the trout. I had to work at it at first, but now I prefer it that way.

So, he can't understand why I'd quit when there was even one more trout to be stuck and I can't understand why he can never quite get enough, but I guess it's one of those things that, in the long course of a friendship, seems to matter less and less. I mean, no one understands everything, right?

And it could be a lot worse. Over the years I've fished with frustrated drill sergeants who absolutely have to be in charge of everything; phony experts who always have to be right; competitors who keep score so they can win and you can lose; headhunters whose biggest trout has to be longer than yours for reasons that seem suspiciously Freudian and so on. In the grand scheme of things, someone who makes you wait at the truck for an hour or so is nothing.

The other man and I were still watching the river. I'd finished my coffee and accepted one of his cold beers, which tasted so wonderful I almost fell off the tailgate. My friend out on the water had taught me that years ago: When you're tired, have a cup of coffee first so you can stay awake to enjoy the beer. The night had turned cold and I'd put on a sweater.

I said, "This guy you're fishing with, have you known him long?"

"Oh, God," he said, "I've known him for years. He can be an asshole at times, but we get along."

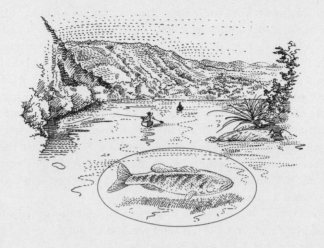

Texas

T H E Texas hill country north of San Antonio struck me as wildly foreign
and strangely familiar at the same time. The rolling topography forested in
live oak, pin oak, walnut, pecan and such reminded me of the Midwest
where I was born, as did the humidity and the small, old towns built
around shady courthouse squares, but of course there are differences. Try
to picture rural Ohio but with armadillos, ringtails, rattlesnakes, cactus,
great Mexican food and hardscrabble goat ranches instead of farms.

And then there's *poco tiempo:* the slow pace, of which Texan English is
one example. It's a lovely language to hear spoken, and after a few days of it
you come to realize that you'd drawl too if you had plenty of time to speak
your piece and could assume your listeners were too polite to interrupt.
Pause to search for the right word, and everyone waits patiently. It's amazing. You find yourself saying pretty much what you meant to say instead of
just blurting something out.

Ed Engle and I drove down there in April to do some "real" bass fishing,
as opposed to whatever kind of bass fishing it is we do back home in Colorado. The possibility of bigger fish was part of it, but more than that we

wanted to catch bass in a place where they belong—as opposed to a place like Colorado where they've been introduced—in the company of people who grew up there and really know how to do it.

This is important because to catch a certain kind of fish you must come to understand them, and that understanding becomes part of the character of a place. That's why fishermen are almost as interesting as the fish themselves.

We were in Ed's old Datsun pickup with my new Mansfield canoe strapped on top. This truck doesn't have a proper boat rack on it, so we had jury-rigged one with foam blocks and lots of rope. If we hadn't had to stop to retie the canoe every hundred miles or so, we might have cut a few hours off the trip. As it was, it took the better part of two days.

Ed and I aren't kids anymore, but we still believe in the hip romance of long road trips—you know, the boredom, risk, sense of purpose and the distance from all that stuff that, before you left, seemed too damned important.

The first night we slept in a park somewhere near Big Spring, Texas. We'd spent an hour in town asking people where we could camp and no one seemed to know what we were talking about.

"You mean park a camper?"

"No, we mean 'camp,' you know, sleep on the ground."

We were a little road-burned and I suggested getting a room, which we both usually consider to be the same as giving up, or at least giving in to lazy, middle-class comfort. But Ed held out for a quick, cheap camp. Our road trips have always been low-budget by necessity, and at this stage of the game a room just seems like a needless extravagance. And, as Ed the pragmatist says, "You should always scrimp early on a trip because you never know what you'll run into later."

Finally a woman at a gas station said it would be all right if we slept in the park just down the road. It wasn't clear whether it was all right officially or just all right with her, but it was dark, we were tired and we didn't pursue it.

It took about ten minutes to toss out the sleeping bags and set up the camp stove. Then I started supper while Ed drove back into town to call home. Seems his wife, Monica, was having some trouble at work serious enough that she might lose the job. Ed had offered to cancel the trip so he could be there during the crisis, but Monica had said, no, go, staying won't make any difference. Bless her heart. I've always liked Monica.

I was sitting at a picnic table under a street light surrounded by a thousand bugs, drinking a Lone Star beer and trying to keep at least the larger insects out of the stew. I've made some of those calls myself—the ones where you feel like you really should be home, even though you probably couldn't be much help, but instead you're on a trip, supposedly having fun, although you're not having as much fun as you might ordinarily because you really should be home. You feel slightly irresponsible, but you know in your heart that life is short and responsibility is overrated.

I could picture it: Ed calling home from an outside pay phone to see about the trouble, the trucks on the highway drowning out parts of the conversation. First she'd ask, "Where are you calling from?" and Ed would say, "Big Spring." That probably wouldn't mean anything, but she'd try to picture it anyway. Was it a nice little town or a neon shithole along the highway?

All the calls I've made like that seemed crucial at the time, although now I can't remember what a single one of them was about. All I remember is the feeling. It's not loneliness; more like just the experience of distance.

Ed was back in fifteen minutes. He got a beer from the cooler and said, "It's okay, at least for the time being. *Now* I'm glad I came." That's about as specific as Ed ever gets about things like this. He's a bit of a cynic (he once told me his only retirement plan was to have a massive heart attack) but he's not a whiner, so it's: "Well, there's a little trouble, but when isn't there?" and then some time later, "Oh, that. I guess it turned out okay."

It's not that Ed won't bitch if you get him started, but about personal matters he exhibits a kind of restraint I've always admired: a sort of things-are-a-mess-but-I'm-okay attitude that makes him more likely to argue than complain.

We made Mason, Texas, by late afternoon the next day, and checked into the motel where we were supposed to meet our unofficial guides, Bud Priddy and Joe Robinson. The drive seemed to go quickly. The conversation was more spirited because we were getting closer to actually going fishing and because Ed had a load off his mind. And then there was a lift, literally and figuratively, as we drove up out of the scrubby plains into the forested hills around Mason County.

Bud showed up in time for supper—burritos at a little cafe on the corner—and Joe arrived some time after dark. It was a hot night, so we sat in the air-conditioned room to discuss our strategy. The first order of business was to float the Llano River in canoes for two days, camping overnight on an island. That's permissible. "Islands are considered no man's land," Bud said.

Ed and I were concerned about what was permissible because there is almost no public land or water in Texas. Everything is so uniformly private—and trespassing is so universally frowned upon—that most land isn't even posted. The assumption is that you will exhibit the proper respect, and if you don't you'll learn damned quick and in no uncertain terms. This made us a little nervous, coming from Colorado, where there's more public than private land to wander around on.

So in our midwestern Germanic way, Ed and I wanted to know the rules. Bud said, "Well, there's things that'll get you yelled at and things that won't." Joe added, "It's best not to go acting like a hippie *in front of people.*"

Officially, you can put your canoe in and take it out at road crossings on navigable rivers. In between, you'll probably be okay if you conduct yourself like a gentleman. You'll naturally get out of the canoe from time to time to wade, cast from the bank, have lunch and relieve yourself, and all of that *may* be illegal. If you want to do this yourself, don't just bring a copy of this book. Contact the State of Texas Parks and Wildlife Department.

These lush, pretty, spring-fed hill country rivers are perfect for a canoe paddled by people who are less than experts: mostly slow flowing and lazy, but with enough rocks and rapids to make things interesting. Ed and I were using my new Mansfield canoe, a sweet little boat with thin cedar strut construction inside and an equally thin fiberglass shell. It's pretty and delicate looking, and when we lifted it off the top of the truck Joe said, "Nice boat. I hope you don't bust it up in here."

I thought he was giving us some of that good-natured grief, but when I looked at his eyes I realized he was honestly wishing us well. He really hoped we wouldn't bust it up.

These streams are not only pretty, they're also rich in fish: several species of sunfish (called "perch" locally), catfish big enough for head mounts, carp, alligator gar and some largemouth bass, but the definitive fish is the Guadalupe bass. These are small, stream-dwelling bass native only to a few rivers in Texas.

Guadalupe bass are somewhat troutlike in their habits, even to their tendency to feed daintily on mayflies below riffles, and local fly fishermen like to call them "Texas brook trout." They even look a little like trout in the water. The coloration varies, but many Guadalupe bass have distinct spots and bronzish-green backs; actually more like a cutthroat than a brookie.

The only catch is that they seldom grow to more than two pounds, so many bass fishermen overlook them and, as near as I can tell, the trout fishermen who would appreciate them don't usually *go* to Texas.

Fly-fishing is considered a minor angling method in Texas, and fly-fishing for small stream fish with light tackle is a downright rarefied sport. Before this was over we'd spend four days on rivers, and in that time we'd see one other boat, from which no one was fishing.

So there was that cockeyed familiarity again. The Llano was wider and slower than most Rocky Mountain streams, but there were rock cliffs and it was flowing water with bright, spotted fish, and so completely recognizable. But then when you got out to wade and fish you didn't need waders because the water was warm, and you usually fished something like a deer hair frog instead of a mayfly—although you *could* fish a mayfly during a hatch and do well.

The banks were forested with deciduous trees filled with cardinals and, unless you count the odd trotline set for catfish, there were no signs of civilization. If I wasn't casting a little cork or deer hair froggie along the banks and picking up fish, I was paddling with long, slow strokes trying to keep Ed in the best casting position. If you're fond of canoes, one is about as much fun as the other. The newness of the place sank in quickly and I became pretty happy.

We took turns paddling and fishing and tried to look around as much as possible, knowing that you'll never see enough of a new river in just a couple of days. I saw a snake that could have been a cottonmouth and a mature white-tailed deer no bigger than a Great Dane. The deer are tiny here, stunted because there are so many of them.

We each caught our first Guadalupe bass, first yellow-bellied perch, first long ear. You couldn't tell what kind of fish you had by the strike, but once hooked the largemouth bass would often jump, Guadalupe bass would jump higher and the panfish would plane heavily with their flat sides against the current.

Sometimes we'd beach the canoe to admire and photograph these fish, and then there'd be a strange bird we had to get a look at. I saw a little green kingfisher: another first.

Often the two canoes were far apart, but sometimes you'd catch bits of conversation. Once, after an hour of virtual silence, I heard a thump and Joe's slow voice saying, "Bud, I believe that bass just took a bite out of your boat."

The first night we camped on an island of bleached round river stones that would not take a tent peg. Bud cooked steaks and beans and made biscuits in a Dutch oven while Ed and I went through the guidebook trying to identify, from memory, some of the unfamiliar birds we'd seen. We turned the canoes over to drain. Mine had taken a few scratches, but we hadn't busted it up.

The island is accessible by car over a narrow bridge, and just as we were all crawling into our tents a pickup with two young couples pulled in. They saw our camp, talked it over for a minute and left. In the polite way Texans have, Joe suggested that they'd driven out there to "look at the moon" and required a little more privacy.

A few days later we were in south Texas looking for the entrance to a private fishing camp. In between there had been a party at a Mexican restaurant in San Antonio with great food, lots of beer, many wild fishing stories and an awful mariachi band. I'm as multicultural as the next guy, but I draw the line at mariachi bands with no sense of rhythm and two flat trumpets. One of the guys at our table went over and tipped the band leader. When he came back I asked, "You like that?" and he said, "Hell no, that's how you make them go away."

Joe had gone home and we'd picked up a man named Tommy and his huge, apparently oceangoing, metal flake red bass boat with white Naugahyde swivel seats and chrome steering wheel. There were no dingleberries only because there was no place to hang them. This thing was towed, at great speed, by one of those enormous pickups with the four wheels in back.

The camp consisted of one big building—which was mostly kitchen— that you might call the main lodge, surrounded by several trailers, outbuildings and a collection of possibly abandoned trucks. There was a small airstrip off to the side with a limp orange wind sock hanging from a pole and cracks in the paving through which weeds were growing. As we pulled up, a flock of maybe twenty wild turkeys darted off into the mesquite and cactus.

People in Texas sometimes use a kind of enviable economy in their conversation. Bud could have warned me specifically about rattlesnakes, water moccasins, scorpions, poisonous spiders, wild boars, catclaw bushes, killer bees and such, but instead he just said, as we were getting out of the car, "Now, be careful. Everything down here will either sting you or bite you."

Ed now refers to that first afternoon as the Comanche Tank Disaster. (There are no bass ponds in Texas, but there are plenty of "tanks.") While Bud and I were getting the aluminum john boat into the water, Tommy backed his trailer way too far and too fast out into the tank and got both the trailer and the truck stuck in the deep, clinging mud.

Bud told me to get into the john boat, cranked up the outboard and said he thought the fishing would be best way over there on the other side of the six-hundred-acre lake. As we pulled away, Tommy was gunning the pickup. You could see the rear wheels sinking deeply into the mud, the dual exhausts blowing big bubbles in the muddy water.

I got most of the rest of it secondhand from Ed. Tommy fought the truck and trailer until they were both stuck up to the axles, but the trailer still wasn't deep enough to float the bass boat and it was too heavy to push off. Tommy tried, and he might have done it. He was about seven feet tall, weighed several hundred pounds, and looked strong, but that was offset by many old injuries from a few seasons of playing professional football, as well as numerous other accidents before and since.

Once Tommy was out deer hunting at this very camp. He was riding a dirt bike with a scoped .270 slung over his shoulder when he spotted a big rattlesnake and decided to run over it. (Rattlers are killed on sight in Texas.) But the snake got caught in the front tire, flipped up into Tommy's lap and the whole assembly—bike, snake, rifle and rider—did half a dozen forward somersaults. Tommy was unhappy about that because he "busted the damn gun."

Ed suggested calling a wrecker to pull the truck out of the tank (there was a phone in the pickup), but Tommy said, "They'd never find us out here," which seemed true enough.

Sometime during the struggle Ed's graphite rod got broken, he lost track of his Hardy reel, and then Tommy called someone on the car phone, said, "Hi. Oh, we're stuck in the lake, what're you up to?" and chatted for half an hour.

Then they decided to walk back to the camp for help, took a short cut and got lost.

Bud and I had a nice time catching some bass and watching the pelicans. Later, when Ed accused me of abandoning him, I thought of several excuses, but finally just said, "You're right, I'm sorry."

Then Ed said, in an admiring tone, "You've always been good at sidestepping the weird shit."

Over the next few days we fished the big Comanche Tank and several smaller ones where fly-fishing was a little more reasonable, places like the Frog Tank, Rock Tank and a few others the names of which I either didn't catch or wasn't told. We were in the company of half a dozen middle-aged men who, apparently, had all played high-school football together. Football is a big deal in Texas. You can drive through many small towns without learning their names, but you'll by God know they're the home of the Cougars or the Trojans or whatever.

One of these guys took us aside and said that, although Tommy seemed big and dangerous, he was really just accident prone, but otherwise gentle as a lamb. "Just give him plenty of room," the man said.

The standard tactic in these tanks was to fish a floating bug with the diving fly routine. You start by cutting off half of the sinking portion of a sink-tip fly line and throwing it away. Then, on the part that's left, you tie on a short, stout leader—maybe four feet of fifteen- or twenty-pound monofila-ment—and attach a bass bug to the business end with a Duncan Loop, a knot that lets the fly wiggle around, even on a stiff leader.

Bud's flies of choice are Dahlberg Diver–style deer hair bugs. The stan-dard froggie is good, but Bud also has some patterns of his own design, in-cluding an injured baitfish and a neat little baby catfish with rubber whiskers. Bud ties some of the best-looking deer hair bugs I've ever seen. They're right up there with the ones tied by Dave Whitlock and Jimmy Nix: trim but buggy, tails perfectly matched, deer hair spun tight as cork.

Anyway, you cast the bug up against the bank, a weed bed or flooded stump. When the sinking tip of the line has bellied out under the surface of the water, you give it a good pull and the floating deer hair bug dives with a beautiful wiggling, swimming motion, kicking its feather legs behind it. I tried other flies, but it only works right with a Dahlberg Diver. I don't know how Larry Dahlberg figured this out, but it was a stroke of genius.

Sometimes the bass do hit like outdoor writers say they do—"like a freight train" is what you usually hear—but more often the take is so subtle you can think the fly has just bumped a weed or a waterlogged stick. Con-sequently, you set up on everything, and you set up hard, pulling line with your left hand and raising the rod tip with your right. "The harder the bet-ter," Bud said. "You want to cross his eyes."

We caught a lot of what I think of as big largemouth bass, but of course the locals outfished us, which is only right and proper. Most of these guys were Ugly Stick and rubber worm fishers, and they were good. Some of them, when they saw that Bud, Ed and I were fly-fishing, dug into their in-credible piles of gear, got out their own fly rods, to be polite, and outfished us *that* way.

The often-written-about style of bass bugging, where you fish a floating deer hair bug on a floating line, letting it sit perfectly still on the surface for two, three minutes between gentle twitches, is not much thought of here. "That was invented by some goddamn outdoor writer from up north," Bud said. "These fish are aggressive and you gotta go after 'em aggressively."

He seemed to be right about that, but then this was the way I knew to fish for bass, and in a tank that was so choked with weeds they said it would be unfishable in another couple of weeks, I tried it. I cast a big Near Enough deer hair froggie to the edge of a five-foot-wide pothole of open water, let it sit there for two, three, maybe four minutes and then gave it a twitch.

The fly went down in a rise that looked like a toilet flushing. That's what bass fishers say. It's not the prettiest analogy in angling, but, I'm sorry, that's exactly what it looks like.

I was fishing a stiff, nine-foot, nine-weight rod and had already learned that if you gave a fish even a foot or two of line in these overgrown tanks you'd lose him in the weeds. So the fights were short and brutal. You'd grab the rod in both hands and haul, figuring you had spare rods back in the car, so you could break one, which would at least make for a good story. The bass would either throw the hook or come to the apron of the belly boat still thrashing. That day I got a case of tendonitis in my right elbow that lasted most of the season.

I think that bass weighed eight pounds, so figure seven. I held it up for Bud at a distance and he later said, "Now that was a *big* ol' bass." He was probably being kind. Usually the technical term "big ol' bass" refers to something in the ten-pound class.

That was the prettiest of all the tanks we fished. It was set in flat mesquite country with an enormous horizon and was full of tough weeds, bleached flooded timber and water moccasins they said you should watch out for because they like to crawl up on your belly boat. There were big white-winged whistling ducks that made an eerie, piping call that sounded like the first few notes of a sad folk song. Tommy said that if you got up on the dam and looked west over the tops of the mesquite bushes you could see Mexico. "And if you see dark-haired people running through the bushes," he added, "don't wave."

That night we ate home-cooked tacos at another camp that seemed abandoned, except that the electricity was still on. It was just dark and a storm was coming in from the southwest, so we stood at the open door for a while and watched the lightning. A guy who had made a comment about animal rights nuts two days ago picked up a gallon tub of guacamole dip and said, "Just think how many guacamoles had to die to make this."

The conversations in these fishing camps had less to do with fishing than I'm used to. These men were there to catch bass, but it was generally known where the fish were and how to catch them, so there just didn't seem to be a lot to discuss. Instead there was a lot of catching up. Those who hadn't played football together were distantly related or had once worked for or worked with or been the neighbor of a cousin or great-uncle or had shot deer on the same ranch as boys or *something*. When two strangers meet in Texas they pick each other's pasts apart until they find that connection, a whole universe of discourse opens up, and then they're buddies, if not actual relatives.

Once that's done, conversations take place in which little is apparently said. One night the name of a girl everyone had known in high school came up. A quiet smile went around the room that I thought I recognized as the prelude to an off-color story, but instead someone said, "Well, she was a pretty girl and she's grown into a handsome married woman." Everyone agreed. "Yes sir, a *hand*some married woman."

One of the best parts of this leg of the trip was all the fish we ate. These tanks are extremely rich in food organisms and the climate is such that bass will spawn several times in a season, so the prevailing management philosophy is that they need to be harvested heavily so they won't overpopulate. "Now kill all the little bass you catch," they kept saying.

"What's 'little'?" I'd ask.

"Oh, say five pounds."

"Back home we'd think about *mounting* a five-pound bass," I said.

"Yeah, I know."

Tommy turned out to be the best cook. He didn't exactly teach me how to make mustard beer battered fish—when I asked him how he did it after the fact he said he couldn't remember—but I watched him do it a few times and picked it up. You mix equal parts mustard and yellow cornmeal, add a dash of baking powder and maybe some hickory salt or whatever else is lying around in the spice department and enough beer to make a thin paste. Then batter the fish and deep fry them in hot Crisco until they're just brown. And watch out for the spitting grease.

I never did land the ten-pound bass on a fly rod—which you can do in south Texas—but I had one on. At least that's what a gentleman named Dan said from the seat next to me in the big red bass boat one day. I was fishing some kind of streamer on a sink-tip line and had gotten a little lazy, as you can do on a hot day, fishing from a plush seat, roll casting with your right hand and holding a cold Lone Star in your left.

The fish hit, I struck and had him on for about as long as it took for him to come to the surface, jump and throw the hook. "That would have gone about ten," Dan said casually. "You shoulda set up harder."

I was trying to fix in my mind that fleeting glimpse of the biggest large-mouth bass I'd ever seen alive and I almost said, "How the hell am I supposed to set up harder with a beer in my hand?" but of course the answer was obvious. You *can* fish and drink at the same time, but you can't do both well.

Later I told Ed about the big bass that had gotten off. He said, "Well, that's another one you can think about for the rest of your life."

A day or two later, Bud, Ed and I were back in the hill country, staying at a campground on the Nueces (pronounced "new aces") River. We were a few miles from Camp Wood, the little town where Bud, who now lives in San Antonio, was born. Ed and I were beginning to show signs that the trip was winding down—wondering what was happening at home, talking about work. If we'd stuck to the original plan, we'd have been in northern New Mexico by then, but this was one of those trips that takes on a life of its own. When Bud suggested canoeing one more river, we'd gotten a second wind and called home to say we'd be a little late.

Ed said, "Well, one of us is still employed," meaning Monica. Ed makes a living as a writer and fishing guide, but he wisely doesn't think of either as "employment."

We were a man short for the float the next day—you need a fisherman *and* a paddler per canoe—so we spent a few hours locating Bud's friend Don, who, Bud said, "needed to go fishing." Don was a tall, wiry man with a handlebar mustache and one of those silver belt buckles the size of a saucer. He had apparently done many things in life, judging by his stories, but was now happy to be an ostrich rancher. He told us about ostriches in some detail in camp that night, as huge Hexagenia mayflies from the river collected on the picnic table and flying beetles the size of golf balls buzzed the lantern.

The Llano River had been clear, as someone said, "in that pea green way those warm rivers have," but the Nueces was as limpid as any trout stream I've ever seen. Glancing over the gunnels of the canoe in a deep hole, you could count the scales on a bluegill at ten feet.

Bud said the river was fishing a little slow. The water did seem a bit cool and, as clear as it was, it was running a little high. The weather had been chilly for spring in Texas—in the eighties—and there'd been a couple of horrendous rains. In fact, we'd talked about floating the Guadalupe River, but it was blown out by high water.

The Nueces *was* slow in the morning, but it was a bright, almost hot day and by noon the water had warmed and we started getting into fish. Sometimes we'd stop and wade, but more often we'd drift along a shady bank with one man paddling and the other casting. The river was slow enough in most places that if you hit a good bank you could paddle back upstream and drift down again.

We portaged around a few rapids on the Nueces, but I had already put some scratches on my no-longer-new canoe on the Llano, so I had gotten a little braver by then.

Maybe the fishing *was* a little slow, but then Bud has fished these rivers off and on all his life, so he has a different perspective. You have to understand that when a local fisherman tells you how a river usually is, he's describing the best day anyone ever had there. It seemed fine to me and, it being toward the end of the trip and all, I'd have been happy enough just to float and look around, experiencing that edgy sadness you feel when it's almost over, but you still have a hard, two-day drive ahead of you. We did catch fish, but I considered them a bonus.

I guess I had finally achieved the regional pace. I didn't really notice that until I got back home, decompressed for a day, and then forged ahead at what I thought was my normal speed, which is none too fast anyway. Down at the cafe someone asked, "Are you still tired from your trip?" and I said, "Why, no, darlin', I'm just relaxed," remembering too late that "darlin'" is politically incorrect in Colorado.

I also found that I wasn't bragging. When asked if I got into fish, I allowed as how some folks had been nice enough to show me how to do it and, yes, I did catch a few.

For a couple of days there I was even hesitant to criticize people, tending to say either nice things or nothing at all, as in, "Oh, I don't think he's incompetent, he's probably just in the wrong line of work." It wore off eventually, but for a week or so I was actually acting like a gentleman.

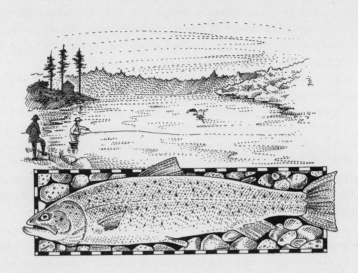

Scotland

F O R once it was exactly as I'd pictured it, which is something a fisherman doesn't get to say very often. There were real castles and slate-roofed stone cottages scattered around a green river valley, ghillies in knee-high breeches and leather vests, a water bailiff in a deerstalker cap who slept days and only ventured out in the gloaming when poachers were about. Hundreds of pheasants strolled the fields and roosted in the oak forests where the deer live, waiting for the driven shoots in the fall.

We dressed in jackets and ties for dinner, drank the good whiskey they don't export to America and, of course, our party of five fished hard for six days and caught one fish among us.

We were fly-fishing for Atlantic salmon on a private river in Scotland in late June—a good river at a pretty good time of year, by all accounts—but this was what everyone had told me to expect. "Even if you do everything right, you might not catch one. *You've got to understand that*," they said, or words to that effect.

The thing about Atlantic salmon is, once they've run out of the sea and into their home rivers to spawn, they don't feed. As always, there's a logical reason for that. If these big salmon came into the rivers hungry, they'd eat up all the salmon parr from the previous year's spawn and wipe out the whole next generation of fish. Perfectly logical, when you think about it.

So a salmon comes into a river carrying enough nutrients in its tissues to last it many months, its digestive system ceases to work and physical changes occur in the fish's hypothalamus that bring on what Lee Wulff called "a loss of appetite or nausea." This is not the moodiness you sometimes see in trout; these fish really don't eat, so they're really not supposed to bite.

This is something a fisherman has to think hard about and get firmly in mind.

Hugh Falkus, in his inch-and-a-half-thick, three-pound *Salmon Fishing: A Practical Guide,* says, "What is surprising is not that salmon are hard to catch, but that any are caught at all." Every salmon-fishing book I've ever peeked into has said something like that, usually right near the beginning so you won't get the wrong idea. This has been known to work, but you've gotta understand that it's not *supposed* to work, okay?

I'd never fished for Atlantic salmon before and in the end it was the very unlikelihood of catching one—the exciting weirdness of that—that finally attracted me to it, or at least that's what I thought. Looking back on it now, I realize I didn't believe I'd actually get skunked. I thought I'd experience the epitome of sport everyone talks about, work hard, confront frustration and otherwise take my lumps, but I also thought I'd eventually catch a fish.

I should have known better, because the sport is lousy with stories not just of blank days but of entire blank seasons. A man in Scotland told me he'd caught five salmon the first time he'd fished for them (that's unheard of and it cost him a fortune in scotch at the pub afterward) and then he didn't catch another fish for three years.

Once a story like that is told among salmon anglers, everyone else trots out *their* story. It's a form of competition, the winner being the guy who went the longest without a fish, but still didn't give up.

When I said okay, sure, it's just that I couldn't remember the last time I'd fished for six days straight without so much as a strike, I was told, "A bad week is nothing, lad, nothing a'tall."

This river had been held privately for the last six hundred years—the whole river, not just a piece of it—but an English company had recently bought the fishing rights from the estate and was offering them for sale on a time-share basis: one week in perpetuity for seventy thousand pounds, or about twice that many American dollars. There were six of us altogether: five

American writers—Tom, Scott, Don, Clive and me—plus Laine, Clive's photographer (although Laine might have said that Clive was *his* writer). Some of us were magazine staffers, some were on assignment and others were freelancing, but that was the story: time shares on a salmon river in Scotland, a cultural hybrid of an idea that was supposed to make Americans dive for their checkbooks.

Since only five rods were allowed on a beat, Laine couldn't fish, but he said he wouldn't have even if he could. He thought fishing was insane. He hated the boredom, couldn't stand getting wet or cold and didn't care much for fish anyway, except maybe kippers. Turning to Clive he said, "Remember when I covered that sea trout story with you? Night after miserable night in the freezing rain, in a leaky boat, not even the paltry excitement of catching a fish, and having to put up with you the whole time."

But, he added to the rest of us, as a professional photographer he could, and would, take pictures of anything, and they'd be damned good, too.

We began downstream at the Downie beat. Our ghillie, Matthew, put me on The Breaches pool and asked to see my flies. I had a single box of brand-new wets: Copper Killers, Thunder and Lightnings, Undertakers and General Practitioners that a man who'd fished Scotland had recommended, plus a brace each of Jock Scotts and Green Highlanders for local color.

"Did you tie these?" asked Matthew.

"No, I bought them."

"In America?"

"Yeah, from a place called Hunter's."

"Well," he said, "they're terribly pretty," as if prettiness was a nice enough touch, but it wasn't going to make any difference.

He broke off my tippet and retied it—because no guide anywhere likes *your* knots—then selected a small General Practitioner on a double hook and tied that on for me, too. There's no reason in the world for an Atlantic salmon in a river to bite any fly, but among the people who fish for them this way there's still something that clicks, making one pattern look better than another.

Laine was photographing all this: the American fisherman being instructed by the Scottish ghillie with Croiche Wood as a backdrop and good morning light. He hated to get wet, but to achieve the right angle he had waded into the river up to his shins in tennis shoes.

There are subtleties to Atlantic salmon fishing (there must be, there have been so many thick, ponderous books written about it), but when you don't know what you're doing, you do what you're told. In this case, you "work the water."

You start at the top of a pool, make a quartering downstream cast, fish it out, take a step downstream and do it again. The fly is fished on an across and downstream swing, so you end up covering the entire pool in what would look, in an illustration, like a series of sickle-moon-shaped stripes about two feet apart.

At the bottom of the pool you get out, walk back to the top and start again. You're fishing with a floating line, so your unweighted wet fly swims very shallowly, within an inch or two of the surface. Of course the salmon usually lie much deeper than that so, as unlikely as these fish are to bite in the first place, they have to make the full commitment and move for the fly. It seems like an outside chance, but that's how a gentleman fishes.

I asked if maybe a guy shouldn't concentrate on places where salmon would likely be lying. "Yes," said the ghillie, "that would be all right."

"So where do you suppose that would be?" I asked.

"Oh," he said, making a gesture that seemed to include the whole pool, "all through there."

You think the ghillie should have more to tell you about this, but he doesn't, or at least you assume he doesn't because you don't see much of him. I had assumed the ghillie was there to be helpful, like an American guide, but then I was from out of town.

I fished down the pool, letting the fly hang in the current for a minute or so at the end of each swing because sometimes a salmon chases it and hits it when it stops. I fished through the pool maybe five times. On the third or fourth pass two men on horseback trotted into a clearing on the far bank and sat watching me. I waved, but they didn't wave back. That was the most exciting thing that happened all morning.

A friend of mine said he'd been salmon fishing once and had actually enjoyed the mindless, repetitive nature of it. He didn't mention whether he'd caught a fish or not, which means he didn't. He also said he can spot the Atlantic salmon story in which the writer got skunked by the first paragraph. "It's all about the castles, cottages, ghillies and deer forests," he said.

We were staying at the Cruvies House, a large cottage on the river at the bottom of the Falls beat, complete with a tile-floored fishermen's changing room and a heated drying closet for waders and rain gear. The river side of the dining room had a line of French doors looking out on the cruvies themselves—a set of V-shaped stone dams with cribs used for netting salmon in the old days. The old days in this case dated back to the 1400s.

Lunch was served at the hut on whatever beat we happened to be fishing, but we ate breakfast and dinner in that room overlooking the river, usually with Dick, who was president of the company that owned the fishing rights.

Dick was charming, quick with a joke, always in charge in an even-handed, British way and, he said, a student of all things American, even to doing most of his riding on a western saddle. He gently instructed us in the ways of salmon fishing—more the etiquette than the technique, although some of us were weak on both—and occasionally corrected our speech.

When the subject of priests came up, someone asked, "What do you mean by a 'priest'?"

Tom said, "In this context, it's a little weighted club you use to bonk a salmon on the head to kill it."

"I wouldn't put it quite that way," Dick said.

"Why not?"

"Because here 'bonking' means 'screwing.'"

He also tried to explain cricket, but gave it up when I said I didn't even understand baseball.

These dinners were at least three courses, prepared and served by Jane, who is probably the best fancy meat and potatoes cook I've ever met. She was self-employed, working sometimes for Dick and sometimes for other parties of salmon fishers who rented cottages in the valley. She was the best cook in the county, she said, and these rich folk, being used to the best of everything, often bid against each other for her services.

One day I got to talking with one of these guys, a wealthy sport who was a tenant on half a dozen of the country's best salmon and sea trout rivers, and who seemed to stop fishing only long enough to do a little driven grouse and pheasant shooting. He seemed like a nice man—if nothing else, he was spending his money right—but he also gave off a certain air that's hard to describe: almost as if he thought he could have you beheaded if the mood struck him. Anyway, he'd told Dick he wanted to meet some of these American writers who were such hard-core fishermen they weren't even stopping for tea.

He asked me about the Frying Pan River in Colorado, which he'd heard about.

"Now, when you go over there and camp for a week," he said, "do you bring your own cook from home or do you engage someone locally?"

I had to tell him that, as far as I knew, there was no one like Jane in Colorado. He winced slightly when he heard the name. She was cooking for us that week, which apparently meant he and his party were getting by on cold porridge, stale bread and cheap wine in bottles with screw caps.

I liked Jane immediately—we all did—and not just for the great food she
put out. She was a genuine wild Highlander who pointedly took no crap
from anyone, addressed no one as "mister," liked to refer to us as boys, her
boss included—although she was younger than most of us—did not engage
in false modesty and managed the kind of dignity that allowed her to serve
meals without seeming like a waitress. She made you want to hang out in
the kitchen, even though (or maybe because) that seemed to be frowned
upon.

Jane could do a great impression of a midwestern American accent, complete with appropriate dialogue ("Hey, Bob, get a load of this here
church"). She said, "You can always spot Americans by their wide arses and
small heads." She also happened to be pretty: willowy, but not anorectic-
looking like a model.

I noticed right off that Scott was hanging out in the kitchen more than
the rest of us, but I thought maybe he just had a domestic streak and was
pumping her for recipes.

I think that cottage is the most comfortable place I've ever stayed while
fishing. We each had our own big, homey, high-ceilinged room with a huge
bed, down comforters and a private bath (with English plumbing, but then
nothing's perfect). My room looked out on the river, and since the nights
were only chilly, I slept with the windows open. We put in long days fishing, drank some and ate large meals, but I still think it was the river that put
me away each night. The sound of it hissing through the cruvies had the
same effect as morphine.

Laine seemed happy enough for a day or two. We fished methodically and
he took pictures. Fishermen casting, or wading, or tying on a fly while
standing conveniently in front of an ancient churchyard. He'd pose you
carefully one minute and then tell you to just do whatever it was you were
doing the next.

At first he'd be saying, "Yes! Great! Perfect!" all the time he was shooting,
but then he started muttering things like, "No," "No good," or "Nope, not
weird enough."

"Not weird enough?" I asked.

"Any idiot can take a picture of a man fishing," he said. "Anyway, the magazine likes weird photos. That's why they hired me. And by the way," he
added, "is someone going to catch a fish soon?"

Don did catch a fish the next day when we rotated up to the Falls beat. It
was about eleven o'clock in the evening, just dusk that far north, and he

was casting to a salmon that had boiled several times more or less in the same spot. Tom said, "Now that's a taking fish," and Don had started down the bank saying, "Let's see."

A "taker" is the salmon everyone is looking for. It's the one fish in God knows how many that, for reasons of its own, will take your fly. This may have to do with habit or the memory of feeding, aggression, curiosity, playfulness, the fish's freshness from the sea, time of day, time of the most recent tide, weather, water conditions, fly pattern, a defective hypothalamus or some combination thereof. It's a mystery but, since it ultimately has to do with sex, the odd moodiness of it also seems vaguely familiar. One thing is clear: A taking fish is defined after the fact. As Matthew told me, "A taker is the one you caught, if you catch one."

"How do you know that's a taker?" I asked Tom.

"Just a guess," he said.

And then Don caught the fish, a lovely fourteen pounder. It was what they call a "bright fish," fresh from the ocean with sea lice still on it and shiny as a chrome bumper. We all ran down to watch him land it and take some photos, even though the light was almost gone. All of us except Scott, that is. He hadn't come out with us after dinner. In fact, it seemed as if he vanished about the time Jane went home.

Come to think of it, Laine wasn't there either. Earlier that day he'd begun mumbling about taking a different approach and needing some props. No one had seen him since.

It turns out that Laine had driven into the nearest town and, after hours of haggling, had rented an ornate old grandfather clock from the suspicious owner of an antique shop. When we came in that night it was lying in pieces in the front hall.

"What's it for?" Dick asked at breakfast the next day.

"I don't know exactly," Laine said, "but, you know, it's about time shares, so I felt I needed a large clock."

Dick nodded thoughtfully. There *was* a certain logic to it.

We were late getting on the water that day because it took an hour or more to drag out Don's salmon and pose it and him in every way any of us could think of. Then someone else would have to pose with it so Don could get some shots. After all, it was his fish. And then you'd have to do everything both with and without the ghillie, who would have been happy to get done with this foolishness and get on the water. "This is a good deal of excitement over one fish," he said.

Laine followed us around for another day and a half, taking candid shots, posing each of us in turn at the scenic Back of the Castle Pool, fooling with fill-in flashes and reflectors and generally waiting for someone else to catch a fish.

It seemed as if all of us fishermen were waiting for the same thing. That's what it feels like: the repetitive, almost hypnotic cast, drift, step; cast, drift, step. You're not so much fishing as you are waiting for a fish.

Of course as writers we had other things to think about. Presumably Don had at least the germ of his story, but what about the rest of us? Fishing with fishing writers is strange enough anyway, but when almost everyone is getting skunked and searching for a new angle, the conversation can get pretty weird. You'll make some idle comment like, "Well, it's a pretty spot anyway, with those castle towers poking up above the trees," and someone will say, "Yeah, man, there's your lead."

Scott seemed to be sublimely above all this, taking the lack of fish philosophically, but he *was* under some strain. In the evenings he'd say he was bushed and was going to turn in early. Then in the morning we'd come down to find him in the kitchen chatting quietly with Jane as she cooked breakfast. But it was all just a little bit *too* discreet, and peeking into his room was too much of a temptation for some of us. Sure enough, the bed hadn't been slept in, not that it was any of our business, of course.

Then later, out on the river, Scott would turn up missing again, only to be found curled up in the tall grass sleeping like a baby. When he'd get caught at it he'd say something like, "Gee, this salmon fishing is more strenuous than I thought."

One day Laine and some of the others decided to photograph one of the great lunches we were having catered at the fishing huts. (The angle everyone seemed to be working on now had more to do with cuisine than fishing.) We hauled the table outside—for natural light and the river as a background—and Laine, Tom and Don began arranging food, wine, wicker picnic baskets, two-handed fly rods and Dick into the perfect *Gourmet Magazine*-style composition.

Of course no two photographers think alike, so there was some disagreement about what should go where. I didn't have an opinion, so I was standing off to the side, out of the way. Scott sidled up beside me and asked, quietly, "Ever hear the expression 'high-speed goat fuck'?"

I said, "No, but I like it."

Someone commented that the only thing missing was a salmon, at

which point Matthew jumped into his little pickup with the dog kennels in
the back and roared off down a dirt road. I thought he'd gone to the cottage
to get Don's fish, but instead he came back in ten minutes with a nice grilse
(young salmon) of about seven or eight pounds. The fish was so fresh that,
although he'd killed it, it was still twitching.

Someone said, "Perfect!" but I thought, Wait a minute, if the ghillie
knows where a fish can be caught that easily, shouldn't he be putting one
of us on it? One of us like me, maybe?

It was just an idle thought. The grilse did complete the photograph and
Dick, who'd been standing at the head of the table holding a glass of wine
and wearing a frozen smile, seemed relieved to finally hear the shutters
clicking.

"May I drink this now?" he asked.

On the fifth day we trudged back to the hut on the Home beat for lunch and
Dick, who looked a little confused, said that before we sat down to eat,
Laine would like to see us all up at the cruvies, in waders, with our rods.

We drove up to the house, and when we got out of the van I heard bagpipes. They were faint, but unmistakable.

"Scott," I said, "do you hear pipes?"

"Yeah, I do," he answered sleepily, "but I wasn't gonna say anything."

It seems that the same day Laine had rented the clock, he'd also engaged
the services of a piper; an authentic Highlander in a kilt, bearskin hat, dag-
ger in his boot, the whole catastrophe. By the time we arrived Laine had
the clock sitting in a shallow riffle out in the river with a battery of lights
and reflectors trained on it. Don's salmon had been resurrected and was lying on the bank. It was a couple of days old now; its eyes were glazed, its
jaw was locked open and it was starting to look pretty dead.

The piper was standing back in the trees to keep out of the light drizzle.
He was playing his heart out because, as near as he could figure, that's what
he'd been hired to do.

I've always loved the sound of bagpipes—played well, they make me
want to either cry or fight—but I noticed Matthew cringing every time the
guy launched into another tune.

"Don't you like this stuff?" I asked.

"Well," he said, "a little of it goes a long way, doesn't it?"

I thought, of course: punk rock, spiked hair, pale girls dressed in
leather. Our immediate surroundings notwithstanding, this is still the twentieth century.

Over the next two hours, in a steady light rain, Laine posed every possible combination of one grandfather clock, one piper, one dead fish, five fishermen and one bored ghillie with a long-handled landing net. He was the only one not wearing rain gear and he was soaked to the skin.

"This is it!" he kept shouting. "Time! Salmon! Scotland!" Then he'd rush to adjust some small detail. "What time should the clock say?" he asked of no one in particular. I guess we were watching genius at work.

Dick was a little puzzled by all this, but he wasn't shocked. Over the last few days you could see him slowly getting used to us. We asked some impertinent questions, but then we were writers. Sometimes our language was a little rough, especially after a few drinks, and we seemed to prefer the company of the help instead of the rich sports, but then we were Americans.

I didn't think Dick cared about Scott "taking up with the cook," as he put it, until we rotated back up to the Falls beat on the last day and Scott wasn't there because he'd disappeared with Jane again. Dick didn't say much, but he was clearly scandalized, so I asked, "Does this really bother you?"

"Who's bonking who isn't my business," he said, "but one simply *does not* give up a salmon beat."

As near as I can tell from the little bit of reading I've done, fly-fishing for Atlantic salmon is based on the premise that anything that can happen will, eventually. There are many theories on when, where and on what fly pattern salmon will bite, but, by all accounts, no theory produces fish often enough to be proven true.

Even the experts speak in italics. There *should* be a fresh run off this last tide; this fly *should* work in this pool, if only because it has, off and on, for generations. When salmon aren't caught—which is most of the time—these people take a kind of sly comfort in the fact that, given the circumstances, you really ought not to be able to catch them at all. Meanwhile, the accommodations are posh, the food is good, the booze flows freely and there's the general feeling that things are as they should be.

This would seem like an expensive snipe hunt except that you see fish. Some are boiling and porpoising, others are jumping to dislodge sea lice. Jumpers won't bite, they said, and that was the only statement about salmon I heard that wasn't followed by several contradictory footnotes.

You put yourself through this because some fishermen say catching an Atlantic salmon on a fly is as good as sex, even though you know in your heart it isn't. I agree with a friend of mine who says that if fishing is really

like sex, then he's doing one of them wrong. Still, there do seem to be similarities.

For one thing—as the salmon fishers tell it—either you catch a fish way
too soon, before you're fully able to appreciate it, or you have to wait much
longer than you think you should have to, so that when you finally hook
and land one the elation is tempered by a profound sense of relief.

And, of course, repeated failures don't lead you to the logical conclusion; they only whet your appetite.

Back at the cottage in the evenings, the more experienced salmon fishers—Clive, Dick and Tom—would hold forth. The river flowed by just outside the French doors. It was clear but, because all its water had first
filtered through peat in the Highlands, it was slightly whiskey-colored in
the deep pools. The way to catch salmon, they said, is to keep your fly in
the river and be of good cheer. They didn't seem to understand it either,
but they still appeared to possess a kind of wisdom.

It reminded me of when I was a kid and some grown man would decide
to take me aside and give me the kindly lecture on women. He'd fall into
this vague, humorous mode, trying not to let on that, although he had considerably more experience than I did, he still didn't know what the hell he
was talking about.

Apparently, the genuine salmon fisher takes pride in his acquired tastes,
strength of character, fine sense of irony and apparent craziness, which he
and a few other aficionados know isn't really craziness but, well, something else entirely. As a trout fisherman, I used to think I understood that,
but salmon types look down on us trouters as dilettantes. I mean, we catch
what I now think of as quite a few fish. Small ones by comparison, but fish
nonetheless.

We fished for six days and took Sunday off, not because we were tired or
discouraged, but because it's illegal to fish for salmon on Sunday. I asked
why, but no one knew. It's just always been that way. We took the rented
van and, with Dick as guide, drove up into the Highlands to look around.
All of us except Scott, of course. By now, no one had to wonder where
Scott had gone.

I kept dozing off in the backseat. When you've fished long and hard and
it's become obvious that you're not going to catch anything, it's a relief to finally stop and let it all sink in. As it sank in, I tended to lose consciousness.

On the flight over, Tom had gone into that old salmon-fishing refrain:
You've gotta understand you might not catch one, and I'd said, maybe a

little impatiently, that I understood that. "You understand it intellectually," he said, "but if you really *don't* catch one, there's a hump you'll have to get over."

Right. I could see that now. You have to learn to see yourself not catching fish as if from a great theoretical height.

I also realized that I liked it and that I'd probably do it again, and then again if I had to, until I finally hooked and landed one of the damned things. To prove something, to be able to say I'd done it and because I knew it would be beautiful somehow; not like sex, of course, but in a way so weird that that's the only fair comparison. I also knew that this is how a life can be ruined by sport, and just as I was dozing off I had a vision of myself on a street corner with a tin cup and a sign reading, "NEVER COULD CATCH AN AT-LANTIC SALMON ON A FLY ROD—PLEASE HELP."

The next morning, Dick drove Don and me to the airport at Inverness. Clive and Laine had left early, and Tom was staying on for a day and then heading to Russia, where there were bigger, dumber salmon that hadn't seen six hundred years' worth of flies. We could only guess at Scott's where-abouts. He hadn't been seen for at least a day and a half.

Dick was in a good mood. He said he'd enjoyed having us. "There was a lot of laughter this week," he said, "much more than usual. To be honest, some of the people who fish here are a little stuffy."

Then he asked, "Do you think we'll see Scott at the airport?"

There was some shrugging and throat clearing, and I thought, Would *I* be at the airport?

Dick drove on quietly for a minute and then said, "Well, if he turns up in the next few days, I'll see if I can find a little job for him."

(Author's note: Five months later, in Virginia City, Montana, Scott and Jane were married.)

The Storm

I T was a good spring to be self-employed and a fisherman. From early April all the way into June the weather had been flipping back and forth more wildly than usual, even for Colorado—warmer when it got warm, bitter when it got cold, snowing when it should have just rained—but if you averaged it out it still amounted to what you'd expect: Things were waking up and, when you could catch it right, the fishing was good. But if you wanted to fish in the proper conditions, you had to be in a position to drop everything and go when things fell into place. At those times when things weren't as right as you thought, it was good if that wasn't your only day off.

The rocky weather muddied the trout streams early, broke some freshly leafed-out cottonwood trees with wet snow, pleased some farmers, worried some ranchers and brought complaints from spring turkey hunters, as well as the usual pissing and moaning from big-haired local television newscasters who can't understand that the American West is not the Bahamas.

Local bass fishers weren't whining because it's undignified, but they did say the largemouths never really got on the spawning beds "in a meaningful way."

That's where it stood when Steve, Larry and I went to a private bass pond out east to try to re-create an earlier performance. We'd fished there a week before, dodged the weather successfully for a few hours and caught some good-sized fish before getting rained out. These bass were in exceptionally fine shape—chunky and heavy—and we thought maybe the aborted spawn had saved them from getting beat up and then having to recover. In the long run, there'd be a missing generation of bass in the waters where they manage to reproduce naturally, while in the short run the fish were fatter and prettier than usual. In the interest of playing the ball where it lay, we thought we'd try them again, even though the odds are against pulling it off that well twice in a row.

On the long drive out to the pond, things seemed to be shaping up into a nice enough spring day. The air was warm and there were scattered puffy white cumulus clouds against a blue sky so perfect it looked like the underside of the universe. Driving east, away from the foothills and out toward the Plains, the country always strikes me as enormous, but in that first bass-fishing weather it seems bigger yet, as if doors you'd forgotten you'd closed had been flung open. The conversation was louder than usual, both from happiness and because the windows in the pickup were rolled down.

The big, dark thunderstorm to the south looked as if it would blow past us by quite a few miles. Judging by the angle of the gray veil of rain trailing behind it, we figured it was going roughly west and a little north, while we were going east and a little south. There was no telling how far away it was without knowing its size, but I claimed—based on its purplish-black, almost eggplant color—that it was a great big one and, therefore, many miles off. With the air of a man who has just heard what he wanted to hear, whether he's completely convinced or not, Steve said, "No question about it," and quickly moved to a different subject: canoes, I think.

But by the time we got to the pond the storm had changed direction (or we'd guessed wrong in the first place), and it looked as if it was wheeling toward us. We stood watching it for a few minutes and agreed that we'd just get clipped by the extreme eastern edge of it—a cool, twenty-minute squall at the worst.

A breeze was already ruffling the pond, and it seemed the smartest thing to do would be to cast streamer flies from the bank, working the rough water in the shallows where fish might come in to see what was being stirred up. Little fish to eat the bugs, big fish to eat the little fish—the old by-the-book theory that works more often than most. We were still in sunlight, but the sky was troubled and the bright air felt chilly and damp. This was no time to launch Steve's and Larry's belly boats, let alone my fragile little canvas canoe.

By the time we had our rods strung up, the wind had gotten a little too strong for fly-casting. Steve tried, but no. When you have to hold your hat on your head with one hand and dodge your streamer fly, it's too windy. But the weather wasn't threatening enough yet to drive all three of us into the cramped cab of the pickup, so we took a walk. It was something to do, it would be bracing and we wouldn't get so far from the truck that we couldn't make it back in one good dash.

This pond lies in a low spot in an expanse of classic western high plains country. At first glance it's dry, open, rolling and scrubby—dramatic and severe—but of course it's populated by most of what are now the appropriate creatures, native and otherwise, many of which are attracted to the scattered, cottonwood-lined ponds. This is where you see herons, ducks, geese, pelicans and ibis and where the white-tailed deer you never see in daylight seem to grow up out of the ground at dusk.

This is settled, owned country where it's almost impossible to step off the road bed without permission and not be trespassing, but it's also pleasantly empty: few buildings, few paved roads, a couple of scattered oil wells. The fabled Rocky Mountains are back on the western horizon looking lower and closer than they really are.

This is not great pheasant country, but we saw two and heard at least another cock. The cackle of a cock pheasant sounds like the squeak of an oil well in need of lubrication and also the sound a loose, rusty barbed-wire fence makes in a gusty wind, but you do learn to tell the difference after a while.

As we strolled past a windbreak of trees, a mourning dove flapped off across the ground doing the injured-bird distraction routine, and we were able to find the nest. There were two young doves in it, just starting to get flight feathers.

There were all the usual magpies, cowbirds, blackbirds, starlings and such. And there was a western tanager and also a blue grosbeak, which was a new bird for me, one I'd always wanted to see.

I've always liked the way birds chatter when weather is moving in. They're like humans then, pointing out the obvious, having conversations like, "Hey, look." "Yeah, I see." Not long ago I read that the Tlingit Eskimos in Alaska think owls say, "Get under trees," when a storm is coming, and whenever they say that a storm *does* come.

The wind was really up by then and we decided to head back to the truck, which was the only real shelter in sight. For a while the sky had been blue with lit-up clouds almost yellow above the purple underside of the storm, but suddenly it was gray and somber, with just a line of bright weather to the north. I was carrying my hat because it wouldn't stay on my head, and I could feel a few raindrops on my bald spot.

Back at the pickup we ran into a pair of big peacocks. They came out of the trees to meet us, clearly used to people, but then realized we weren't who they thought we were and shied off a little. We knew the guy who owned this spread raised some exotic birds, but we didn't expect to see them two miles from the house.

We stood by the truck watching the edge of the storm slide in toward us. At a distance it looked almost stationary, but right above us the disk of cloud was scudding by pretty quickly. The tall, slate-gray part of the storm went right to the ground about two miles off in solid curtains of rain. On the edges we could see either filmy rain squalls or the beginnings of funnels, we couldn't be sure which.

The center of the storm was full of lightning, and we counted the seconds between the flash and the crack to see how far away it was. Not far. We noticed that the peacocks had hunkered down under the truck, so we decided to get into the cab ourselves. We were starting to get wet and the temperature seemed to have dropped by about twenty degrees.

It was a wonderful storm: The sky was dark, the rain was in nearly rhythmic, pulsing sheets that laid the cattails down flat. The pickup was broadside to the wind and it was high profile, a big, square '78 Ford with a topper on the bed and a canoe on top of that. It caught the air like a sail and rocked on its springs, making a sound like, oddly enough, a cock pheasant. To the south and west was a purple wall, but what we could see of the sky behind us to the north was clear, so we were just into the edge of this thing.

At the height of it there was some small but dangerously driving hail. Larry pointed at the roof of the cab and asked me if I was worried about my canvas canoe up there. I said, "Maybe a little, but I'm not gonna go out there and do anything about it."

"Yeah," he said, "that's probably wise. I was just asking."

We had a good time sitting in the truck for about forty-five minutes, not talking much because of the din of wind, rain, hail and thunder; just taking the occasional small nip from the flask of Southern Comfort and now and then yelling, "ISN'T THIS GREAT?" or "SON-OF-A-BITCH," or "IT'S GETTING KINDA COLD, ISN'T IT?" It occurred to me that this is something you have to look for in fishing partners: the quality of uncomplaining acceptance, or at least the ability to have a decent time even when things aren't going too well. To put it another way, you don't want to be trapped in a storm with a whiner.

Then I thought I saw something on the water, a funny movement, a shape that wasn't waves: something. I turned on the windshield wipers, which helped only a little. We were parked facing the pond, maybe ten feet from the bank.

I said, "Are there fish rising out there?"

Steve said, "No."

Larry leaned forward, squinting, and said, "I think I see what you see, but I don't know what it is."

I turned the wipers to high and we all leaned up over the dashboard. Yes, it was hard to see, but there appeared to be greenish-bronze shapes moving at the surface. Not logs, not weeds, too substantial to be water shaped by the wind, too green to be carp (and there are no carp in there that I know of), too big to be panfish. I opened the door and leaned out. Before I could even focus I was soaked all down the right side, but I could just make it out.

"God damn it," I said, "there are bass rising right in front of us."

Larry opened his door, leaned out for a second, then slammed it closed again and said, "Yeah, maybe."

Steve sat between us holding the Southern Comfort and said, "No."

"Get out and look," I said.

"No."

We got on the water when it was all but over. The storm had bashed off to the northwest and the thunder had gone from loud cracks to dull, retreating rolls. Gusts of cool wind were blowing themselves out in the trees. The pond was nearly still and the sun was back out, even though a thin drizzle was still sifting down from a great height. The peacocks seemed blissfully unconcerned. They were high-stepping through puddles of clay-colored water and pecking at seeds and bugs. The air was sweet and magical, and I thought of a line written years ago by my old, mad poet friend Marc Campbell: "Peacocks strolled beside the lake/Like illuminated manuscripts."

I launched my canoe while Steve and Larry were getting into waders and flippers and skidding their float tubes down to the water through the dripping grass. The canoe's caned seat was wet from splattered rain, but there was no hail damage to the leathery hull.

I made a quick, ten-minute tour of the pond just to feel the little boat glide, passing Steve and Larry twice as they paddled their tubes over to the good bank. I like belly boats when I'm in one, but when I'm next to them in a canoe I feel like a swan.

Then I tied off to a bleached stick and flipped a little cork popper into the flooded timber. After a few casts I had a big bluegill and then, out of thicker cover, I got a heavy, fifteen-inch bass. I held him in the water for a few seconds before letting him go and thought, That's what I saw boiling around in the shallows during the storm; same shape, same color, only bigger than anything I've ever seen or caught here before.

It wasn't what you'd call useless information, just too small a piece to too large a puzzle, like when, once every two or three generations, it rains frogs. Okay, but if you *want* frogs, there are better ways to get them than standing in the backyard with a bucket. A friend tells me that trying to figure out things like this is like teaching a pig to sing. It may be interesting, but in the end it's a waste of time and it annoys the pig.

We all caught some fish, but the storm had cooled things off, so there wasn't the usual flurry of feeding right at dusk. We fished until dark anyway, going the last half hour or so without a strike. The pond was like a smooth disk by then, but rainwater was still dripping from the trees and spattering in the shallows near shore, making a narrow band of muddy water. Both the bluegills and the bass seemed to be cruising along the edge of it, right where the water cleared.

The closest town was closed up and pretty much deserted, but Larry said he knew of a good, cheap Mexican joint that might still be open. It was two blocks off the one-story main street, with a warehouse on one side and railroad tracks on the other.

"La-something," he said.

"Cocina?" I said. (Half of all Mexican restaurants in the west are known as "The Kitchen.")

"No," Larry said, "La-something else."

They had just closed when we walked in, but when all three of us looked pitiful the guy told us to sit down while he saw if he could still whip something up. When he came back with some beers, he nodded at the bass bug stuck in Larry's baseball cap and said, "You been fishing?"

"Yup."

"Where?"

We told him, vaguely: "A pond sort of near Such-and-Such."

"That tornado out there give you any trouble?" he asked.

"Not much," Larry answered.

"Well," the guy said, "we still got some enchiladas."

Alaska

T H E backcountry of Alaska is a perfect silence broken by the sound of motors: generators, outboards and especially the droning of float planes. Up there the single-engine plane is the equivalent of the pickup truck. Once you're away from the state's handful of roads—in the bush where the fishing is really good—a plane is your only way of getting anywhere, not to mention getting back.

I was in Alaska not too long ago with my friends DeWitt Daggett and Dan Heiner. DeWitt is a publisher and Dan is the managing field editor of an outdoor magazine (which means he manages to get into the field as much as possible). I'd never been to Alaska before and DeWitt had just moved to Anchorage, so this was a first good look around for both of us. Dan was the local boy with all the connections.

We fished from three different lodges—technically, two lodges and a hotel—and spent a lot of time in the air, which is standard procedure. There would be the flight in and then, most days, weather permitting, we'd fly out to this or that river in the morning to be left with a guide and maybe an inflatable raft or a boat stashed on site. Then we'd be picked up at a predetermined place and time to be flown back to the lodge in the evening.

Or what passes for evening. In the Alaskan summer there's a little bit of duskiness in the wee hours, but nothing those of us from "down below," as they say, would call night. I found that if you really want to see darkness you have to drink three or four beers just before going to bed at around eleven o'clock. When you get up to pee about one, it's as dark as it gets, but not so dark you can't find the toilet in a strange cabin. That's important, since by then the generator has been turned off and the lights don't work.

Most days we spent two or three hours flying over genuinely trackless country, often at altitudes of two hundred feet or less, which is low enough to see bears, moose, caribou and even tundra swans clearly, not to mention stream after stream running red from spawning sockeye salmon. I must have asked a dozen people why the salmon turn red in the rivers, and the only one who knew was a native guy. "It's so the bears can see 'em," he said.

We often had the rivers we'd chosen entirely to ourselves, and that sense of loneliness was enhanced by the knowledge that now and then the plane doesn't show up to take you back to the nice, cozy lodge. This doesn't happen often (it never happened to us) but there *is* weather to consider, or engine trouble, and every now and then a pilot will get sick or even just forget he was supposed to pick you up, only to slap his forehead in a bar two days later, turn to the guy on the next stool and say, "Oh, shit." Fishermen are seldom lost forever, but they've been known to get stranded for a while.

At the time it seemed like an outrageous odyssey, but back in Anchorage I found that we'd only gone a couple of inches down the Alaska Peninsula on a map of the state that would cover the average kitchen table. I went out on the front porch and tried to extrapolate the feeling of vastness from our own little trip to all the rest of that game- and fish-infested, largely roadless open land as an exercise in meditation. I sat there through two cans of beer and couldn't do it, but I did remember something Wallace Stegner had said on an audiotape DeWitt's company produced: something about how you don't even have to go into the wilderness to get its benefits; just knowing it's out there is a great comfort.

When we boarded the Alaska Airlines flight from Anchorage to Iliamna, the stewardess got on the intercom and said, "Fasten your seat belts and, yes, the reds are running." That was welcome news because I was psyched to catch salmon, as was everyone else on the plane. There were sixty-some passengers and exactly that many rod cases. No briefcases, no lap-top computers. We were there in late July so any salmon caught would probably be sockeyes, aka "reds." These are a marginal fly rod fish, many people said, but that hardly mattered.

For one thing, I'd spent a week fishing for Atlantic salmon in Scotland that same summer and had gotten skunked. I wasn't exactly looking for revenge—although going after, but not catching, a certain kind of fish does give you a long-lasting itch—there was just the idea of those millions of big fish that live somewhere out at sea and then run up into the rivers once a year, past orcas and seals and bears, to spawn and then die. When you come from a place where there are fewer fish and they pretty much stay put, that's romantic stuff.

And then there was the book tour I'd just finished. It was a mercifully short one, three cities in three days, but it was hell nonetheless. I'd be up too early to get breakfast, and with only one or two cups of coffee under my belt I'd be talking to a motor-mouth morning disc jockey who'd never fished and didn't seem to have read the book.

Then it was more or less constant media for the next six or seven hours. I'd appear on the noontime television talk show as a five-minute segment right after how to buy the perfect gift and just before household tips from kids. The interviewer had fished once as a kid, but he also didn't seem to have read the book. He'd read the press release, though.

"It says here that you're 'the undisputed bard of fly-fishing.'"

After a pause that's too long for television I said, "Yeah, I read that, too."

Despite my anarchistic tendencies, I was intimidated, so I lacked the courage to say, "Look, it's just some bullshit cooked up by the publisher, okay?" Back home some friends had started calling me the undisputed bard of fly-fishing, and then laughing hysterically.

Then came the reading/book signing. It's July in the Northwest, so it's warm and humid anyway. Then I get up on the podium in this stuffy room and they turn a battery of lights on me. These are the same lights they use to keep hamburgers hot in fast-food restaurants.

I'm thinking, If I'm gonna suffer this much, maybe I should get into something that really pays. I'm also thinking, In another fourteen hours I'll be in Alaska where I will burn this sport coat on DeWitt's front lawn. There are shuffling noises coming from the small crowd because I'm thinking instead of talking.

I got into salmon on our first day on the water. I was a little short on sleep and felt jet-lagged, even though I'd only crossed one time zone between Seattle and Anchorage. I guess it was the flying. I'm not as terrified of flying as I once was because I do more of it now. Then again, I can't shake the feeling that every time I fly and live I've used up a bit more luck.

We'd flown into the mouth of the Tazamina River and then motored upstream a mile or so. The water was full of sockeyes, but that didn't seem to interest anyone much except me. Dan, DeWitt and the guide were calmly speculating on where the rainbows and grayling might be, while I kept leaning over the gunnels saying, "Jesus Christ, look at all the salmon. Stop the god damn boat!" Most of the fish were nice and silvery, still fresh from the sea.

When we finally beached on a sand bar the guide got the other two guys going with streamers and then led me to a huge pod of sockeyes. He told me to rig a pink Polar Shrimp with split shot, as if I were fishing for trout with a nymph. One thing about the Alaskans: Unlike the Scots, they fish for salmon as if they actually want to catch them, with sink-tip lines and lead.

When the guide saw that I was rigging up an old Payne nine-and-a-half-foot light salmon rod with a brand-new Peerless #6 reel, he said he'd never seen one of those and asked to try it.

"Shoot," he said, "this is a little heavy, but it casts real nice."

There were fifty salmon in a pool not ten feet from where I was standing. "I'm glad you like the rod," I said, "but give it back."

I had a fish on for a minute or two and lost him. Then I got a good hookup, but the fish was snagged in the back. It weighed six or seven pounds and took longer to land than it should have.

I thought, Yeah, I've heard about this. There are those who say the plankton-eating sockeyes don't take flies and the best you can do is foul hook them, and there are others who say they do too take flies if you do it right. The rules say the fish is a keeper if it's hooked somewhere in the face, ahead of the gill covers.

If I remember right, I landed seven salmon that afternoon, four of which were hooked in or so close to the mouth that I'd say they either ate or tried to eat the fly. And that's as far as I care to delve into that controversy. I will say that when a sockeye is hooked near the front it fights real good, especially on a bamboo rod.

Those first few days we fished from the Iliaska Lodge, owned by Ted and Mary Gerkin. There's a long story here, and if you'd like to hear it you should read Ted's book, *Gamble at Iliamna,* because he tells it much better than I could. Anyway, it was here that I began to understand how sockeye salmon were viewed by Alaskan fly fishers.

The sockeyes, along with the kings, silvers, chums and pinks, form the basis for the entire ecology of these watersheds. The numbers of fish in these runs are astonishing: 6 million in this drainage, 19 million in that one, and there are hundreds of drainages.

Salmon often run all the way up into the smaller rivers and creeks, many of which are connected by large lakes. There are resident grayling and some Dolly Vardens in these streams, but the big rainbow trout and arctic char are only in the flowing water in significant numbers when they follow the salmon runs up out of the lakes. Sometimes a fisherman will say that Such-and-Such River isn't good for big rainbows yet because the salmon aren't in. If you're new at this you'll have to ask him what the hell he's talking about.

The trout, char and grayling feed on salmon eggs that are dribbled by the ripe hen salmon as they run up the rivers and then later on the ones that wash out of the spawning redds. This sounds like an incidental dietary foot-note until you multiply the salmon by millions and get tons of protein from stray eggs alone.

The fish are really onto these things. It's said that big rainbows will swim over and nudge ripe hen salmon to dislodge eggs. Every guide and bush pi-lot I talked to claims to have seen that.

Still later, after the spawn when the salmon all die, these same game fish feed on bits of rotted salmon meat dislodged by the current. It's hard to pic-ture, but in this scheme the pretty rainbow trout, char and grayling fall into the same ecological niche as maggots and vultures.

The standard flies are salmon egg patterns and sickly beige-colored "flesh flies," tied from rabbit fur. Naturally, these are fished on a dead drift. This may not be what you'd call classy stuff, but it does match the hatch perfectly.

The dying and dead salmon are also eaten by gulls, ravens, eagles, otters and such, not to mention aquatic insects, which then go on to feed the salmon parr and smolts before they return to the sea, as well as the grayling, trout, char and such during those times when there are no salmon in the rivers. Then the young salmon themselves form part of the diet for other game fish. In the middle of all this, you can go to the places where rivers enter lakes and fish streamers for big char collected there to feed on migrat-ing smolts. The schools of char are often under flocks of excited, hungry gulls and terns.

That's the obvious stuff you can see from a boat or while wading a river. There's also the plankton/salmon/seal/orca connection out at sea. In the grand scheme, that's what salmon do: They bring the nutrients from the ocean far up into the freshwater rivers, lakes and streams and there's no way I can convey the magnitude of it. It's just something you have to see.

And then there are the bears. Alaskan brown bears—along with rainbow trout—put on a large part of every year's growth gorging on salmon, and once you've stepped in a huge, steaming pile of bear crap you begin to see that their droppings are not an insignificant contribution to the fertilizer needed to grow the grasses that are fed upon by the caribou that are now and then eaten by the bears—and so on.

This is efficient, economical, messy, smelly, mystically circular and temperamental. It's especially temperamental if you count the commercial netting of salmon—the "nylon curtain," they call it—that can screw things up seriously when it's not properly regulated, as most people will tell you it, in fact, is not. Take away the salmon, as some would gladly do for a single year's profit, and the ecosystem would die.

They say that the silvers and, in some circumstances, the kings are the real fly rod salmon in Alaska. The sockeyes are loved as a food fish and for their overall contribution to the food chain, but in the circles we were traveling in—fly fishers and fly-fishing guides—they don't seem to be too highly rated.

One morning at Iliaska when the weather was too socked in for flying, some of the guides drove a crew of us over to the Newhalen River to join seventy-five or so other fishermen who were dredging for sockeyes. This is called "combat zone fishing," and one of the guides told me the Newhalen was nothing. "You should see the rivers you can drive to from Anchorage," he said.

I got into it after a while, even though I claim not to like fishing in a crowd or chunking lead. I mean, what the hell; these were big fish and this was Alaska, where things are sometimes done differently. In the true spirit of things, I got deeply interested in killing some fish to take home.

By the way, I believe that "chunking" is the proper, common term. It's onomatopoetic, coming from the distinctive "chunk" sound split shot makes when it hits the water.

When the ceiling lifted after a few hours, Ted and another pilot flew over to pick us up and take us to a secluded little river to catch big rainbow trout, possibly on dry flies. "You're about to go from the ridiculous to the sublime," Ted said.

Rainbows are what the guides and lodge owners brag about most—in terms of both numbers and size—and they're what many visiting fly fishers are looking for. After all, this is one of the few places on earth where, at the right time, with some skill, a little luck and maybe the right guide, you can bag your ten- or twelve- or (if the stories can be believed) even your fifteen-pound rainbow on a fly rod. The fish will be scavenging behind a run of salmon instead of sipping mayflies but, if you connect, it will be a by God, double-digit wallhanger.

Not far from Iliamna Lake by float plane, on a river the name of which I've been asked not to mention, I landed a six-pound rainbow on a dry fly. It was a nice fish, big enough to make the lodge book (volume III), in which, among other things, you can record for posterity any trout over four pounds caught on a dry fly.

It was a nice fish, but not a great one by Alaskan standards; memorable only because it was hooked on a floating caddis pattern instead of on a sunken salmon egg, flesh fly or streamer. On the other hand, it was probably the biggest trout I've ever caught on a dry fly.

People have written pages in that lodge book about a single, good fish—eloquent stories filled with keen observations and humor—but I couldn't think of anything more profound than, "Six-pound rainbow on a #14 olive Stimulator," dated and signed. It's not that I wasn't happy, I was just a little tongue-tied.

We caught salmon on wet flies and split shot, nice-sized arctic char on eggs and Woolly Bugger streamers, rainbows on streamers and eggs, and one day I got into some pretty Dolly Vardens, once again on eggs. Apparently you don't do a lot of dry fly fishing in Alaska and I understand some fishermen on their first trip there are a little disillusioned by that.

I won't say I was actually disappointed, but there were a few times when I got enough of lead and sink-tips and flies that looked less like bugs or fish and more like bangles from a stripper's costume. And, yes, those did happen to be the few times when we weren't catching fish. I've noticed that certain fishing tactics seem a lot more acceptable when they're working.

Still, that day on the river Ted Gerkin asked me not to write about—the one where the big rainbows would come up to a dry caddis fly—was a tremendous relief, and so was our first afternoon at Wood River Lodge on the Agulawok River.

There were fish rising right in front of the cabin as we lugged our gear from the plane, and when we rushed down there we found that they were rainbows and grayling, both up to eighteen or twenty inches, rising to a this-and-that hatch of caddis, mayflies and small stoneflies. The fish weren't too picky, but we did have to fish flies that at least approximated the appearance of the real bugs. I was already in the water with my five-weight rod strung up, DeWitt was playing a fish and Dan had just missed a strike, when I learned that I had to run back to the cabin and dig my dry fly boxes out of the bottom of the duffel bag. At that point in the trip I had caught countless big fish, but it almost killed me that, for five minutes, Dan and DeWitt were getting them while I was looking for those damned fly boxes.

The next day we could have flown out once again to catch great big something-or-others someplace else, but we unanimously voted to stay and fish the river right in front of the lodge. They gave us two guides with boats, and we fished from right after breakfast—say, 8:00 in the morning—until dusk, which would have been going on midnight. Sure, we broke for a shore lunch and dinner at the lodge, but that's still a long day. In fact, this has happened to me at least once every time I've gone north. I say, "Jeeze, I'm kind of tired for some reason," and the bright-eyed guide says, "Well, we *have* been fishing for about sixteen hours now . . ."

We caught rainbows, some nice big arctic char and my biggest sockeye of the trip (ten pounds) on streamers, but what I remember most clearly now are the grayling.

They were almost all good-sized, maybe fifteen to twenty inches, and throughout the day we'd find pods of them rising in the slack water beside faster currents. "That's because they're a lazy fish," Duncan said. That's Duncan Oswald, one of several guides at Wood River who specialize in fly fishing. He also ties the flies for the lodge and knows the river's hatches. That's significant because in Alaska you don't *have* to know the hatches to catch fish.

I fished for the grayling with a seven-foot, nine-inch Mike Clark bamboo rod and Dan broke out a sweet little Pezon & Michelle Parabolic. Neither rod raised any eyebrows and, in fact, I was surprised at how many cane rods I saw on that trip. Apparently, many Alaskan fly fishers have a darling little bamboo stashed away for just these kinds of occasions.

As I said, the hatches were scattered, but the best was a fall of size fourteen dark stoneflies. The grayling would execute a refusal rise to a #14 Royal Wulff, *sometimes* eat an Elk Hair Caddis, Irresistible or Stimulator, and absolutely hammer an elegantly simple deer hair and calf tail stonefly of Duncan's own design. I brought a few of these home with me to copy.

Some people will tell you that grayling are an easy fish—the bluegills of the north—but I've never found them to be like that. The few times I've fished for them in their native range, they've been catchable, but far from pushovers: easy enough that you can usually get some, but still hard enough that each fish is an event. And, of course, they're unbelievably, iridescently beautiful. The perfect game fish, in other words.

That night at the lodge over gin and tonics, one of the other guides said it was too bad we hadn't gone off with him to catch the pigs but, more for Duncan's benefit than ours, I think, he said he did realize that a salmon egg is "chunked," while a dry fly is *presented.*

I'm sorry to say I don't remember that guide's name now. We met so many guides and bush pilots I don't remember half their names, and I don't have them written down anywhere. Since I claim to be a professional writer, I should probably keep better notes but, looking back on previous trips, I sometimes think I've missed what could have been pure moments because I was busy scribbling in a damned notebook, making sure I'd be able to spell the name of the river when I got back home.

Of the pilots, a man with Branch River Air Service was the most overtly professional. Before takeoff, shouting over the racket of the engine, he told us how the doors opened and the location of the life vests and first aid kit. There was even an abbreviated version of the notorious seat-back safety card: a silhouette of the plane with arrows pointing to each side labeled "door."

That was the first time we flew with him. The next morning he said, "All the safety stuff is the same as it was yesterday, okay?"

Then there was the guy flying for Iliaska who could give you a quick, appraising glance and guess your weight within a few pounds, and then do the same with your gear. Payload weights are constantly on the minds of bush pilots.

John, with Wood River Lodge, was the most acrobatic flier. Usually if you pointed out wildlife while in a plane, everyone would look and nod approvingly, but John would shout, "Yeah, cool!" and go into a diving spin to get a closer look. The first time he did that it took me by surprise. I was squashed down in the seat and my cheeks felt heavy from the increased gravity of the spin. The ground was wheeling directly off my right shoulder and coming up fast. John asked, "Anyone here get airsick?" I said, "Not until now," but I don't think he could hear me over the roaring of the engine.

Bernie had the crazy bush pilot act down pat. He turned the engine over and yelled, "Jeeze, it started!" Then he looked down at his instruments and said, loudly but apparently to himself, "Hell, I guess all these little switches are in the right place." Then, turning to me in the copilot's seat, he asked, "You ever fly one of these?"

Once in the air he launched into a fishing story. The motor was howling. We were both wearing headphones, but all I could hear through mine was static, which is kind of what Bernie's voice sounds like anyway. I could see

his lips moving. He made casting motions with his right hand, line stripping motions with his left and then held his palms up in front of him to indicate a fish (salmon? rainbow?) about three feet long.

I shouted "Far out" into my microphone, which is all you ever have to say
to a fish story.

Bernie yells on the ground, too, as do many Alaskans. It's a survival tactic. A ranger at Katmai National Park told me about a park employee who
had recently been mauled by a bear. "She's a very quiet person," the ranger
said. This wasn't an idle comment on the victim's personality; he meant she
wasn't talking loudly and constantly to herself as she walked through the
woods, so she had come upon the bear unannounced. Bears don't like that.

We saw lots of bears in Alaska. They were following the salmon runs, as we
were—inadvertently or otherwise—so it was unavoidable. These animals
are called Alaskan brown bears, although there's some disagreement
among the scientists about whether they're a separate species from the grizzly. The main difference is size. A big brown bear looks just like a grizzly,
but stands a foot taller and weighs as much as six hundred pounds more.
When you're sharing a gravel bar with one, size does seem to be a defining
factor.

A big sow and a yearling cub came down to the Newhalen River the first
day we fished it. I was about fourth in the line of fishermen upstream from
the spot the bears wanted. When one of the guides hooted, "Bear!" I
looked, broke off the eight-pound salmon I was playing without a second
thought and began wading slowly but deliberately upstream, as they tell
you to do. Dan, who doesn't like bears much, was just ahead of me. He
didn't say anything, but he was making a quiet noise deep in his throat that
sounded like the cooing of a pigeon.

Later, DeWitt said it was interesting to see the "ripple of recognition" go
through us when the bears waded out into the river.

We saw bears almost every day, and there are three things people tell
you about them: that, nine times out of ten, the bear will decline a confrontation; that if he *doesn't* decline, it's probably your fault; and that a
bear's personal space is no less than fifty yards. That seemed awfully close. I
found that I had to be at about two hundred before it would occur to me
that the adults were handsome and the cubs were actually pretty cute.
Bears scare me badly, but I still like them a lot, which I take as evidence
that I've negotiated something heavy.

We only had two bear encounters that seemed ticklish. One day we flew into the Morraine River, a beautiful but bleak tundra stream known for big rainbows. We were dropped off at a small lake with our guide and the light inflatable raft we'd use to float a few miles of river down to the pickup point.

It was an unsettled day with gray, scudding clouds and winds between thirty and forty knots. The last thing the pilot said was that the weather would "probably" allow him to pick us up that evening. To understand Alaskan weather, all you have to do is look at one of the weather maps they sell in souvenir shops up there where various parts of the state are labeled partly shitty, mostly shitty, moderately shitty and so on.

Of course the wind made for grueling fly-casting, but we were still picking up a few big rainbows on Woolly Buggers and a thing I think they were calling an Electric Egg Sucking Leech, although I might not be remembering that correctly.

We'd stopped for lunch on a little stretch of sandy beach and the guide was talking to me about some other writers he'd guided. "They all wanted something for nothing," he said. "They expected to spend a day with me and come home with all the secrets I've learned in ten years in the bush." I was just beginning to explain that all I wanted to know was what fly to tie on when a bear popped out of the brush about forty yards away.

He stood up on his hind feet and squinted at us. Bears don't see well, but he knew there was something on this sand bar that wasn't there the last time he'd looked. The wind was blowing hard at right angles between us and the bear, so he couldn't get our scent.

When the bear dropped to all fours and came a little closer—cautious, but seized by curiosity—I asked the guide, "Should we launch the raft?" He said, "What good would that do?" and I remembered what someone had said a few days before: "You think you're safe in a boat until you see one of those guys trot across a deep, fast stream as if it wasn't even there." The Morraine was a small river, swift and deep here and there, but wadable by humans in most places.

Then the bear walked into the underbrush and we lost sight of him. Dan asked, "What should we do now?" and the guide said, "Finish your lunch."

Another day we flew into a spot where a small creek entered a lake. The plan was to wade up the creek a half mile or so to a place where, we'd been assured, there were huge rainbows and grayling, but there was a sow and two cubs around the first bend, so we had to turn back and work the inlet, where there didn't seem to be too many fish.

I won't try to describe the whole, grim dance in detail, but eventually a young male bear came down to the inlet and made it known that we had blundered into his personal space and that he wasn't pleased. Since he was on shore and we were already up to our armpits in the lake, we had a little trouble getting out of his way, although we tried. At one point the bear gave us some negative body language—lowered head, flattened ears. This doesn't sound like much on paper, but on site it's pretty damned impressive.

That bear herded us back and forth across the inlet a few times, and at one point Dan and DeWitt both lost their footing and went under while trying to move a little more deliberately than was possible in deep water and slippery rocks. At that point I was closest to the bear—I can't say how close, but far less than the prescribed fifty yards—and I kept my footing not because I'd remained calm exactly, but because I'd already come to terms with a horrible death and was wondering how badly I'd be missed back home.

Throughout the whole thing our guide, Nanci Morris, spoke in a calming voice, first to the bear, then to us, and she never unholstered her Smith and Wesson .44 magnum. She was the picture of composure, and said later she was more worried about that sow getting nervous because bears are known to attack cubs.

It turned out okay, but I was glad to hear the deep, unmistakable drone of the DeHavilland Beaver Nanci calls the Cream Puff coming to pick us up. It occurred to me that having an airplane come and save you from a bear is a great way to get over your fear of flying. When the plane taxied in, Dan waded out and kissed a pontoon, able to kid around now because it seemed we'd live.

Nanci is the head guide (excuse me, "Director of Sportfishing") at the Quinnat Landing Hotel in the town of King Salmon. Her specialty is trophy-sized kings, and in some magazine article or brochure she was once dubbed "the queen of the king salmon guides." Naturally, that stuck, as embarrassing publicity always does.

When I said something about getting to be head guide at a place like that at an obviously tender age, Nanci said, "Yeah, and, not to put too fine a point on it, try doing it as a woman."

I could see that. Competence is admired in a place like King Salmon, but men far outnumber women and at times the horniness is almost palpable. And it's a little rough—in a pleasant way for a tourist, but rough nonetheless. Over some beers in the hotel bar a pilot named Red told me, "We try to make a year's living here in five or six months, so we fight sleep deprivation half the year and depression the other half." He also said, gazing wistfully out at the Naknik River, "Ah, Alaska. She seduces you every summer and then abandons you every winter."

Anyway, Nanci does seem to love that plane with something close to a passion. As head guide, she almost always manages to schedule it for her own trips and, although she talked about other things in the two days we all spent together, she kept coming back to the Cream Puff. When we walked down to the dock to board it or when it banked in to land and pick us up, she'd say, "Just look at it. God!"

It *is* a sweetheart. You see all kinds of other aircraft, but the Beaver is the classic, workhorse bush plane, the one everyone wants. They were discontinued in the 1960s, but they're still widely in use because, like only a handful of other things in life, they are absolutely perfect as is. This one is painted deep purple with a silver lightning bolt down each side, and it's a "cherry rebuild"—might as well be brand new. A plane is everything in Alaska, and a great plane is sublime.

The first time I saw the Cream Puff it was sitting at a dock on the Naknik River and we were sitting in the bar at Quinnat Landing, near the big picture windows, eating thick steaks and talking about the fishing. During a lull in the conversation, Nanci gazed out at the Beaver and said, "See that plane out there? I love that plane. If that plane was a man, I just might say 'I do.'"

At which point every man in the joint looked out the window at the lovely old purple Beaver. Its big radial engine was idling. At that range it sounded like the purring of a large, happy cat.

A Few Days Before Christmas

A few days before Christmas last year, A.K. and I drove down to Pike National Forest and hiked into the Cheesman Canyon stretch of the South Platte River. The weather had been chilly for at least a week (meaning the water would be cold, even for trout), word was the flow was down to about thirty cubic feet per second (too low) and the grapevine hadn't had anything to say about the midge hatches in a while, which meant they were probably off. If there was any good news, it was that the river wasn't frozen bank to bank.

All the signs pointed to poor fishing or, as A.K. would say, in the tone of a schoolteacher correcting your grammar, "poor *catching*," since the fishing itself is always good. Now that I think about it, I guess that was the whole point.

I hadn't been out fishing—or doing much of anything else—in almost a month, and I was beginning to think all my friends were getting too old. All are at least in their forties now, and they seem so damn busy. No one had called to say, "Well, nothing much is happening, but let's at least go look at the Frying Pan River," or, "It's pretty cold, but let's see if we can shoot a couple of rabbits." When *I* made the calls, people were saying, "Oh, I don't know, this is happening, that's happening . . . I don't know . . ." God, I thought, I'm hanging out with a bunch of old men.

And for about that same month, A.K. had been back at his family home in Iowa. His father had died, and there were all those sad, final chores to be taken care of, including the selling of the farm where A.K. was born. In a typical example of understatement, he said it hadn't been much fun.

We talked about it a little when he got back, but I've noticed that in situations like this there's often surprisingly little to say. The late Mr. Best had lived a good, long, honest, largely uneventful life farming the land he was born on; hunting rabbits with the .22 rifle he'd bought used in the 1920s because it would have gone against his practical, Protestant upbringing to pay seven whole dollars for a new one. This kind of personal history is all but obsolete now and, aside from everything else, *that's* a damned shame.

I won't presume to speculate about what A.K. was feeling or what he had to "work through," as they say, but I knew he was not in a good mood. As for me, real trouble should show me that my own little problems are really nothing, but I'm more likely to see it as proof that a festering cloud of doom is settling on everything.

Anyway, when A.K. called and said he needed to go fishing, I said, "Yeah, I do, too," and I understood it wasn't going to matter much if the trout weren't biting.

We walked into the canyon at the fastest pace we could manage on the dangerously icy trail. On the drive down we had carefully established that there wasn't much chance of catching any fish, but once we were there a little of the old excitement began to kick in. We noted that there were no cars at the trailhead parking lot and no fresh tracks on the trail. That meant—for what it was worth—that we'd probably have the whole three miles of river to ourselves.

After looking at a few good pools, we settled on an old favorite spot. The day was chilly with a low, solid overcast and the water temperature on A.K.'s stream thermometer read thirty-six degrees, or four degrees below the trout's lower avoidance level. When the water temperature drops below forty, the trout become sluggish and so do the aquatic insects they feed on. It's a matter of predators evolving to match the habits of their prey, or at least that's how I like to see it.

And fishermen, bundled in three times the clothing they'd need for a hike on a cold day, can get a little sluggish themselves. You think of evolution because on a cold trout stream in midwinter, time seems numbingly huge. We stood there for a few minutes looking at the river. "This is going to be tough," I said, and A.K. replied, "Well, we knew that."

The fly to fish at a time like that is a String Thing. This is no more than a layer of white thread wrapped on a #20 hook, but it's almost an exact copy of the little wormlike midge larvae that are so numerous in that stretch of the Platte. Even on days when the food chain is turned down as low as it will go and the fish are sulking, you can sometimes get them to inhale a String Thing if you're persistent enough and your drifts are close to perfect.

This fly is so simple as to be offensive to A.K.—who's a professional fly tier, after all—but he sometimes has a few of them tucked into a corner of one of his fly boxes where maybe no one will notice them.

This is the kind of repetitive, meditational fishing that requires not so much skill as something I've heard called thoughtless, harmonious concentration. It's the kind of job that doesn't take all your wits; just enough of them to keep you from thinking very rigorously of anything else. On a cold day it also requires a twig fire and a pot of coffee on shore, which you repair to just *before* your feet actually go numb.

Wading out of the water to sit by the fire for a while is easy when the fishing is slow, and at those times the conversation wanders all over the place, from politics to fishing to sleeping bag design to the proper way to make boiled coffee. A.K. didn't say anything about his father that I can remember now, but, because it was in the air, I caught myself thinking about *my* dad a little when the talk petered out.

It occurred to me that I'm now a better fisherman than he was— maybe even a better outdoorsman in general—but that's only because I've had the time to put into it. I never did have the family or the regular job or his sense of "what a grown man's responsibilities in life ought to be." I still recall bits and pieces of the lectures, and I guess those memories aren't exactly fond ones.

Dad and I didn't see eye to eye about a lot of things, but that's only natural. When you grow up seeing one way in life, you're very likely to choose another for yourself, if only for some variety. But I think he'd have liked it that I moved out to Colorado where I fish a lot and make a decent living writing stories about it. He might even have come to understand why I didn't get all clobbered up with a lot of dependents and responsibilities. Dad liked to hunt and fish, but he never did as much of either as he'd have liked. He planned to make up for that after he retired, but he never made it that far. Many of the fathers of my generation did this same thing: They gave up what they thought of as childish things because they thought they were supposed to, and it killed a lot of them.

If Dad had lived, he might not have ended up sharing my bohemian views on life, but when he saw that the result was a lot more fishing time, I'll bet he'd at least have stopped bitching at me.

So I didn't grow up to be my father (that's a kind of victory for most boys), but in some ways I may have become the man my father wanted to be, which is, I guess you'd say, interesting.

I did get one thing from him, though: the worst kind of workaholism. That's the kind where you're not always busy, but you always feel that you should be, so it can be hard to goof off effectively. One of the few times I can do nothing with a clear conscience is when I'm sitting next to a twig fire on the bank of a trout stream. And that, I suppose, is because nothing is all you can do when you're waiting for the fishing to pick up—even if it probably won't pick up for a month.

A.K. and I did well that day when you consider that, by rights, we shouldn't have caught anything at all. There was a period of less than an hour in midafternoon when the water temperature must have reached up into the low forties. I was fishing along on automatic pilot when a big trout bit my fly, bent the hook almost straight and got away before I could even think of giving it line. A few minutes later I hooked another one and got it almost to the net before it threw the hook. I really wanted to land that fish, but then when it got off I was glad I didn't have to freeze my hands releasing it. It was a nice rainbow. Maybe sixteen inches.

I switched to a little dry fly when I saw a single trout rise twice near the far bank, but by the time I got the knot tied the fish had stopped. I made a few casts anyway, notwithstanding the feeling that it was useless.

Fifty yards downstream, A.K. also had a few risers. He missed one and hooked and landed another on a dry fly. When he got that fish to the net, he gave a quiet little "whoop" so I'd notice. On a day when more fish were being caught, this wouldn't have been necessary.

After that the river went dead again and pretty much stayed that way until dark. We doused the fire and wandered around a little, doing more looking than fishing and making some tentative plans. In the coming year, aside from the fishing we'd naturally do around Colorado, there was the possibility of bass in Texas, trout in Montana, various game fish in Alaska and Atlantic salmon on a river somewhere in Canada.

Well, maybe these were just ideas instead of plans, but there comes a time when the former has to be bravely turned into the latter. Otherwise, you just talk and think and eventually they dissolve, either because other things pile up or because it just gets to be too late to do anything about them.

And there's another wrinkle to all this. The possible Alaska trip had to do with some friends who were moving there soon and who had already invited several of us to come up. "As soon as we get a line on something" (meaning good fishing), "we'll let you know," they said.

These folks are good planners, but they're also enthusiastic and quick to seize the moment. It wouldn't surprise me to get a phone call from them saying, "Be here in a week, the something-or-others are running."

This involves a fine point in the art of planning: maintaining the mental balance and self-confidence it takes to let you go at a moment's notice. Ed told me once that when he was younger he'd automatically say "yes" when some frantic fisherman called with little more than a rumor, while now he sees this creeping tendency to say "no" just as compulsively.

"It's something you need to pay attention to," he said, and I agree. Half of getting old is inexorable biology, but the other half is attitude.

My father liked to have things planned out in detail and I see that tendency in myself, but I've also learned to like the idea that I really don't know what's going to happen. I might as well like it because that's the way it is.

Ed again: "If you knew exactly what was gonna happen on a trip, you wouldn't even have to go."

So A.K. and I wandered the river like this, strolling, talking, making a few halfhearted casts here and there. The day had stayed that same, uniform damp gray, with the rock cliffs and the sky both looking like the undersides of old iron ships. If it had been warmer, it would have been great fishing weather.

We saw two ravens perched in a dead ponderosa pine tree. Every now and then one of them would turn to the other and poke it hard with its beak a few times. The bird getting poked didn't seem to respond in any way. I'm only an amateur bird watcher, which means I know what a raven is, but I have no idea why one would poke his partner like that.

There might have been another short flurry of feeding activity from the trout, but it was unlikely. It seemed as if it had gotten colder, although it may have only felt that way because we'd been out in it for so long. I do carry a little thermometer/compass gadget on my day pack, but I've found that I don't need an instrument to tell me when I'm cold.

We didn't stay until the light was almost gone out of desperation for more trout, but simply because that's what one does, probably in part because both our dads had that linear view of things. We're here to fish, so we fish. A equals B, period.

So in one way we were just going through the motions. On the other hand, we ended up at a pool called the Ice Box because that was the most likely place to find feeding trout late on a cold December afternoon. You stay the whole day as a kind of observance, but you don't entirely blow off the fishing either.

On the way down to that last pool we had to cross a little rip in the current, and A.K. pulled out ahead. He's thirteen years my senior, but he still wades better than I do in fast water, although both of us have gotten a little more careful in recent years. It's funny, but I didn't notice that a little of the spring had gone out of his step until it was back.

West

N o t long ago A.K. Best and I found ourselves in West Yellowstone, Montana, on what we'll call, for official purposes, a business trip.

The Federation of Fly Fishers Conclave was in town, and Jim Criner, now owner of Bud Lilly's Trout Shop, asked us to come up and sign copies of our books in the store for a couple of mornings. Mornings, that is, so we could sneak out and fish in the afternoons. He also said he'd put us up and we could stay as long as we liked. Jim had thought this through. He understood we weren't going to be on expense accounts from our publishers, so he felt we might need a little incentive to make the thirteen-hour drive from Colorado.

The book signings were actually very successful, but there were still some of those inevitable doldrums to get through. A good way to stay humble about being a writer is to sit at a table with your life's work in front of you and wait for, say, an hour and a half for an adoring fan to show up. Finally a guy does walk over. He smiles and says, "Hi, you got a public toilet here?"

Some years ago A.K. and I both spent time working in fly shops, so when there didn't happen to be anyone wanting an autograph, our tendency was to go on automatic: helping people try on waders and select flies, which beats sitting around trying to be famous when things are slow.

I also bought a new hat from the shop. A few weeks before, while we were camped at Roy Palm's place on the Frying Pan River in Colorado, Roy's sweet little bird dog pup had eaten my old one.

I wouldn't have kicked the dog even if she wasn't worth a reported four thousand dollars and even if Roy hadn't been very good to me over the years. Puppies will be puppies and fishing hats, even old favorite ones, are expendable. The only thing that bothered me was, a new fishing hat cost almost forty dollars. I must be getting old. I remember when you could buy a Hardy reel for forty dollars.

In fact, that's about what a good fly reel went for the first time I came to West Yellowstone in the 1970s, back when Bud Lilly still owned Bud Lilly's Trout Shop. There's a gentrified covered mall in town now (at least it's small) and at a neat little bookstore called the Book Peddler you can actually get a cup of cappuccino, but aside from a few things like that, the place hasn't changed much. It's still a small, funky, honestly rustic, somewhat touristy, largely one-story western town that grew up haphazardly at the west entrance to Yellowstone National Park.

When mail first started arriving there in 1908, the town—or at least the post office—was called Riverside. The following year it was changed to Yellowstone and then, in 1920, it became *West* Yellowstone. Now, in regional anglers' shorthand, it's often referred to simply as "West."

West Yellowstone is arguably the capital city of American fly-fishing. It's a town with 924 year-round residents that supports five fly shops, countless guides and fly tiers and the Federation of Fly Fishers international headquarters. Not every business in town has stuffed trout on the walls, but those that don't seem oddly stark. World-famous western trout rivers like the Madison, Yellowstone, Gibbon, Firehole and Henry's Fork, not to mention many lesser-known streams and lakes, are within easy day-trip range.

The trout-fishing in the area is wonderful, or, fishing being what it is, let's say it *can* be when the conditions are right. Whether it's as fabulous as it once was is a matter of some debate. There's always the suspicion that it was better in the good old days, and Al McClane, one of the early jet-set angling writers and an undisputed expert in such matters, has said, "Montana fishing has survived as well as can be expected against the onslaught of civilization."

Then again, Bud Lilly, who was born in that country and should know, said, "When the fishing around West Yellowstone started to get a lot of attention from the fishing writers in the late 1960s and early 1970s, those of us who lived there noticed a surprising increase in the size of fish being reported (but not seen or photographed) from some rivers."

It's a scandalous implication, but then fishermen—let alone writers—*have* been known to exaggerate.

So let's just say that the fishing is better than average at the very least and, more important, it is legendary. Even if the trout you catch are only a few inches longer than the ones you get back home, they are nonetheless from rivers that are, as they say, part of the literature of the sport. That's important. In certain circles, the names of famous rivers can be dropped as impressively as those of movie stars.

So fly-fishing in the West Yellowstone area amounts to a kind of pilgrimage. An unofficial survey of license plates reveals that most of the visitors are from states west of the Mississippi, but you see plates from all over—Florida, Kentucky, Maine, pick a place—and in years past I've run into anglers from England, Australia, Germany, Japan and New Zealand.

One of the New Zealanders, with a deadpan delivery worthy of a native Montanan, said he was having a nice time, even though, compared to back home, the beer was watery and the trout were small.

When I asked Vicki Eggers at the West Yellowstone Chamber of Commerce how many fishermen the town saw in a season, she said she couldn't say, but it was "a sizable number." To the same question, a fly shop owner or a guide will say, "Plenty," and a fisherman may say, "Too many."

Even if you didn't know beforehand, you'd spot this as a fishing town before you'd driven two blocks. Maybe it's the businesses that cater to anglers in one way or another or all the obvious fishing vehicles, ranging from official-looking pickups towing Mackenzie boats to decrepit Volkswagens with float tubes strapped on top.

Or maybe it's the fishermen themselves. As you walk or drive down the main drag, you keep thinking you see people you know, but before you can turn to whomever you're with and say, "Isn't that . . . ?" you realize it's not the specific person you recognize, but the type: ageless—say, forty on up—male or female, fit, tanned, dressed in a practical, sporting sort of way, often wearing the expression Ed Engle calls the hundred-mile stare. Fly fishers. It's hard to explain, but they don't have to be wearing hip boots. You pick them out the way members of any subculture can spot each other pretty much at a glance.

And it works the other way around, too. I can't remember ever buying gas, coffee or anything else in West without being asked, "How's the fishing?" I don't know how they can tell I'm not there to look at the geysers; it's just obvious somehow.

Of course, sometimes you do recognize someone, either a friend from somewhere or one of the many angling celebrities who show up in town on a fairly regular basis. On any street corner or in any bar, cafe or fly shop you might spot Ernest Schweibert, Doug Swisher, Gary LaFontaine, Nick Lyons, Dave Whitlock or almost any other face you've seen on the dust jacket of a fly-fishing book. In years past it might have been Lee Wulff or Arnold Gingrich. Everyone shows up there sooner or later.

I've been told that angling notoriety is the best kind in that, although certain people may know who you are, you can still walk down any street in any town in the country without being recognized—except maybe in West.

A.K. and I did slip out those first two afternoons. We drove the ninety-mile round trip to a place we know on the Yellowstone River in the park and dragged back into West between 10:30 and 11:00 at night, just in time to get supper at Thiem's Cafe.

When we arrived in town we'd asked a couple of local contacts the two questions one must have answered immediately, namely, where are the fish biting and what is the current fisherman's cafe? Both things change from time to time. The consensus was, the Madison and Yellowstone rivers, and Thiem's.

The right cafe must be casual and cozy (pine paneling is nice, but optional), have good food served in generous portions, have quick service (at least in the morning when you're in a hurry), have waiters and waitresses who can stand up to the endless, corny wisecracks, and keep fishermen's hours.

It also helps if the place has the proper history. Thiem's, like many other establishments in West, displays the obligatory collection of snapshots dating back at least to the 1950s showing the building in winter. On the wall near the bathroom door there are shots of Thiem's—formerly Chat's, formerly Huck's—buried in snow up to the eaves, with just the sign visible at the top of the drift. If no one gets married or catches a huge trout, this might be the only photograph a West Yellowstonian takes in a year. It's a way locals have of reminding us summer tourists that we're dilettantes compared to those who spend their winters there.

The right cafe provides not only food, but gossip. It's rare for a fisherman you don't know well to tell you precisely where he caught a lot of big trout and what fly he was using, but it's just as rare for him to be able to entirely contain himself if he's done well. Consequently, if you pay attention and read between the lines, you can deduce that certain insect hatches are on and that people are generally "doing okay" on a stretch of a certain river roughly between this bridge and that roadhouse. This is B-list stuff, but valuable just the same.

You can also learn who's staying in whose spare cabin, guest room or back porch, borrowing whose drift boat or guiding for which shop, although trying to look anyone up is usually a waste of time. Someone you know may be "in town," but of course that's a euphemism. They're actually out fishing, dawn till dusk, and if they're into something good, they probably didn't tell anyone where they were going. You learn to say, "Well, maybe we'll run into him."

And you really do want to run into him because it's the people you know who give you the best tips about where there are big fish that are currently biting and that everyone isn't onto: the A-list material. There can be mobs of fishermen in and around West in the summer, but there are also countless miles of good water in the immediate area, which, depending on how hard you want to drive, includes the park (which is in Wyoming), a good chunk of Montana and a sizable corner of Idaho. There are always secrets to be learned.

Around West, the best fishing tips often come with the standard boiler-plate grizzly disclaimer: "You park at the bridge, cross the river, hike downstream until the trail peters out, then go on for another two miles and start fishing at the big bend in the river. Now, there *are* some bears down there . . ."

This is done for a number of reasons. First, there really are a few grizzlies around, although they're hardly ever seen. Statistically, your chances of getting stomped by a bison or hit by a car are far greater than those of being attacked by a bear, but it does happen, and a bear attack can be extremely definitive. If you sent some tenderfoot to a fishing spot where grizzlies had been seen a time or two over the last few seasons and a week later the search party turned up a broken fly rod and a single, bloody hiking boot, you might feel a little funny about it if you hadn't issued the usual warning. So local etiquette demands that you say, "Now, there *are* some bears down there . . ." so if anything happens it won't be your fault.

And I think there's also a subtle character check involved. When a guy gives up a great spot, he wants to think you're worthy of it. If a little thing like a grizzly bear is going to scare you off, it's probably just as well.

In some hands this whole bear business can be yet another one of those subtle digs that locals really do have a right to. Sure, you had a good trip and caught lots of trout, but a competent local smart-ass can send you home thinking you probably could have gotten into even bigger fish if you'd only had more guts.

I guess you just have to understand the relationship between the residents of a tourist town and the tourists themselves. Locals can be like cow-boys: They may love the life and the region, but they can eventually get tired of the cows.

People who like trout have the same kind of affection for West that other people have for, say, Paris. That is, it begins as a kind of cultural condition-ing before we've even seen the place, and then once we've been there a few times we begin to feel like honorary citizens, strolling its sidewalks with a proprietary air. After all, we're fly fishermen, and this is a fly-fishing town.

To be honest, we tend to look down a little on the regular tourists who only come to view the wildlife from the car and maybe do some shopping in town because they are there as spectators, while we're there to partici-pate. Granted, fly fishers are an arrogant bunch as a rule, but when people stop their cars, run down to take your picture while you're fishing, and then ask you things like, "Where do they keep the buffalo in the winter?" it's hard not to feel a little superior.

On the other hand, I can't say I know the town itself well. Over the past fifteen years or so, I've been in all the fly shops, some of the gas stations and cafes, the Laundromat, a book store and the post office. Once, years ago, a bunch of us rented a room in the Alpine Motel for an afternoon so we could take showers, but we didn't stay the night, and I have now had a cup of authentic West Yellowstone cappuccino, which was real good.

I'm told there are one or two decent restaurants, but I've never eaten in them because they don't stay open late enough. On this last trip, one of our publishers told A.K. and me that, although he wouldn't spring for the trip, he would reimburse us for a dinner. We wanted to stick him good—and he fully expected that—but the best we could do was a couple of chicken fried steak specials at Thiem's.

I can't remember offhand the numbers of the highways leading out of town in three directions, but I know where they go. To the east is the road into the park that takes you to the Firehole, upper Madison, Yellowstone and such. The road north goes to Bozeman and the Gallatin River, crossing the Madison, Cougar Creek, Duck Creek and so on. (Duck Creek is pretty good, but there *are* some bears.) The Idaho Road goes south, toward the Henry's Fork and beyond.

Like most fishermen who show up in West on a more or less regular basis to eat, sleep, buy trout flies and ask directions, I know the surrounding rivers better than the town. That's not to say I'm anything but a normal duffer, but I've been there often enough—and been out with enough good guides—that I do have some spots.

A "spot" doesn't have to be remote (some good ones are within sight of roads) and it doesn't have to be completely unknown. It just has to be a good place to fish that isn't a regular stop for half the guides and fly fishers in three states; a place you stand a fair chance of having all to yourself and that you wouldn't tell just anyone about.

Like that stretch of the Yellowstone A.K. and I know about. It's miles from the famous spots on that river that everyone fishes. There are fewer cutthroat trout there, but they are bigger and healthier. A friend who spends his summers in West took us there years ago, but we now think of it as our spot. In all the time we've been fishing it we've seen two other anglers and a bull moose.

That's not to say we always catch fish there. Once a guide asked me if catching those big, dumb cutthroats in the Yellowstone wasn't a little like shooting fish in a barrel. I had to say, "Not to me."

We fished that spot those first two afternoons after the book signings and we caught some nice big trout. Then on the second night, over buffalo burgers at Thiem's, we ran into an East Coast guide that A.K. knows. A.K. is a professional fly tier and by now he knows half the people in the business.

This guy knew we'd been fishing the area off and on for quite a few years, so he naturally assumed we knew what we were doing. After all, fly-fishing is one small part of American culture where it's still assumed that experience and a little age naturally bring wisdom. After the usual pleasantries, the guy asked how we'd been doing—the standard opening move.

"Oh," I said, "we've been getting into some fish," trying to sound as if, you know, we'd been holding up our end, but it was nothing really fabulous or anything, while at the same time leaving open the possibility that it *had* been fabulous and I was just being cagey.

"Where?" the guy asked casually, and A.K. answered, "On the Yellowstone," glancing at me now because we were getting into a sensitive area.

"Oh," the guy said, "where exactly on the Yellowstone?"

At this point in these classic, ticklish conversations, the questioner usually gives up on innocence (he knows he's just asked an impertinent question) and tries for just the right note of brazenness. The interviewee is then faced with either telling him or ending it right there without being too rude.

A.K. looked up from his buffalo burger and said, with finality, "Not where you think."

By now we have a handful of places like this between us. Most were gifts from friends, a precious few are ours alone and were hard won. We don't tell other visitors about them because we don't want the word to get around, and we don't tell locals for fear these spots aren't as secret as we think they are. In this town you want to feel plugged in to the local fly-fishing mystique, if only for a week or so out of every summer, and nothing will deflate you quicker than hearing someone say, "Oh, hell, everyone knows about *that.*"

So we assume that recognizable West Yellowstone pose: modest, seasoned and ever so slightly self-satisfied. The implication being, yes, I guess we do know a thing or two about the fishing around here, and, no, we don't really care to go into it. If nothing else, we know how to fit in here. We understand that the less you say about fly-fishing, the more people will assume you know.

Another Lousy Day in Paradise

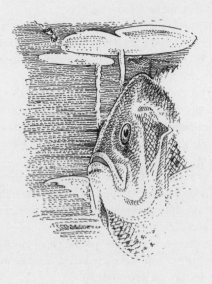

Rock Bass

A couple of seasons ago, a fisheries biologist with the Colorado Division of Wildlife asked me if I could get him some rock bass. It just came up by accident in conversation. He was asking me about some of the warm-water ponds I fished—out of professional curiosity, since he's in charge of managing most of them, and also out of the common (though often mistaken) idea that fishing writers know more about this stuff than regular old fishermen. In the course of things, I happened to mention that, in addition to the largemouth bass and the various kinds of sunfish I was getting, I sometimes caught rock bass.

He perked up at that, said he'd been trying to get a few rock bass as specimens, but in all the netting and shocking surveys he'd done, he hadn't been able to turn any up, even though he knew there were some around.

The rock bass is a pretty common sunfish, as sunfish go, but there are so few of them in Colorado they're not even listed in the fishing regulations, and not every fisherman recognizes them. They're a little fatter and more robust than most of the sunfishes, but otherwise they just look like a chunky, dark-colored bluegill.

"If I gave you a jug of Formalin, do you suppose you could get me a few?" he asked. "They wouldn't have to be big."

I said sure, I could do that. The guy had helped me out with tips and information a few times, and I guess I was flattered that he couldn't get a couple of little rock bass with all his scientific collection techniques, but he thought I could with a fly rod.

After all, as an official biologist for a state agency, this guy had some serious resources at his disposal, not to mention a federal permit that—although I don't remember the exact wording—allowed him to catch, trap, snare, shoot or otherwise take any species by any means at any time, period, no exceptions.

He showed it to me once. Considering that it was the cosmic fishing and hunting license, it was a small, deceptively modest-looking document.

I said, "I know a couple of guys who could use one of those."

"I'll just bet you do," he replied.

So I picked up the 5-gallon plastic pickle jar of Formalin—a solution of formaldehyde, methanol and water used to store specimens temporarily—and got the short lecture on how to use it.

"Now you want to put them in here alive," he said, "so they pump the stuff through their systems before they die, but you probably don't want to *watch* that. And don't get any of it on you."

I did know of a couple of ponds that had some rock bass, and I even knew where in the ponds to look, not that that was much of a trick. For reasons of their own, these fish like riprap banks—stone rubble and large rocks—hence their name.

This was no big deal—just a small, return favor for a nice guy—but, driving home with that jug of gunk in the bed of the pickup, I really enjoyed being someone you could ask to locate and identify a certain obscure little sunfish. When it comes right down to it, I think that's the secret ambition of every fly fisher: just to be someone who knows the territory.

When I moved out here to the Rocky Mountains, almost exactly a quarter of a century ago now, I didn't do it entirely for the fly-fishing, although that was part of it. A larger part, I think, was the idea of learning the place and making myself at home here. It wasn't until later that I fully realized how much fly-fishing had to do with that.

Sure, I could have stayed in the Midwest and learned to be at home *there,* but I think I saw things in the heartland going in the wrong direction, so I came out West to start over. After all, that's what dissatisfied Americans

have been doing for the last two hundred years, never mind that if you
come West now you'll meet the eastward migration of Californians who've
sold their surfboards and are now trying to retrace their steps.

I did want to learn how to fly fish, but there were other considerations—most of which I've all but forgotten by now—and because of them I
rattled around Colorado for a while, working odd jobs, living in odd places
with odd people, and finally ended up on the outskirts of a small, foothills
town on the East Slope, a stone's throw from what, in the grand scheme of
things, you'd have to describe as a fair to middling little trout creek.

Besides the creek, there's a lot of other fishing nearby, and if none of it is
downright fabulous, there's at least a good variety.

And this is also a great jumping-off place. Within a day's drive of here are
maybe a quarter of the best trout streams and rivers in the West. Add a second day on the road and you're probably in range of over half. More water
than a guy could adequately fish in a lifetime.

Hell, I still haven't even fished all of the 300-some miles of the nearest local drainage—although I'm still working on it—and even after all this time,
I could probably make a longer list of places in the region I'd like to fish
than of places I *have* fished. But I still feel like I know the area pretty well.

For instance, it took me a few trips to get my friend his elusive rock bass,
but I did finally manage it. He'd said all he wanted were little ones and that,
actually, little ones were all he'd ever seen. So I pickled five dinks and one
nice big one, just because I thought he'd appreciate that. Under "location"
on the form he gave me, I wrote "Nameless pond in Boulder County." To his
credit, he never asked me to be more specific.

I've lived in the same old house since 1977, but of course it's not quite as
sleepy and quiet here as it was when I moved in eighteen years ago. That little town down the road has grown out to meet me, and although I'm officially still in the county, the town limit now lies up against my property
line, which strikes me as a little too close for comfort. They keep asking me
to annex and I keep saying, "If I'd wanted to live in town, I'd have bought a
house in town in the first place."

Okay, that's a technicality, but it seems important because where you
live in relation to a town is a lot like where you place yourself in society in
general. That is, you don't have to be completely outside of it, but you
should stay close enough to the edge to be able to see out.

If a handful of people have their way, the town will grow more and faster
than it has already, against the wishes of almost everyone who lives here,

but then it's always possible that certain greedy developers and politicians *won't* have their way. That does happen, you know.

Since I've lived here I've been involved in an effort that killed one development, another that just recently mounted a referendum and reversed a 40-acre annexation for a monster housing project, and also an ongoing movement to put a little water back into the creek for the trout, although the jury is still out on that last one.

Not long ago a town official pointed out that I was, after all, just a county resident and accused me of being an "outside agitator" in the town's affairs, an epithet I haven't heard since the 1960s. Luckily I had the presence of mind to say, "Right. What's your point?"

Any grass-roots political effort is so easily derailed by money, influence, arrogance and bureaucracy on the opposing side and by laziness, rage, egotism and cloying attempts to "achieve solidarity" within your own ranks that it's almost not worth doing. But then if you stay in one place long enough, you become part of the community—like it or not—and eventually you have to pitch in, especially when the things that are going wrong where you are now are the same ones you had to escape from twenty-some years ago.

But politics is ugly, and it won't be long before you find yourself up a spiritual box canyon: You began with the best intentions, only to end up as ruthless as a paid assassin because that's what you have to do to win. So you have to wonder, Are those the only two choices: complete bastard or helpless victim? There are those who'll tell you not to let it get personal, but the dirtiest secret in politics is that it *is* personal.

And then there are those eerie reversals. One day someone asks you to annex into the town again, but this time it's not so they can gouge you for hook-up fees and taxes but so they can run you for mayor. You think, My God, are these people fools, or are things really that desperate?

Naturally, all of this can cut deeply into your fishing time.

Still, it *is* sometimes possible to achieve one single small thing that could make a difference, at least for the time being. When it comes right down to it, I hate politics as much as I love writing and fishing, but in all three of those endeavors it's possible to momentarily achieve the kind of clarity and precision you'll never see in your day-to-day life.

So I guess I've reached stage three in the long, slow process of becoming a bona fide local. Stage one was when no one knew or much cared who I was, and that went on for a long time, as it often does in small towns.

Stage two came when something clicked and people started speaking to me, usually asking how the fishing was.

Stage three came when I got involved in local politics (always on the pro-environment, anti-growth side, of course) and now, in some circles, I am known as "that son of a bitch Gierach."

I don't mind that. I figure, if you think you're right and you're making enemies of people you think are wrong, you're doing okay. And anyway, it's sort of a family tradition. If you go to a certain small town in Wisconsin and ask for that son of a bitch Gierach, you'll get directions to my uncle Al's place.

I've written some stories about the little creek here (sometimes trying to disguise its name and location, though not always successfully), and when I met a man who'd read some of them, he said he was disappointed when he finally saw and fished the thing. Interesting. I thought I'd described it pretty accurately, right down to the gas station next door to the house, the cement plant on the stream and the small trout you catch.

I like it, even though the trout aren't that big and parts of it aren't entirely picturesque. That's because I've come to believe that life isn't, can't be and probably shouldn't be perfect, and that you'll be a lot happier if you live as much the way you want to as possible, while at the same time not having to cross every t and dot every i. But then I suppose some romanticism inevitably creeps in when you're talking about your favorite trout stream.

Then too, some of those stories go back a few years, and although you don't always notice when you're right in the middle of it, things do change.

The first Good Old Days parade I saw here consisted of a flatbed truck full of drunks from the Sundance Saloon with a hand-painted banner reading LIFE IN THE FAST LANE, a handful of guys in buckskins from the local blackpowder gun club and the Pet Parade: a woman leading a golden retriever bitch that was clearly nursing, and four kids, each carrying a puppy.

They formed up in one block of Main Street and marched down the other block in front of an audience of twenty or thirty people. It was so much fun they went around the block and did it again. Then everyone went home except the drunks, who went back to the saloon.

Now, Good Old Days has a craft fair, flea market, carnival rides (cheap, little ones that don't look very safe), third-rate rock bands, loud cars, drunken fistfights and other elements of the full catastrophe. The city fathers and mothers are real proud of it, but a number of us make it a point to be out of town fishing the weekend it happens.

For a while the little sign you passed as you came into town said HOWDY, FOKS, but they changed it. I think someone realized it would only be funny if it was clear that the spelling error was intentional.

More to the point, down here on the lower stretch of the creek, there's

392   D E A T H ,   T A X E S ,   A N D   L E A K Y   W A D E R S

more traffic than there used to be, more noise, more people fishing and so on. Don't get me wrong. It's still the Rocky Mountains and, compared to much of the country, it's pretty idyllic. But, still, it just ain't quite the same.

When I break down and complain about that (I try not to, but I'm only human), people sometimes ask me why I don't just move someplace where there are fewer people and better fishing. "In your line of work," a friend pointed out, "you could live anywhere. All you need is a phone and a mailbox and a generator for the word processor."

I do think about it sometimes. In the course of twenty years spent writing about fly-fishing, I've been to some neat places where—at first glance at least—it looks like a guy could live a quiet, pretty much undisturbed life with lots of space, few human neighbors, fish and game right out the back door and so on. It can be tempting, especially when you're experiencing that nervous, anything-could-happen freedom you feel when you're far from home.

Parts of western Montana are also not what they once were, but there are still some backwaters the movie stars haven't discovered yet. Wyoming, Utah, Idaho and, for that matter, parts of Colorado still have little one-horse, one-cafe, one-gas-station burgs that are near decent trout water but still nicely off the beaten path.

I really liked the Texas hill country north of San Antonio, with its rolling, forested hills, acres of wildflowers, polite people and lonesome limestone rivers full of bass and panfish, but then I was there in April, and I'm told the summers are kind of grim.

On the farther edge (unlikely, I suppose, but still sort of tantalizing) there's, let's say, King Salmon, Alaska, where there are fish the size of small canoes, or Goose Bay, Labrador, where one could spend time with some of the biggest brook trout in the world. Or, for less-terrifying winters, how about the bull trout and west-slope cutthroats around Fernie, British Columbia?

There's an interesting pattern here. All the places I'm thinking of have good fishing, but they don't have fly shops yet. I dearly love a good fly shop, but the presence of a new one is a symptom of growing popularity and all the nostalgic heartaches that come with it.

But then I keep coming back to the episode with the rock bass and all the other bits and pieces that would fit into the same category: things I know about now only because I've been kicking around here for twenty-five years, and I mean kicking around in a way I probably wouldn't do in a new place because I'd be in my late forties instead of my early twenties when I got there.

Not that I'm exactly a doddering old fool, but if you're in middle age yourself you know what I mean, and if you're in your twenties, trust me. If nothing else, you get a little smarter, take fewer risks, pace yourself better and run up fewer mountains just to see what the view is like.

Then again, you ran up some of those mountains once, so you already *know* what the view is like. Age doesn't necessarily bring wisdom, but you do build up a backlog of useful experience.

There are great fishing spots I know about and still go to, the likes of which I might not find in new country. And when I do go, I know—or at least have some ideas—about the best season, time of day, the weather, where to start, where to end up at dusk, approaches, tactics, fly patterns and I don't know what all else.

Sure, most of this is stuff that would work on any similar water, but I know from fishing similar water in other places that there's a subtle, intuitive, bioregional angle to it. A stream in British Columbia can be exactly like a stream here in northern Colorado in almost every way you can put your finger on, but I still fish the home water better. And it doesn't feel frozen in time the way a new stream can to a tourist who fishes it only once. If the home water is better or worse than it was ten years ago, I know that, and sometimes I can even tell you why.

Now, I'm not claiming to be such a great fisherman. In fact, that's probably the point. Without being a Dave Whitlock, Lefty Kreh, Joan Wulff or Dave Hughes, to name a few, and without knowing all that much about casting or entomology, I still do okay because I have a comfortable old familiarity with the place that fills in the large gaps in my skill with . . . well, I don't know what exactly, but something just as useful.

I didn't even have to work at it in the way I usually understand that word. Sure, I've expended, and continue to expend, a lot of time and effort, and I do sometimes get deeply philosophical about it or claim I have to do it because it's my job, but I also love every minute of it.

My girlfriend Susan thinks it's interesting that, although most of my friends and I are fairly serious travelers, when we're *not* traveling we tend to be homebodies: apparently happy to kick around in a 20- or 30-mile radius of home, hang around the house and haunt the local cafes. There's always a little wanderlust in evidence, she says, but there's also a kind of satisfaction.

In the last year, two friends have told me they envied my sense of community. Both of these guys have spent the same years I've lived here mov-

ing restlessly from place to place, leaving behind pages in my address book
with dozens of crossed out P.O. boxes and phone numbers. One of them,
after a day's visit, said, "You know, I bet you've waved at or said hello to
thirty people today."

A nice detail: one I wouldn't have noticed on my own. Luckily, on that
particular day no one from the pro-growth side gave me the finger.

Now that I think about it, I also know who's a good carpenter, fly tier,
rod maker, auto mechanic and gunsmith; who'll return a favor and who
won't; which cafe makes the best coffee and where I might even be able to
get a free cup now and then: the same sorts of things I know about the fishing.

So maybe I don't move because I'm lazy. Or maybe by now I enjoy the familiarity of it all as much as anything else, and I'm afraid it would take me
the rest of my life to get back to the same thing somewhere else—or that I'd
never get it back at all.

And anyway, if I did move it would probably take my new neighbors a
decade or more to recognize me, take me in and then finally realize I'm an
outside agitator and a son of a bitch.

The Kindness of Strangers

I T had been a busy summer so far: lots of fishing (which I sometimes say is my job) with a little bit of frantic writing (which really *is* my job) wedged in between. When I got back from twelve days in Alaska, I found that I was still mentally exhausted from the work, but also refreshed and invigorated from the fishing, which left me sort of stuck in neutral: weary, but not exactly ready to rest.

I guess there was a little sleep deprivation in there, too. Summer days in Alaska are so long you can end up fishing for eighteen hours and sleeping four or five. You don't actually feel tired, but after a week or so you start walking into trees and forgetting your friends' names.

Anyway, that's how I was feeling—pleasantly bushed and a little disoriented—when A.K. called to see if I wanted to go over to the Frying Pan River. I said I should stay home and work, but he didn't want to know what I *should* do, he wanted to know if I was going fishing. I thought for a minute and said, "Yeah, okay."

You have to understand that this is the annual trip; a tradition. Every season, sometime in late July or early August, the Green Drake and Pale Morning Dun mayfly hatches overlap perfectly on the Pan, and A.K., Ed and I have been hitting that—or at least trying to—for quite a few years now.

We always set up a comfortable camp at Roy Palm's place—whatever bird dogs he has around at the moment move in with us as camp mascots—and we fish hard, but also manage to relax a little, too. After all, the Pale Morning Duns and Green Drakes keep banker's hours, so there's no reason to be on the water at dawn, and a leisurely breakfast in fishing camp—drinking a third cup of coffee while scratching a retriever behind the ears—is pleasant if only because it's so rare.

I've fished the Pan long enough now to have seen it change some. The hatches are a little different than they were a dozen years ago—heavier here, lighter there—and I've seen fish sizes and numbers go up and down, though never so far down that it wasn't still a great stream.

But the biggest change has been a kind of gentrification. There are more houses along the river now, and most of the new ones are palatial numbers (rumored to have cost millions) with commanding views, lots of glass and, in the foreground, along the river, NO FISHING signs.

This is something I hate to see on general principles, and the first question that comes to mind when I come upon one of these huge, overbearing monstrosities of a house is, Who the hell do those people think they are? If it turns out that there's an afterlife, the owners of these things are going to have to account for having taken up a lot more than their fair share of room.

Then again, it *is* good for the environment, as holders of private water are always quick to point out. "A trout stream is better off being fished by a select few than being hammered by the mob," they say. As a dues-paying member of the mob, I've never liked the sanctimonious sound of that, and those who use it as an argument don't seem to realize how flimsy it sounds. As a friend of mine says, "If I'll never get to fish it, why the hell should I care how good it is?"

On the other hand, the three of us have fished the Frying Pan long enough to have some loose connections over there, so we can occasionally get on some of that private water. Sometimes we're invited out of the blue, so we don't even have to suck up. We do it when the chance comes along because, well, who wouldn't? But it sometimes makes me feel funny.

On this last trip, A.K. and I got on an especially good private stretch. Ed had already left, and it was my last day there—I really did have to get some work done—but A.K. would be staying on for a few more days to camp and fish by himself, which he likes to do. I knew he'd call me when he got back, just to let me know how great it had been after I left.

We drove up to our benefactor's house, past a sign that read, NO FISHING, DON'T EVEN ASK, and got a couple of big orange buttons to wear on our vests so that whoever needed to know (hired thugs? snipers?) could tell at a distance that we were legitimate guests of one of the landowners controlling that stretch of river.

I don't know if it was the haughty language of the sign or the big, gaudy buttons, but although the fishing was good with a Green Drake dry fly and an emerger on a short dropper, I didn't feel quite right about being there. This is not a new feeling for me, and it's never a simple or even a predictable one. It just pops up now and then to bother me. To be honest, though, it often conveniently bothers me on the drive home, after I've caught a bunch of big, private fish.

But not always. Sometimes when I'm fishing private water I see it as what it probably is—an example of the kindness of strangers—and I just enjoy it. When I pay a rod fee, I usually experience the righteousness of the capitalist: Maybe the fishing is better than on public water and maybe it's not, but by God I purchased the right to be there.

But then there are other times when I feel . . . well, if not actually guilty, then at least embarrassed, hoping no one I know sees me fishing behind the Keep Out sign or recognizes my truck parked up at the Big House. Sometimes I'll try to think of what I'm doing as a populist raid on the ruling class: After all, it may be a private stretch of river, but these are still the People's trout. Other times I'll amuse myself by planning to fish the place *without* permission: figuring out how one could best sneak in, stick some fish and slip back out without getting caught.

For the record, I haven't poached or trespassed since I was a foolish boy, but I find an odd sort of comfort in the idea that I haven't forgotten how to do it. On that stretch of the Frying Pan it would be easy. Anyplace that makes such things could copy that big, campaign-sized button you have to pin on your vest. There are enough landowners involved that anyone who saw you would assume you were a guest of someone else. You'd fish out in the open, standing erect, and wave happily at anyone who happened to pass by. By the time they realized their mistake, you'd be long gone. You could probably only get away with it once, but if you were doing it just to prove a point, once would be enough.

But, as I said, I'm not a poacher. These are just entertaining mind games in the same league with, say, sexual fantasies.

I can't tell you exactly where the embarrassment I feel on private water comes from, but it's real enough that it comes from somewhere. Maybe it's because I spent so many years gazing longingly at private water I thought I'd never get on and alternately hating and envying the people I saw fishing there. I was doing that in my twenties when, typically, one's sense of idealism takes shape. As you grow older you get either more realistic or more cynical (two shades of the same color), but that perfection you once saw sometimes comes back to haunt you.

I know it's not a perfect world, but if it was there'd be enough good water for everyone and all of it would be public; open to the mob, that is, because the water and the fish would be considered the property only of God and the People. If the fishing wasn't good for everyone who wanted to wet a line, then the fishing would not be considered good for anyone.

But of course the mob wouldn't *be* a mob, they'd be a loose society of sporting ladies and gentlemen, each with good manners and the environmental conscience of a saint, so there'd be no vandalism, no garbage and only the occasional fish kept as needed for food.

Naturally, there would be lots of water and so few people (courteous people, at that) that crowds would never be a problem.

In this Utopia there might not be such a thing as money, but even if there was, it wouldn't be used to buy privilege or to close land and water, so there'd be no hard feelings, no class warfare.

Where was I? Oh yeah, back in the real world where the number of anglers is growing while the amount of fishable public water shrinks, and where, just that year, I'd fished a private trout club in Colorado, some private bass tanks in south Texas, private spring creeks in Montana, a private salmon river in Scotland and so on. After all, as I keep telling myself, it's my job.

Okay, but then I know how my luck runs. Anytime I start thinking I'm actually getting close to some kind of inside track, something happens to remind me that I am, as always, just another guy standing on a stranger's front porch with his hat in his hand.

My friend Jack called me once and said he'd wangled permission to fish a spring creek that he (and the precious few others who have fished it) tell me is easily the best trout stream in Colorado and probably one of the best in the country. And there's no aesthetic sidestepping here. It's the best, they say, in terms of numbers of large trout that can be caught on dry flies between about mid-April and the end of June, and then again in late summer and fall.

So Jack and I were scheduled to fish this thing, and it hadn't been an easy matter; at least not for Jack. I was just along for the ride, having done nothing more than pick up my phone when he called.

To get on the stream, you have to not only know the owner but also somehow get on his good side, which I'm told isn't a snap and can't be done with money. Then you have to negotiate with the old guy who sold

the place to the current owner a few years ago, but who still lives there raising his horses, caretaking the stream and, of course, fishing.

The old man is in his eighties and, like all old cowboys, he is bent,
gnarled and gimpy from being kicked by and thrown off of large animals all
his life, but I'm told he's still a great fly caster.

We were supposed to fish there on Thursday, but we stopped in Wednesday just to say hello to the old man and let him know we were in the area.

"How's the stream look?" Jack asked.

"Not good," the old man said.

He told us the flow was down and he was afraid his fish might be getting
stressed. He wasn't sure we should fish it.

We all went over to have a look at the stream, and Jack and I both
thought it had a good head of water in it. There were five or six trout rising
in the first pool we came to, and at least two of them looked very large.

I said, "It doesn't look bad to me," and the old man said, "Yeah, now that
I look at it, I guess it'll be okay."

"Okay," Jack said, "we'll see you in the morning."

That was about one o'clock in the afternoon, and we spent the rest of
the day fishing another nearby creek that was also said to be very good.
Jack said it was a little low, too—though not dangerously so for the fish.

The famous Mother's Day caddis hatch we'd hoped to hit wasn't quite on
yet (there were a few caddis flies in the air, but no rising fish), so we
worked weighted nymphs in some of the deeper holes.

It was the kind of fishing I say I like best: dramatic and a little bit
painstaking, so that every fish caught stands out as its own small victory.
We worked the stream for about five hours, and I landed four trout. The
smallest was 19 inches.

The next morning we drove back to the fabled creek where, Jack said, I
should be ready to achieve Nirvana. "Even on a mediocre day," he said, "it's
like nothing you've ever seen before."

We were putting on our waders in the driveway when the old man hob-
bled out. He said that the owner had come by yesterday to look at the stream
and had decided it was in fact too low and we shouldn't fish it. Sorry.

Jack, who is well known for his wisecracks, was speechless. I, just along
for the ride, as I said, was now just along for the ride home.

That's how it is with private water. You fish—or not—at the whim of the
owner, and I accept that because somewhere in my straight line of radical
populist leanings there's a snarl of respect for private land. It would have
been nice if the guy had changed his mind before we made the five-hour
drive and stayed overnight, but those, as they say, are the breaks.

I guess I was a little pissed when we were turned away, but by the time I was driving up the last stretch of highway toward home I'd convinced myself it was probably for the best. I mean, if I fished the finest trout stream in Colorado now, everything else would be downhill, and I'm too young for that.

Does that sound a little hollow? Well, so be it. That's my story and I'm sticking to it.

Not long after that, A.K. and I were doing a book signing at a fly shop in Denver. A young guy came in, bought a book and said he was taking the whole summer off to fly fish before he went back to school to do some graduate work.

He was clean cut and well dressed, so I took a wild guess and said, "Law school, right?"

He said, "Uh, well, yeah," looking around a little guiltily.

I said, "Don't worry about it. In ten years you'll own a nice little spring creek somewhere and A.K. and I will be knocking on your door asking to fish it."

He smiled. He probably thought I was kidding.

That was all last season. This year, Steve and Larry and I suddenly have a little piece of private water of our own. It's a small bass and bluegill pond, and it doesn't seem very elitist to us if only because it was a gift. One day the woman who owns it said casually, "You know, if you guys want to stock and manage my pond, you can have it to fish in." No lease, no money changing hands, no strings, just the rare logic of generosity: I own a little pond, I know some fishermen who seem like nice enough guys, why not put the two together?

This is a plain, small stock pond, just big enough to be more than a puddle, just deep enough for fish to winter over, with year-round water from a spring, a small island and cattails on the uphill bank. It's not beautiful, but it's handsome in a homespun, practical way, and it's a ten-minute drive from my house, two dirt roads from the highway.

The pond bottom is a little on the featureless side, so the first thing we did was make five big bundles of brush to sink at the deep end for cover. Then we stocked it with 8-inch bass and lots of fathead minnows. At this writing we're in the process of transplanting crawdads, frogs and a variety of warm-water insect nymphs from surrounding ponds and lakes. We want as natural a fishery as we can get while still stocking three thousand fatheads as fish food.

For a while we considered getting a shipment of hybrid bluegills from a hatchery in Georgia—a kind of designer panfish with a high growth rate that don't overpopulate and stunt because they're sterile—but in the end we decided on plain old, garden-variety, sexually active sunfish.

The pond will take a few seasons to develop, but in time it should be okay and it *could* be great. The hardest part will be not fishing it for a while so the fish can settle in and start to grow up.

Once the woman who owns it said she thought it was kind of sad that these fish only existed to be caught. I said, "Look, it's also kind of sad that as far as the government is concerned, *we* only exist to fight the wars, pay the taxes and believe the lies." I'm sure that made her feel better. Anyway, she never mentioned it again.

We will take our friends to the pond once it's up and running—we've already agreed on that—and I think we'll be generous about who our friends are, but even if the woman who owns the place would stand for it, we won't put up a sign reading, BASS POND—OPEN TO THE PUBLIC—EVERYONE WELCOME.

The pond won't have to be posted because it's out of sight of the road, and the driveway, though long, clearly *is* a driveway, complete with mailbox. There's usually someone around, and if not, anyone who just wandered in there would have to deal with Khan.

Khan (or Khan the Magnificent, as I like to think of him) is a large, black, impressive Great Dane. He was taken in a few years ago as a sick, hungry stray, and the theory is he was mistreated as a pup, because he doesn't like men.

The first time we all went out to the pond, it took Khan about ten minutes to decide to let us out of the car, and then there was a moment when we didn't think he'd let us back in.

A few days later we came back with the five bundles of brush, a box of large-size Milk Bone dog biscuits and Steve's young son, Julian. It's men Khan doesn't care for. Children and women are okay. So while Steve, Larry and I tied up the bundles with nylon cord and weighted them with rocks, Julian fed Khan the whole box of treats.

Since all dogs are basically whores, the deal was struck. Now when we drive up to the pond and Khan comes roaring out like the Hound of the Baskervilles, all we have to do is roll the window down a crack and slip him a Milk Bone. You can almost see the light go on as he remembers: Oh yeah, I don't like men *in general,* but I'll make an exception for men with dog biscuits. So Khan is now our buddy, proving once again that everyone has his price.

Carp

I do fly fish for carp and I'm not here to apologize for it, which is how a lot of these stories begin. (That there *have* been other stories should tell you something, but never mind about that.)

I will admit that the first carp I caught on a fly rod was an accident and that, after I saw it and realized it wasn't an enormous largemouth bass, I was pretty disappointed and even a little hesitant to touch the thing. And when I first stumbled upon a couple of local fly fishers who were actually catching carp on purpose, I thought it was either a joke or maybe another little campaign in the sport's ongoing class wars.

But either way, I figured I'd better try it, and when I did, the most natural thing in the world happened: My aesthetics adjusted themselves to fit the situation. I mean, the fish were big (a 5-pound carp is nothing special), they were spooky and sometimes discriminating, the fishing itself was visual and stealthy and I couldn't catch them at first, even though a carp-fishing dentist I know had given me the dressing for his secret, killer carp fly.

Beyond that fly pattern, advice was hard to come by. There was no hot young carp guide down at the local fly shop, no standard carp-fly selection in any tackle catalog and no book entitled *Selective Carp*.

I guess that was the most exciting part: So few people fly fish for carp that very little is known about the sport. If you want to learn how to do it, you have to pick the brain of one of the rare people who's into it, or just go out cold and try it for yourself. In *Carp in North America,* published by the American Fisheries Society, Ronald J. Spitler says, "When it comes to fly-fishing [for carp] we are drifting a bit into the unknown . . . " I don't know about you, but I kind of like the sound of that.

Where I've fished for them the most—in the warm-water ponds and reservoirs of northeastern Colorado—you can usually find carp tailing like bonefish in the shallow flats on hot summer days. They're beautifully camouflaged against the silty bottom, but you can pick them out by the faint, lazy puffs of mud they blow through their gills as they suck in food, or by their tails waving slowly under the surface like big brown flowers. In deeper water you can sometimes locate them by the trails of tiny bubbles they leave while feeding. (I once asked a carp fisher what exactly caused those bubbles, but he didn't know. Apparently, further study of carp physiology and pond bottom ecology is needed.)

Anyway, then it's a matter of casting a weighted fly ahead of a fish, letting it sink to the bottom and retrieving it in front of him, slowly or briskly, depending on his mood. I'm told it's just like fishing crab flies for bonefish, right down to sounding a lot easier than it really is.

Sometimes you'll spot pods of four or five carp slowly cruising off the bottom in clear water. They're as easy to spook as brown trout would be in the same situation, but if you cast quietly and far enough ahead of them, one may peel off and take a slowly sinking or gently retrieved nymph.

And, naturally, rising carp will take dry flies. By the way, a carp rising to insects or whatever floating on the surface is said to be "clooping."

When it comes to choosing fly patterns, the boilerplate logic of fly-fishing works as well as anything. That is, the more convoluted logic and poetry you can cram into it the better, but unless you have a better idea, just copy the food organism.

Carp feed mostly on aquatic and terrestrial insects, crustaceans, crawdads and such—pretty much what trout would eat in the same water. For tailing carp, I've had my best luck with size 8 or 10, drab-colored, weighted flies tied upside down so that their hooks ride up. This keeps you from fouling on the bottom and, since the fish comes at the fly from above, you want the hook on top anyway—a nice coincidence.

One of my favorites is the Tarcher Nymph, invented as a trout fly by Ken Iwamasa of Boulder, Colorado. Tom Austin, lately of Austin, Texas, does well with bonefish flies like Crazy Charlies and Epoxy flies ("Carp don't know there ain't no crabs and shrimp in here," he once told me), and Steve has come up with a neat little Clouser Minnow variation he calls a Blood-shot Charlie—one of only three or four patterns I know of that are tied especially for carp.

The carp I've caught, and seen caught, on dry flies ate trout patterns that more or less copied what was on the water: grasshoppers, mayfly spinners and so on. Then again, the first carp I ever hooked on a dry fly took a #14 Royal Wulff, even though he seemed to be eating cottonwood seeds.

I didn't know about it then, but one of the carp patterns I've run across *is* a cottonwood seed. Another is a deer-hair mulberry. Like the man said, "we are drifting a bit into the unknown."

I guess I didn't do this entirely for its own sake right at first. In the beginning, it was just a hoot to do something that some of my colleagues considered beneath their dignity, although, to be fair, few of my real friends worry much about dignity, and most of them who aren't into carp respond the way A.K. does. "I think a guy should do whatever the hell he wants," he once told me.

"Do you want to go carp fishing tomorrow?" I asked.

"No."

Okay, but then, when I couldn't catch one right away, hooking a carp fairly on a fly became a mildly interesting problem. Then I caught a little one, weighing maybe 3 or 4 pounds, and it nearly took me into the backing on a 6-weight bamboo rod and put a set in one of the tips. When I took the tip over to Mike Clark's rod shop to have it straightened, he asked, "How'd you do this?"

"On a big brown trout," I said.

"Bullshit," he said. "You did this on a carp, didn't you?"

It turns out that as a fly rod game fish, the average carp is far bigger than the average bass or trout and more widely distributed than both put together. He can be difficult to hook, and he'll usually fight with great strength. In the best carp water you stand a better than even chance of hooking and landing a 10-pound or bigger fish and, since most American fishermen (and especially fly fishermen) don't much like carp, you'll probably have the best water all to yourself.

You know how other fishermen sometimes casually drift over in your direction when they see you catching fish? They do that when you're catching carp, too, but when they see what you're into, they just drift away again. I wish I could make them do that with trout.

Oddly enough, America is one of the few places where carp are generally disliked. In Europe they're highly regarded as a food and game fish and were once reserved only for royalty. In China and Japan they are traditional symbols of strength and nobility. Poets write about them, painters paint them and samurai warriors once rode into battle carrying carp banners.

Carp were introduced to America in the late 1800s to replace some of the native fish populations that we had all but destroyed through pollution, commercial fishing and general habitat destruction. They did well because they were hardy enough to live in the now warm, muddy water that other game fish couldn't handle, and they were well received at first.

But by the early 1900s carp began to fall out of favor as a food fish, probably because Americans didn't understand how to raise them commercially. In Europe, carp for eating were kept in clean, cool water, but here they were farmed in, or caught from, any old hot, murky pond, and they tasted like it.

We eventually came to miss the fish the carp had replaced, but, although it was our fault the water wasn't clear and clean enough for them anymore, we somehow managed to ignore that. According to Rob Buffler and Tom Dickson, in *Fishing for Buffalo,* the American prejudice against carp developed as follows: First we trashed our waters to the point where nothing but carp would survive in them, and then we blamed the carp for trashing the water.

That's unfair, but I guess it's not all bad. The thing I like most about fly fishing for carp is, it's not popular and, with any luck, it never will be. In a way it reminds me of the way fly-fishing itself was way back before it became fashionable. If you were heavily into it, you were considered sort of a nut, and those of us with antisocial tendencies felt pretty comfortable with that. If nothing else, people would leave you alone, and being left alone is one of the great underrated pleasures of life.

Once Steve and I were out in a boat, casting to some big carp that were feeding up against a dam face. A couple of guys wandered out on the walkway above us and watched for a while. Finally one of them called down, trying to be helpful, "Them are carp, you know."

"Yeah, we know," we said in unison.

"Okay," the guy said, and he and his friend walked away.

So, although I've come to think of these critters as big, handsome, graceful, intelligent, wary fish with a kind of quiet, understated classiness about them, they're still "just carp" and most people can't understand why you'd want to catch them. It makes it hard to take all this seriously—and that's how fishing should be. If people don't occasionally walk away from you shaking their heads, you're probably doing something wrong.

***

In fact, the only fishing contest I've seen that makes any sense to me is the Big Lip Invitational, fly-fishing's only carp tournament, held every summer in Fort Smith, Montana. Steve and I have fished in it as a team for two years now. At first we just saw it as a joke, but after the first one we began to see it as a more refined, intelligent joke: a genuine tournament that is, nonetheless, a spoof on tournaments.

The saving grace is that there's no prize money. The winning team (the one that boats the most carp) has their names engraved on the traveling carp trophy and gets to bask in ten or fifteen minutes of local glory before the picnic breaks up and everyone goes home. That's it.

There are also awards for the biggest carp, the carp with the biggest lips, and a few booby prizes for things like the carp with the *smallest* lips. The rules themselves are simple: two-person teams, fly-fishing only, catch and release, no motors, no chumming, carp must have both lips to qualify.

The field is small—there were sixteen boats in 1993, a few less in '94—and the entry fee is just enough to cover a picnic supper and official T-shirts.

Of course Steve and I—not to mention the other Colorado team, Larry and his wife, Donna—have our own T-shirts. The motto reads, "Carpe Carpio," which we thought was Latin for "Seize the Carp." We learned later it should have been "Carpe *Carpium*," thought about changing it, then decided that a grammatical error in a dead language was somehow appropriate for an event like this.

The contest began six years ago as the logical extension of a typical guide's day off. Some of the people who guided trout fishers on the Bighorn River below Yellowtail Dam took to going up above the dam to Bighorn Lake to fly fish for carp on their days off—to relax, to get away from the crowds and to have some yuks. It was fun, it wasn't easy and, guides being guides, some discussions arose as to who was the best carp fisher. Hence the tournament, organized by the Bighorn Trout Shop in Fort Smith.

A few teams from out of state have entered in recent years, but this is still essentially a small, local event held in a sleepy little fishing town in southern Montana—sort of an elaborate guides' day off. It draws no spectators, teams aren't sponsored by tackle manufacturers and this is probably the only thing resembling press coverage you'll see on it. And, although more than one fisherman in Fort Smith or at the nearby Cottonwood Campground will tell you, "We take our carp fishing seriously around here," something in his manner will suggest that isn't completely true.

Considering that the winners of this thing probably qualify as the fly-fishing-for-carp champions of North America, it's all surprisingly casual, although this year we did receive a warning. A guy took us aside and said, "Keep an eye on your boat." It seems that the first year we were newcomers and so had been treated as guests, but by coming back a second time we've become regulars. "Someone could, you know, steal your drain plug or hide your oars," the guy said.

Apparently tricks are played now and then, although it's not always clear what's a practical joke and what's not. On the morning of the last tournament, John Keiser showed up with a primitive-looking carp painted down each side of his drift boat. "Is that a case of vandalism?" I asked. "Oh no," he said proudly, "I did that myself." Someone standing nearby said, "You'll be able to wash that off, won't you?"

Incidentally, hanging on the wall of John's trailer is the only mounted carp I've ever seen in the flesh. It's huge. He says it weighed 20 pounds. Actually, he said, "All I know for sure is, it bottomed out a 15-pound Chitillion scale. Twenty anyway, maybe more."

I don't know if a mount indicates seriousness or not. If I remember right, that *was* the only stuffed fish in the place, but I guess that's understandable. After all, once you've got a 20-pound carp on the wall, even a 10-pound trout would look puny by comparison.

Steve and I have never won the tournament, but then we've only been in competitive carp fishing for two seasons, so we're still rookies. The first year we were in a three-way tie for second place, which was not a bad showing for a couple of newcomers. Last time we finished farther back, but I caught the biggest carp: a 6½ pounder on a dry fly, for which I was awarded a set of carp notecards.

Still, we plan to keep at it until we can bring the traveling trophy—and the glory—back to Colorado for the winter, although it's always in the back of our minds that no one really cares much one way or the other.

But the best thing about the tournament is the fishing itself. The water in Bighorn Lake is gin clear and cool; the banks are either rubble rock or sheer cliff and there's no bottom feeding, because, at the lower end of the reservoir where the tournament takes place, the bottom is 400 feet down. This is by far the best dry-fly carp water I've ever seen.

The best way to find carp that will take dry flies is to cruise around the shoreline, looking for their snouts quietly poking up through windblown rafts of organic and semiorganic matter where insects, among other things, collect.

This stuff is not exactly classic trout-stream foam and I didn't know what to call it until Steve suggested "schmoots." I like the sound of that and, after all, we do need the terminology. This is a fairly new sport, but it's still fly-fishing, so we have to be able to say things like, "It was a hot, windless afternoon and carp were clooping in the schmoots."

Any bug is fair game for a carp, and matching the hatch does work, but on warm summer days a fair number of grasshoppers get on the water, and Steve and I have found that a small hopper pattern or a light Elk Hair Caddis (either in about a size 12 or 14) is a good bet. The contestants in the Big Lip Invitational are pretty secretive about their fly patterns, so I can't tell you what the real pros use. Last year one guy went so far as to spray paint the lid of his clear plastic fly box so no one could even catch a fleeting glimpse of his carp selection.

Carp feeding on the surface are fairly easy to spot—at least once you know what to look for. The rise is so subtle it usually leaves no ring, even on dead smooth water, and that round, dark nose looks like a waterlogged pinecone bobbing on a gentle swell.

The trick is to put the fly in front of the fish, close enough that he'll see it, but not so close that it will spook him. It takes steady nerves. Carp don't charge the fly, and the actual take is slow and deliberate. The fly disappears, you tighten the line slowly until you feel pressure and *then* set the hook.

The fishing is delicate, demanding and visual, and the carp fight unusually hard in that cool water. Several times now I've been taken well into the backing by carp that weren't all that heavy. Fish over 10 pounds are sometimes landed in the reservoir, but most run around 5 to 6 pounds. That's not terribly large for carp, but it's bigger than the average trout caught in the Bighorn River.

The local guides have mostly kept this to themselves, but I did hear of at least one party of paying clients who were taken to the reservoir for carp after several good days in a row on the Bighorn. One of these guys hollered "Whoo, hoo, hoo, hoo!" every time he hooked a carp. He'd done that with trout on the river, too, but up at the reservoir there was no one to hear him so, the guide said, "It wasn't quite as embarrassing."

This last time, Steve and I arrived a couple of days before the tournament and checked into the campground. We planned to spend a day scouting the lake before the contest and maybe a day floating the river for trout. But then after a great day of carping with caddis and hopper patterns, and considering reports that the river was only fishing well with nymphs, we asked ourselves, "Why nymph fish in a crowd when you can catch bigger fish on dry flies in solitude?" and headed back to the lake.

Come to think of it, I never have gotten around to fishing for trout in the Bighorn River. I should do that one of these days. I hear it's actually pretty good.

Desperation Creek

F O R once I don't have to make up a phony name for the stream I'm talking about because the man who owns a nice long stretch of it has already done that. He calls it "Desperation Creek." Things being as they are, there may actually *be* a Desperation Creek somewhere in the Rocky Mountain West, but of course this isn't it. Or at least not yet. I'm sure the name began as a combination joke and smoke screen, but now the owner uses it with a straight face, which is how real place names evolve.

There's no great story about getting on the stream. I met a man at a party a few years ago, and in the course of things he said if I was ever in the area again I should come by and fish his little spring creek. So last summer when I was back up there, I called and asked if the invitation was still open and, if it was, could it please include Ed, who I was traveling with.

The answer was yes, and that was that: almost too easy to be fun.

Desperation is an archetypal small western spring creek. Looking out across the meadow from the road, you don't see the stream. If you didn't know it was there, this could just be another several hundred acres of rough pastureland, although it should go without saying that on this stretch at least, no big, stupid, clumsy cows muddy the water or break down the banks. So unless you know better, that's the only clue: no cows.

The creek meanders in its shallow cut through open country where the tallest scrubby bush is no more than waist-high. When I saw it, I thought it was lovely and perfect, but I also thought it would benefit from a little shade. Then I remembered a Xeriscaper telling me how a grove of hundred-year-old cottonwoods could suck a little stream like this dry in the summer. Okay, forget the shade. It's perfect as it is.

Our host assigned each of us half the stream—starting roughly in the middle, Ed worked upstream and I worked down—but first he took us around to show us where the fish were. Some of the spots were obvious, like a deep bend pool with a cut bank, but others were more obscure, the kinds of places where, on strange water, you'd inadvertently spook the fish if you hadn't been warned.

We'd walk from place to place far out away from the creek. Then, coming up on a spot, we'd crouch and finally kneel, and the man would outline the proven approach to each spot: "Stay low from here on down, don't get any closer than that bush and cast from your knees—sidearm." This is a guy who knows his fishing, and I could tell he really hoped we'd do well. (The stream itself is very small, but there are some big trout in it.) He couldn't tell us everything in a few minutes, but he wanted us to fully understand the delicacy of the situation.

Then he wished us luck and left, saying he was too busy to fish. Maybe he was, or maybe he just knew that three people would be one too many. Real generosity isn't always obvious.

Ed and I had been traveling and fishing for at least a few days by then, so we'd worked out most of the kinks. We were as sharp as we get and feeling confident. As we split up, Ed gave me a clenched-fist salute and advised me to "have courage."

I went to the first spot I'd been shown: a gentle riffle with a fair-sized pool below it, where four or five trout were rising. I couldn't see the fish themselves because the light was wrong, and I'm not that good at guessing fish size from rise forms. I crept over to the stream at a shallow, fishless stretch downstream to see if the bugs on the water were really Pale Morning Dun mayflies as I suspected. They were. Good.

Then I crawled up toward the pool, knelt by the bush and began working out line for my first sidearm cast. I hooked a shrub on a back cast and had to crawl back there on my knees to get my dry fly. When I was younger, I used to do this kind of fishing in roofers' knee pads. Now that I—and my knees—are older, I seem happy enough to crawl around unprotected, chewing gravel holes in my waders and sometimes hurting myself. Who knows why? Maybe I finally realized that life is going to cause some damage and there's nothing much I can do about it.

I cast for the bottom trout first. One cast was short, the next not quite so short and the third was pretty much right on. The trout moved 6 or 8 inches and took the fly daintily. When I set the hook, he wiggled once and shot out of the pool toward me. I saw him go by, heading downstream, as I was trying to gather line to take up the slack. It was a rainbow, 20 inches long or more, but by the time I got control of the line he was gone.

There were two more trout still rising in the pool, one about a yard ahead of the other. I neatly hooked and landed them both. The first was about 10 inches long, the second more like 8. I tried to make myself think: Look, they're trout, they're real pretty and you caught 'em. This is great, right? Never mind that you blew the big one.

At the next spot there were two fish rising tight to the far bank, one so close he was making a half-moon–shaped ring, the other maybe a foot out and 2 feet upstream. You naturally assume that the more difficult fish is the bigger, so I got into position and planned a cast that would put the fly almost, but not quite, on the bank, and then let it drift past the first fish and within an inch of the feeding lane of the second one.

It nearly worked. I couldn't have been off by more than a fraction of an inch, but that was enough to stick the fly securely on a wet, rubbery, pencil-sized root. Before I could think of what to do, the leader bellied heavily in the current and the two fish stopped rising.

I broke the fly off and then took a few minutes to calm down and to replace my 6x tippet and size 18 Pale Morning Dun thorax dry fly. I thought about waiting the fish out, then realized that the sparse hatch had been on for a while and wouldn't last forever. So I moved on to the next spot, where I hooked and landed a nice 14- or 15-inch rainbow out of a pod of several risers. The fish jumped twice, spooking the rest of the pool.

A little farther downstream I spotted a trout rising near the bank in a spot I hadn't been shown. It was there that I started hearing the voices: a man and a woman, clearly angry, though I couldn't make out what they were saying, and also the occasional sound of a slamming screen door. It had to be coming from the little house, half screened by Russian olive trees, about 200 yards away, just over the fence line on the next property. I hadn't noticed it before.

I cast from my knees and caught the trout on the third or fourth drift. It was a chunky, silvery rainbow about a foot long.

Then, as I was walking on downstream to the next pool, staying far back from the stream so as not to spook the fish, the woman's voice carried clearly through the still air. It said, "You *bastard!*" I could see now that they were hauling furniture from the house to a pickup parked out back. I thought, Okay, the main thing here is, this is none of your business.

I remembered the next pool. It was an L-shaped bend with a steep bank on the outside and an open gravel bar on the inside. Kneeling in the grass 30 or 40 yards away, I could see a few trout rising near the head of it; casual, sporadic dimples. I couldn't recall how my host had told me to approach this one, but it looked as though if I crept up the long leg of the L on the inside, right at the water's edge, I could get to a spot far to the side and a little below the fish. A slight right hook would keep the line out of the gravel, and the back cast looked clear.

I slithered down the bank and began crawling upstream toward the pool. The same openness that would leave plenty of room for a back cast made me feel awfully exposed, so I stayed as low as I could, on my knees and one hand, carrying the rod low, moving with an awkward, hopping limp like a dog with a bad foot.

At about 40 feet the angle of the light changed so I could see the fish. One second the stream was a dull silver sheet and the next the water was clear as air, green bottomed at a depth of roughly 3 feet, with mottled brown rocks. There were only two trout that I could see and they were both huge: easily 20 inches, possibly more. One fish was pale—probably a rainbow—and the other looked very dark, almost black. They seemed to have divided the pool exactly in half, lengthwise, and each one was dancing around in its own half, casually eating mayflies.

From next door, only about 75 yards away now, the man's voice said, "Goddamn it, that's just like you. That's why—" And then the door slammed again.

I crouched there for a few minutes, watching the two fish. Whenever I see game like this—going about their business, unaware that I'm there and that I'm about to catch them or shoot them or (just as likely) do something stupid and scare them away—I often hesitate, savoring it. In some ways, the most beautiful moments in sport are the ones just before you act. You know, open-ended, full of promise, often better than what actually happens in the next few minutes.

Then I cast to the near fish, making a few short false casts first to make sure I'd judged the range and the drift right, and then dropping the fly about 2 feet ahead of him. It was lovely. The fly went past the fish less than a foot to his right. He saw it, turned, followed it downstream and took it gently near the tail of the pool. When I set the hook, the trout shook his head and wallowed on downstream, out of the pool and into a long glide. I didn't want to spook the other fish by standing up, so I followed the run in what must have been a pretty comical knee-walk, but I had just enough time to glance back and see that the other trout was still rising.

I played the fish out in the next pool, far enough downstream that I could lurch to my feet and stand. I suppose you could say it was an unspectacular fight—no blazing runs, no jumps—but when I have a big trout on light tackle, I'm grateful for that. It means I might be able to get him.

When I waded into the water to land the trout, my boots sank in thick mud and a cloud of black muck billowed into the clear stream. My beautiful trout vanished in this crap momentarily, and I experienced panic, but it was okay in the end. The fish was covered with mud, but he was in the net.

I waded out to clear water and washed him off. He was wonderful: as deep-bellied and hump-backed as a little sockeye salmon; olive, purplish red and bluish silver with big spots; 22 inches easy, maybe 23, maybe even . . . Well, I've gotta start carrying a tape measure. Anyway, it was the biggest trout I'd seen in a hell of a long time, and I was real happy.

"You can't take that!" the woman's voice said. "That's *mine!*"

I crawled back up to the pool on knees that felt bruised and that I knew would be sore for days to come, thinking, Hardware store in Bozeman, knee pads, twenty bucks, tops. Sure enough, the other fish was still rising.

When I put the thorax dry fly over him, he executed a heartbreaking refusal rise: He saw it, turned and came for it with his mouth beginning to open and then flashed away at the last minute. It was all I could do not to strike.

The fish ignored two more good drifts with the same fly, so I knew I had to change. For no other reason than that it looked good, I tied on a Harrop's captive dun pattern I'd bought at a local fly shop a few days before. I couldn't see it on the water, but when the fish rose to take something on the surface, I thought it was about where my fly should have been and carefully set the hook.

This trout did exactly what the rainbow had done. He shook his head, ran slowly but heavily down the long run and let himself be played out in the next pool. He was almost an exact copy of the bow: let's say 22 inches, fat and heavy, except he was a lovely brown, the color of burnt butter.

When I released the fish, he cruised to the edge of the main current, belched some mud from his gill covers and then darted under a cut bank. I stood there watching that plume of ugly black muck drifting out of sight around the next bend and wondering how I'd tell Ed about this. Lead up to it? Blurt it out?

I remember my emotions about this being mixed, as they tend to be now that I'm no longer a kid. I was happy about those two big trout, but also vaguely sorry about all the mud I'd stirred up. You can't live without causing some damage, but it occurred to me that maybe over the years I'd caused more than my fair share, although I guess I'd also learned that regret is usually a waste of time. Then again, I knew that when I told Ed the story I'd leave the mud out.

The screen door slammed and the man's voice said, "Aw, fuck you!"

I almost yelled back, "Yeah, well fuck you, too!" but then decided against it. In a situation like that it's best to remain hidden; best for everyone that they never even knew I was there.

STORY CREDITS

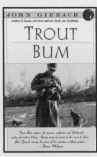
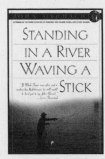
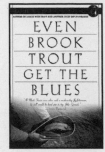
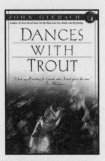
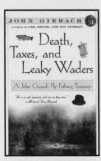

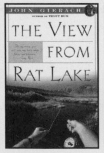
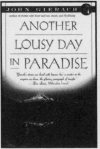

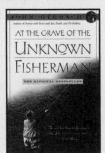